RUNS WI!
WHATEVER THE WEATHER

The Official Centenary History
of the
Scottish Cross Country Union
1890 — 1990

COLIN A. SHIELDS

SCOTTISH CROSS COUNTRY UNION
1990

© COLIN A. SHIELDS 1990

I.S.B.N. 0 - 9516681 - 0 - 2

This manuscript is copyright and no part of it may be reproduced, stored in a retrieval system, or transmitted, in any form or by any means, electronic, mechanical, photocopying, recording or otherwise, without the prior permission and consent of the author.

Printed by
McNaughtan & Sinclair Ltd, Glasgow. Scotland

COLIN A. SHIELDS

to
My Mother, Janet, who always encouraged me
in my love of athletics and cross country
and
My Wife, Linda, who always believed that I would
write this book and helped greatly throughout.

Born in Shanghai and educated in Greenock and at Strathclyde University, Colin Shields is a qualified civil engineer and town planner being in charge of transportation planning at Glasgow District Council Planning Department. He has been involved with athletics and cross country running since joining Greenock Glenpark Harriers in 1952. He takes an active interest in all forms of the sport, with involvement and interest in events as diverse as the decathlon and long distance road and cross country running.

He has always been fascinated by the statistics and results of the sport, being a member of the National Union of Track Statisticians and a founder member of the Scottish Association of Track Statisticians, assisting in the compiling, collation and publishing of annual ranking lists. He is currently Convener of the SAAA Records and Statistics Committee and a former Convener of the SCCU Rules Committee.

A Past President of the Scottish Amateur Athletic Association, he has been a member of the SAAA General Committee for 15 years. In cross country circles he was the Hon. Secretary of both the South Western and Western Districts of the Union over a period of 13 years, and has been a member of the General Committee of the Union for 16 years. He is currently Chairman of the Western District.

A long term fascination with the history and personalities of cross country, since its inception in 1885, has led him to carry out the lengthy research and investigations necessary to compile this detailed history of the Union and cross country running in Scotland.

He is a freelance reporter on athletic and cross country meetings and was the Scottish correspondent of "Athletics Weekly" for almost a decade. He now contributes a comprehensive results service to "Scotland's Runner" magazine.

D.M. DUNCAN

It is with a sense of honour that I accept the invitation to write the foreword to this, the Centenary Book of the Scottish Cross Country Union of Scotland, of which currently I am privileged to be the Honorary President.

We are indebted to the foresight of those gentlemen who, 100 years ago, decided that the future and progress of Cross Country Running, already active in several areas of Scotland, be administered by a National body.

The wisdom of this decision, discussed in more detail in the book, is evinced by the improvement in facilities, training and coaching with the introduction of more competitive events at Club, District, National and International level. As a direct result, we saw the emergence of such outstanding athletes as James Wilson, James Flockhart and Ian Stewart who each won the International Cross Country Championships and many other great runners whose distinguished performances are fully documented in the book.

The constant aim throughout the past century has been to provide, with adaptability to changing circumstances, the best service to the athletes, be they winners or losers, in the enjoyment of their sport. Also, let us not forget the officials, mostly former participants, who freely give so much of their time.

Material change is again knocking at the door. We have now lost the right to be separately represented in certain International events and I would hope that in the proposed changes, at present under discussion, our legislators will ensure that the Union does not lose its identity or autonomy so that we may extend our Best Wishes for continued success during the next 100 years.

Finally, appreciation should be recorded of the author, Colin Shields, and those who supplied information which helped him in the compilation of the book which I heartily commend to all interested in the sport.

Hon. President

INTRODUCTION

This book commemorates the centenary of the Scottish Cross Country Union but also details the history of cross country running in Scotland from the early days when the sport was first organised in 1885, together with biographical sketches of the great National champions of the past 100 years. The chapters which follow are in chronological order, taken a decade at a time, with coverage of District, National and International championships, together with significant races and events outside the championships. The great champions of the past, Andrew Hannah, Duncan Wright, J. Suttie Smith, James Flockhart and more recently Nat Muir, span more than one decade, and it is possible to trace their progress from their early running exploits to their championship victories from one chapter to another.

The fascinating history of the unique Edinburgh to Glasgow relay race, over its 60 years of existence, is contained in a separate chapter with detailed results of the race. A special statistical appendix is included, giving detailed results of all the races of District and National level, together with a complete list of all Junior and Senior athletes who have represented Scotland in the ICCU and IAAF International races between 1903 and 1987, and a unique record of their finishing positions in each race.

While the numbers of clubs and competitors have increased over the years, the struggle for success in championship races has always remained intense between the challenges for an ever growing number of National and District honours. When the hardy runners of Clydesdale and Edinburgh Harriers gathered at Lanark Racecourse for the first National Championship in 1885, little did they think that, over 100 years later in the Centenary Year of 1990, there would be over 1,500 runners contesting six National individual and team championships with a further four National relay titles being contested throughout the season.

The growth of the competitive side of the sport throughout the decades is fully charted in this authoritative and definitive book, together with anecdotes and stories of the social side of the sport.

What makes a runner run is sometimes a mystery to non running people, in a similar manner to the non understanding of why mountaineers climb mountains or yachtsmen sail the seas. The introductory poem, "To a Harrier", expresses the enjoyment experienced by fit athletes running across the countryside, and the stories of endeavour and success found in the succeeding pages of the book, amply express many good reasons why runners run and greatly enjoy it!

Despite the great care and meticulous research taken to ensure the accuracy of the statistical and editorial text of the book, it is possible that some errors may have occured. I would request readers, in the words of Shakespeare (Henry V) to, "piece out our imperfections with your thoughts". The selection and arrangement of all photographs and editorial content has been my own responsibility throughout and I hope that the final result satisfactorily covers the history of the Union and cross country running in Scotland.

COLIN A. SHIELDS
Glasgow 1990

ACKNOWLEDGEMENTS AND BIBLIOGRAPHY

I gratefully acknowledge the help of numerous people who supplied information, newspaper cuttings and photographs which assisted me in the compilation of this book. I would mention especially Walter Banks and Alex K. McDonald for details of cross country in the Northern District and information on the War time activities of the Scottish Cross Country Association respectively; Val Clement of Computype Services; J. Provan and the office staff of A.G. Barr plc. for producing the typescript from my hand written copy; Nora McBain and Gordon Stevenson of McNaughtan and Sinclair for their great assistance in printing the book and my wife Linda, for her endless patience, tolerance and assistance while I spent so great a time in researching and writing. My thanks are also extended to the following people who, over the three years of compiling this book, helped in various ways:- G. Aithie; A.H. Brown; N. Campbell; J.E. Clifton; F. Clyne; B. Covell; Mrs N. Dallas-Crane; R. Devon; E. Donnelly; J.E. Farrell; A. Forbes; J. Freeland; W. Fulton; D. Gillon; J.M. Hamilton; C. Haskett; D. Hunter; A. Jackson; C.R. Jones; E. Knox; S.B. McAusland; A. McFarlane; D.F. Macgregor; The Mackenzie family; D.V. McLaren; R.L. McSwein; J.T. Mitchell; D. Morrison; A. Naylor; G. Pickering; H. Robertson; W.J. Ross; N.R. Short; G. Spence; A.S. Stevenson; J.L. Stewart; J. Swindale; E. Thursby; B. Webster; J. Young; D. Yuill, together with the staff of the Glasgow Room at the Mitchell Library, Glasgow and the library rooms of the Glasgow Herald, Scotsman and Greenock Telegraph.

I wish to acknowledge the supply of photographs by the Glasgow Herald, the Sunday Post, Scotland's Runner and numerous individuals.

Valuable information was also obtained from the following sources:

Newspapers and Magazines — Scottish Athletic Journal, Scottish Umpire, Scottish Sport, Scottish Referree, Scots Athlete, International Athlete, Athletics in Scotland, Athletics Weekly, Athletics Today, Scotland's Runner, Athletics Review, Glasgow Herald, Scotsman, Dundee Courier, Greenock Telegraph, Evening Citizen, Evening Dispatch, News of the World, Bulletin, Sunday Standard, Sunday Post, Sunday Mail.

Books — J.W. Keddie: Official Centenary Book of the Scottish AAA 1883-1983; D.A. Jamieson and K.M. Whitton: Fifty Years of Athletics 1883-1983, An Historical Record of the SAAA; C.M. Usher: Story of Edinburgh University Athletic Club 1866-1966. S.B. McAusland: History of Clydesdale Harriers 1885-1985; T.N. Richardson: Jubilee History of the International Cross Country Union 1903-1953 and Championship Results Supplement of the ICCU 1954-1965; Duncan Scott: Borrowed Time — Centenary History of Salford H and AC 1884-1984; G. Dunn: Centenary History of the English Cross Country Union 1883-1983; D. Wallechinsky: The Complete Book of the Olympics; D. Jamieson: Edinburgh Southern Harriers, The First Fifty Years.

Other Sources — District Committee and General Committee Minutes and Finance Books of the National Cross Country Union of Scotland and the Scottish Cross Country Union; Handbooks and programmes of the Scottish Cross Country Union (various); Eastern District Cross Country League Records and Dallas Trust Newsletters.

CONTENTS

	Page
Foreword (D.M. Duncan, Hon. President)	iv
Introduction	v
Acknowledgements and Bibliography	vi
Poem "To a Harrier"	viii
Milestones in Scottish Cross Country Running	ix
1885 - 1890	1
1890 - 1899	12
1900 - 1909	24
1910 - 1919	35
1920 - 1929	49
1930 - 1939	70
1940 - 1949	91
1950 - 1959	102
1960 - 1969	122
1970 - 1979	140
1980 - 1989	167
1990 - Centenary Year	193
Edinburgh to Glasgow Relay Race	200
Cross Country in the Northern District	227

Statistical Reference Appendix

National Championships	233
Eastern District Championships	245
Northern District Championships	252
New Western District Championships	254
Former Western District Championships	257
Midland District Championships	258
South Western District Championships	262
International Championships	
a) ICCU Senior	266
b) IAAF Senior	274
c) ICCU Junior	276
d) IAAF Junior	277
Principal Officers of the Union	280
Clubs Affiliated to the Union	281

TO A HARRIER

This poem "To a Harrier", expresses the feelings and emotions of those who love cross country running and partially answers the question so often put by ordinary, non running people, "Why do you do it?". The poet Sorley supplied a partial answer when he wrote "They run because they like it, through the broad, bright land", but this poem is a lyrical statement of the enjoyment and exhiliration experienced by Harriers during their runs across the open countryside.

Some fellow men seem lucky, yet
I yearn to change with few,
But from my heart this afternoon
I needs must envy you,
Mud splattered runners, light of foot,
who on this dismal day
With rhythmic stride and heads upheld
go swinging on your way.

A dismal day? A foolish word,
I should not years ago,
Despite the drizzle and the chill,
have ever thought it so,
For then I might have been with you,
your rich reward to gain,
That glow beneath the freshened skin,
O runners through the rain.

All weather is a friend to you, rain
sunshine, snow or sleet,
The changing course - road, grass or
plough - you pass on flying feet,
No crowds you need to urge you on,
no cheers your efforts wake,
Yours is the sportsman's purest joy -
you run for running's sake.

O games are good - maneouvres shared
to make the team's success
The practised skill, the guiding brain,
the trained unselfishness,
But there's no game men ever played
that gives the zest you find
In using limbs and heart and lungs to
leave long miles behind.

I'll dream that I am with you now
to win my second wind,
To feel my fitness like a flame,
the pack's already thinned,
The turf is soft beneath my feet,
the drizzles on my face,
And in my spirit there is pride,
for I can stand the pace.   Anon.

MILESTONES IN SCOTTISH CROSS COUNTRY RUNNING

1885 First organised club cross country run on "hares and hounds" principle staged by Clydesdale Harriers at the Black Bull, Milngavie.
1886 First National Cross Country Championship staged at Lanark Racecourse, with just 2 clubs competing in the team championship. Alex P Findlay won the individual title - the first of 11 titles won by members of Clydesdale Harriers in the first 12 years of the Championship.
1887 Scottish Cross Country Association formed to govern cross country running in Scotland.
1888 A sporting "Civil War" existed between the Scottish Cross Country Association and the rival Scottish Harriers Union, with each body staging separate National Championships under different rules.
1889 National Championships held for first time at Hamilton Park Racecourse. Cost of hiring Racecourse and attendant facilities was £6 for the day.
1890 Formation of Scottish Cross Country Union after dissolution of rival Scottish Cross Country Association and Scottish Harriers Union.
1891 National Junior Championship inaugurated with W H Lowson (Dundee Harriers) winning individual title, and Edinburgh Harriers winning team championship.
1892 D S Duncan of Edinburgh Harriers, the grand old man of Scottish athletics, elected President of the Union after being Secretary/Treasurer for the first 7 years.
1893 Maryhill Harriers proposed to the Union that cross country running would be more popular if a league competition, as in football, was held to maintain interest for smaller clubs not strong enough to enter the National Championships. The idea was dropped as it was considered that harriers would not keep in strict training all season for this purpose.
1894 The Fourth National Junior Championship was held in the grounds of the Ducal Palace at Hamilton. As usual in a championship race of this nature where so many runners have entered (16 clubs!), it was some half an hour after the advertised starting time that the competitors gathered at the starting line.
1895 Western District Junior Championship inaugurated, with A McCallum (Partick Harriers) winning the individual title and Wishaw Harriers winning the team championship.
1896 Advice from national champion Andrew Hannah to aspiring harriers included, "Training means getting the body into the best possible health and condition. Be temperate in all things and keep regular hours, retire to bed as soon after 10 o'clock as possible. Take good, substantial food, partaking sparingly of soups and potatoes and avoid liquors of all sorts, and this is one of the hardest but most necessary things to do".
1897 Andrew Hannah (Clydesdale Harriers) elected President after winning the National Senior title the previous year for a record fifth time in 7 years.
1898 George Hume (Berwick and District Harriers) elected President of the Union - the only member of an English club to have the honour.
1899 The rift between the SCCU and the SCCA Western District is resolved after a conference in Edinburgh, with the SCCA affiliating to the SCCU but retaining the right to control the Western District Junior Championship in the future.

1900	J Paterson (Watsonions Cross Country Club) wins his third successive National Senior title, with his club being the first to break the monopoly of Clydesdale Harriers and Edinburgh Harriers by winning the team championships.
1901	J J McCafferty of West of Scotland Harriers, who won the Scottish Junior Championship at Larbert, chose to run in the Irish National Championship rather than contest the Scottish Championship.
1902	The National Championship at Myreside, Edinburgh was delayed by over 1 hour awaiting the late arrival of teams from West of Scotland due to a delayed train.
1903	First International Cross Country Championship between Scotland, England, Ireland and Wales held at Hamilton Park Racecourse. Change of name from Scottish Cross Country Union to National Cross Country Union of Scotland.
1904	George MacKenzie (West of Scotland Harriers), who won 9 International caps, and was one of the Union's benefactors over a long number of years, won the National Junior Championship.
1905	George Hume (Berwick and District Harriers), previously President of the Scottish Cross Country Union seven years earlier, becomes President for the second time. The only person in the 100 years history of the Union to be President on two separate occasions.
1906	Sam Stevenson becomes the eighth member of Clydesdale Harriers to win the National Senior Championship and finishes tenth in the International Championship in Wales to lead Scotland to third place in the team contest.
1907	I.C.C.U. International Championship held at Scotstoun, Glasgow, with Tom Jack (Edinburgh Southern Harriers) being first Scot home in 5th position, after winning both the National Junior and Senior titles in the same year. George Hume became the first Scot to be President of the I.C.C.U.
1908	Only one of the 26 clubs in membership of the Western District did not compete in the Championship at Scotstoun Showgrounds, where runners were supplied before the race with cloth numbers to be sewn on the breast of the club's vest.
1909	Complaints received from Lanark golf clubs that harriers had been seen running over golf courses and stealing balls from fairways and greens. Trail layers were warned not to lay paper over private land where trouble could result from land owners.
1910	George Wallach (Greenock Glenpark Harriers) was deprived of Individual victory at his first appearance in the I.C.C.U. International Championship at Belvoir Park, Belfast when pulled out of race in the final stages by a policeman due to wearing badly torn shorts.
1911	George Wallach (G G H) became the first Scot to win an Individual medal in the International Championship when finishing 3rd at Caerleon Racecourse in Wales.
1912	The I.C.C.U. International Championship was held at Saughton Park, Edinburgh - the only time that the Championship was held in the East of Scotland in the 70 year history of the event. George Wallach (G G H) was the first Scot to finish in 4th position. William Laing (Edinburgh Harriers) became the second Scot elected President of the I.C.C.U.
1913	William Struthers (Greenock Glenpark Harriers), later to become the first Hon President of the Union, serves second term as President. Archie Craig (Bellahouston Harriers) wins National Senior Title and leads his club to their first ever team championship title.

1914 Start of the First World War. The District and National Championships suspended for the duration of the War. George Wallach won the silver medal in I.C.C.U. International Championship at Chesham Park, Bucks.
1915 All cross country running suspended for the duration of the War with an Emergency Committee appointed to keep the Union in existence till the War is over.
1919 Restart of normal competition after 1914-18 War. National Novice Championship introduced and the club annual subscription doubled from 10/6 (52½p) to £1.1/- (£1.05p).
1920 James Wilson (Greenock Glenpark Harriers) records first Scottish Individual victory in the I.C.C.U. International Championship at Belvoir Park, Belfast after winning the National Senior title at his first attempt.
1921 George Dallas of Mayhill Harriers elected Hon. Secretary of the Union, a post he was to hold for 39 years. George Hume (Edinburgh Harriers) elected first permanent Hon. Secretary/Treasurer of the I.C.C.U.
1922 I.C.C.U. International Championships staged at Hampden Park, Glasgow, starting at half time of a football match before 25,000 spectators. George Wallach (GGH), at 41 years of age, was first Scot home in a remarkable 4th place after winning the National Senior title 8 years after his first victory in the event. J Howieson (Shettleston Harriers) became third Scot elected President of the I.C.C.U.
1923 Raffle organised by Union to finance International team travel to France to compete in International Championships at Maisons - Laffitte, Paris.
1924 Inauguration of Eastern District Cross Country League. First race staged at Portobello Baths.
1925 Duncan McLeod Wright (Clydesdale Harriers) wins National Senior title, the first of 4 titles in five years.
1926 George Aithie (Edinburgh Northern Harriers) became Secretary/Treasurer of the Eastern District League, a post he was to hold for over 50 years.
1927 George Sandilands from Kirkcaldy, a former member of Edinburgh Harriers, gifted a trophy to be known as the "Sandilands Shield". This trophy was contested by the Senior Club teams in the Eastern District League with Edinburgh Northern Harriers being the first winners.
1928 I.C.C.U. International Championship held at Ayr Racecourse with J. Suttie Smith (Dundee Thistle Harriers), after an earlier career as a gymnast, winning the silver medal as first Scot to finish. He had earlier won the National Senior title to start a record series of five consecutive victories. J.C.A. Bodie (West of Scotland Harriers) became the fourth Scot elected as President of the I.C.C.U.
1929 Due to the large number of clubs in the West of Scotland the Western District was divided into the Midland District and the South Western District.
1930 Edinburgh Northern Harriers won the MacKenzie Trophy in the Eastern District Relay Championship, starting a series of eight victories broken only in 1936 by Dundee Thistle Harriers. Inaugural Edinburgh to Glasgow relay race won by Plebian Harriers.
1931 Tom Jack (Edinburgh Rover Scouts), winner of three National Senior titles between 1907 and 1912, elected President of the Union.
1932 Maryhill Harriers won the National Senior Team Championship for the sixth year in a row, setting a record that stood for 46 years until equalled by Edinburgh Southern Harriers in 1987.
1933 James Flockhart (Shettleston Harriers) won the National Junior and Senior titles

in his first year of competition in cross country running. He went on to take the Senior title 4 times in 5 years. Youth championship introduced to National Championship programme with J McDonald (St Peters AC) winning the Individual title and Maryhill Harriers taking the Team championship.

1934 I.C.C.U. International Championship held at Ayr Racecourse with James Flockhart (Shettleston Harriers) being first Scot to finish in 6th position. C Chalmers (Garscube Harriers) became fifth Scot elected as President of the I.C.C.U.

1935 Anniversary of 50 years of cross country running in Scotland. George Craig (Shettleston Harriers) wins National Youth title for second time and, after the War, gains Scottish International cap to join father Archie, 1913 National Champion, and elder brother Archie as unique family of Scottish cross country internationalists.

1936 Duncan McSwein (Greenock Wellpark Harriers), one of Scotland's greatest athletics officials and administrators over half a century, was appointed President of the Union.

1937 James Flockhart (Shettleston Harriers) records Scotland's second Individual victory in the I.C.C.U. International Championship at Brussels.

1938 John Emmett Farrell (Maryhill Harriers) won the National Senior title at Ayr Racecourse and led his club to team victory in the club's Jubilee year.

1939 Last National Championship until 1947, due to Second World War, held at Lanark Racecourse with 19 year old Robert Reid (Doon Harriers) winning the National Junior and Senior titles after winning the Youths title just one year earlier. First Scottish Universities Cross Country Championship held at Garscadden Estate, Glasgow. The National Cross Country Union of Scotland set up an Emergency Committee to look after cross country running in Scotland for the duration of the War.

1943 The war time Scottish Cross Country Association was set up to maintain interest in cross country running in Scotland during the War with muster runs and open races.

1944 Unofficial War time National Championship held at Renfrew with George Burdett (Shettleston Harriers) winning the Individual title and Maryhill Harriers taking the Team Championship.

1945 Dunky Wright keeps cross country running going by supplying runners with pre-war sandshoes without the need of clothing coupons.

1946 Scotland stages I.C.C.U. International Championship at Ayr Racecourse for the third time. In the first event since 1939 James Flockhart (Shettleston Harriers) was the first Scot to finish in 15th position in a disappointing team performance. James Fallon (Kilbarchan AAC) becomes the sixth Scot elected as President of the I.C.C.U. Duncan McSwein (Greenock Wellpark Harriers) elected Hon. Treasurer at the first post war A.G.M. - a post he held for the next 26 years.

1947 The first National Championship since 1939 held at snow covered Lanark Racecourse with Andrew Forbes (Victoria Park AAC) adding the National Senior and Junior titles to the Midland District title he won earlier in the season. Bellahouston Harriers retained the team championship they won in 1939.

1948 John Emmett Farrell (Maryhill Harriers) wins National Senior title at Ayr Racecourse - 10 years after his first Senior title at the same venue. Final Novice Championship staged at Hamilton Park Racecourse. The event, which had been in existence for 30 years, was discontinued.

1949 First Scottish Inter Counties Championship held. Resumption of Edinburgh to Glasgow relay race held twice, in April and November, before establishing a permanent date in November each year.
1950 Robert Reid (Doon Harriers and Birchfield Harriers) wins National Senior title - 11 years after his first victory before the War - the greatest time gap between Senior victories in the history of the Championship.
1951 A plea made for the introduction of the disc recording system allocating places at the National Championship rather than the manual recording system. A progressive innovation that is still awaited almost 40 years later.
1952 I.C.C.U. International Championships held at Hamilton Park Racecourse for the first time since 1903. Eddie Bannon (Shettleston Harriers) was the first Scot to finish in 14th position, after winning the National Senior title, starting a series of three consecutive victories. George Dallas (Maryhill Harriers) becomes seventh Scot elected as President of the I.C.C.U.
1953 John and Tommy Stevenson of Greenock Wellpark Harriers finish 3rd and 4th respectively in the Scottish National Championship and become the first brothers to represent Scotland in the I.C.C.U. International Championship in the same year.
1954 John McLaren (Shotts Miners Welfare Club) wins both the Scottish and English Junior titles - an unprecedented double.
1955 Joe McGhee (Shettleston Harriers), who won the Empire Games marathon title at Vancouver, Canada the previous year, showed excellent finishing speed to win the closest ever finish in the Nigel Barge Road Race with Eddie Bannon (Shettleston Harriers) and Alex Small (Plebian Harriers) also sharing the winning time of 23 mins 24 secs.
1956 William Armour becomes President of the Union in the year his club, Victoria Park AAC, wins the National Senior team Championship - the first of three consecutive victories. Youth's Individual and Team races introduced to the Eastern District League.
1957 Harry Fenion (Bellahouston Harriers), nine years after winning the National Youths title, wins the National Senior title and completes a notable race double when winning the Scottish Marathon Championship later in the Summer.
1958 Senior Boys Championships introduced to National Championship programme. First title won by Lachie Stewart (Vale of Leven AAC), with George Heriots School winning the first of 3 consecutive team championships. Andrew Brown (Motherwell YMCA) wins his only National Senior title with Victoria Park AAC winning the National Senior team title by just 8 points from Bellahouston Harriers.
1959 R.A.F. Officer Alastair J Wood, Scottish 3 and 6 mile track champion, wins the National Senior title at Hamilton Park Racecourse and leads Shettleston Harriers to the first of four consecutive Team Championships. Individual and Team Senior Boys races introduced to the Eastern District league with Junior Boys races starting in 1962.
1960 I.C.C.U. International Championship held at Hamilton Park Racecourse with Alastair Wood (Shettleston Harriers) being first Scot to finish in 7th position. Duncan McSwein becomes eighth Scot elected President of the International Cross Country Union.
1961 Doubts expressed at the Annual General Meeting of Scotland's ability to afford the cost of travel to compete in the International Championship now that Morocco and Tunisia are added to the Championship roster of venues.

Suggested restriction of travel to compete only in Championships staged in the Home Countries and possibly France and Belgium.

1962 Jim Alder (Morpeth Harriers), in his first championship appearance, won the first of three National Senior titles at Hamilton Park Racecourse. Championship distances reduced; Senior race from 9 miles to 7½ miles and Junior race from 6 miles to 5 miles.

1963 Tom Cochrane (Beith Harriers) gained selection for Scotland in the I.C.C.U. International Championships after winning the South Western District Senior Championship for the first of 6 victories in 7 years.

1964 Name change from National Cross Country Union of Scotland to Scottish Cross Country Union - the title which still exists in centenary year. Ian McCafferty (Motherwell YMCA) becomes first Scot to win the I.C.C.U. International Junior title, winning by 25 seconds - the largest winning margin in the history of the race.

1965 Ian McCafferty wins Second National Junior title. This win, in addition to his Youths victory in 1963 and National Senior win in 1972 makes him the first athlete to win these three National titles - a feat repeated by Nat Muir (Shettleston Harriers) between 1975 and 79.

1966 Fergus Murray (Edinburgh University) won the National Senior title for the third year in a row and led his team to victory in the National team championship.

1967 Edinburgh University, with the strongest team in their long history, won both the National Senior and Junior team championships, Eastern District relay and League titles and the Edinburgh to Glasgow relay race. Foot and mouth epidemic forced S.C.C.U. to cancel all cross country races over grassland and confine all races to the road. Edward Knox (Springburn Harriers) wins I.C.C.U. International Junior title at Barry, Glamorgan.

1968 Junior Boys Championship added to the National Championship programme. First title won by James Mulvey (Shettleston Harriers) with Springburn Harriers winning the team championship.

1969 I.C.C.U. International Championships held at Clydebank with Ian McCafferty (Law & District AC) being the first Scot to finish in 3rd position. He became the first athlete to receive the Walter Lawn Memorial Trophy as first Scot to finish in the Championship. National Championships held at Duddingston Park, Edinburgh - the first time in over 20 years the championships were not held at Hamilton Park Racecourse.

1970 Jim Alder (Edinburgh AC) wins National Senior title at Ayr Racecourse after a wait of 8 years since his first title success.

1971 The Scottish National Championships return for the first time in 50 years to Glasgow. Held at Bellahouston Park they were commercially sponsored for the first time in the Union's history by Lees of Coatbridge.

1972 The I.C.C.U. International Championship, held for the first time in Scotland, was staged for the final time at Cambridge. Scotland completed their unbroken record of entering and completing a team in every race since 1903, led home by 3rd placed Ian Stewart.

1973 Scotland compete in the inaugural I.A.A.F. World Championships at Waregem, Belgium. Senior team led home by 13th placed Norman Morrison (Shettleston Harriers). Jim Brown (Monkland Harriers) won the Junior title after finishing 3rd in 1971 and 2nd in 1972. Robert McSwein (Paisley Harriers) elected Hon Treasurer in succession to his father Duncan McSwein - a post he has held for the past 17 years.

1974 Senior 4 x 2½ miles cross country relay championship added to the National Championship programme, with the first title being won by Clyde Valley AC at Bellahouston Park, Glasgow. Springburn Harriers dominated the Scottish National Team Championships winning 4 team titles - Junior Boys, Senior Boys, Youths and Junior team championships, missing only the Senior event - the first time a club ever won so many National team titles in the same year.

1975 Commonwealth Games 5,000 metres champion Ian Stewart records Scotlands first individual victory in the IAAF World Championships at Rabat, Morocco.

1976 Administration reorganisation results in the integration of the Midlands and South Western Districts into the Western District covering all the West and South West of Scotland. A new Northern District formed to control cross country running in the Highlands. Jim Alder (Edinburgh AC) competes for Scotland for the 14th and final time in 15 years in the ICCU/IAAF Championships - a Scottish record of International appearances.

1977 Young Athletes 3 x 2 miles cross country relay championships, in running order of Junior Boy, Senior Boy and Youth, introduced to the National Championship programme. Springburn Harriers won the first title.

1978 IAAF World Championships held at Bellahouston Park, Glasgow with Nat Muir (Shettleston Harriers) being first Scot to finish in 7th position. Edinburgh AC, led by National Champion Andy McKean, won National Senior team title for the fifth time in six years.

1979 Senior 6 Stage Road Relay Championship introduced to National Championship programme. First title won by Edinburgh Southern Harriers who won the title for the next 4 years.

1980 John Robson (Edinburgh Southern Harriers), winner of 1978 Commonwealth Games 1500 metres bronze medal, finished 5th in the IAAF World Championships at Paris, after winning Eastern District title and leading his club to National and Eastern District team championships.

1981 An inaugural Inter District contest between the Eastern, Western and Northern Districts of the Union was held for Young Athletes. Races for Youths, Senior Boys and Junior Boys were staged at Stirling University. Objections to the standard of District and National Championship awards were made at the Annual General Meeting.

1982 Ian Clifton (Edinburgh Southern Harriers) elected as Hon. Secretary of the Union, a post he still holds in Centenary Year. Edinburgh Southern Harriers complete a clean sweep of National Senior honours, winning the National Individual and Team titles, the 4 x 2½ miles cross country relay title, the Six Stage road relay title and the Edinburgh to Glasgow relay race.

1983 Nat Muir (Shettleston Harriers), after winning 3 Senior National titles in a row between 1979 and 1981, won the National Senior title and went on to equal Suttie Smith's record of 5 consecutive victories between 1983 and 1987.

1984 IAAF World Championship held for the first time in America. Scottish athletes catch mystery illness on flight across the Atlantic to New York and no Scottish runner finishes in the first hundred home. Lawrie Spence wins the Walter Lawn Memorial Trophy in 112th position.

1985 Veterans Individual and Team Championships introduced to the National Championship programme after a period of club championships staged by the Scottish Veteran Harriers Club. First title won by Richard Hodelet (Greenock Glenpark Harriers), with Shettleston Harriers winning the team championship. Clydesdale Harriers, the oldest club in Scotland, celebrate their centenary.

1986 John Fairgreive appointed as the first Scottish Athletics Administrator. The Union joins the SAAA, SWAAA and SWCCU in a Scottish Athletics Administrative group in effort to streamline and improve administration costs.
1987 Final appearance of Scotland as a seperate country in the IAAF World Championships in Warsaw, Poland. This ended an unbroken run of appearances at ICCU and IAAF Championships since 1903. Edinburgh Southern Harriers win National Senior team title for the sixth year in succession and equal the record held by Maryhill Harriers. The age group structure was altered with the qualifying date changed from 1st April to 1st January each year.
1988 Neil Tennant (Edinburgh Southern Harriers) won the National Senior title at Beach Park, Irvine, preventing Nat Muir (Shettleston Harriers) from setting a new record of six consecutive individual victories. Cambuslang Harriers, who had recorded their first victory in the Edinburgh to Glasgow Relay race the previous year, won the Senior team championship for the first time in their history.
1989 Teviotdale Harriers and Dundee Hawkhill Harriers, in their Centenary Years, win honours in National competition. Teviotdale Harriers, after staging the National Championships for the first time, won the Senior 4 × 2½ mile relay title for their first ever victory in National competition. Six age group championship categories introduced to National Veteran Championships. Thomas Murray became first Greenock Glenpark Harrier to win Senior National title in 69 years.
1990 The Union celebrate their Centenary season with a series of functions throughout the winter season from October to March. An opening season pack run in 1890's costume was staged at Strathkelvin with civic receptions for the Union held at Dundee, Edinburgh, Inverness and Glasgow. Dundee Hawkhill Harriers were the most successful club of the year, winning the National Road Relay Championship and the Edinburgh to Glasgow relay race, together with wins in the Eastern District Relay and Team championships.

1885 to 1890

Although Cross Country Running is generally accepted as starting in Scotland in 1885 with the emergence of Harriers Clubs based on the "hares and hounds" principle there had been runs over the country in earlier times. In Carnwath in Lanarkshire the "Red Hose" cross country race, an annual event stretching back to the early years of the nineteenth century, was well established with local competitors. In Edinburgh there are accounts of a one mile steeplechase over the country, held at Hunters Tryst in May 1828, by the Edinburgh "Six Foot" club, and paper chases and other cross country events were held at Public Schools as part of their rigorous sports programme.

The Scottish Universities also staged cross country runs and the Edinburgh University magazine of 1871 includes a complaint by Robert Louis Stevenson that "no more does the merry medical student run eagerly in the clear wintry morning up the rugged sides of Arthurs Seat". It is recorded that Edinburgh University Harriers were running in 1874-75 and the club was a lively body although one of its members, left at headquarters as timekeeper, betrayed his trust and fell asleep. In 1881 the sport was not too popular among students and only three turned up for the first organised run in February. These runners were "attacked by quarrymen and a large black dog and accosted by gardeners" during their outing and no further information on the sport in University annals is listed until 1887 when there was a large influx of students into the ranks of Edinburgh Harriers.

However, the first advent of organised cross country races in Scotland, as described by the late George Dallas in Fifty Years of Athletics (1883-1933), An Historical Record of the Scottish AAA was "cross country running in Scotland, as we know it today, began with a meeting in Glasgow on 4th May 1885 at which it was decided to form a club to be known as Clydesdale Harriers". This meeting, attended by a number of gentlemen interested in athletics, agreed to form a harriers club for Glasgow and the surrounding district devoted to promoting the sport of cross country running in the hares and hounds form. While other athletic clubs, devoted to track and field athletics and cycling, existed in membership of the Scottish Amateur Athletic Association, Clydesdale Harriers were swiftly followed by Edinburgh Harriers who were formed on 30th September due to the efforts of D S Duncan, the Scottish Mile Champion who became Hon. Secretary of the SAAA at the age of 24 years, a post he was to hold for the next 40 years.

In October 1885 cross country running began with a run from the "Harp" Public House near Corstorphine on 17th October. The runners had a very enjoyable spin over 6 miles of country and decided that they would meet the following Saturday at the Volunteer Arms, Morningside at 3.30 p.m. for their next outing. It was agreed to organise an outing over the country every Thursday afternoon for the special benefit of those members who played football on Saturdays.

A few days earlier, on 8th October, a Springburn club called Towerhill AC staged what was described as "a rather novel departure from the ordinary run of athletic sports, a hares and hounds run of 17 to 20 miles taking in the countryside around Lenzie and Kirkintilloch". This appears to have been a sort of rambling run in the countryside rather than an authentic harriers run following a paper trail laid by hares.

The "hares and hounds" principle has now passed into disuse in cross country running since the Second World War and the following account details the old "pack run" traditions of the sport. Two or three runners were selected as the "hares" to lay a trail for the main pack of "hounds" to follow. The hares, carrying bags of paper strips slung over their shoulders, set off with an agreed start and the hounds pack followed. The hounds, usually divided into fast and slow packs, were controlled by a "Pace" who generally wore a green sash and always kept a lead of three yards from his followers. The pack was controlled by the "Whip" who wore a red sash and in Clydesdale Harriers tradition, communicated with the leading "Pace" by means of a hunting horn to speed up or slow down the speed of running. Other means of communication were by blowing a whistle or by shouting instructions to speed up or slow down the running speed of the runners in the pack.

The hares generally used white paper for laying the trail although coloured paper was kept in reserve for use when snow covered the ground. They were allowed, indeed encouraged, to lay false trails for the following pack. Generally the "false" trail consisted of a hare continuing past a point where the "true" trail would go off at right angles, and continue to lay paper until it petered out at a point where the hare would stop laying paper, and then he would cut across country to join his partner at a pre-arranged point on the true trail. The hares became very devious in their tricks and often added considerable extra distance for the hounds to run on their outings. On one occasion the hares, on arriving at a marshy area, wrapped the trail paper round rocks and threw them into the bog. The stones sank, leaving the paper on the surface, and the hares carefully ran round the hazard and continued the paper trail on the other side as though there had been no obstacle. The following hounds, keen to catch the hares, ran straight into the marsh without pause!

Clydesdale Harriers waited until 21st October for their opening run from the "Black Bull" in Milngavie. This run was described in the "Scots Umpire" as follows -

"The Clydesdale Harriers engaged in the first of their series of cross country runs at Milngavie. A goodly number of runners and friends took part in the run and returned home delighted with the afternoon's sport. On arriving at the "Black Bull", J Henderson and Wm Walker were despatched as the Hares and, being well acquainted with the district, they led the pack through the estates of Campbell Douglas, Baron Graham and Sir J Buchanan. A number of people watched with interest the start of the Hounds who, led by W S Legge, followed the paper to a field at one end of the town, and on entering they had a fine run across fields for nearly a mile when some time was lost finding the trail, a "false" having been laid. The paper was at last found again and the pack started in hot pursuit. Several miles were traversed before the hares were sighted and this seemed to put new life into the hounds and they, keeping well together, kept a steady pace and lessened the gap between them and the hares. The hares were soon again lost to sight and it was some time before they were seen on the top of a hill having still a good lead. The pack, when about a mile from the town, were drawn up in a line and a race home took place which ended in S Walker (who started as whip) coming in first, being closely followed by A M Campbell and W S Legge, the others being close up. The hares got home a few minutes before the pack with the distance covered being over 13 miles. A very pleasant evening followed".

The two clubs who started the sport were particular in their attention to dress for their runs over the country, with Clydesdale Harriers sporting "Black knickers and a white jersey with the club badge of a five bar gate on the back". Edinburgh Harriers decided at their opening meeting on 30th September 1885 to wear dark blue jerseys with a gate worked in crimson on the back and white knickerbockers or knee breaches. Runners were advised to acquire dark blue caps with monogram E H on the cap.

The sport began to be noticed in the athletic press and in November 1885 the Scottish Athletic Journal commented "cross country running, if carefully nurtured, is certain to become one of our leading sports," but clubs were warned of the danger of "having too many football men on their committees".

On 12th December Edinburgh Harriers held the first cross country handicap ever run in Scotland from the "Sheepshead" in Duddingston over a distance of 4 miles, with D S Duncan and W M Gabriel running from the scratch mark with the limit man running from a 4 minute advantage.

Clydesdale Harriers held their first club championship from the Ranfurly Hotel, Bridge of Weir through heavy snow with thick mist limiting visibility to just 30 yards. The course was 7 miles in length - 3 miles less then originally intended and W M Thomson won the Championship by 10 yards from James Campbell with J Henderson third.

During the winter the Lanarkshire and Langside Bicycle Clubs each formed harriers sections and held several runs, but conditions like those encountered at Bridge of Weir soon persuaded them that the sport was too strenuous and tough and the sections faded out.

Naturally, with two clubs in existence, an inter club run was to be expected and in February an inter club pack run took place at Govan with 27 runners taking part.

The inaugural Scottish National Championships were organised by a Sub-Committee of the Scottish AAA, with just three weeks elapsing from the first consideration of the proposal to the Championships being staged at Lanark Racecourse on Saturday 13th March. There was some discussion that the date be changed as the Edinburgh runners would not turn up due to the Rugby International match being held in Raeburn Place, Edinburgh on the same day. But it was the Clydesdale club which suffered most with only four of their nominated fourteen runners turning out while Edinburgh fielded seven men. The eleven runners started at 4.15 p.m. in miserable conditions in front of a paltry crowd of spectators whose entry fees resulted in total gate receipts of 2/- (10p)!!

THE CROSS-COUNTRY
Championship of Scotland
WILL BE HELD ON

Lanark Racecourse

On SATURDAY, 27th MARCH, 1886,
At 4 15 p m.

Admission 6d. Grand Stand 6d. extra.

The Ayr footballer A P Findlay of Clydesdale Harriers, a stonemason by trade, led the eleven runners through the pouring rain and covered the 10 miles of heavy grassland in 62 min 57 sec defeating D S Duncan (Edinburgh H) to give Clydesdale the first of their 9 consecutive individual titles, with Edinburgh Harriers gaining the team title. Claims that betting was permitted on the day were strongly denied by D S Duncan who also rebutted a claim that "the course was under distance, by stating that "the course was over the stated 10 miles and that up to a dozen Scots runners could cover 10 miles of cross country in under an hour".

When the news of Findlay's victory reached his home town of Ayr preparations were made to meet him on the arrival of the Glasgow train at 9.12 p.m. He did not turn up and a still larger crowd met the 11.20 p.m. train, but again there was no Findlay! The crowd dispersed and it was not until 7.40 a.m. the following morning that Findlay arrived, footsore and weary, having walked from Barrhead to Kilmarnock to catch the first train to Ayr on the Sunday morning.

Edinburgh Harriers winning team in the inaugural National Championship at Lanark Racecourse in March 1886. T. Fraser (back left); D.C. Macmichael, D.S. Duncan, W.M. Gabriel and J.W.L. Beck (respectively third, fourth, fifth and sixth in second row); P. Addison, R.C. Buist and J.M. Bow (first, third and fourth from left, seated).

The following season the sport expanded with West of Scotland Harriers being formed on 14th September 1886, mainly from runners who left Clydesdale Harriers, with new members from cycling, rowing and football clubs rapidly joining up. The athletic press again mentioned the new and growing sport critically, saying "the only fault with cross country running is its severe exclusiveness. Though having all the physical advantages it has none of the entertaining merits of football as it is a sport which gives gratification only to those who engage in it and must always suffer from a lack of public patronage for that reason".

The three clubs carried out missionary exercises, holding their Saturday afternoon pack runs in different parts of the countryside, partly for the enjoyment of their members and partly to bring the sport to the attention of potential recruits outside the main centres of population. Clydesdale Harriers, though centered in Glasgow, held weekly club pack runs in Rutherglen, Chryston, Uddingston,

Cathcart, Newton Mearns, Bothwell and Milngavie. This travel was made possible by the comprehensive railway system existing in West and Central Scotland, with trains running at frequent intervals and providing easy and cheap travel. West of Scotland Harriers travelling to Helensburgh, were advised by their Committee, "special rail coaches have been hired and special tickets have been taken out for the whole party at reduced rates, so members are requested not to purchase tickets at the station".

The second National Championships were held on 19th March 1887 at Hampden Park, organised again by the Scottish AAA Sub-Committee. The race was over 12 miles on this occasion and a Grand Football Match between East and West Harriers was scheduled during the race. This, together with the promise that "the half time and final results of the International football match between England and Scotland will be published in the ground", attracted 600 spectators who paid 6 d. (2½p) admission with a further 6 d. (2½p) charge to the stands.

At that time Hampden Park was situated in the middle of the countryside and the trail consisted of four laps of the cinder track, out of the stadium to the country over Mount Florida, past Hundred Acre Park into Castlemilk Estate, then back through Rutherglen to the stadium, with one lap of the cinder track to complete the first of four laps. The race was won by James Campbell (Clydesdale H) in 1 hour 14 min 24 sec from his clubmate W Henderson, with W Jack in third place leading Edinburgh Harriers 42 pts. to a repeat victory over Clydesdale Harriers 49 pts. with West of Scotland H third with 89 pts.

CROSS-COUNTRY CHAMPIONSHIP OF SCOTLAND,
AND
GRAND FOOTBALL MATCH.

EAST
V.
WEST HARRIERS,
At HAMPDEN PARK, GLASGOW
(By kind permission of the Queen's Park F.C.),
On SATURDAY, 19TH MARCH, 1887,
Commencing at 3.30 P.M.
Admission, Sixpence.   Stands, Sixpence Extra.

NOTE.—The half-time and final results of the International will be published on the ground.

By this time the three clubs all had healthy memberships with Edinburgh Harriers boasting over 300 members, Clydesdale Harriers a total of 420 and the year old West of Scotland Harriers having 48 members on their books.

The active harrier clubs felt strong enough, in season 1887/88, to set up a Scottish Cross Country Association, breaking clear of the Scottish AAA Sub Committee of Management which had organised the first two National Championships.

At this time the sport of cross country running was very much in its infancy with few rules or regulations governing the growing sport. The new Association, under the Presidency of J M Bow and guided by Secretary D S Duncan (both of Edinburgh Harriers), set about introducing rules and establishing control of the existing and new clubs which were being set up throughout Scotland. Two of the new rules, which aroused immediate antagonism from Clydesdale Harriers, were:-

1) Only athletes resident within a 20 mile radius from a Club's Headquarters could be members of that club.
2) Athletes must have completed 5 qualifying Saturday runs from Club Headquarters before being eligible to represent the club in the National Championships.

Clydesdale Harriers had their Headquarters in Glasgow but had established satellite "sections" throughout Central and West Scotland to encourage the growth of cross country running in outlying country areas. Most of these sections'

Headquarters were well outside a 20 mile radius from Glasgow but Clydesdale Harriers used the top runners from their "sections" in their National team, thus accounting for their domination in the early years when they gained 9 individual and 6 team titles in the first 10 years of the National Championships. Most of the runners in the sections ran from their own local Headquarters and only visited Clydesdale's Glasgow Headquarters for an official pack run outing or participation in the club's annual championships. This practice precluded runners achieving the necessary total of 5 qualifying runs from the Glasgow Headquarters to be eligible to run in Clydesdale's team in the National Championship at the end of the season.

Feeling threatened as to the continued growth of their club which was directly affected by the distance radius for membership rules, Clydesdale felt that the legality of their country "sections" was being challenged by the new S.C.C.A. Clydesdale opposed the new governing body, refusing to join the S.C.C.A. at the outset as it considered that the influence of the club was likely to be diminished by the new rules of the Association. However they decided to participate in the National Championship organised by the S.C.C.A. as it was the only formal competition available in Scotland at the time.

The domestic season saw the well established clubs Edinburgh Harriers and West of Scotland Harriers, together with Clydesdale Harriers and the country sections from Falkirk, Ayrshire, Dumbartonshire, Renfrewshire and South Lanarkshire, sharing inter-clubs runs with Dundee Harriers, Hamilton Harriers, Kilmarnock Harriers, Penicuik Harriers, Lochee Harriers, Dennistoun Bath Harriers and many other new clubs.

Clydesdale staged their club championship from the Racecourse, Paisley with the Headquarters section and all sections, except Falkirk, fielding teams of 10 runners with the unusual number of 5 to count in the team contest. It was intended that the runners cover an 8 mile course but, after a fast start in which the leaders ran the first mile around the Racecourse in under 5 minutes, the race was accidently extended and a 12 mile trail was covered. A P Findlay, the winner of the inaugural National title at Lanark in 1886, scored a narrow victory finishing just 2 seconds in front of R Graham, with W Henderson third a further 2 minutes behind.

The 1888 National Championships were staged at Hawkhill trotting track in Leith just 5 weeks after a S.C.C.A Committee Meeting on 4th February appointed a sub committee of Messrs Bow (President), Duncan (Secretary) and Meikle to organise the event and lay out the course. In spite of the short organising time available an excellent event was held at Hawkhill with 7 of the runners in the inaugral 1886 Championship competing. Four clubs contested the championship - Clydesdale, Edinburgh, West of Scotland and Kilmarnock Harriers - covering a varied two lap 9 mile course. The runners covered 600 yards of the cinder track, onto Restalrig Road, across ploughed fields to Craigentinny Meadows to the Leith end of Portobello Road. A homewards turn was made at Craigentinny Farm passing by St Margaret's gasworks and Lochend Road to enter by the main gate. After half a lap of the cinder track the runners covered the course again. A P Findlay led from the start, being closely followed by a pack of 6 Clydesdale Harriers and A Robertson (Edinburgh). Findlay eventually finished a clear winner with Clydesdale scoring an overwhelming team victory with J Campbell 2; A Hannah 3; R Graham 4; W Henderson 5 and A Colquhoun 8 for a team total of just 23 points to defeat Edinburgh Harriers and West of Scotland, with Kilmarnock Harriers, who had just 5 men finishing, failing to complete a team.

A football match between teams representing East and West Harriers Clubs was held while the runners were out of the Stadium and, although the East team was said to contain members who were of International standard, the West team won by 2 goals to 1. A football match was held as an integral part of the early National Championships, mainly to attract a crowd of spectators and provide interest while the runners were out of the park for upwards of an hour.

Clydesdale Harriers antagonism and opposition to the new Association were voiced at the presentation of prizes in the Prince of Wales Hotel that evening. Mr Mellish, Secretary of Clydesdale Harriers, stated that his club was determined not to change the position which they had already taken up against the restrictive laws of the S.C.C.A. This statement was received with marked signs of disapproval by the majority of the company including those who were members of his own club.

Scottish Cross-Country Association.

THIRD ANNUAL
Cross-Country Championship
AT HAWKHILL GROUNDS, LEITH,
ON SATURDAY FIRST.
ADMISSION SIXPENCE.

Domestically the sport was growing rapidly and almost 30 clubs were in existence at the end of the 1887/88 season. Edinburgh had 297 members, with Clydesdale totalling 514 members and the Edinburgh club had an attendance of 64 members at an inter club match with West of Scotland (22 members) at Granton, resulting in the largest assembly of harriers ever seen in Scotland. Edinburgh Harriers were a very social club, holding inter club runs often during the season, and one such event with Penicuik Harriers was recorded as "after an enjoyable run, and even more enjoyable social evening, the horses were yoked and the old Stockbridge bus made tracks homeward". In 1888 the Loretto Challenge Cup was presented to Edinburgh for competition between athletes over 27 years of age to encourage veteran runners. The donor considered that runners gave up active participation in outside sports at far too early a stage in life and he wanted to encourage veterans to keep competing. He would be extremely gratified at the current scene where veterans between 40 and 80 years of age are competitively active on most weekends throughout the year.

Difficulties grew between the S.C.C.A. and Clydesdale Harriers and its satellite sections, and relations deteriorated to such an extent that Clydesdale formed a rival breakaway group to run their version of the sport under their own rules. At a meeting in the Bath Hotel, Glasgow in December 1888 Clydesdale proposed the formation of a body whereby individual interests were to be subordinated to the general interest of Harriers clubs and the sport in general. The result was the formation of the Scottish Harriers Union (S.H.U.) with the intention of carrying out competitions on more modern and improved lines, and fostering and encouraging cross country running with as few restrictions as possible.

Both the S.H.U. and the S.C.C.A. had firm objectives of developing interest in cross country running throughout Scotland and encouraging the formation and ultimate affiliation of harrier clubs. The S.C.C.A. took the unusual step, at a Special General Meeting in the Royal Hotel, Glasgow in February 1889, of amending their constitution to enable Berwick and District Harriers to join the Association. Only clubs with headquarters in Scotland were eligible to join the S.C.C.A. and, for the purposes of the Association, Berwick was declared to be part of Scotland and the new club was welcomed into membership.

Both bodies held National Cross Country Championships of Scotland during the two seasons of "civil war" between the two rival bodies. In 1889 the Scottish Harriers Union held their championship in February at Parkhead, Glasgow with the cooperation of Celtic F.C. Six teams took part in the event, with 10 men teams from the Glasgow HQ and the Lanarkshire, Dumbartonshire, Renfrewshire, Ayrshire and Stirlingshire sections of Clydesdale Harriers competing. The event was staged under the aggregate time method with 5 men (not 6) counting for the team championship. All the runners were timed and the best average time for the first 5 counters of the team decided the team championship, instead of the more usual individual places total. This was the first time in Great Britain this method of scoring was used.

Club Advertisements.

SCOTTISH HARRIERS' UNION.

GREAT FOOTBALL MATCH
CELTIC
Versus a Select Team of
CLYDESDALE HARRIERS
(Similar to that which defeated Preston North End), and
Cross-Country Championships
CELTIC PARK, PARKHEAD.
SATURDAY, 23rd FEBRUARY.
Admission Sixpence. Grand Stand Sixpence extra. Kick-off at 3 p.m. Championships at 4 p.m. (Half-time). Admission Tickets may be had from H. & P. M'NEIL, W. G. BELL, and Officials.

The SAAA 4 mile champion and record holder, J W McWilliams (Ayrshire section), won the 10 mile race, finishing 8 seconds in front of A G Colquhoun (Glasgow), with C McCann (Lanarkshire) third. The team competition resulted as follows:

1) Glasgow 81 min 23 sec average time (40 place points); 2) Ayrshire 83 min 00 sec (55 points) 3) Lanarkshire 84 min 49 sec (77 points); 4) Renfrewshire 85 min 57 sec (86 points) and 5) Dunbartonshire 86 min 39 sec (92 points). It is interesting to note that the team order was the same under both the traditional place points scoring system and the innovative average time system. The usual football match was held between Clydesdale Harriers team, which had beaten Preston North End and Third Lanark earlier in the season, and Celtic F.C. the Scottish Cup Finalists. This was probably the main reason for over 5,000 spectators attending the Championship and Clydesdale's day was complete when their team defeated Celtic by 3 goals to 0.

The S.C.C.A. Championship was held at Hamilton Park Racecourse 2 weeks later. This was the first time a National Championship had been held at Hamilton and it is possible that the unfortunate events of the Championship deterred organisers from using it again for the most important Championship of the year. For, except for the staging of the inaugural International Championship in 1903, Hamilton Park Racecourse was never again the venue for a National Championship when staged in the West

---

Scottish Cross-Country Association.

FOURTH ANNUAL
CROSS COUNTRY CHAMPIONSHIP
OF SCOTLAND AND
GRAND FOOTBALL MATCH,
EAST v. WEST OF SCOTLAND.
At HAMILTON PARK RACECOURSE, HAMILTON,
On SATURDAY FIRST at 4 p.m.
ADMISSION SIXPENCE.   GRAND STAND SIXPENCE EXTRA.

SCOTTISH FOOTBALL ASSOCIATION.

---

of Scotland until 1926. From that time the highly suitable location was utilised as a championship venue on 28 of the 36 occassions in the period between 1926 and

1968, when championships were held. The S.C.C.A. National Championship was contested by Clydesdale, Edinburgh, West of Scotland, Ayr and the local Hamilton club. Motherwell Y.M.C.A Harriers laid the trail on the morning of the race but unfortunately the leaders followed an old paper trail which had been laid by Motherwell for a race the previous Saturday and went off course, adding almost 2 miles to the required distance of the race.

Thomas Thorburn, one of four brothers in the Hamilton team, with local knowledge of the intended trail as laid by the organisers, knew which was the new paper trail and followed the correct course. Unfortunately only 12 of the 54 starters followed him around the correct course. Thorburn led the 12 runners home with SCCA Secretary D S Duncan (Edinburgh) in third place, but the remaining runners finished over 10 minutes later, having covered a longer trail. No club had 6 finishers in the leading group which covered the correct distance with Hamilton and West of Scotland both having 5 men; so no club had a complete team to claim the championship. Due to an outcry from the leading runners who went off course the SCCA declared both the individual and team race null and void and ordered a re-run in 2 weeks time.

Hamilton Harriers, disgusted at the decision of General Committee, did not compete at the second running of the Championship but the other 4 clubs again turned out. Without any incidents the runners covered the same trail as the first race and C McCann (Clydesdale) won in 54 min 46 sec, finishing 9 seconds in front of A Robertson (Edinburgh) with Andrew Hannah (Clydesdale) making his first appearance in the National in third place in 55 min 21 secs.

It is important to note that Thomas Thorburn, who was first home in the void race, finished in 54 min 19 sec - 27 seconds faster than the winning time recorded by C McCann in the re run race. It is the only occasion in the history of the National Championship that a runner ran the correct championship course as determined by the organisers, defeated all his rivals in the race and recorded a faster time than any one else recorded over the official course - and still was not acknowledged as the National Champion. History may have forgotten Thomas Thorburn's achievements and he is not recorded in the official list of Scottish Champions but his victory is acknowledged and recorded over 100 years later.

In season 1889/90 two separate National Championships were again held with the SHU introducing a "Junior " Championship restricted to competitors who had never taken part in the Senior Championship race organised by the S.C.C.A., SHU or the English CCU. This "Junior" Championship was in line with the declared intent of the S.H.U. to increase opportunities for competition and, with members of the first 3 teams being declared ineligible for further competitons as "Juniors", it was intended to act as a feeder competition for the Senior Championship and increase the number of individuals and clubs taking part in the National Championships.

The Junior Championship was held at Ibrox Park on 21st December 1889 with 11 teams and over 100 competitors taking part in the largest competitive event seen in Scotland. Most of the teams were from Clydesdale Harriers and its country sections but other teams from Argyll, Strathblane, Motherwell, Greenock, Dennistoun and Paisley entered also. Jack Wright (Dumbartonshire) won the 7 mile race in 50 min 59 sec, finishing 24 seconds clear of A McDonald (Paisley), with the Paisley team recording an average time of 51 min 59 sec to defeat Dunbartonshire 52 min 37 sec and Motherwell 52 min 37 sec.

The SHU Championship was held in February 1890 from Cathkin Park with Charles Pennycook, despite losing a shoe 2 miles from the finish, winning by 21 seconds from Andrew Hannah.

The SCCA Championship was held 2 weeks later from Tynecastle Park, Edinburgh. Contemporary reports detail "a cold, bleak, miserable day, not encouraging for runners to race a gruelling 10 miles across country". Nevertheless, 46 of the 48 entered runners from four clubs started the race. The final of the Edinburgh Cup, held elsewhere in the city, caused a meagre crowd of spectators at the race, and not even the attraction of the usual football match between St. Bernards and Queens Park, while the runners were out of sight over the country, could attract a large crowd. The Scottish Sport newspaper commented "the tastes of the Scottish sporting public have yet to be educated to the fierce delights of harrier racing".

A fast start, by the Clydesdale pair Andrew Hannah and James Campbell, speadeagled the field. The Clydesdale runners, together with A Robertson and D McKinlay (both Edinburgh), led at half distance, and it was with just 2 miles to go that Hannah raced clear of the leading group to win in 56 min 52 sec, over 120 yards in front of A Robertson, with 1887 champion James Campbell in third position.

Clydesdale Harriers, with their counting six runners in the first nine home, totalled 34 points to retain the team championship, 10 points in front of Edinburgh, with West of Scotland finishing third for the fourth year in a row ahead of Motherwell YMCA. Besides winning the individual championship Hannah had, in the 3 weeks prior to the championship at Tynecastle, finished second in the SHU Championship and ninth in the English National Championship at Sutton Coldfield near Birmingham despite suffering from a bad cold.

With the SCCA being the Association affiliated to the Scottish AAA, from whom it had official delegated control of the sport, the SHU was just an independent, unofficial body. After various unofficial meetings between the two cross country organisations to discuss their points of difference, the SCCA called a meeting to resolve the situation and consider amalgamation to form a representative cross country governing body to control the sport in Scotland.

This initiative was encouraged by the sporting press who advised "it must be obvious to Clydesdale Harriers that it cannot control the rest of the clubs in Scotland outside its own membership. The time has come when it should lay aside any feeling of umbrage it may have against the SCCA and join forces with the other leading clubs in an effort to govern and popularise the sport whose interests all have at heart".

A meeting between the two bodies was held in the Royal Hotel, George Square, Glasgow on 1st February 1890 with the aim of bringing into existence one body to amalgamate all the governing elements. During the two seasons of discord the SCCA was shown as being mainly concerned with staging and supervising the National Championship, and not greatly interested in actively developing the sport throughout the country. The SHU, on the other hand, had definite objectives in fostering the sport as they assisted and encouraged minor clubs to become established, inaugurated a "Junior" Championship, in addition to the National Championship, and staged other competitive events to develop the sport.

The main points of concern which caused the split could be regarded, in this day and age, as being relatively trivial and no reason for the rivalry which resulted in the establishment of two governing bodies in Scotland. The main points of dissension were:-

1) SCCA ruled that only athletes resident within a 20 mile radius of a club's headquarters could be members of that club. (Not accepted by SHU who viewed this as an intention to break up Clydesdale Harriers).
2) SCCA ruled that athletes must have completed 5 qualifying Saturday runs from club headquarters before being eligible to represent the club in the National Championships. (SHU required that only 3 qualifying runs be necessary).
3) SCCA ruled that 6 runners count in a team in the National Championships with place points determining team victory. (SHU ruled that 5 runners count in a team with the aggregate time method determining team victory).

These 3 main points of principle separated the two bodies until the February meeting in Glasgow when concessions were made by both sides in an effort to resolve the situation. Points agreed were as follows:-

1) SCCA agreed to accept SHU Junior Championships.
2) SCCA agreed that the National Senior Championships be open to all Scottish amateurs as in SHU constitution.
3) SCCA agreed to 3 qualifying runs instead of original 5 qualifying runs.
4) SHU agreed to the 20 mile radius qualifying clause to determine club membership.
5) SHU agreed to place points deciding victory in team competition and dropping the aggregate time method.
6) SHU agreed to 6 counters, not 5, in team competition.
7) SCCA agreed to adopt SHU rule re representation:-

"That each affiliated club be entitled to send a representative to the A.G.M., and clubs with a membership of over 100 members be entitled to an additional representative for every 50 members or fraction thereof, with a limit that no club be entitled to have more than 3 representatives".

The meeting agreed that both existing bodies be dissolved and an entirely new Union would assume control of cross country sport in Scotland as the sole governing body. This new Union would be called the Scottish Cross Country Union and D S Duncan was requested to officiate as Interim Secretary, draft a new constitution and rules, and call a meeting to establish the new body at the end of March.

Contemporary reports of the meeting state, "In sporting circles there is a feeling of general satisfaction that a dispute has been removed from the sphere of athletics which has prevented the full and free development of the comparatively new sport of cross country running". It was also stated that "the new Union will be the means of concentrating all the energies of the different harrier clubs in Scotland to support and develop the sport".

It is important to realise that both the SCCA and the SHU were dissolved to allow the formation of the Scottish Cross Country Union. The 5 year period between 1885 and 1890 was a period of development, experimentation and "trial and error" before the sport stabilised and the new SCCU was formed to become the first true National governing body of cross country running in Scotland.

1890 to 1899

After the formation of the Scottish Cross Country Union there was a commitment to extend the range of National championship events. This had been agreed during the discussions between the Scottish Cross Country Association and the Scottish Harriers Union, and consequently the new body extended the National Senior Championships to all amateurs in Scotland and instituted a new Junior individual and team Championship. This Junior Championship, open to all Scottish amateurs who had never competed in the Senior championship, included a team championship in which clubs could enter a team of 12 competitors with 6 men to count. This Junior race was to prove very popular, encouraging clubs and athletes who would never have taken part in the Senior championship to enter the Junior race.

In the final decade of the nineteenth century there was a clear division between the "Senior" and "Junior" clubs in Scotland. The "Senior" clubs consisted of Clydesdale Harriers and Edinburgh Harriers, who were the constant entrants and winners in the Scottish Senior Championship, together with West of Scotland Harriers, Edinburgh Northern Harriers, Watsonians CCC and Motherwell YMCA Harriers who entered the Senior Championship on occasions when they were strong enough to offer a challenge to the top clubs. The remaining 40 or so clubs in Scotland were titled "Junior" clubs and their members took no part in the Scottish Championships on any occasion. This state of affairs did nothing to encourage the growth of the sport as, for other than the top 6 clubs in Scotland, cross country running was an enjoyable pastime with no spice of competition at all.

The new Junior championship provided a competitive outlet for runners from the vast majority of harrier clubs in Scotland who had never had any intention of entering the Senior championship and racing against Clydesdale and Edinburgh Harriers, who had dominated both the individual and team titles since the inception of the Championship in 1886. Contemporary newspaper reports in Scottish Sport stated that "cross country running in Scotland is quite a new sport and is trying to excite public interest. But it will be a long time before the public turn out in large numbers to watch it, for there is not sufficient excitement generated by the races to arouse enthusiasm and Scots, more than Englishmen, need their emotions aroused before forming an attachment to any departure from the normal, accepted variety of physical recreation".

The inaugural National Junior Championship staged by the S.C.C.U. was held at Hawkhill Stadium in Leith on 7th February 1891, approximately a month before the National Senior Championship. Eight teams competed, four from the East (Edinburgh H, Edinburgh Northern H, Edinburgh University H & H and Dalkeith H) with the West also fielding four teams (Clydesdale H, West of Scotland H, Paisley H and Dennistoun H). The 7 mile race was held over a 2 lap course with a good assortment of plough and grassland intermingled with fences, hedges, walls and ditches. Many of the runners were new to cross country running, though experienced in other sports, and were racing for the first ever time.

To help them, an article entitled "Advice to Intending Runners" was published in

Scottish Sport, urging competitors to "take a moderate amount of exercise the day before the race so as to induce a fatigue which will yield a cool, refreshing sleep and avoid a sleepless, restless night. When you go to bed don't think about the race the next day. If you do you won't get any sleep before dawn. If you fear this will be the case a good tumblerful of hot toddy will work the trick if taken on a light, but not empty, stomach. On race day eat a lean chop or steak and dry toast, two or three hours before the race and you will be well provided. Suck a lemon at half distance in the race if you are dry, but don't take too much as it could induce vomiting and spoil your performance".

Despite the above advice, or maybe because of it, a good few runners were satisfied with one lap of the course and dropped out at half distance when returning to the trotting track at Hawkhill. W J Lowson, an individual entrant from Dundee, proved the stronger to win by 3 yards from J Taylor (Clydesdale), with W Muir finishing third and leading home an Edinburgh team, all of whom were under 20 years of age, to victory over Edinburgh Northern and Clydesdale. The winners received their medals at a smoking concert in the Continental Hotel, Meuse Lane, Edinburgh that evening.

With two National Championships it was decided to stage them alternately in the East and West of Scotland each year. Accordingly the Senior National race was held at Cathkin Park, Glasgow on 14th March, with Motherwell YMCA joining the ever present trio of Clydesdale, Edinburgh and West of Scotland. Scottish Sport wrote indignantly that "there were over 50 cross country clubs in existence in Scotland, at least 12 of which were fully capable of fielding experienced teams in the National Championships. Why were there only 4 clubs willing to enter the Championships and challenge for honours?"

It seemed that the Junior clubs were content to leave the race for National individual and team honours to others. However, this problem was not only apparent in Scotland, for in England the previous year only 9 clubs had competed in their National Championships - and one of these was from Dublin!

Of the 46 runners lined up on a warm, sunny day more reminiscent of June than March, only D S Duncan, Union Secretary, and P Addison (both Edinburgh H) had taken part in the first championship race at Lanark five years earlier. Andrew Hannah, the greatest cross country runner of his generation, repeated the previous year's victory after leading by a large margin at half distance and going on to finish "fresh as paint" for a 500 yard margin of victory with the Edinburgh pair A Robertson and W M Carment taking the other medals. This good start to the team contest enabled Edinburgh to break the Clydesdale run of three team championship victories and win by 6 points from their Glasgow rivals.

The sport continued to grow rapidly with new clubs starting up regularly. They included a club in Edinburgh restricted only to total abstainers - though there is no record of how many joined - and Whiteinch Harriers who utilised the Corporation Tramway Stables in Whiteinch for their Saturday runs.

A Glasgow sports shop advertised an equipment price list for Harriers containing such items as:-

Clydesdale Harriers singlets from 1/- (5p) to 2/6 (12½p)each
Clydesdale Harriers nickers from 2/6 (12½p) to 4/6 (22½)per pair
West of Scotland Harriers jerseys 4/6 (22½p)each to 4/6 (32½p)each; badges 2/- (10p)each

Harrier shoes with rubber soles 3/6 (17½p)per pair; spikes on soles 6/6 (32½p) to 9/6 (47½p) per pair. Caps and berets for Harriers available.

At the 1891 Annual General Meeting of the SCCU Mr Honeyman (Clydesdale) tried to get the Cross Country team championships decided by the average time of counting runners - the strange method utilised by the SHU - but failed by a large margin and this system was never raised again in Scotland.

The attraction of a football match between Rangers and St Mirren while the race was in progress ensured a crowd of over 2,000 spectators at the 1892 National Junior Championship at Westmarch Grounds, Paisley. Eleven clubs entered for the 7 mile race (3 more than the previous year) and Edinburgh H, keen to repeat last year's team victory, arranged for a special rail carriage for team and supporters at a return fare of 3/9 (19p) from Edinburgh to Paisley.

After finding that the stripping accommodation was totally inadequate for the large number of runners, complaints were loud in the air from the shivering runners huddled together waiting for the start of the race at 4pm. After 2 miles the leading runners encountered a burly farmer, who after discovering a paper trail laid over his land, stood guard over the entrance to his fields and with scythe in hand, threatened to decapitate the first runner to step on his land. The runners, who decided that discretion was much better than foolish valour, made a detour around his fields and continued on their way. P. T. Lewis, to the cheers of the large contingent of Clydesdale supporters, finished 200 yards clear of his nearest rival with Edinburgh Northern winning the team title by 9 points from Clydesdale.

The Senior Championship was held 5 weeks later at Tynecastle but no clubs from the Junior Championship entered in addition to the usual contenders. It had previously been suggested that the winners of the Junior individual and team titles be reclassified as Seniors and become ineligible to compete again as Juniors, but this proposal was to wait for a considerable period of time before being implemented. Charles Pennycook interrupted his club mate Andrew Hannah's bid for a hat trick of individual titles but continued Clydesdale's domination of the individual race. He scored a convincing victory over Hannah with Carment (Edinburgh) third and Clydesdale scored 37 points to defeat Edinburgh by 7 points.

After an enjoyable smoker concert in Edinburgh there was an eventful journey home for the Glasgow teams, who captured an Italian organ grinder and bundled him on to the Glasgow train against his will to provide the musical accompaniment for a sing song on the homeward journey.

In season 1892/93 David S Duncan, the guiding mentor behind cross country who had acted as Hon Secretary and Treasurer since 1885, became President of the Union with his club mate W M Carment taking over as Secretary while still an active competitor. Duncan showed he was still active when laying the paper trail on the morning of the National Junior Championship at Musselburgh Racecourse. It is perhaps indicative of the time, and the intimate, growing nature of the sport in the final decade of the nineteeth century, that the President could take so active a part in the championship's organisation compared to modern times when the President's activities are confined to chairing the Reception Committee for guests on race day.

The race was won by Stewart Duffus of Arbroath Harriers, who later joined Clydesdale and went on to win the Senior title in 1897. Third placed J Thin led Edinburgh Northern (6 men in the first 12 home) to a repeat team victory over

Clydesdale. Edinburgh Northern, encouraged by their two consecutive National Junior team championship wins, entered the 1893 National Senior race at Hampden Park for the first time. The very high wind on the cold, blustery afternoon blew away much of the paper trail laid in the morning. Andrew Hannah was in the lead at the point where the paper trail disappeared and, with his intimate local knowledge of the course, waited for the rest of the field to catch up with him. He then led the runners home by a circuitous route, adding a mile to the correct distance, and passing some of the trail layers who had waited to act as stewards to guide the runners where the paper was sparse.

At the end of the first lap, confident that the others now knew the correct course to follow, Hannah set out on his own and quickly

David S. Duncan
the "Grand Old Man of Scottish Athletics"
He was President of the Union in 1892/93 after being Hon. Secretary and Treasurer for the first 7 years of the Union's existence.

established a lead of 100 yards in the next mile. From there on the race was settled and Hannah came home an easy winner over a course that was more like 12 miles than the expected 10 miles after his added distance on each lap. Hannah scored his third National triumph with former Junior Champion P T Lewis (also Clydesdale) finishing 60 yards in front of the Union Secretary W M Carment. Clydesdale, with 6 in 16 home, totalled 48 points to win by 12 points from Edinburgh Northern, with Edinburgh 66 points in third place.

William Robertson scored Clydesdale's second individual victory in the Junior championship when he won the 1894 title at Hamilton Racecourse by 20 yards from W Hay (Edinburgh), with J Hamilton finishing third to win the first National honour for Maryhill Harriers. Clydesdale, with their 6 men in the first 19 runners to finish, won the team championship from the other 10 competing clubs. The most surprising performance came from Watsonians Cross Country Club, formed only four months earlier, who had just 30 members, as membership was restricted to former pupils of George Watsons College. The Watsonians finished as third team on this occasion and, within 4 years, were to provide the National individual champion and twice win the team title.

Andrew Hannah continued on his winning way with another easy victory in the National Senior Championship at Musselburgh Racecourse. Running over a short course (less than 9 miles), which had only one half mile stretch of plough to test the runners, Hannah defeated the previous year's Junior Champion Stewart Duffus (Arbroath) and led Clydesdale to victory by 10 points over Edinburgh Northern who finished well clear of city rivals Edinburgh Harriers. The Edinburgh club supporters were well positioned around the course to supply sponges and drinks to their members competing in the race. Although complaints were made by the Glasgow clubs no action was taken as no rules had been broken.

Hannah received his winners medal from Union President Alex McNab of Clydesdale Harriers, who was the first Clydesdale man to hold this proud position. In the six year period from 1887 there had been 4 Presidents from Edinburgh and 2 from West of Scotland Harriers. Andrew Hannah, who became President in 1897-98 on his retiral from active competition, and Alex McNab were the only Clydesdale men to be President in the 100 year history of the Scottish Cross Country Union.

It is very strange, taking account of the pre-eminent position of Clydesdale in both the competitive and administrative sides of Union activities, that in the long period between 1898 and 1990 no Clydesdale man was ever appointed President. It would seem that the Clydesdale led "Scottish Harriers Union" episode rankled deeply and long in the memories of the General Committee for them to carry out such a prolonged period of exclusion of Clydesdale members from Scotland's top honour in harrier circles. However, Clydesdale did not seem to carry any grudge at this attitude as one of their members, A Ross Scott, served as Secretary and Treasurer of the Union between 1898 and 1911, with his long period of 13 years service being exceeded only among the 10 Secretaries of the Union by George Dallas (1921-1960).

The 1894 SCCU Annual General Meeting was held in the Continental Hotel, Edinburgh with a membership of 16 clubs and a cash balance of just £8.00 reported. This compared unfavourably with the report of Clydesdale Harriers cash balance of over £80 and further cause for concern was given at the founding meeting of the Western District Junior Cross Country Association in Ancells Restaurant, Glasgow in September, 1894.

This meeting was attended by representatives of over 20 clubs in the West of Scotland. The Association had held a 7 mile race from the Couper Institute, Cathcart the previous February in which 7 clubs, Bellahouston, Carluke Beagles, Clydesdale Juniors, Elderslie Wallace, Springburn, Strathblane and Whiteinch, took part together with individuals from Greenock Balclutha and Greenock Juniors. This race, organised by James Walker of Clydesdale Juniors, provided competition for Junior runners from young clubs in the West of Scotland not yet ready for National Championship competition. The need for such a race for young and inexperienced runners had long been talked about as necessary for the continued development of individuals and clubs to a higher standard.

However no action had been taken by the SCCU. who pointed out that there was a National Junior Championship race held annually and did not see the need to provide a race for Junior athletes in the West of Scotland. The large number of clubs in attendance at the inaugural meeting of the Western District Junior Association demonstrated the need for a District race. But on requesting the SCCU to undertake responsibility for the race on an official basis, the fledgling Association received a blank refusal from General Committee who told the Western District clubs to carry on and organise their own championship race.

This decision, contrary to the declared SCCU policy of developing and encouraging the sport, was a big mistake, for within 4 years the new Association had a larger membership of clubs than the SCCU itself. Indeed, matters had grown to such an extent that a second split in the administration of the sport, similar to the SCCA/SHU conflict, was imminent, with the SCCU being challenged as to its control of all levels of competition in the West of Scotland.

However in the 1895 Western District Junior Championship 13 clubs entered teams, a greater number than seen in the National Junior race. The race, held in Cathcart, was won by A McCallum (Partick Harrriers) from J Barclay (Whiteinch) with Wishaw winning the team contest from Springburn.

The National Junior Championship at Musselborough Racecourse attracted 12 teams which competed on a bitterly cold day. The 7 mile course, which consisted of $3\frac{1}{2}$ miles of flat, frost bound race course with a further $3\frac{1}{2}$ miles of surfaced road, was judged a poor substitute for a genuine cross country course. But the race itself proved exciting with three runners, who had led the race throughout, entering the final straight together. The lead changed hands several times in the last 50 yards, with Edinburgh University student F Bruce winning by inches from Hugh Welsh who led Watsonians, 67 points to team victory over Edinburgh Northern, 115 points and Clydesdale, 121 points.

The Senior National was disappointing with Andrew Hannah missing the race due to an attack of influenza and Clydesdale's top Junior runners refusing to run so that they would have another year of eligibility for the National Junior Championship. Edinburgh, on the other hand, were at their strongest as Edinburgh Northern, runners up for the past two years, did not enter and their top runners competed for Edinburgh. The Arbroath runner Stewart Duffus led for the entire race shadowed by R Hay (Edinburgh) but, when they entered for the final circuit of the Hampden Park track, Hay sprinted past the tired Duffus to win easily, with his clubmate A Reid third. Edinburgh not only won the individual title for the first time in the 10 year history of the championship but defeated Clydesdale by 10 points to win the team title.

Discussions were held between the Home Countries, Wales excepted, regarding a cross country International race. A March meeting in London agreed that the race would be run in Ireland, England and Scotland on consecutive years with the host country paying the expenses of the travelling teams. However the first race, to be held in 1896, did not take place as the Irish authorities said it was impossible to get a suitable enclosure in Dublin for the International at the beginning of April as agreed at the initial meeting. Any later date would mean the runners would be "stale" and off form, so the race was abandoned, with Scotland expressing strong regrets and hoping that better arrangements would be made the following year. The arrangements for the proposed 1897 International race failed to materialise and the proposal was dropped until future discussions resulted in the first International race being held at Hamilton Park Racecourse between all four Home Countries in 1903.

The 1896 National Junior Championship at Hamilton Park Racecourse was a closely contested team race with just one point covering the first 3 teams. Clydesdale and Motherwell YMCA each scored 94 points in a tie for the team title, with Edinburgh Northern just one point away in third place. As no tie breaking rule operated at this time the SCCU General Committee ordered a re-run between the two tieing clubs. The draw resulted in the race being held over Motherwell's home course, but Clydesdale won by the narrow margin of just 2 points and became the undisputed team champions.

Despite the handicaps of a sprained ankle from a club race in early February and an attack of neuralgia, Andrew Hannah recorded his fifth victory in eight years in the Senior National Championship held on 14th March from Stewart's College grounds at Inverleith, Edinburgh. Because of his injuries Hannah was not in his usual dominating form. For, after the first 5 miles run at a very fast pace, Hannah was fully 400 yards behind the leading group. However his experience told and, paced by clubmate David Mill, he worked his way back into contention with the leaders. With 2 miles to go Hannah struck over a long stretch of ploughed land and only Stewart Duffus (who had switched allegiance from Arbroath to Clydesdale) was strong enough to go with him. They ran the last 2 miles shoulder to shoulder until, with 250 yards to go, Hannah made his winning effort to finish 10 yards clear of Duffus who finished runner up for the third year in a row.

Clydesdale won a disappointing team contest with Edinburgh, the only other club in the race, finishing only five men and thus failing to register a team score. Perhaps spurred by this debacle of a championship the SCCU, at their September Annual General Meeting, decided that the individual winner and the six members of the winning team in the National Junior Championship would become Seniors and ineligible to compete again in the Junior Championship race.

At this meeting Andrew Hannah , who had retired from active competition after his fifth National Championship win, was appointed Vice President of the Union and was President in the year 1897-98. He had a wonderful record of competition in the National event, finishing with 2 silver and 1 bronze medals in addition to his 5 victories. He was just as successful on the track, winning the SAAA 4 miles title four times and the 10 miles seven times between 1889 and 1896. In the 10 miles he brought the Scottish record down from 55min 33.0sec to 53min 26.0sec - a record which stood for 12 years.

Hannah was just as successful an administrator as he was a competitor, being SCCU President in 1897-98 and SAAA President in 1909-10 after 11 years service as SAAA Western District Secretary. He also served as an athletics official for a long

*Andrew Hannah
(Clydesdale Harriers)
National Champion 5 times between 1890 and 1896*

number of years and was a track judge at the 1908 Olympic Games in London. He was a lifelong member and supporter of Clydesdale Harriers, being a member from 1887 to his death in December 1939. One of the legends of Clydesdale tell of Hannah's exploits after a club dinner at St Georges Cross, Glasgow. After an argument Hannah challenged some other club members to a race from St Georges Cross to Maryhill Baths - a distance of approximately 2 miles. Dressed in his dinner suit Hannah set off on foot with his rivals in a horse drawn hansom cab. The dinner and refreshments were too much of a handicap even for the redoubtable Hannah, and the cab won, but only just!

Hannah's new status became apparent when, the following season, he wrote an article in Scottish Sport advising on distance training and racing for aspiring Junior athletes. The training philisophy and practice of the 1890's is fascinating and far different from that practised by runners of the present day. "Training means getting the body into the best possible health and condition. This can only be achieved by being temperate in all things and keeping regular hours - retiring to bed as soon after 10 o'clock as possible. Take good plain substantial food but partake sparingly of soups and potatoes. The most important thing to avoid is liquor of all sorts, and this is one of the hardest things to do; especially at first, as after a run and a good sweat one gets very thirsty. But to go and drink freely would just spoil all the preparations. If you must drink take only a few sips to quench your thirst; do not drink for the pleasure of drinking.

A quiet stroll before breakfast is all that I would advise, as training in the morning on an empty stomach can only do harm. As it is understood that business has to be attended to during the day, training must therefore be confined to the evening, say 2 hours after tea. Run every night if possible. Begin with a distance of 2 miles, at a quiet, easy pace and do not distress yourself trying to see how fast you can cover the distance. In fact never distress yourself when training, rather cultivate style and length of stride. Continue this for the first week, then gradually increase the distance to 3 or 4 miles. A fortnight of this systematic work and all the preliminary aches and pains will have disappeared. The distances can now be varied from 1 to 4 miles and run at a smarter pace - the longer distance not to be run more than once a week.

This, with the usual Saturday outing over 5 to 7 miles across country, should make one as fit as a fiddle inside 6 weeks. Take matters easy in training the final week so that you may arrive at the start of your race full of life and spirits".

A change of title in 1896 to the Scottish Junior Cross Country Association, followed the following year by dropping the word Junior from the title which became the Scottish Cross Country Association (Western District), showed the growing aspirations and ambitions of this body of clubs in the West of Scotland. Their annual meeting agreed to apply for membership of the Scottish AAA, rejected affiliation to the SCCU as they regarded themselves the equal, if not superior, to the SCCU as they had a greater number of clubs in membership and promoted a more successful Junior Championship.

These claims were not borne out by their 1896 championship race at Cathcart where a great deal of trouble and protests resulted from poor organisation. Objections from participating clubs included:

1) Changing quarters were unacceptable and inadequate for the large number of competitors taking part.
2) Vast crowds of supporters were allowed to roam at will in the stripping rooms.
3) Wild disorder resulted at the finish as supporters were permitted to pace their men home to the finish line.
4) Finishing positions were wrongly recorded with competitors being omitted and the wrong team results announced.

In addition the Wishaw runners, brothers W and J Rainey, were known professionals, having competed at unpermitted athletic meetings in the summer. However the SCCA Committee claimed not to have had enough evidence to stop them from competing in the race and allowed them to compete. This resulted in the SAAA having to grant a mass pardon and agreeing not to take any action against athletes who had run against the Rainey brothers.

The following year the championship race moved to Hamilton Park Racecourse with an entry of 17 Western clubs making it the largest race held in Scotland -

compared to the SCCU Junior championship at Musselburgh Racecourse where 10 clubs, including the newly admitted Berwick and District Harriers, competed.

The SCCU Junior race was notable for the victory by Jack Paterson of Watsonians who went on to win three National Senior individual titles and lead his club to two National team titles. The 1897 National Senior race was held from Underwood Park, Paisley with Watsonians CCC, twice National Junior team champions, joining the holders Clydesdale, Edinburgh and Edinburgh Northern.

The pace over the three lap 10 mile course was set by William Robertson of Clydesdale, who had earlier in the season won his clubs Open Handicap 7 mile race - the first open, non championship race staged in Scotland. On the second lap Robertson suffered a mishap on negotiating a barbed wire fence, quaintly described in contemporary reports as "bursting his unmentionable nether garments". Robertson lost considerable distance due to splitting his shorts and Stewart Duffus (also Clydesdale) displayed good pace judgement to score his first victory, after three times finishing runner up, winning by 180 yards from the unfortunate Robertson, with A McLagan (Edinburgh Northern) third. Poor training and preparation by Edinburgh and Watsonian runners resulted in numerous withdrawals during the race and neither club finished six runners for a counting team. Clydesdale thus won easily from Edinburgh Northern for whom P Addison, who ran in the inaugural 1886 championship and every one of the 12 succeeding events, finished 14th and fifth counter for his club.

The developing nature of the sport, which was little known or followed by the general public, was illustrated by a warning issued to Harrier clubs in the south of Glasgow. "Members of Greenhead Harriers had their Saturday run abruptly terminated at Aitkenhead Estate grounds by the appearance of a brutal gamekeeper armed with a formidable stick and a ferocious guard dog. After threatening and abusive language he brutally assaulted one of the runners who had become detached from the pack, knocking him to the ground, kicking him and causing blood to flow freely from his mouth. Clubs who run in the district are warned to keep clear of this estate."

Hamilton Racecourse was the venue in 1898 for both the SCCU and SCCA Junior championship races. The SCCU race, with 11 teams, was won by Arthur Pitt (Motherwell) by 40 yards from J K Hamilton (Maryhill), with Motherwell easily winning the team championship from Edinburgh Northern.

A much larger entry of 20 clubs contested the SCCA race. William McConville of the newly formed Celtic Harriers was favourite and led the field of over 170 runners out of the Racecourse. He had the misfortune to jump into what looked like a dry ditch, only to find himself up to his neck in very dirty, cold water. He emerged from his soaking "in a shocked frame of mind not conducive to further effort or success" and did well to eventually finish fifth. William Marshall won the 7 mile race from his Springburn clubmate Walter Leggat and their club won the team championship from Bellahouston.

Five clubs competed in the National Senior championship at Musselburgh Racecourse - the largest entry in the 13 year history of the event. Clydesdale started the race in a much depleted manner, fielding only 8 runners and their top performer, Stewart Duffus, appeared with a bad cold after a restricted period of just 9 weeks training since he restarted at New Year after injury.

Jack Paterson forced the pace from half distance and had a large lead with just 2 miles to go, followed by the Clydesdale pair William Robertson and Stewart Duffus. Paterson held a 100 yard advantage as he crossed the finishing line for the first of three consecutive victories, with Robertson holding off the defending champion Duffus for second place. Clydesdale, despite finishing with just seven counters, scored their third successive and ninth overall team championship victory, defeating Watsonians by 27 points with Motherwell YMCA, at their first appearance in the championship, finishing third.

The dispute between the SCCU and the troublesome SCCA was worsened that autumn when both bodies held their annual meetings. They both approved restrictive new rules which attempted to strengthen their position and weaken the rival body.

The SCCU announced a membership of 13 clubs and a credit balance of just £2-10/9 (£2-54p). A new rule, requiring all clubs or associations not in membership of the SCCU intending to hold open or championship races under the laws of the SCCU to apply to the Hon Secretary for a permit prior to staging the race, was approved. A permit fee of 10/6 (52½p) was required to be paid 28 days before the race was held but, if granted, the applying body was then registered as an associate club of the SCCU.

The fledgling SCCA, in just its fourth year of operation, had 27 clubs in membership from the West of Scotland and a credit balance of £15-4/8 (£15-23½p). They decided that membership would be restricted to clubs in the West of Scotland not in membership of any other cross country association. It was agreed that the annual championship be open to all amateurs in the West who had not competed in any other cross country championship. Details of a conference between the SCCA and the SCCU, at which the SCCU, in the interest of the sport, had requested an amalgamation between the two bodies, were reported to the meeting. It was decided by a large majority neither to amalgamate with nor to affiliate to, the SCCU, and the strength of the Association was confirmed when 5 new clubs were admitted to membership.

The two bodies were on a collision course reminiscent of the SCCA/SHU dispute a decade earlier. How the General Committee of the SCCU must have longed to reverse their fateful decision of 1894 when they rejected the request by the Western clubs to take charge of their championship race and control the organisation. Control of the numerous clubs in the West of Scotland seemed to be slipping away from the Union, with the majority of clubs in the "Junior" category favouring affiliation to the SCCA rather than the older SCCU.

The matter was brought to a resolution by the Scottish AAA who refused to consider the application from the SCCA for affiliation. D S Duncan, SAAA Hon Secretary, intimated that the SCCU was recognised as the governing body of cross country running in Scotland and recommended that the SCCA apply to the SCCU for a permit to hold their annual championship at Hamilton in February 1899. The SCCU, anxious to avoid a similar situation arising in the East of Scotland where clubs were loyal to the SCCU championships, established an Eastern District Committee which would organise a District "Junior" championship as a feeder race to the National Junior Championship. The SAAA action seemed to be decisive, as the SCCA applied to the SCCU for a permit to hold their championship race and agreed to attend a conference after their championship race had been held in February.

The District championships were staged successfully. The SCCU Eastern event was held with 10 clubs competing on a bitterly cold day at Inverleith, Edinburgh with John Harcus (Kirkcaldy) winning narrowly from C Morrison who led Edinburgh to team victory over Waverley Harriers and Bonnybridge Harriers. The Western District race was contested by just 15 of the 27 clubs in membership of the SCCA. The restricted entry was due to the rift between the SCCA and SCCU with many clubs awaiting the result of the post race conference before committing themselves.

John McCafferty, 10 mile club champion of the three year old Celtic Harriers, won the 7½ mile race over a difficult course around Hamilton Park Racecourse. He finished in 45min 20sec with W Lawson (Whiteinch) runner up 23 seconds behind and Wishaw winning the team championship from Bellahouston. The SCCA medals, of hallmarked gold with a lion rampant in the centre on a white background, were awarded to the first six finishers and members of the first three teams. McCafferty was richly rewarded for his victory, receiving three gold medals - one from the SCCA, one from Celtic Harriers and a further medal and velvet cap from Mr F Lumley of the well known sports shop.

The National Junior Championship was run from Edinburgh University ground at Craiglockhart in drizzling rain and heavy mist. W T Marshall (West of Scotland) led from the early stages to win by 40 yards from R F Steel (Paisley). Maryhill Harriers, loyal supporters since joining the SCCU in December 1891, recorded their first major success by winning the team championship from West of Scotland and Edinburgh.

The Maryhill club trained mainly from the local military barracks and Maryhill Baths and held most of their country runs in the north and north east of Glasgow around Summerston and Bearsden. On a season's opening run, attended by a record field of 36 runners, the hares led the Maryhill runners a merry dance. Approaching the final stages of the run, and needing to cross the River Kelvin to reach the haven of the dressing rooms at Maryhill Baths, the runners found the paper trail ending at the toll bridge across the Kelvin. The hounds, who had cunningly provided themselves with the halfpenny toll to cross the bridge, had crossed the river dry footed. The angry runners, without the necessary fare, were refused entry to the bridge and had to wade waist deep through the river to chase the wily hounds home to the finish.

The Maryhill club were among the record entry of 6 clubs for the 1899 National Senior Championship at Hampden Park where Jack Paterson started favourite to retain his individual title. Paterson was a lazy trainer, preferring the more leisurely game of golf to running - being almost as good at golf as he was at running - and it was his natural ability in athletics that enabled him to win SAAA track titles at 1 mile (2), 4 miles (3) and 10 miles (1) as well as 3 National individual titles and 2 team championship medals in the National Senior Cross Country Championship.

Clydesdale, severely weakened by an SAAA investigation into professionalism in athletics which resulted in the suspension of three of their top runners - Stewart Duffus, his brother James and William Robertson - for professional activities in Ireland, were not expected to have any chance of retaining their team title.

The runners covered two laps of the tough trail leaving Hampden by the eastern exit gate, up by Hangingshaw to Aitkenhead House, across to Old Cathcart and then circling round Langside, through Queens Park recreation ground and into Hampden for a circuit of the cinder track. Paterson ran a sensible, well judged race, being content to let others do the pace making throughout the race before making his final effort in the final 300 yards on the track. He sprinted home to finish 40 yards clear of David Mill (Clydesdale) in a time of 64 min 36.5 sec for the 10 mile course. The monopoly in team championship honours held by Clydesdale and Edinburgh since 1886 was finally broken by Watsonians as Paterson led his clubmates (all 6 finishers in the first 21 home) to a team victory over first time entrants Maryhill (6 in 18 home).

The Scottish AAA convened a meeting between the rival SCCU and SCCA in Edinburgh in May with great argument taking place during a lengthy meeting. Agreement was finally reached that:

1) The SCCA Western District Association would affiliate to the SCCU.
2) SCCA proposed to change the rules of their championship to require more individuals and teams to compete in the National Senior race.
3) The SCCA Western District Association would retain sole control of the Western District Championship.
4) The SCCA would have the right to appoint members to sit on the SCCU General Committee.

The SCCU annual meeting in September 1899 announced a membership of 21 clubs - 6 more that the previous year - and a satisfactory balance of £4 - 11/8½ (£4-58½p), despite making a loss of £4 -15/2 (£4-76p) on the promotion of the National Senior Championship at Hampden Park. The first claim rule was amended to read "In the event of any competitor's name appearing in the programme for two or more clubs, such competitor shall only represent the club of which he is a first claim member. The priority of claim shall be decided by the date of members admission to the club as shown in the club membership book".

The SCCA held their annual meeting a week later with a reduced membership of 24 clubs - still 3 more than the SCCU - and a credit balance of £13 -10/- (£13-50p). They confirmed the decision to affiliate to the SCCU and still indicated a measure of independence by adopting the English CCU version of the first claim rule for their championship race which stated:- "A first claim member is one who can show original or period of unbroken membership of any club". The meeting also ruled that the first six runners home and the first three home in the winning team would become Seniors and not eligible for further Junior championship races.

The dispute, mainly of the SCCU's own making by their reluctance to extend the level of competition and thus develop and open the sport to more competitors, was thus settled.

The Western and Eastern District Committees thus established control of their own championship races, elected their own representatives from District Committees to General Committee and established a semi-autonomous form of self government in the Districts. This has continued, though in a much more mellowed manner with specific General Committee influence exerted through financial control, to the present day.

1900 to 1909

In the early years of the twentieth century there were no races for club runners outside the championship races organised by the Union. These consisted of "Junior" championship races for both the Eastern and Western District clubs and the National Championship race, with clubs holding club trial races to decide the twelve men to represent the club in the championship event. Other than those two championship races for clubs in each District the sport consisted entirely of non-competitive outings in pack runs based on the "hares and hounds" principle. Most members of harrier clubs ran for fitness, with an enjoyable outing over the open countryside in the company of fellow runners and the prospect of a racing finish over the final mile being the spice to their afternoon's sport. Of course in those days Saturday afternoon outings usually continued to a high tea in a nearby hostelry, followed by an enjoyable "smoker" concert with communal singing, throughout the entire Saturday evening. Other than home fixtures, when training runs and races for club trophies were the usual events, inter club runs on a home and away basis throughout the season predominated. The season of friendly inter club fixtures was much enjoyed and most clubs took pride in laying on entertainment evenings after the various packs returned to the clubrooms.

A fixture card of Falkirk Victoria Harriers, dated soon after their founding in 1901, makes interesting reading. A list of 16 patrons included three names from abroad - J Lundie from Ontario, Canada; D McCulloch from Illinois, USA and W Kerr from Sydney, Australia - full evidence of the wandering spirit of the Scots of the era who left their homeland to colonise the British Empire and the rest of the world to make their fortune.

The 26 Saturdays on the fixture list were divided up as follows:- 15 club pack runs, 6 inter club runs with Grange Harriers, Stirlingshire Central Harriers, West of Scotland Harriers, Edinburgh Harriers, Edinburgh Northern Harriers and Heriots CCC on a home and away basis. There were also 5 racing fixtures including the club 8 mile championship, a 10 mile road race for the Thule Trophy, a 5 mile handicap race for the Lyon Medal and a club trial for the team to compete in the Eastern District Championship race - the only outside competitive event Falkirk took part in at that time. The Falkirk club had an interesting item under their cross country rules. This stated that "no trail be laid or followed across water more than eight feet in breadth, or across or alongside railways of any description."

Edinburgh Harriers, a larger club and one of the powers in the sport at that time, also had an interesting fixture list. It included 10 inter club runs, with away trips including Galashiels and Glasgow, and an inter club run and football match with Watsonians at Myreside on Christmas Day. Club races ranged from a $2\frac{1}{2}$ mile handicap to the 10 mile club championship and teams were also entered in both the Eastern District and National Championships.

George McKenzie, who was to be Hon President of the Union and gain nine international vests for Scotland in the period 1904-14, was always an enthusiastic advocate of cross country running. In a newspaper interview he said "It is distressing to see the number of young men in our public parks on a Saturday afternoon watching a football match, blue in the face and shaking with cold. Compare them with the athletes who, with the blood coursing through their veins, are enjoying healthy exercise with a harrier pack".

He explained that on Saturday afternoons three packs - slow, medium and fast - covered the laid trail through the country with beginners naturally starting with the slow pack and working their way up as they felt more capable of covering the distance. At the beginning of the season in October the usual run was about four miles. "Any young man who cannot run four miles with a harriers slow pack should see a doctor at once," said Mr McKenzie. During the season the distance was gradually increased until by the end of March, when the runners were in form, the packs covered distances up to 10 miles.

Recommended training was road runs twice weekly, together with the usual country run on Saturday with a long walk at a good pace being desirable on Sunday. Rubbing was regarded as important and this was usually done by the club trainer, in most cases an old "ped". Regarding diet it was accepted that the athlete should be able to eat almost anything though moderation in all things was the watch word of the athlete. Cigarettes and alcohol were tabooed by the wise runner. Mr McKenzie emphasised that the sport was carried out in the lonely, quiet, out of the way countryside where runs could be completed undisturbed. There was thus little or no opportunity for participants indulging in "gallery work", even if they were so inclined, because spectators were somewhat lacking in numbers, except in championship races where the public were starting to appreciate the sport and turn up in greater numbers to watch the top runners.

In February 1900 the National Junior Championship was held from Scotstoun Agricultural Showgrounds in Glasgow with 9 clubs competing over the 7 mile course which consisted of plough and fallow with no objectionable hedges, fences or barbed wire to hinder the progress of the competitors. In poor weather conditions Andrew Forrester won by 250 yards from his Coatbridge Harriers clubmate Robert Pettigrew, with Andrew Bone third and all the runners finishing splashed in mud from head to toe. Bone led Clydesdale to the team championship defeating Coatbridge and Maryhill.

In the District Championships John Ranken (Watsonians CCC) won the second Eastern District Championship to be held, with Stirlingshire Central Harriers taking the team title, while in the longer established Western District Championship G. Cunningham (Greenock Wellpark) won the individual title with rivals Greenock Glenpark defeating over 20 clubs to win the team championship.

Only 37 runners from four clubs finished the National Championship held before a large crowd of spectators at Musselburgh Racecourse. A pre race summary stated that J W Paterson was favourite but noted "if fit he should again win the individual title as easily as he did the previous year, but he takes matters less earnestly than most other runners and on that account one never knows how he will perform". Paterson was on form and won the 10 mile race for a record third consecutive time ahead of W Neil (Clydesdale) with R Gribb (Watsonians) third. With such an excellent start of two runners in the first three home Watsonians repeated their 1899 victory scoring 37 points to defeat Clydesdale 46 points. The other two clubs entered, Edinburgh Harriers and Maryhill, did not have enough runners to complete counting teams.

Next year, following the established rota of the Senior National being held annually in Edinburgh and Glasgow, the event was held from Maryhill headquarters at Lochburn Road, Glasgow. The course, by way of St Kentigern's Cemetery, across fields to Summerston, Blackhill and Lochburn Farm, was twice covered for a testing 10 mile trail. Watsonians did not defend their team title and Coatbridge Harriers, who had run so well in the Junior National the previous year, were the only club to challenge the big two, Clydesdale and Edinburgh, who had won 13 of the previous 15 titles between them. Duncan Mill became the seventh Clydesdale runner to win the individual title, leading from half distance to win from Arthur Pitt, an individual entrant from Motherwell YMCA, with former Junior Champion Andrew Forrester (Coatbridge) third.

Clydesdale, with four in the first eight home, narrowly won the team title by just one point from Edinburgh. Whereas Edinburgh Harriers shared the Edinburgh District catchment area with another half dozen clubs, Clydesdale had a much greater catchment area than any other club in Scotland. Their team was drawn from Clydesdale sections from towns in Lanarkshire, Dunbartonshire and Renfrewshire and, being a "District" club rather than a "City" club, as long as they had such extensive provincial resources to call upon, they would always stand a better chance of winning championships than their rivals. Duncan Mill completed the double the following year in 1902 at Myreside, Edinburgh with Clydesdale again displaying their dominance in the team championship.

In early 1903 discussions between the Welsh and Irish Associations regarding an International race were enthusiastically supported by the Scottish Union despite early opposition by England, who at first held aloof from supporting the idea. They suggested that the English National Championship could be used as it was open to all comers and could be utilised as a British Championship.

There was a lot of anger against England's arrogant opposition to the proposal and the Glasgow Herald expressed the view that "England cannot dominate matters as she once did, and by degrees the Rugby Union, the Football Association, the Cross Country Union, the Swimming Association and the Amateur Athletic Association are gradually being cut down to their proper level in the national administration of sport. It is only right that these bodies should be deprived of the arrogant appropriation of the International significance which each claims for its special event and at the same time it is appropriate that England should be reminded from time to time that she does not possess a monopoly of administrative talent and legislative wisdom".

England, apprehensive that the status and dignity of their championship would be impaired, only agreed to participate when they saw that the other three countries were determined to proceed with the race regardless of their attitude. No mention of this is given in the 1983 brief history of the English Cross Country Union which states "the 1903 minutes mention support for the first official International Championship when it was resolved to send 12 competitors plus the three Area Presidents and the Hon Secretary of the Union to Hamilton Racecourse, Glasgow".

With all countries in agreement that the race be held that year, Scotland's offer to host the inaugural event at Hamilton Park Racecourse was accepted and the date fixed as the 28th March as the climax of the season. This date was fixed at the insistence of the English Union as their National champion Alfred Shrubb was running in an International race in France on the 21st March which was the first suggested date for the race, and England refused to compete unless the date was arranged to accomodate Shrubb's racing programme.

The National Championship, from which Scotland's team for the International would be selected, were held over a 10 mile course at Scotstoun Showgrounds with eight clubs taking part. The race also included "Juniors" for the first time for the National Junior Championship, previously held as a separate championship event, was combined with the Senior National race. The first "Junior" to finish in the National gained the "Junior" title. Heavy rain had created heavy underfoot conditions but the weather for the race itself were pleasant, with a nip in the air. The race was a test of endurance and speed and P J McCafferty (West of Scotland) proved the strongest on the day, just one week after winning the Irish Junior Championship, to take both the National Senior and Junior titles.

McCafferty, who opted to run for Ireland in the International, won the race by fully 150 yards from John Ranken (Watsonians CCC), the 1900 Eastern District Champion, who was to win the National title for the next two years. Duncan Mill, who won the National title in 1901/02 when running for Clydesdale, finished in third place when representing Greenock Glenpark. He had the misfortune, after being selected for Scotland's team for Hamilton, of being injured in an accident at work and having to withdraw from the team. After a gap of eight years Edinburgh won the team championship for the fifth time scoring 72 points to defeat old rivals Clydesdale 103 points, with third placed West of Scotland totalling 118 points - just 5 points in front of Greenock Glenpark Harriers.

Alfred Shrubb, the greatest distance runner of his day, climaxed an unbeaten season by adding the first International title to his earlier victories in the Sussex county, Southern Counties and English National Championship races. Held in miserable conditions the heavy rain confined spectators to the shelter of the Racecourse grandstand where they witnessed a most one sided event in both individual and team competition. Shrubb's only challenger was the Irish Champion Joe Daly, and the comparison between the two was a feature of the race. The compact, stylish Shrubb strode over the country in effortless style while Daly, a big heavy man over six foot in height, pounded over the ground gaining distance at each hurdle cleared, with Shrubb, a poor hurdler, easily closing the gap between obstacles. Daly was broken by Shrubb's relentless pace before half distance, eventually finishing third 48 seconds behind Shrubb, with England having their counting six men in the first seven runners home to score an overwhelming team victory ahead of Ireland and Scotland.

Although the history books always record the first International as being held at Hamilton Racecourse, it is necessary, in the interests of strict accuracy, to state that it was run in the adjacent grounds of the Duke of Hamilton's Palace. The race started and finished in front of the grandstand and after 300 yards of running over the racecourse turf the runners exited to the ducal grounds where they covered four 2 mile laps before returning to complete the course in the racecourse finishing straight.

The top Scots disappointed with J Crosbie (Larkhall YMCA) 10, receiving the medal for the first Scot to finish ahead of J Ranken 14, with the Scottish Champion P J McCafferty only finishing twentieth for Ireland.

There was much praise for Shrubb, who was described as "a running machine who trained as hard in winter as he did in summer" and critics went on to say that "until Scots runners started training as systematically as their English rivals and became more devoted to the drudgery of winter training they would meet with little success in International competition."

At the dinner after the race Shrubb said that Daly must have considered him an unsociable person because he did not reply to his constant flow of chatter during the race. He then offered the Irishman a bit of advice - to conserve his wind by remaining silent during a race and his running would undoubtedly improve. Also during the dinner the keen sportsman and patron of athletics, Fred A Lumley, offered to present a trophy for annual team competition. Thus came into being the coveted Lumley Shield - a magnificent trophy of which A Ross Scott, Union Secretary said "I have just seen the Shield which Mr Lumley is presenting. It is very handsome and I am only sorry that so far as Scotland is concerned we have probably seen the last of it for a number of years".

Unfortunately his words were all too correct for, in the 70 years of competition in the ICCU International championship, Scotland was never to win the Lumley Shield. Valued in 1903 at 65 guineas (£68.25p) it was a splendid specimen of repoussé work, being of solid silver, with the National emblems of England, Scotland, Wales, Ireland, France and Belgium in enamel on gilt discs. Scrolls were mounted on the side for the names of winning countries and the six counting members of the team. The Shield was enclosed in a fumed oak air-tight case with a bronze ornament mounted on top. The race was so successful that discussions on the train journey from Hamilton back to Glasgow afterwards led to an understanding that a similar race would be held the following year at Haydock Park, Lancashire, where the International Cross Country Union (I.C.C.U.) was established.

In spite of the poor weather the Scottish organisers made a profit of £8- 4/4 (£8-22p) which was equally divided between the participating countries to the tune of £2-1/1 (£2-05½p)each. The following year England made a profit of only £4-8/- (£4.40p) but in the next two years the championship was run at a loss by Ireland (£6-00p loss) and Wales (£15-71p loss) before Scotland, at Scotstoun in 1907, returned a profit of £10-11/2 (£10-56p). France joined the ICCU that year and, in the first year the championship was held in Paris in 1913, returned a large profit of £45-6/2 (£45-31p) with each country receiving £11-6/6 (£11-32½p) as their share of the profit.

After the 1903 Annual General Meeting it was agreed that the Union title be changed to the National Cross Country Union of Scotland. A Ross Scott remained Hon Secretary/Treasurer, a post he was to hold for the next 8 years, and W A McCaa of Garscube Harriers started a two year term as President of the newly named NCCU of Scotland.

Hamilton Racecourse hosted the 1904 Western District Championship, with the District Committee paying six guineas (£6.30p) for the use of the grounds and attendant building facilities. The race attracted 228 starters but, being run in the most miserable weather conditions of heavy rain and gale force winds, only 163 brave runners finished the 7 mile course. Sam Kennedy won the race by 5 yards and led Garscube to the team title with William McFarlane, the runner up, heading the Motherwell YMCA team in second place. Wet and boisterous conditions spoiled the Eastern District Championship at Inverleith where 12 clubs started. Over a course tough enough to test the staying powers of competitors, J A Jamieson (Watsonians) won from J Arnott who led Falkirk Victoria to the team championship.

Racing was keen in the National Championship at Scotstoun Showgrounds with 7 clubs entered. John Ranken of Watsonians followed in the footsteps of his clubmate J Paterson when winning the individual title from T C Hughes (Edinburgh) and Sam Stevenson (Clydesdale). George McKenzie (West of Scotland) made his first appearance in the National honours list, finishing in sixth place just two years after winning his club's Novice Championship in his first outing over the country and gaining the National Junior title in a race where just fifty runners finished. Edinburgh Harriers, with their counting six runners in the first seventeen to finish, retained the team title from Clydesdale, six in thirty three, with Garscube third ahead of Greenock Glenpark.

Alfred Shrubb (England) scored his second International victory at Haydock Park but never competed again as he turned professional soon after, racing extensively in Australia, USA and Canada. Ranken was the first Scots runner home in eleventh position - over $3\frac{1}{2}$ minutes behind the winner and Scotland was again third team behind England and Wales. A caustic note was sounded at the disappointing Scottish team performance after finishing behind Wales with a contemporary report stating "with greater devotion to training, there is nothing to stop our runners finishing even higher in the race in future years".

George McKenzie
(West of Scotland Harriers)
Scottish Junior champion in 1904 and ICCU member of Scottish team in ICCU International Championships 9 times between 1904 and 1914.

The following year, 1905, the death of Alex P Findlay, the winner of the first National Championship at Lanark in 1886, was announced. Findlay, a two time cross country champion, had also run with distinction on the track winning the SAAA 10 mile track title three times, with a best of 55 min 16.8 secs - very good running in those early days. He never allowed his interest in athletics to drop and was always an interested observer of every athletic meeting near his home town of Ayr.

The National Championship was held for the third year in a row at Scotstoun Showgrounds with the race, attracting seven clubs and ninety runners, being delayed by almost an hour due to the late arrival of Edinburgh Harriers. John Ranken won for the second time, running with the leading group for most of the race, but making his break for home as he crossed Great Western Road for the second time and opening a winning gap over the final stretch of ploughed land between Anniesland and Scotstoun Stadium. He eventually won by 100 yards from P C Russell (Bellahouston) who became the National Junior Champion, with Sam

Stevenson (Clydesdale) in third place.

Fifth placed George McKenzie, who was trained by Danny Williams, father of comedian Dave Willis, led West of Scotland to their first ever team championship. Since the inauguration of the National event West of Scotland had sent a team to compete with few exceptions, displaying loyalty to the Union when they had no real expectations of winning. Their victory was a surprise in an event in which only Clydesdale, Edinburgh and Watsonians had won the team title, and the Glasgow club had their six finishers home in the first twenty seven for a total of 79 points to win by 36 points from the holders Edinburgh, with Clydesdale third.

West of Scotland were only the fourth team to win the team title and it is worth noting that, since the first championship race was staged at Lanark Racecourse in 1886, only 19 clubs have had the honour of being National Champions. The most prolific winners are Shettleston, with 16 titles between 1920 and 1972; followed by Clydesdale with 14 titles between 1888 and 1910, with Edinburgh Southern being the most successful club in modern times with 12 titles between 1964 and 1987. Edinburgh AC (1973 to 1981), Edinburgh Harriers (1886 to 1911) and Maryhill Harriers (1927 to 1938) all have 7 titles to their credit, with Victoria Park AAC 6 titles in their fine post war run of success between 1951 and 1958.

In the 1905 International race at Baldoyle Racecourse, Dublin, Scotland had their first three runners inside the first dozen with Sam Stevenson 6; Tom Johnston, an Anglo Scot from Highgate Harriers 11, and John Ranken 12, to give them second place for the first time. Each country was allowed to field 12 runners with the first 6 home counting for the team score - a practice which lasted until 1910 when the number of runners in each team was limited to 9 men.

The Scottish team had its headquarters at Jury's Hotel, College Green in Dublin and a large party travelled to Dublin as each country supplied 1 timekeeper, 2 judges, 2 lap scorers and 3 stewards - a total of 8 officials to help in the organisation of the race on the day. Clydesdale Harriers celebrated their coming of age in 1906 with a Twenty First Anniversary Dinner attended by a galaxy of top names from Cross Country, athletics and other sports. Union Secretary A Ross Scott said that the primary aim of a Harrier Club was not to train runners for competition in the athletics arena but to encourage healthy, strenuous open air exercise.

Tom Jack, of Edinburgh Southern Harriers, who was to become a three times National Champion, made his first appearance in the Eastern District Championship at Colinton, Edinburgh and was involved, as was so often the case, in a sprint finish to the race. Jack entered the grounds neck and neck with P J Melville (Watsonians) and, in a very close finish, Melville won by a yard with Jack runner up one second behind and J R McLagin (Edinburgh Northern) third, a further two seconds behind.

John Ranken failed to complete his hat trick of wins in the 1906 National Championship at Scotstoun Showgrounds where Sam Stevenson won from 60 runners and led Clydesdale to victory in the team race defeating Edinburgh Harriers. David Cather, who had run so well in the earlier Western District Championship when leading Hamilton Harriers to the team title, won the National Junior title in second position, with P J Melville (Edinburgh) third. Stevenson proved his National form when being the first Scot in tenth position in the International at Caerleon Racecourse, Wales, closely followed by the surprising D Cather 13, but Scotland slipped to third team behind England and Ireland.

In 1907 Borderer A J Grieve (Teviotdale) won the Eastern District race and Alex

McPhee, running for Paisley Junior Harriers, won the Western District title. McPhee, after this success, was quickly signed by the powerful Clydesdale club to strengthen their team and won his two National titles in their colours.

The National Championship was held at the newly opened ground of Hibernian F C at Portobello Road with six clubs competing. The 10 mile race was held over two 5 mile laps with the runners leaving the Football Park to run over open countryside to the village of Niddrie, then passing Duddingston Golf Club House and returning, by Willowbrae Road, to Portobello for the start of the final lap. Running in dry, but very cold, conditions the runners found the ground frosty and very hard underfoot. In an exciting race former champions Sam Stevenson and John Ranken were running abreast with the young challenger Tom Jack at the head of the field. Ranken led entering the football ground but Jack, with a strong finishing sprint, overtook him with 30 yards to go to win by less than a yard with both runners sharing the slow winning time of 65 min 38 secs. In his first appearance in the Championship Jack won both the Senior and Junior titles. Sam Stevenson finished third, leading Clydesdale to a nine point margin of victory over West of Scotland, with Motherwell YMCA, in their first appearance in the team championship, finishing a close up third.

Sam Stevenson (Clydesdale Harriers) National Champion in 1906 and a member of the Scottish International team in 1904/05/06.

The International race was held at Scotstoun Showground over a four lap 10 mile course for the benefit of the 2,000 spectators who attended the event. Newly crowned National Champion, Tom Jack, finished fifth over a tough course which included fences and water jumps on each lap. In a fast run race, won by A Underwood (England) in 54 min 26.4 secs, Jack split the English team, finishing less than a minute behind the winner, and the entire Scottish team finished inside the first 18 home to take second place behind England and finish well clear of Ireland and France who made their first appearance in the race.

The intensively developed West End of Glasgow, where Scotstoun Showground is located, was very different in 1907. George Dallas, watching the first of over forty International Championships, recalled running in the company of his Maryhill clubmate George Barber to meet the race and seeing the competitors streaming across the fields to the small cross roads at Anniesland Cross (now one of the largest and busiest traffic junctions in Europe) before running down Crow Road to finish on the track around Scotstoun Showground.

The District Championships, held in February each year, were the main racing opportunity for club competitors who never aspired to take part in the National Championships. In 1908 the Western District Championships at Scotstoun had an entry of 25 clubs - all the clubs affiliated to the Western District taking part with the exception of Dumbarton YMCA Harriers.

For the first time competitors were issued with cloth numbers in the week before the race and these were to be sewn to the front of the club vest before race day. Club entries of 12 runners per team were carefully vetted by the District Scrutiny

Committee. Each runner had to complete four qualifying runs with their club on an official Saturday pack run, or three Saturday and one mid week runs, to qualify to run in the Championships. Another qualifying condition was that runners had to be from within a 10 mile radius from the official clubhouse.

The scrutineers were knowledgeable and strict, and runners with only three qualifying runs to their credit were deleted from the entry form. A claim by Glasgow YMCA that their entered team "had been running regularly with the club all season" was rejected as being not specific enough and the entry form sent back to the Club Secretary to detail the dates of the required four qualifying runs. The position of entered teams on the starting line was drawn by lot before the race day and teams lined up in the pre-determined order, not in alphabetical order as in modern day assembly of teams. Concern had been expressed at the fast growing, undesirable practices of pacing and assistance to runners during the race. Judges were authorised to go out on the trail and, "with the assistance of a few other vigilant gentlemen from the Committee", try and stop pacing and assistance to competitors.

It is worth while detailing the Championship Bye Laws for the old time District Championships:-

1) Secretaries of competing clubs must declare the composition of their teams before 3 o'clock on the day of the race.
2) A bell will be rung 10 minutes before the start of the race.
3) All competitors must turn out on the starting line on hearing the bell.
4) Competitors must have their official number securely fixed to their vest.
5) No attendant shall accompany any competitor on the start line or in the race. Nor shall a competitor be allowed to receive any assistance or refreshments from any one during the progress of the race.
6) The Committee shall have full powers to deal with any infringements of the rules. Every club entering a team shall receive 14 competitors tickets and 2 tickets to the stripping boxes for the club trainers.

The Committee decided to have four policemen plus two commissionaires on duty at the ground to control the crowd who were charged 6d (2½p) admission with 800 programmes at 2d (1p) printed for sale on the day. Arrangements were made for free Oxo drinks to be distributed to competitors after the race. Over 280 competitors competed in the race won by George Culbert of Monkland Harriers with Motherwell YMCA gaining their third team championship in four years.

Heartened and encouraged by this success, Motherwell entered their strongest team in the National Championship the following month, being one of seven teams entered. In a closely contested race Alex McPhee (Clydesdale), 1907 West District champion, looked the likely winner, only for Jack to catch him on the final circuit of the cinder track in the stadium and snatch victory on the line by less than six inches with both runners sharing the same winning time. McPhee had the satisfaction of winning the National Junior Title.

Thus Jack won for the second year in a row with his combined margin of victory in both races consisting of just one second and a distance of less than three feet - but gaining the National Title on each occasion - surely proving himself the master of the close finish!

Motherwell, despite not having a finisher in the first five home, won their first ever National team championship, scoring 79 points to defeat Clydesdale by the narrow margin of just 3 points, with West of Scotland third.

The International, held for the first time in France to celebrate their participation in the ICCU Championship, was staged at Colombes, near Paris. The race, usually held on a Saturday on the previous occasions in the British Isles, was unusually staged on a Thursday. The next time the French staged the race in 1913 they kept the other four competing countries on the hop by holding it on a Monday!

George McKenzie, who finished third in the 1908 National, competed in the International at Colombes and his invitation to represent Scotland, written on a postcard, went as follows:- "You have been selected to represent Scotland in the International at Paris. Please say if you accept. We propose to leave Glasgow Central Station on Tuesday 24th March at 11pm and return to Glasgow 9am on Saturday 28th March. Your International jersey will be supplied but please bring your own white knickers, together with spikes and rubber shoes". Signed A Ross Scott, Hon Secretary/Treasurer NCCU. The Scottish International kit, which consisted of a royal blue vest with a thistle on the breast and white knickers, was obviously not freely handed out by the Union. Unlike modern days there was no branded running kit, no sweat shirt, track suit, wet suit or warm up and competition running shoes supplied to team members.

A Scotsman won the Individual Title at Colombes! But unfortunately he was not a member of the Scottish team. Arthur J Robertson, an Anglo Scot running for Birchfield Harriers who had earlier won the English National title, now won the International title at his first and only attempt when competing for England. Robertson, who was born in Sheffield of a Scottish father, was educated in Glasgow and lived most of his life in Peterborough. The most versatile and successful Scottish distance runner of the first decade of the century, Robertson started as a moderately successful racing cyclist - in a similar manner to James Flockhart almost thirty years later - before taking to track and cross country running.

Later in 1908, competing in the Olympic Games at London, he showed he was truly a world ranking athlete with a great display over a variety of distances. He gained three Olympic Medals; a silver in the 3,200 metres Steeplechase and another silver as an individual in the 3 mile team race where he gained a gold medal when leading Britain to victory in the team contest over USA and France. Robertson also ran in the 5 mile race where he finished fifth in the race in which Sam Stevenson (Clydesdale) also represented Britain.

Robertson finished runner up in the 1909 English National Championship, but did not run in that year's International race at Derby, and never ran in the Scottish National on any occasion, unlike James Wilson who, after representing England once in the International race, became a stalwart supporter of Scottish cross country running for the rest of his career.

John Ranken, in his final international appearance for Scotland, finished third team counter. He served as a corporal in the Royal Scots regiment in the First World War and died of wounds sustained in the Dardanelles campaign.

Scotstoun Showgrounds was once again the venue of the National Championship in 1909 and seven clubs took part. Running over an easy course with good going underfoot Alex McPhee broke clear of the field of 72 runners early in the race and established a 130 yard winning margin over John Templeman (Bellahouston) with defending champion Tom Jack (Edinburgh Southern) another

100 yards behind in third position. Glasgow runners dominated the race, filling eight of the first ten places, with James Duffy (Edinburgh) finishing tenth to win the National Junior title just three seconds in front of J Torrie (Gala), the Eastern District Champion. West of Scotland, with four in seven, scored 64 points to win the team title by just one point from Clydesdale with Edinburgh taking third place and the defending champions, Motherwell YMCA, fourth.

Scots runners disappointed in the International at Derby Racecourse with National Champion McPhee falling at a water jump and, badly winded, dropping back to eventually finish thirty fourth with Tom Jack finishing three places further behind. Sam Stevenson lost a shoe early in the race and dropped out. It was left to William Bowman (West of Scotland), only sixth in the National, to finish first Scot in eleventh place, with Scotland finishing third behind England and Ireland but four points in front of France.

1910 to 1919

To those who knew him George Dallas was the administrative rock on which the National Cross Country Union of Scotland operated. For twenty five years, between 1921/22 and 1946/47, he held the post of joint Hon Secretary and Hon Treasurer, and then remained as Hon Secretary for a further period of fifteen years until 1961, with Duncan McSwein having taken over the separate post of Hon Treasurer in 1946.

But Dallas was also a very successful competitor on both the track and country as well as being an able administrator and reporter of the sport in most of Scotland's newspapers. It was general for runners to turn to distance running and competition over the country after a period of track competition over shorter distances. But Dallas was different in his approach to competition. Returning from army service in the First World War he was in the peak of physical fitness after a year in the army of occupation in Germany had given him plenty of time for training. In his first summer home he ran 52.0 seconds to win the SAAA National 440 yards title at Powderhall Stadium in Edinburgh.

This short distance sprint victory came, unusually, after a pre war period of cross country running. In 1910 Dallas won Maryhill Harriers 9 mile club championship, bettering the course record by two minutes with three other clubmates also inside the old record. This run established him as favourite for the Western District Junior title and he justified this position by winning the seven mile race in 41 minutes 05 seconds. In a close finish he was three seconds clear of A Austin (Greenock Glenpark Harriers) with D Peat (Motherwell YMCA Harriers) third, just one second behind. Dallas led Maryhill to their first ever team victory in the championship.

George Dallas
(Maryhill Harriers)
Western District Junior Champion in 1910
and Scottish AAA 440 yards champion in 1920.

In the Eastern District Championships, staged from Edinburgh University athletic fields, 124 competitors found the race a test of strength with strong winds and heavy rain slowing the runners over the 8 mile course. W R Grant of Waverley Harriers won, with Edinburgh Northern Harriers dominating the team contest, placing nine runners in the first thirty to finish, and scoring a convincing team victory with 46 points to defeat Falkirk Victoria Harriers by 87 points. It is an example of the simplicity of race organisation at that time that just seven officials - one referee, two timekeepers and four judges - were required to stage the championship, compared to modern times when up to ten times that number of officials are required to successfully stage a major championship meeting.

Clubs staged their own programme of low key pack runs, club trophy races and inter club runs throughout the season with the only competitive fixtures, outside the Championship events, being the Christmas cross country race staged by Edinburgh Harriers in the East, and Clydesdale Harriers individual and team race, open to all other clubs, in the West.

Seven clubs entered for the National Championships held at Glasgow Agricultural Showgrounds at Scotstoun, which at that time was in the middle of the countryside outside Glasgow. The small entry of clubs in the team championships was partly due to the concept that only the top clubs with a chance of winning the title should enter, but possibly the high team entry fee of £1.00 deterred clubs from entering. The same year the English Cross Country Union defeated a proposal to reduce the team entry fee from £2.00 to £1-1/- (£1- 05p) - a reduction that was agreed after the First World War and only increased back to £2 as recently as 1970.

The runners covered a two lap course starting with two circuits of the Showground cinder track and then passing by way of Scotstoun Hill, Bankhead Farm, Cloverhill, Knightswood, Anniesland and Jordanhill for a total of ten miles. In favourable weather conditions Alex McPhee of Clydesdale Harriers, described by contemporary reports as "one of the best distance runners Scotland has given to amateur athletics", effectively spanned the two decades by repeating his victory of 1909 when winning by seventy yards in 58 minutes 17 seconds from J Duffy (Edinburgh Harriers) with former champion Tom Jack (Edinburgh Southern Harriers) finishing third over a minute behind.

There was obviously no tie break rule in existence at this time, for in a close and exciting team contest Clydesdale Harriers, led by Alex McPhee, and West of Scotland, led by fourth placed George McKenzie, tied for first place with each scoring 83 points ahead of Edinburgh Harriers 106 points. George Dallas, in his first race as a "Senior" after winning the Western "Junior" title, finished tenth and was selected as reserve for the Scottish team for the International Championships at Belvoir Park in Belfast.

Anglo Scot George Wallach of Bolton United Harriers, who finished third in the English Championship at Derby one week later, was selected for the Scottish team having been born in Scotland but lived for most of his life in England. At 28 years of age this was Wallach's first appearance in the Scottish team though he was to run for Britain in the 10,000 metres in the 1912 Olympic Games at Stockholm. He was to show remarkable consistency over cross country, gaining nine international vests in the period ending in 1924 - and that was without the opportunity of competing during the war years between 1915 and 1919. Wallach competed for Greenock Glenpark Harriers in Scotland and turned out regularly over the years in the National cross country and track 4 and 10 miles track championships.

National champion Alex McPhee was the first Scot to finish in the International Championship, but he was 2 minutes 37 seconds behind the winner, and it was the desparately unfortunate experience of George Wallach that was the main feature of the race.

Wallach looked certain to join the illustrious band of runners who won the International title at their first attempt when he entered the approaches to Belvoir Park with a clear lead. However he had extensively torn his shorts when climbing over a barbed wire fence out in the country section of the course and a sharp eyed policeman near the finish stepped out, physically tackled him, and pulled him out of the race on the grounds of indecent exposure in a public place. Wallach calmly acquiesced with the actions of the officious policeman and watched his rivals stream past to the finishing line.

It is difficult, in these days of appearance money and sponsorship for athletes, when large sums of money depend on the performance of athletes in major International championships, to realise how calmly Wallach accepted the police action which deprived him of almost certain victory. It is more than possible nowadays that an International athlete, in the same circumstances that Wallach found himself in Belfast, would tear himself free of the policeman's arresting embrace and run on to victory. The enhanced publicity about his torn shorts and resistance of arrest would give him an increased monetary value for future competitive appearances and result in fame and fortune. Who can say which is the better state of affairs but it certainly gives an example of the changing times in our sport.

The following season there were thirty one clubs affiliated to the Western District of which twenty seven competed in the District Championships at Carntyne Racecourse which cost £2-10/- (£2-50p) to hire for the event. The organising committee decided that it would not be necessary to have any policemen on duty at Carntyne in the East End of Glasgow compared to four policemen and two commissionaires on duty the previous year at Scotstoun in the West End of Glasgow.

Paisley Junior Harriers, who won Clydesdale Harriers open team contest earlier in the season from Motherwell YMCA, showed the advantage of a familiarising run over the course the previous week when they again defeated the Motherwell club to lift the team championship. Archie Craig of Bellahouston Harriers, who was to win the National championship two years later, finished third in the race behind D Peat (Motherwell YMCA).

Sam Watt of Clydesdale Harriers, won the National championships from 100 competitors representing eight clubs at Sheep Farm Park in Pollok Estate, Glasgow where a large and enthusiastic crowd of spectators lined the course. Watt won by fifty yards from J Duffy who finished runner up for the second time and led Edinburgh Harriers to victory over Clydesdale and West of Scotland in the team championships.

The close, friendly link between football clubs and cross country running was evidenced when donations from Celtic FC £3-3/- (£3-15p) and Rangers FC £2- 2/- (£2-10p) helped the Union to send a team to Wales for the International championships held at Caerleon Racecourse in Newport. Caerleon Racecourse, where the Welsh staged the championships on six of the seven occasions they hosted the event in the first half century of the International, had a weather jinx which recurred in different forms time and time again.

In 1911 snow had fallen heavily for several days prior to the race but a trail of coloured paper had been laid over the thick layer of snow. However, just an hour or two before the race started a snow storm covered the laid trail. The organisers immediately recruited a number of Welsh cross country runners who were present as spectators, provided them with running kit, and stationed them as stewards with hand flags at strategic points around the Racecourse to guide the competitors round the trail.

In 1927 appalling weather conditions again caused race problems with torrential rain falling throughout the race. Six years later heatwave conditions applied, and so eager were spectators to enter the ground that they broke down the barriers and rushed into the Racecourse grounds, depriving the promoters of much needed gate money. The tropical weather conditions resulted in amazing sights. Runners cast off their vests, in contravention of the International rules that athletes must be properly clothed, others had not the strength to continue over the rough ground and collapsed in scenes of complete exhaustion, falling by the wayside and having to be brought to the dressing room by ambulance men. Finally, in 1951, heavy rain for days before the race turned the Racecourse into a quagmire and parts of the trail, which were entirely under deep pools of water, had to be deleted from the planned course.

In 1911 Jean Bouin of France took the lead at half distance over the treacherous course and went on to win by 70 yards from D Baldwin (England) with George Wallach gaining partial compensation for his disappointment at Belfast the previous year when he finished third a further 100 yards behind. This was the first of six occasions that Wallach finished in the first eight in the International race - a remarkable display of consistent running throughout the years. Scotland, with National Champion Sam Watt finishing a disappointing fourteenth over two minutes behind Wallach, took third place thirteen points behind second placed Ireland, but ahead of France who were still developing their cross country strength for future successes.

West of Scotland closed their season with a pack run from the village of Netherlee, the runners covering a distance of between 16 and 20 miles. They then celebrated their 25th Anniversary with a dinner in the St Enoch Hotel. The club's patron Sir John Ure Primrose was in the chair and, it was said "the speeches were excellent being, in most instances, commendably brief". The dinner attracted a distinguished attendance with the speakers including the President of the Scottish AAA, the Presidents of both the Scottish and English Cross Country Unions and the President of the Scottish Football Association.

It is certain that no one present at the Dinner would have been in any fit state to go for a run the following day after the vast menu presented for their enjoyment. The following details give a mouth watering description of the ten course menu:-

          Royal Native Oysters
     Consommé Célestine or Asparagus Soup
Salmon, Sauce Mousseline or Fillet of Sole, Sauce Tartare
          Balotine of Duck, Clemard
                Haggis
   Sirloin of Beef, or Roast Lamb, Mint Sauce,
               Vegetables
        Chicken Cocotte, Salad
          Saxon Pudding
         Croûte Cambridge
              Dessert
               Coffee

Sir John donated a silver trophy to West of Scotland which was contested for over 60 years until the club sadly went defunct in the 1970's and it is now presented by the SAAA as the prize for the Indoor Pole Vault Championship. Edinburgh Northern Harriers continued the celebratory season with their Coming of Age Dinner (21st Anniversary) at Milne's Hotel with Fred Lumley in the chair.

Falkirk Victoria Harriers, the previous years winners, hosted the 1912 Eastern District Championships at Victoria Park in Falkirk. Twelve teams entered for the event with the eight mile course covering a great deal of ploughed land made heavy by a thaw after heavy frost. W Menzies of Edinburgh Northern scored a 500 yard victory with Edinburgh Harriers, placing their scoring six runners in the first eighteen finishers, winning the team title for the fifth time.

A record entry of twenty seven clubs contested the Western District Championships at Scotstoun, running over the course to be used for the National Championships the following month. On this occasion a keen frost made the going hard with large numbers of competitors having accidents due to the underfoot conditions and retiring from the race. Alexander Loch (Clydesdale Harriers) won the title by three seconds from R Bell (Motherwell YMCA), with a strong, enthusiastic young team from Bellahouston Harriers equalling the Motherwell YMCA record of three team championship wins.

A much smaller field of just six clubs took part in the 1912 National at Scotstoun with defending champion Sam Watt setting the pace over the two lap 10 mile course over the country to the west and north of Scotstoun. Tom Jack (Edinburgh Southern Harriers), winner in 1907 and 08, took over the lead in the latter stages and held off a strong challenge on the final circuit of the Showground track to win by just one second from A Kerr (Motherwell YMCA) with Watt finishing third in the closest finish ever seen in a National Championship with just four seconds covering the first three finishers. West of Scotland, with four runners in the first ten home, won the title for the fourth and final time, defeating Clydesdale Harriers and Edinburgh Harriers with Bellahouston Harriers, who were to win for the next two years, finishing in fourth position.

Edinburgh hosted the International Championship race, the previous two times it had been held in Scotland being in the West, but representatives of the competing countries had expressed strong desires to see the beauties of Scotland's capital. The organisers acquiesced and chose Saughton Park, the venue of the sports programme of the Scottish National Exhibition held in Edinburgh four years earlier. Early in March, just three weeks before the event took place, the Glasgow Herald commented "It is not generally known that the ICCU Championship will be held in Edinburgh on March 30. Cross country running has generally a firmer hold in Glasgow and the West of Scotland but in other respects there could not be a more delightful venue for the race. The trail will probably embrace the Corstorphine Hills though that is a matter of detail still to be decided by the Scottish Union at an early date".

In modern days, when the organisation of a major championship starts at least a year or more before the event, it is difficult to realise that the trail was not settled with course maps sent to competing countries months before the race itself. But events were conducted in a more leisurely manner in the early years of the century, although they still, somehow, were implemented in a manner satisfactory to all concerned. The runners were half an hour late in appearing at the starting line but

Union President William Struthers soon sent them on their way over a 9½ mile course which consisted of 1 mile round the track before leaving the Park to cover 5 miles of rough cart track and 3½ miles of grassland.

Bouin of France led from the early stages to score a repeat victory from two English runners with George Wallach finishing fourth for the Scottish team which, with all their six counting runners finishing in the first twenty two, finished runners up to England. Tom Jack had a disappointing final appearance for Scotland, finishing only fifth counter in twentieth position, but going on three weeks later to win the SAAA 10 mile track title for the seventh time in nine years.

Jack retired from competition after this run to become President of the Scottish AAA the following season. He followed well known names from cross country circles such as A Ross Scott, who was President in 1903-04; G Hume 1904- 05; C Pennycook 1907-08 and A Hannah 1909-10 in an era when the cross country influence was stronger in the SAAA than it is nowadays.

Tom Jack was one of Scotland's most distinguished and successful distance runners in the pre First World War period. Of West Calder farming stock Jack was born in 1881 on his father's farm in Brotherton and enrolled as a student teacher at Moray House Training College with subsequent graduation as MA from Edinburgh University.

Joining Edinburgh Southern Harriers in 1900 his early running gave no signs of the future greatness he was to display, finishing runner up for four successive years in his club's championships. He blossomed forth as a National Champion in 1904 when winning the SAAA track 10 mile title, a title he was to win seven times inside the nine year period from 1904 to 1912. His best victory came in 1907 when he set a Scottish record of 53 minutes 04.0 seconds and recorded best performances at the intermediate distances of 5,6,7,8 and 9 miles, with the 6 mile record of 31 minutes 18.8 seconds lasting 13 years until James Wilson bettered it in 1920 with a run of 30 minutes 45.0 seconds.

Tom Jack
(Edinburgh Southern Harriers)
National Champion in 1907/08 and 1912 and a member of the Scottish International team 5 times between 1907 and 1912.

Winning the Senior title in the 1907 National cross country championships while still a Junior he became the second athlete to win the dual Senior and Junior titles at the same time. He repeated the Senior title victory the following year and again in 1912. He gained International selection for Scotland on five separate occasions between 1907 and 1912, with his best effort being on his international debut in 1907 when he finished in fifth position and led Scotland to second position in the team contest.

In the 1908 Olympic Games Marathon at London Jack represented Great Britain but, after leading the field for the first 5 miles at a suicidal fast pace, he was forced to drop out of the race with exhaustion.

On the administrative side of the sport, after seven years as an SAAA Council member while still an active athlete he became the only President (1912- 13) while still an active competitor. He became President of the Cross Country Union in 1930-

31, completing an administrative career which was every bit as distinguished as his competitive one. He died, aged 79, in Edinburgh in 1960 after maintaining his connections with the sport to the end.

The 1913 Eastern District Championships were held in splendid weather at Galashiels with 98 runners from nine clubs taking part. The local club had chosen a tough 7 mile course, starting from Gala Policies and thence by way of Scott Street and Wendyknowe to Mosilee cricket pitch; over by Mosilee Farm to Fairnalee Moor and returning home by Hollybush to the starting point. Borderers found themselves very much at home in the rugged conditions winning both individual and team titles with J Grierson winning from his Teviotdale Harrier teammate T Hamilton and Gala Harriers, led by third placed C Abbot, easily winning the team championship by 47 points from Falkirk Victoria Harriers.

The Western clubs were not so favoured in their Championships at Scotstoun where, for the first time in living memory, the Championships had to be called off due to the weather. The weather was fine for the start but an earlier snowstorm had left a thick covering of snow on the higher ground. The hares, although provided with sacks of coloured paper, had not enough to satisfactorily lay the trail over the snowy sections with the result that many of the runners lost the trail and went off course.

The organisers declared the race null and void as the first entrants to Scotstoun were a large group of runners who freely confessed to losing the trail and taking a short cut back to the finish. When the race was re-run two weeks later 26 clubs took part, with only West of Scotland, holding their club championship, and Mauchline Harriers, who found a second long journey from Ayrshire to Glasgow inconvenient, missing from the full District membership.

In order to prevent competitors going off the laid trail course marshalls were positioned at strategic locations around the course. R Bell of Monkland Harriers confirmed his position as favourite when winning from clubmate A McDonald and the Airdrie club, with four counters in twelve, won the team championship for the first time. They defeated Garscube Harriers and Greenock Glenpark Harriers, who fielded three Lang brothers (AH 20th; AG 21st and AJ 27th) in their team.

Going into the National Championships Bellahouston Harriers were favourites to break the domination of National team honours by Edinburgh Harriers, Clydesdale and West of Scotland. The Glasgow club had added fifty new runners to their membership roll in the past year and was gaining the benefit of more modern training methods. Help from Rangers FC, who granted them the use of training facilities on easier terms than in previous years, together with great enthusiasm and discipline in training runs, had brought them to a peak of fitness that had gained them increased honours throughout the season.

Seven teams entered the National championships, including first time entrants Gala Harriers who fielded their Eastern District Championship team. Archie Craig (Bellahouston) moved into the lead after just a mile with former champion Sam Watt and George McKenzie leading a chasing group of runners. Craig was challenged for the lead up to half distance in the 10 mile course, but finished strongly to win by forty yards from A McDonald (Monkland Harriers), who came through in the final mile to finish runner up two seconds in front of Watt.

Early on in the race it was apparent that the team contest would be between the holders, West of Scotland, and Bellahouston, and these two clubs eventually provided eleven of the first thirteen finishers between them. Bellahouston's team, led by A Craig 1, consisted of A Kerr 5, J Templeman 7, G Stephens 10, E Rodgers 12 and A Hendry 15, totalling 50 points. West of Scotland, led by fourth placed George McKenzie, had their other five runners inside the first thirteen home, but were narrowly edged out by just one point by Bellahouston, who recorded their first ever victory in the National team championships.

Bellahouson and West of Scotland each fielded three runners in Scotland's team for the 1913 International championship race at Juvisy Aerodrome outside Paris. Wallach, who finished third in the English Northern championships and in the first 10 in the English National, was selected. He fully justified his position by finishing as first Scot home in eigth position with the Bellahouston men A Kerr 11, A Craig 14 and J Templeman 18 all being in Scotland's counting team while the three West of Scotland runners were all outside the counting six.

Several thousand spectators attended the championships to see their 24 year old countryman Jean Bouin complete his hat trick of wins. This large attendance enabled the French organisers to make a profit of £45-6/2 (£45-31p) which gave each competing country a share of £11-6/6 (£11-32½p) when previous operating profits had never exceeded £11 in total.

The perpetual problem of defining the requirements of a successful cross country course was raised at the International Board Meeting. The British delegates expressed the opinion that there was too little real country in some International events, and too much racing track surfaces where speedy runners had it all their own way, with the strength of real cross country specialists not given a real opportunity.

The Board preferrred not to strictly define the conditions for a course but to leave it to the judgement of the country in which the race was held. A resolution was agreed which stated:- "The country promoting the International race should provide as natural a course as possible and the course should include some hill, natural or other obstacles such as ditches, gates or hedges and a little road if the same cannot be avoided". The French complied well with the spirit of the resolution, providing a well varied 10 mile course including flat meadow land, ploughed fields and long stretches of hilly woodland paths through private parkland.

Wallach, running for Greenock Glenpark Harriers in the SAAA 10 mile track championship at Celtic Park, won the race and set a Scottish record of 53 minutes 01.0 seconds. He broke the record, far outside his personal best of 51 minutes 36 seconds set a few weeks earlier in England, despite a most unusual and unsettling preparation for the race. Having to work as a printer with the Manchester Evening News on the night before, he caught the morning express train on the day of the race, arriving in Glasgow just a couple of hours before the race started. He displayed what a fine distance runner he was by lapping the entire field except for Archie Craig, who finished runner up just outside 54 minutes in a time beaten on only four occasions since the race was first held in 1886.

Wallach won the title the following year at the Hawkhill Grounds with another Scottish record time of 52 minutes 48.6 seconds, setting Scottish records at all intermediate distances from 7 to 10 miles.

Newspaper reports of the era always referred to G C L Wallach when reporting details of his many athletic triumphs. His full name was George Curtis Locke

Wallach, born in Castle Douglas, Kirkcudbright in 1882, the twelfth of eighteen children, and died, aged 96 years, in 1979.. He lived and worked for most of his life in England, competing extensively in English races. He was a remarkable cross country runner who represented Scotland eight times in the International race and finished as first Scot home on six of these occasions. His achievements are listed below:-

Newport	1911	3rd	Chesham	1914	2nd
Edinburgh	1912	4th	Newport	1921	8th
Paris	1913	8th	Glasgow	1922	4th

He was a typical Harrier; tough, rugged and determined - a hard man of athletics who was renowned for his pace and race judgement, with his strength and staying power being his forte, rather than his finishing speed which was always judged to be lacking for the International class runner that he was.

His achievements were uniquely recognised by the NCCU General Committee who minuted their special appreciation of his performance in the 1922 International at Hampden Park by noting:- "Reference to the International would hardly be complete without commenting on the running of G C L Wallach who was again first man home for Scotland in fourth place, an excellent performance for a man who has passed forty years of age. Wallach's performance was truly remarkable and well worthy of the many eulogising press comments and his overall record is testimony of his consistency in the International event".

He won the National title in 1914 and 22, representing Greenock Glenpark Harriers, and the First World War must have robbed him of the opportunity of many more victories. He was also a noted track runner, twice having won both the SAAA 4 and 10 mile track titles.

In those times the majority of roads were surfaced with sets of cobbles which were extremely painful to run on, causing bad blistering and in the evening there was only limited street lighting to illuminate the poor road surface.

Wallach trained mainly on the track in the evenings, and from New Year onwards, utilised Belle Vue track in Manchester where he lived and worked. Admission to the track cost 4d (1½p), with the changing rooms being in a dilapidated wooden structure open to all the winds that blew, with doors that never shut properly. Wallach changed by the light of a candle and, once on the track, there was only the glow from the adjacent street lights to distinguish the grass verge from the cinder track. Baths, showers or adequate toilet facilities were undreamed of luxuries at Belle Vue but Wallach took all the difficulties, that would horrify modern day athletes, in his stride.

His durability, twice gaining international selection when past 40 years of age, is remarkable when one considers that the average life expectancy was 45 years in 1900, rising slowly to the late fifties by 1932. The training carried out by harriers placed them far above the general level of fitness of the ordinary population, as is borne out by the fact that, during the First World War, two thirds of all men examined were declared unfit for active service.

Bellahouston Harriers started the 1914 season in the winning form they finished the previous season. One of their new recruits James Lindsay, a Dreghorn youth who had been running less than two years, won the Western District Championships at Carntyne Racecourse where over 300 runners from 26 clubs -

only two of whom failed to finish full teams in the race - competed over a 7 mile course of plough and stubble fields. Lindsay won by 300 yards from clubmate A Semple with D Cummings (Paisley Harriers) in third place. Bellahouston totalled just 57 points to win by a massive margin from Greenock Glenpark Harriers 163 points who had 5 points to spare from Maryhill Harriers.

The National Championships were also held at Carntyne Racecourse, where the 10 mile course was a real test of stamina, with numerous obstacles creating breaks to smooth racing which upset the rhythm of competitors. Wallach, who had finished third in the English National Championship, made his first appearance in the National and was close behind defending champion Archie Craig in the early stages. The Scottish 4 and 10 mile champion passed Craig at half distance and went on to win by 50 yards from Craig with G Stephens (also Bellahouston) in third place.

With Wallach competing only as an individual, and not counting in the team scoring, Bellahouston had it all their own way in retaining their team title. They scored an overwhelming victory totalling the record low score of just 29 points with A Craig 1, G Stephens 2, J Templeman 3, J Lindsay 5, G Cummings 6 and W Mathie 12. West of Scotland, beaten last year by just one point by Bellahouston, finished second team with 62 points with Edinburgh Northern finishing a distant third with 128 points.

England hosted the International race at Chesham, Bucks where the English Championships had been held over such a tough, testing course that many runners had failed to finish the race. Fourth in the English Championships, after finishing runner up in the Southern Championships, was James Wilson, a Scotsman who was to take up his eligibility to represent his country after the War, but on this occasion chose to represent England in the International Championships.

The fine sunny weather attracted a large crowd of spectators with the runners facing a hilly course with long stretches of ploughed land and many obstacles, including water jumps and hurdles, on each of the three 3 mile laps which provided a most severe test for the competitors. Wallach was in third place in the early stages of the race with Wilson in sixth place. On the second lap Wallach, renowned for his strength and stamina, went into the lead over the long stretches of plough with four Englishmen following, closely in his footsteps. The team race at this point was actually in Scotland's favour for, in an unofficial count, they totalled six points less than England. On the final stretch of plough Wallach was passed by A Nicholls of England and although Wallach held on grimly, a bad fall at the final water jump allowed Nicholls to draw clear in the final half mile to win by 26 seconds with Wallach finishing runner up - the best performance ever achieved at that time by a Scot in the International Championships.

The Scottish team, with a backbone of five Bellahouston runners, finished second in the team contest with their counting six runners finishing inside the first twenty home - actually achieving better packing than the winning English team who had to wait until twenty second position for their final scoring man.

England officially won the team title with their counting runners finishing 1,3,4,6,11 and 22 for a total of 47 points with Scotland, 74 points, having G Wallach 2; J Lindsay 8; A Craig 12; G McKenzie 13; D Peat 19 and S Watt 20. However, looking at the result from purely a Scottish point of view, the knowledge that sixth placed James Wilson was a Scot who was to declare himself as such for the next International race, allows the theoretical re calculation of the team scores on the basis of the first six Scots runners counting for the Scottish team.

With Wilson taken as counting for the Scottish team the official sixth counter in twentieth place can be dropped from the team score. The team counters now become 2,6,8,12,13 and 19 for a readjusted total of 60 points. England, losing Wilson's sixth place from their total, had to take into account their next scorer in twenty ninth position. This gave them a new team score with their team counters being 1,3,4,11,22 and 29 for a new total of 70 points. Thus Scotland, who never actually won the team title in the history of the International Championships, scored an unofficial team victory by 10 points when the eligible scoring Scots in the race were taken as counting for Scotland and outscored the rival English team.

The outstanding achievements of the domestic season was the break through by James Lindsay of Bellahouston who proved the most improved runner of the year. Starting the winter season as an unknown, Lindsay's victory in the Western District Championship promoted him to a "Senior" and eligible to run in the National Championships. His performance at Carntyne, where he finished sixth, was a big surprise. He confirmed this performance with his excellent eighth place in the International where he defeated everyone in the Scottish team except the second placed Wallach.

On the domestic front Springburn celebrated their Coming of Age (21st Anniversary) in January with a supper attended by many influential members of the cross country fraternity. J B Wilson, a member of West of Scotland Harriers, announced his retirement from cross country running, having missed just one run in his 21 years of competition and pack running in the winter sport.

In the final week of the season George McKenzie sponsored an inaugural cross country relay race for Edinburgh clubs at Saughton Park. This novelty event, for such it was, with no relay race ever having been staged as a competitive event, attracted entries from all the Edinburgh clubs except the University Hares and Hounds. The race was over 10 miles with each of four team members running over a $2\frac{1}{2}$ miles course - the classic distance which has remained to this day and is still used for all cross country relay events. After Edinburgh Northern had led for the first three laps, A Peters brought Edinburgh Southern into the lead on the final stage of the race. He entered the track fifty yards in front of J Hendry (Edinburgh Northern), who suddenly collapsed and did not finish. Edinburgh Southern won by 27 seconds from Waverley with Edinburgh in third place. Undoubtedly this race gave George McKenzie the idea to present his trophy to the NCCU for the cross country relay race for Eastern District clubs which eventually became a District Championship event in 1926.

When the First World War started in August 1914 life changed rapidly in Scotland. Young men joined the Services in their thousands and it was the fittest who joined first, with sportsmen to the fore. The ranks of members of Scotland's harrier clubs were depleted and the sport quickly ground to a halt with the usual Championships organised by the Union being cancelled after the 1914 National Championships.

The Annual General Meeting, held on 19th September 1914 in the Christian Institute, Glasgow was attended by 42 delegates from 24 member clubs, of which 20 were from Glasgow and the West of Scotland and the other 4 from Edinburgh. This was in line with the total club membership of 31 clubs in the Western District and 11 in the Eastern District of the Union. A proposal by William Struthers of

Greenock Glenpark Harriers, the retiring President, "that no championships be held during the 1914-15 season owing to so many club members having joined His Majesty's Forces" was approved by an overwhelming majority.

Mr Ferguson (Kilmarnock Harriers) raised the issue of whether the annual subscription of 10/6 (52½p) should be paid to the Union when no championships were organised for member clubs. The AGM minutes record that "a great deal of discussion took place on this matter" before the Chairman resolved the issue by informing delegates that, according to Union rules, all clubs that had not resigned membership prior to the AGM were liable to pay the annual subscription for the forthcoming season. The financial report revealed that the Union's funds totalled £18.14/(£18.70p) and a proposal was made that a donation be made to the Prince of Wales National Relief Fund. A figure of £5.5/(£5.25p) was agreed, but again "heated argument resulted", with alternative proposals as to whether the money should be sent to a Glasgow or an Edinburgh fund. A compromise was reached when it was agreed to send the money direct to the London Fund.

Mr George MacKenzie, a former International athlete and proprietor of a sports shop in Edinburgh, presented a cup for annual competition among Eastern District clubs and was awarded a hearty vote of thanks from the Union. Matthew Dewar of Edinburgh Southern Harriers was elected as President of the Union, a post he was to hold throughout the War years until 1920, when he was succeeded by J.D. McKinlay (Maryhill Harriers), setting a record tenure of six years as President which was not exceeded until the Second World War when J.Follan of Kilbarchan AAC held the post from season 1938/39 to 1945/46.

The programme of a Concert and Cinematograph exhibition, staged by Edinburgh Northern Harriers in the Lyric Theatre in November 1914 in honour of club members serving King and Country, listed 51 harriers who were already serving in the Forces. When it is realised that the Northern Harriers were just one of seven clubs in Edinburgh - the others being Edinburgh Harriers, Edinburgh Southern Harriers, Waverley Harriers, Heriots and Watsonians Cross Country Clubs and the University Hares and Hounds - the large number of harriers who joined the Forces in the first few months of the War left these clubs bereft of members and unable to carry out the normal club programme of events. Club runs were staged in the first year of the War, but lack of club members and travel difficulties made inter club runs hard to organise and long working hours cut down the time for training and club pack runs at the weekend.

By February 1915, of the 42 clubs in memberships of the Union, only 26 clubs had paid their subscription for the current season, 18 from the West and 8 from the East. Eight clubs had resigned from membership due to the national crisis, including such prominent long term members as Teviotdale Harriers from Hawick and Dundee Hawkhill Harriers, with another 8 clubs having failed to respond to the Secretary's communications.

In an effort to maintain the sport of cross country running and spread competition to the large number of troops in training camps in Scotland, approaches were made to the military authorities to hold cross country team races. A race was held at Bogside Racecourse at Gailes in Ayrshire, with entries from the two battalions stationed at Troon and Gailes. William Maley of Celtic F.C., a generous and consistent benefactor to the NCCU of Scotland, presented medals to the winning individuals and teams. 500 programmes were printed, but the turnout of spectators was disappointing, and a deficit of £9.1/.(£9.05p) resulted on the race promotion. Further military races were successfully held at Ibrox and Carntyne with the co-operation of the military authorities, and a similar event was staged at Craiglockhart in Edinburgh, with the individual and team awards, donated by the Edinburgh Evening Dispatch, being won by the Royal Scots Regiment.

The 1915 Annual General Meeting at Milnes Hotel in Edinburgh was attended by 31 delegates from 20 clubs, of which 14 were from Glasgow and the West of Scotland and the other 6 from the Eastern District. A cash balance of £20.16/6 (£20.82½p) was declared by the Treasurer in his Financial Report, with total assets of £46.16/6 (£46.82½p), including the splendid Exhibition Shield, valued at £20, which has now disappeared from the possession of the Union.

After a great deal of discussion, delegates approved the following recommendations from General Committee.

1. That the rules of the Union be suspended for the duration of the War, and that the existing officials and committe carry on the business of the Union for such period, with powers to add to their number.
2. That the Cross Country Union control and arrange all Saturday fixtures through the District Committees.

A recommendation was approved that all clubs that could afford it should pay the Annual Subscription and so keep the Union in a sound financial position for resumption of competition on completion of the War. Clubs struggled with difficult conditions in the following 3½ years with some successfully keeping club runs going on Saturday afternoons. No record is availiable of any competitive events during this period and the next formal activity is recorded in March 1919.

The war had ended four months earlier and a sense of jubilation and desire to return to normality was prevalent at a meeting of Harrier Clubs in the Christian Institute, Glasgow. 28 delegates from 17 clubs appeared in response to advertisements in national newspapers, all of whom were from Glasgow and the West of Scotland,except G M Grant of Edinburgh Northern Harriers. Among those present were Archie Craig, a former National Champion who led Bellahouston Harriers to victory in the National Team Championship in 1913, and Edinburgh University student J Hill Motion of Eglinton Harriers from Ayrshire who was to win both the National Junior and Senior titles in 1921.

The object of the meeting was to discuss the reconstruction and future development of cross country running in Scotland. The record states that "Interesting remarks and debates took place on various matters" and the following recommendations were made to General Committee for consideration at the Annual General Meeting later in the year.

1. The usual Eastern and Western District Junior Championships and the National Senior Championships be restarted.
2. That a National Novice Individual and Team Championships be held (8 to run with 4 to count), with the entry qualification being that a runner should never have won a prize in a cross country race at the start of the cross country season on 1st October.
3. That the annual subscription be increased from 10/6(52½p) to 15/-(75p).

The 1919 A.G.M. was held in the Christian Institute, Glasgow on 29 September with 22 delegates from 13 clubs present. All the clubs were from the West of Scotland, as a railway strike had left the Eastern District delegates, including the President, stranded in Edinburgh. The proposals from the representative meeting of clubs were approved with the exception of the annual subscription where the amount was doubled to £1.1/-(£1.05p). Mr Matthew Dewar of Edinburgh Southern Harriers was re-elected as President, in his absence, for a sixth year of office with William Roxburgh of Hamilton Harriers retaining the post of Hon. Secretary/Treasurer.

1920 to 1929

The 1919 A.G.M. decision to hold a Novice Championship was speedily implemented with the inaugural race being held just two months later at Carntyne Racecourse. The popularity of the event was immediately apparent with 18 clubs taking part over the five mile course. Maryhill Harriers, greatly strengthened by an influx of fit ex-soldiers who had been attracted by a successful publicity campaign organised by the energetic George Dallas, fielded a powerful team. Once outside the enclosure they forged to the front and filled the first four places for a minimum score of 10 points with Garscube Harriers, whose first man home was tenth, finishing runners up with 59 points ahead of Shettleston Harriers 66 points.

The immediate surge of interest, once organised championship events were staged after the War, continued when twenty teams entered for the Western District Championships at Rouken Glen Park. S. Small of Bellahouston won the 7 mile race from Duncan McLeod Wright (Clydesdale H) who was to win the National Junior title over the same course later in the season.

It is not commonly known that Wright, famous for his brilliant marathon running, started athletics as a sprinter. After winning the 75 yards sprint at the Round Toll Foundry Boys Sports he entered the sprints at Barr and Stroud's Staff Sports. In his later training Dunky did everything thoroughly and it was no different at the start of his running career. For a fortnight before the sports he ran two sprints every evening, with the result that his searching training caused him to tie up on the day of the sports and lose a 220 yards race he was quite capable of winning.

He joined Clydesdale Harriers in 1917 and won the club championship four times, was President twice and gained the National Senior title in 1923 before leaving the club to join Shettleston. It is significant that Wright's National victory in Clydesdale's colours of black and white was the last National individual or team honour won by the once great club. From a position in which 14 Scottish team championships and 17 individual wins had been recorded in the first 29 years of the club's history up to the start of the First World War, the best position the club achieved in the Scottish Championships in the inter war years was 15th of 23 teams taking part. In pre war days Clydesdale had been one of the strongest and most successful clubs but, from being a club with a national catchment area centered on Glasgow, they retreated to Clydebank where they became a 'small town" club with limited strength and a smaller catchment area.

Duncan McLeod Wright (Maryhill Harriers) National Champion in 1923/24/25 and 1927, and a member of the Scottish team on 11 consecutive occasions between 1920 and 1930.

After his solitary appearance for the English team in the 1914 International race

James Wilson
(Greenock Glenpark Harriers)
National Champion and International Champion in 1920.
1920 Olympic 10,000 metres bronze medallist at Antwerp.

James Wilson followed the example of his fellow Anglo Scot George Wallach by joining Greenock Glenpark Harriers and assuming international eligibility to compete for Scotland. He quickly took advantage of his new status, winning the SAAA 4 mile title in 1914 and completing a hat trick of wins in 1919 and 20 after the War. Wilson ran in the first post war National Championships in Rouken Glen Park, an event at which the Union expected such a large crowd of spectators to attend that they requested Glasgow Tramways to run extra tramcars through the park for the convenience of spectators and competitors.

Wilson recorded an outstanding win over a muddy course from Dunky Wright, with Shettleston winning the team championship to add to their District team title. Wilson continued his excellent running when taking fourth position in the English National at Windsor Great Park.

Belvoir Park in Belfast was the venue of the International race. Wales did not compete, and England, Ireland, Scotland and France had a four way contest in the team championship. Joseph Guillemot of France started favourite, having won the English National as the first foreigner to take the individual title three weeks earlier, and led for the early stages of the race. The Scottish champion was the only runner to go with the Frenchman and the two were well clear of the field when Guillemot cracked and dropped out in a state of collapse.

50

Wilson ran with fine judgement and style to finish a clear winner by 27 seconds from three Englishmen. Unfortunately there was no back up from a disappointing Scottish team with A Kerr 18 and A Craig 20 being the next Scots to finish. Scotland finished with the same points total as France, in equal last position.

Wilson continued his good form with a track distance double in the Scottish championships, winning the 4 miles in 20 min 22.4 secs and the 10 miles in the Scottish record time of 52 min 04.4 secs. He lapped the Celtic Park cinder track remorselessly with his rivals far behind him from the early stages, setting records at the intermediate distances of 5, 6, 7, 8 and 9 miles. His 6 miles time of 30 min 45.0 secs was not bettered in the Scottish championships until Ian Binnie set a new record of 30 min 04.2 secs thirty two years later.

His fine running gained him selection for the Olympic Games at Antwerp at 10,000 metres over both track and country. Belgium was still recovering from the war but the organisation was exasperating and inefficient throughout. The British team were billeted in an Antwerp school and slept on camp beds liable to collapse, having to drink beer in preference to the suspect water and eating in restaurants until the cooking arrangements improved at their quarters. Transport to the stadium was by army lorry fitted with wooden bench seats, and once there, they found a cinder track which was likened to a well trodden stretch of Flanders mud.

Wilson won his heat of the 10,000 metres from Paavo Nurmi, the ultimate winner, and led the field in the final up to the last two laps. Nurmi went on to win from Joseph Guillemot (France) in 31 min 45.8 secs with the Scot finishing third 5 seconds behind. His bronze medal was the only 10,000 metres medal won by a Briton until Brendan Foster gained a similar medal at the Montreal Olympics 56 years later.

Cross country, at that time, was part of the Olympic Games athletic programme, and three days later Wilson lined up for an underdistance (probably 8,000 metres) cross country individual and team race in which Wilson faced two gold medallists Guillemot (5,000 metres) and Nurmi (10,000 metres). The tiny 5' 3" Frenchman stepped in a pothole 3,000 metres from the finish and was forced to withdraw, leaving Nurmi to win another gold medal with Wilson in fourth position. However he led Britain to second place in the three man team race behind Finland and won a team silver medal. This tally of a silver and bronze medal made him the third most successful Scot in Olympic competition behind Allan Wells (100 metres gold and 200 metres silver) and Eric Liddell (400 metres gold and 200 metres bronze).

The importance of Scottish championship medals was illustrated on two occasions at the end of the season. Paisley Junior Harriers informed the Union that a retiral presentation was to be made to one of their members, J Elliot, who had run in every West District Championship since they started in 1895. Although never gaining a District medal Elliot had a heart felt desire to receive one at his presentation. General Committe agreed, pointing out that it was not to form a precedent, to present Mr Elliot with a first team race medal inscribed 'To John Elliot, for services rendered, from the N.C.C.U. of Scotland". It was also agreed to allow Shettleston Harriers, on the occasion of their team winning the 1920 National team championship, to purchase two additional National medals for presentation to team trainers.

The sport grew in popularity after the War with new clubs constantly being admitted to the Union. These included Dumbarton AAC, Eglinton H, Plebian H,

Mauchline H, Canon ASC, Selkirk H and Beith H, together with the renewal of membership of Teviotdale H, Monkland H and Edinburgh University who had dropped out during the War. Dundee Hawkhill Harriers, another club who resigned during the War, waited until November 1924 to rejoin the Union.

One application caused such controversy that it was referred for consideration to the A.G.M. This was from the Socialist Harrier and Athletic Club and was, after a great deal of discussion, rejected by 19 votes to 14 with the justification that the proposed name and the red flag on their vest was objectionable.

With the entry of newly affiliated clubs to the 1921 Eastern District Championships ten clubs finished teams over a 7 mile mixed country course at Portobello. J.W. Currie scored a 100 yard victory to give Gala Harriers their second individual victory in a row, with Edinburgh University and Edinburgh Northern tying for second team position behind Edinburgh Harriers.

Rouken Glen Park and the open surrounding countryside proved a popular venue for cross country running, for, besides the National Championships, it also hosted the National Novice and Western District Championships. A further event held at this venue was Clydesdale's Open 7 mile race when over 200 runners turned up for a second attempt after a farmer had removed the paper trail which had crossed his land and caused the runners to go off course resulting in the first race being called off. J.G. McIntyre, then running for the newly formed Dumbarton AAC, won the race and his success in this and other events, caused Shettleston Harriers to sign him to strengthen their team.

That summer McIntyre won the first of three consecutive SAAA 4 mile track titles and also won three 10 mile titles. His greatest triumph over the country came in 1923 at Paris, when he finished runner up in the International Championship to C. Blewitt of England - losing the Individual title by just 1.2 seconds in the closest finish ever seen in the event.

J. Hill Motion, an Edinburgh University student running for the Ayrshire club of Eglinton Harriers, had mixed fortunes at Rouken Glen. He finished runner up in the Western District Championships, 300 yards behind David Cummings of Greenock Glenpark, but retrieved his fortunes in the National just one month later.

The National and International champion James Wilson did not defend his title due to illness, but his Greenock Glenpark clubmate George Wallach was forward in the race. Running in wet and foggy weather with heavy, tiring underfoot conditions, Motion set the early pace over the 10 mile course but Wallach was in the lead at half distance with Motion, A Lawrie (Garscube) and D Cumming (Greenock Glenpark) on his shoulder. With just half a mile to go the Edinburgh University student went into the lead and eventually won by 80 yards from Wallach with Lawrie third. Fourth placed A Barrie led Shettleston to retain the team championship by 19 points from Garscube, with Greenock Glenpark third. Motion also won the Junior title, the first runner since Tom Jack in 1907 to achieve the double at the National. Shettleston again showed their team strength when also winning the Novice team championships in a race won by Robert McMillan (Greenock Glenpark).

Wallach was again the first Scot home in the 1921 International at Newport, finishing eighth with Dunky Wright ninth and A Barrie twelfth, but the other team counters were the last three men to finish, causing Scotland to finish fourth and last in the team championship.

At the International Board meeting George Hume was elected as permanent Hon. Secretary and Treasurer of the I.C.C.U., a post he was to hold for thirteen years until his death in 1934. Hume, the only man to be Union President two separate times (1898/99 and 1906/07) and the only President to represent an English club (Berwick and District Harriers), was the first Scot to be President of the International Union in 1907.

At the Scottish A.G.M. William Struthers of Greenock Glenpark was appointed the inaugural Hon. President, having been previously West District Chairman and Union President. Struthers presented a magnificient Shield for competition between West District clubs in a 10 mile cross country relay race which later developed into the District Relay Championships by 1926.

The inordinate interest by clubs in race competition rules was demonstrated when thirteen amendments were considered at the A.G.M., the same number as the previous year, with a total of over fifty amendments being considered in the first four years after competition was resumed after the war. There was always great concern about the marking of championship courses, where on frequent occasions natural conditions such as snow and winds ruined the paper trail, causing disruption and subsequent race re-runs. Edinburgh University put forward a detailed proposal in an attempt to improve the existing situation as follows:-

"The course shall be marked by a line of paper or flags and must be clearly distinguished at all parts. In the event of the course becoming indefinite or misleading at any point, with resulting disturbance to the competitors, the respective Committee shall have powers, on enquiry, to declare the race void and to fix the earliest date for the re-run of the fixture. The committee shall be responsible that official stewards, duly appointed and clearly badged, shall be posted over the course at doubtful positions to direct competitors. Competitors shall be warned against bogus stewards and to recognise guidance only from men carrying the official badge".

Long and detailed discussion revealed that a serious problem existed in all parts of the country and that something required to be done to solve the existing problem. But the meeting decided that the proposal was of far too exacting a nature and could not be adhered to in all respects if it became a rule of the Union - and so it was defeated.

William Roxburgh of Hamilton Harriers resigned after ten years as Secretary and Treasurer, to be followed by George Dallas (Maryhill Harriers) who was to be one of the Union's most able administrators, holding the post of Secretary until 1960. Dallas was immediately faced with a great deal of work. The International race was to be held in Scotland for the first time since 1912 and the Union's funds stood at only £5-13/1 (£5-65½). After considering the venues of Pollok Estate, Rouken Glen Park and Victoria Park, Falkirk it was agreed to stage the race at Hampden Park.

Scotland's team for the International race was chosen from the result of the 1922 National Championships at Musselburgh Racecourse. There, despite a hailstorm during the race, a large crowd of spectators watched George Wallach regain the Individual title he last won in 1914 and become the oldest man, at 40 years of age, to win the National.

After the first lap of 1½ miles over the Racecourse and 3½ miles over open adjacent country by way of Inveresk, Dalkeith Road, Dykehall and Levenhall, Wallach was 300 yards clear of Glenpark clubmates James McMillan and David

Cummings. On the second lap Wallach extended his lead to win by over 400 yards from 1913 champion Archie Craig (Bellahouston), who showed his considerable experience in pacing the race to take second place, four seconds ahead of James Riach (Maryhill), winner of the National Junior title, J.G. McIntyre, who finished fourth, led Shettleston to their third successive team championship.

The team contest was exciting, with Shettleston placing their counting six runners in the first twenty six home to total 88 points, and finish just 10 points ahead of Greenock Glenpark, whose final counter was twenty seventh. It is worth noting that the Greenock club did not have the benefit of Wallach's victory to count in their team total, as Wallach ran only as an individual. This situation was caused by Wallach, who lived in Manchester, not recording the four qualifying runs from Glenpark's headquarters which were necessary for him to be accepted by the scrutiny meeting as a team member.

Admission tickets, priced 1/-each (5p), were distributed for sale among athletic clubs for entry to Hampden Park where the International race was starting at half time in a Scottish league match between Queens Park and Celtic, who stayed top of the First Division by winning the match by 3 goals to 1. Ten thousand programmes, giving details of the International runners, were sold at 3d (1p) each to spectators who watched the International race start with four laps of the cinder track. The runners then headed out to open countryside in the south of Glasgow covering 9 miles of hilly, ploughed and grass meadow land with very little road to be traversed.

Joseph Guillemot of France, whose heart was on the right hand side of his chest, led all the way with Wallach in second place up to half distance. Wallach was passed by W Cotterell (England) and, near the return to Hampden Park, bŷ' J. Schmellmann (France). When the runners entered Hampden they were given a rousing reception from the 15,000 spectators who had stayed to see the race finish after the football match ended.

Guillemot, who had won the English National two weeks earlier, won by 28 seconds and led France to their first team victory over England, who had won every one of the team championships since the race was first held at Hamilton Racecourse in 1903. The French team management had protested, before the race, that the course was too rough and hilly but withdrew their protest after their team victory. Scotland, led by fourth placed captain Wallach who was backed up by vice captain Archie Craig 10 and Dunky Wright 11, finished an excellent third in the five country contest - just 25 points behind second placed England.

Celtic and Queens Park F.C. received thanks from the Union for their sympathetic, moral and material support which included a donation of £20 admission money to the Union's funds. William Struthers, in his first year as Hon. President of the Union, generously gifted the medals for the Eastern and Western District, Novice and National Championships. This helped the Union to announce that the funds stood at the greatly increased total of £62-7/6 (£62-37½p)-a total twelve times greater than just a year earlier.

The 1923 International was held in Paris and the Union, faced with a heavy bill for travelling, made an early start to fund raising. A grant of £50 from the Scottish AAA started the fund and the Union held a raffle 'Trip to Paris", with the first prize being a free trip to the International in Paris, travelling as a guest with the Scottish team. 250 tickets at 6d (2½p) each were sent for sale to leading city clubs with 100 tickets distributed to all other clubs in Union membership.

The Novice Championship at Rouken Glen was won by W Neilson (West of Scotland Harriers) who later won the Western District Championship. James Girvin, later to run for Scotland in the 1927 and 33 Internationals, was second and led Garscube to team victory over the holders Shettleston. The sale of 1,000 raffle tickets to the large crowd resulted in a profit of £15.

Dunky Wright, running for Clydesdale Harriers, won the 1923 National Championships over a 10 mile course at Bothwell Castle Policies - the first of three consecutive and four individual titles in the next five years. This was the last individual or team title won by Clydesdale Harriers in National competition for over thirty years and it is worthy of note that Wright, in his assiduous chase of individual and team medals, was a member of four different clubs during a short five year period.

He ran for Clydesdale up to 1923, for Shettleston in 1924/25, for the short lived, ill fated Caledonia AC in 1926 and finally joined Maryhill in 1927, when he won his final Individual title, but went on to gain six consecutive gold team medals as a member of the all conquering Maryhill team in the period 1927 to 1932.

Wright, running over three 3 mile laps marked by stewards with flags at important turning points, won by 100 yards from J.G. McIntyre (Shettleston), with A Lawrie finishing third and leading Greenock Glenpark Harriers to their first and only National team championship victory. The Greenock club had finished third in 1921, second in 1922 and their team of A Lawrie 3, A Whitelaw 6, D Cummings 15, R Shaw 21, B Dawson 24 and A Pettigrew 26, totalled 95 points, to defeat Garscube by just 5 points, with the holders Shettleston 174 points, finishing a distant third. Twenty teams competed, fifteen from the West and five from the East, with W Moor (Edinburgh University), the 1922 Novice champion and current Eastern District champion, being the first East runner to finish in tenth position.

2,000 spectators watched the race, attracted by the Union's entrepreneurial move of advertising the National championships on local tram cars at a cost of 6d (2½p) per advert. The total advertising cost of £1-18/-(£1.90p) was money well spent, for it allowed a substantial profit to be made from the Championships, in common with other Championships held throughout the season. This allowed the Treasurer to announce a balance of £201-4/-(£201.20p) which was the highest total ever recorded in the history of the Union - a rise of £195-10/11-(£195.55p) inside just two years of judicious financial management by George Dallas.

Only four countries competed in the International race at the small town of Maisons - Laffite near Paris, with Ireland and Wales both absent. The Shettleston runner J.G. McIntyre just lost out in the finishing sprint to English steeplechaser C Blewitt by the narrowest of margins but once again, with the exception of near veteran Archie Craig 13, the rest of the team disappointed badly and Scotland finished last - one point behind Belgium who were competing for the first time.

Gala Harriers celebrated their twenty first anniversary at the end of the season with over 300 members and friends attending an 'at home" and dance where A D Lawson received a gold watch in appreciation of his services to the club.

Shettleston were totally dominant in the 1924 season, winning the Individual and team titles in both the Novice and National Championships and taking the team title in the Western District Championship for the second time since the War. The National Novice Championship was again held at Bothwell Castle where J Stanley won from his Shettleston clubmate T Hart, with Shettleston winning the team title from Garscube and West of Scotland.

The Eastern District championship, held in heavy rain and sleet, attracted 10 clubs to Galashiels. A Hamilton, from one of Edinburgh's lesser known clubs, Heriots C.C.C., won the 7 mile race finishing forty yards in front of T Whitton (Dundee Thistle) and J Mackie (Edinburgh Northern). J W Henderson, a Gala lad who had just turned seventeen years of age, finished a further five yards behind. Henderson, who under modern rules would have been too young to compete, led Gala Harriers to second place in the team contest behind Edinburgh Northern.

Over 200 runners took part in the Western District Championships over an 8 mile trail across varied countryside. The trail, starting at the Tramway Tearoom at Rouken Glen Park, was laid across Deaconsbank Golf Course, crossing the road at Greenlaw Farm, then past the rear of Pollok Castle and round to the south of Gorbals Waterworks and returning by way of Northbrae Farm to Darnley Road at the Fire Station. There was then a straight run home of a mile along the road to the finish at Speirsbridge. It is strange, in these days of intensively developed housing estates in this part of south Glasgow, to realise that this area was all open countryside suitable for cross country running.

Charles Freshwater of West of Scotland Harriers made full use of his local knowledge by sheltering behind the leaders in the exposed parts of the course around the high land at the reservoirs. He saved his energy for the finish along the road to win by 60 yards from clubmate R B McIntyre, with James Mitchell (Mauchline H) taking third place ahead of clubmate Robert Miller. Shettleston won the team championship from West of Scotland, with third placed Greenock Wellpark including seventeenth placed Duncan McSwein, a future Union President and Treasurer, in their team.

Dunky Wright, now representing Shettleston, retained his National Individual title by nineteen seconds from veteran Archie Craig (Bellahouston) and Shettleston narrowly won the team title from Garscube Harriers who, for the second year in a row, were beaten by just five points for the team title. Edinburgh Southern Harriers won the team bronze medals - the first East of Scotland club to figure in the National team championships since the war.

1913 National Champion Archie Craig (Bellahouston) had been a member of the Western District and General Committees since the War, but still continued as an active athlete at the very highest level of competition, representing Scotland in every International race during that time. In the 1924 International race at Gosforth Park in Newcastle, Craig, the captain, finished first Scot in sixteenth position, closely followed by J G McIntyre 17, D Wright 18, J Wilson 19 with George Wallach, nearly 42 years of age, ending a long, illustrious and successful career when finishing 23 in his eighth and final appearance for Scotland. The team finished in third place behind England, who had the first six men home for a minimum score of just 21 points, with France runners up.

This was Craig's farewell performance for he announced his retiral from competitive running after the race. He acted as trainer to future Scottish cross country teams, became President of the Scottish AAA in 1937/38 and watched his two sons Archie Junior and George run five times for Scotland between them in the immediate pre and post Second World War period.

In October 1924 four Edinburgh harrier clubs gathered at Portobello Baths for the inaugural run of the Edinburgh and District cross country league - a title which lasted until 1936-37, when the current title of Eastern Distict Cross Country League was adopted to take account of the competing clubs from outwith the Edinburgh area. The competing clubs, Edinburgh Harriers, Edinburgh Northern, Edinburgh Southern and Heriots C.C.C., raced over a tough course with the current Eastern District 'Junior" champion A P Hamilton (Heriots) winning from University student W Moor (Edinburgh H) and R Paterson (E.S.H.).

The first two seasons of the league had four races throughout the winter before reverting in season 1926/27 to the three races which have became traditional over the 66 years of its existence. W Moor won the second race with R Paterson winning the final two contests. Edinburgh Northern won the team contest, with four men scoring in each team race, defeating Edinburgh and Heriots. The restriction of just four scorers in a team only lasted until season 1926/27, when the usual scoring of six men per team was adopted. Edinburgh Northern won the first five league titles in succession until Edinburgh Southern broke their run of successes in 1928/29.

George Sandilands of Kirkcaldy, a former member of Edinburgh Harriers, presented a shield for annual team competition in 1927 and the Sandilands Shield has been the prized reward for the successful Senior team in league competition ever since.

The administrative duties of the league were carried out by R S Aitken (Heriots) during 1924/26 and Willie Carmichael (Canon) 1926/28 until George K Aithie of Edinburgh Northern took over the post of Hon. Secretary/Treasurer in season 1928/29 - a post he was to hold for over 50 years until his retiral in 1979. During this time he developed the league from a small group of Senior clubs to a highly successful league, embracing more than thirty clubs over the entire East of Scotland, with races for all recognized age groups from Junior Boys to Seniors with a separate category for veteran runners.

Similarly, the growth of clubs in Ayrshire led to the formation of the Ayrshire Harriers Clubs Association and their first championship event was held on 17 January 1925. It was won by Robert Miller of Mauchline Harriers who went on to win the Western District Championship at Thornliebank. He won by 250 yards from clubmate James Mitchell, with P Miller (Kilmarnock H) finishing third a further 100 yards

George K. Aithie
(Edinburgh Northern Harriers)
Hon. Secretary/Treasurer of the Edinburgh and District League for 49 years between 1928 and 1977.

behind for a clean sweep of the Individual medals by Ayrshire athletes. Greenock Wellpark Harriers, in their finest ever performance, won the team championships for the first ever time easily defeating Bellahouston and Garscube.

250 runners from thirty three clubs, only two of which were from the East - these being East Stirlingshire C.C.C. and Edinburgh Northern H - competed in the National Novice 4½ mile Championship at Bothwell Castle. The sodden grass course tested the strength of the runners with Tom Riddell (Shettleston), who was to become one of Scotland's greatest milers on the track in the inter war period, winning the Scottish mile title eight times in eleven years between 1925 and 1935,

winning by eight seconds from C Hamilton (Paisley Junior Harriers). There was no lower age limit for Novice competitors with fourth placed David McKechnie, a slightly built youth from Beith Harriers, having just turned sixteen years of age.

In a welcome change from the pre war tradition of a small entry of clubs in the National Championships the post war years saw an ever increasing number of clubs taking part in the premier event of the domestic season. The 1925 Championships at Ayr Racecourse saw over 200 runners from 19 clubs line up for the start.

Dunky Wright, running for Shettleston, went into the lead at two miles with young James Mitchell and Robert Miller (both Mauchline H) close on his heels. Running strongly, Wright had established a 100 yards lead from the two Ayrshire runners and extended it to 250 yards from Mitchell, who won the title of Junior Champion, with Miller third a further 500 yards behind. Fourth placed A J McMorran led Garscube (four runners in the first nine home) to an easy team championship win after finishing second three times in the previous four years. Shettleston, winners four times in the past five years, were distant runners up ahead of an emerging Maryhill Harriers.

Garscube Harriers, National Team Champions in 1925/26, at club headquarters at Westerton, Glasgow before a pack run. Note the bags of paper strips for the "hares" to lay the paper trail.

The Scottish team sailed by steamer from the Broomielaw Quay in Glasgow to Dublin where Baldoyle Racecourse hosted the International race. The Irish organisers had installed many hurdles and obstacles on the five lap course which consisted of part racecourse and flat, fast grass lands outside the confines of the racecourse. Running at the top of his form Wright, who was to win both the SAAA track 4 and 10 mile titles later in the year, recorded the best performance in his eleven appearances for Scotland in the International Championship.

Wright quickly took position in the leading group of five runners at the head of the field. To the great delight of the large number of Scottish supporters who had sailed to Dublin to support their team, Wright went into the lead at six miles. Although running strongly and well within himself the short statured Wright was at a disadvantage at every one of the obstacles encountered, yielding valuable ground at each clearance of the obstacles and then struggling to regain his position in the leading group.

Wright fell behind in the final mile and, though recovering strongly with a finishing sprint which took him to within just two seconds of the bronze medal position, eventually finished fifth. The 1920 champion James Wilson, in his final appearance for Scotland in the International, finished fourteenth with James Mitchell in sixteenth position to give Scotland fourth position, just 16 points behind second placed Ireland in a close team contest behind runaway winners England.

Dunky Wright was an inveterate collector of medals and titles. After the performance of Shettleston's runners in the National team championship when they failed to provide the necessary back up to Wright's individual victory to secure the team title, he decided that they were not strong enough to win the team championship in the future. Wright therefore resigned and set up Caledonia Athletic Club as his vehicle for gaining more honours. The club was founded for champions and ex champions of harrier clubs in Scotland in an effort to form an elite of runners capable of winning all individual and team honours in championship events staged by the NCCU of Scotland. The application for membership of the Union was strongly opposed by members of General Committee on the grounds that the new club would unfairly attract top runners from the clubs that had nurtured and developed them, and it would not be good for the development of the sport if such an array of talent was gathered together by just one club.

However the constitution and rules of the proposed club were in conformity with the Union's requirements and there was no other course but to accept the application for membership in November 1925. But Scotland's top runners expressed no support for Wright's elitist ambitions and Charles Freshwater, who left West of Scotland for the new club, was the only top ranked athlete to join Caledonia A.C.

The 1926 Eastern District Championships at Portobello witnessed the most exciting and closest finish to a cross country race ever seen in Scotland. Racing neck and neck over the final 100 yards, after a closely contested 7 mile race, G A Farquharson of Dundee Thistle Harriers edged his clubmate J Suttie Smith on the line. This was the first major race that Suttie Smith appeared in and he won the District title the following year before going on to athletic fame, while nothing further was ever heard of Farquharson again. Edinburgh Northern had five runners in the first ten home to win the team championship for the fifth time, defeating city rivals Edinburgh Southern.

National Champion Dunky Wright laid a 7 mile grassland trail for the Western District Championship at Bothwell Castle. Tom Riddell (Shettleston), in one of his rare country outings, scored his expected victory after being chased throughout by British Civil Service champion R Henderson (Glasgow H). Turning on the finishing speed that won him many SAAA mile titles he outsprinted Henderson to win by fifteen yards with the rest of the field far behind.

Maryhill Harriers won the team championship by eight points from Plebian Harriers who showed great improvement after finishing twenty second the year before. Motherwell YMCA, whose team included future well known officials Alex Nangle and Scottish YMCA champion Bobby Craigen, finished third.

After a long absence the 1926 National Championship returned to Hamilton Park Racecourse where a flooding River Clyde prevented the use of the grassland between the river and Hamilton Palace, with the result that the race distance did not exceed 9 miles.

The rapidly improving James Mitchell, now running for Kilmarnock H, who had finished just 10 yards behind Dunky Wright in the previous summer's SAAA 10 miles track championships, quickly went into the lead. At half distance Mitchell had Wright (Caledonia AC) on his heels, with Frank Stevenson (Monkland) and WH Calderwood (Maryhill) a fair distance behind. Over the final two miles Mitchell powered clear from the defending champion to win from Wright by 14 seconds, with Stevenson winning the Junior title in third position. In sixth position, and gaining his place in Scotland's International team, was Scots born Alex Pirie of South London Harriers who lived for most of his life in England. It was a matter of the greatest regret that he did not encourage his son Gordon to take up his paternal eligibility to compete for Scotland. What an encouragement to Scottish athletics it would have been in the 1950's if Gordon Pirie had broken British, Commonwealth, European and World records under Scotland's banner rather than represent England as he actually chose to do.

James Mitchell (Kilmarnock Harriers — No. 181 on right), being congratulated on his victory in the 1926 National Championship by Duncan Wright (Maryhill Harriers — No.32 on left) who finished second.

Garscube Harriers retained the team championship from the Maryhill team which was on the verge of a record series of team championship wins for the next six years in a row - a performance of sustained team strength which has been equalled by Edinburgh Southern Harriers in the 1980's, but never bettered.

James Mitchell continued his brilliant running in the 1926 International race at the Hippodrome de Stockel in Brussels - the same venue at which James Flockhart of Shettleston was to record his International victory in 1937. In the leading group for most of the race Mitchell eventually finished fifth - just 11 seconds outside second place and 6 seconds behind the third placed runner. Scotland, with the two Caledonian AC representatives Dunky Wright 13 and Charles Freshwater 24 counting in the team score of 101 points, took third position behind France and England.

Mitchell suffered a serious injury at Brussels and never again competed at top level in cross country running - a great loss to Scotland who could have expected great things from him in future races. Disappointed with the failure of his concept of a successful Caledonian AC, Wright wound up the club after a short lived and ill fated life of less than a year. Still with his eye on the strongest club to help him to team championship medals Wright then joined Maryhill Harriers - a club he stayed with for the next twenty years until his retirement from active competition.

Wright had a dominant effect on cross country - as a competitor, coach, official and a reporter of the sport, both in the newspapers and on the radio where his enthusiasm for the sport was fully conveyed to the large audience which listened to his Saturday evening race reports on BBC Radio. Wright was a hard worker in training, giving description of his early weekly training schedule during the 20's in a contemporary report as follows:- "A weekend walk of 20 miles, followed by a fast 6 miles on Tuesday, a steady 5 miles on Wednesday, $7\frac{1}{2}$ miles at three quarters speed on Thursday and an ordinary cross country run on Saturday covering the last 2 miles at speed. In addition Wright carried out physical exercises for 15 minutes in the morning and evening." Wright gave further details, in a 1975 interview with Donald Macgregor, of his training after joining Maryhill Harriers. "On week day evenings runners trained from Maryhill Baths, covering 5 miles on Monday, 6 miles on Tuesday, 5 miles on Wednesday with a faster 5 mile run on Thursday. If there was no race on Saturday the runners covered 7 miles - all at an average of 6 minutes per mile with packs of six or more runners taking turns at leading and setting the pace".

His record was a magnificent one, having represented Scotland on eleven successive occasions in the International Championships - a record for any country at that time. In the National Championships he won the Senior title four times inside the five years between 1923 and 1927, was Junior champion in 1920 and gained a total of sixteen medals in individual and team championships. He also had a remarkable sequence of club championship wins, being club champion of Clydesdale four times; Shettleston twice; Caledonian once and Maryhill five times in his peripatetic wanderings around Scotland's top clubs.

R F McMurray, President of the Union, declined an invitation to accompany the Scottish team to the International race at Brussels as the race was held on a Sunday against his Christian beliefs and doctrines. No races were held in Scotland on Sundays at that time, compared to nowadays when an extensive part of the fixture list is staged on Sundays.

The custom was established that all members of the International team required to be medically examined to establish a satisfactory state of fitness to participate. City runners were examined by the Union doctor with provincial runners allowed to submit a medical certificate of fitness to the Hon Secretary.

Twenty four clubs, seventeen from the West and seven from the East, attended the 1926 AGM in Edinburgh. Following the spate of rule amendments from clubs in earlier years of the decade, General Committee submitted a total of 31 rule changes, including a controversial amendment on transfer of club membership as follows:- "A member of a club in Scotland cannot compete for another club in Scotland within 12 months of leaving his last club".

The proposal was rejected by the A G M as it was felt that it was too far reaching to be reasonably workable and was unduly restrictive to athletes whose movements, under certain conditions, were permissable and reasonable. The existing situation, of only six months required between resignation from one club and competition as first claim team member for another club, was retained. This rule was often abused with Dunky Wright changing clubs four times in five years and J Suttie Smith similarly changing clubs five times in ten years.

The financial report gave an end of year balance of £126-16/9 (£126-84p) which, after taking account of the expenditure of £142 for the trip to the International in Brussels, was an improvement on previous years. It is worth noting that with the party of twelve (9 athletes and 3 officials), the average expenditure for assembly, travel and all meals en route from Scotland to Belgium and back was just under £12 per head.

Since the restart of cross country competition in 1919 there had been open cross country relay races staged in both the Eastern and Western Districts. After seven years of competition in the East, when the McKenzie Trophy was won by five different clubs, the first official District Relay Championship was held at Northfield Grounds in Edinburgh in December 1926. Edinburgh Northern led from start to finish, being challenged only by their "B" and "C" teams throughout the first three laps. It was only on the final lap that Edinburgh Southern moved into third position, displacing Edinburgh Northern "C" team to fourth place. Mrs George McKenzie, wife of the trophy donor, presented the trophy and medals to the teams. The Northern club expressed severe dissatisfaction to the Union that the medals supplied were not hall marked, and were of unsatisfactory quality for a National championship event.

The open race by Western District clubs for the Struthers Shield started in 1924, and was first won by Garscube with Shettleston winning in 1925 and then winning the first official District relay title in 1926. Tom Riddel recorded the fastest lap of the day when leading Shettleston home on the opening lap just one second in front of C H Johnston (Glasgow University), who was to win the Western District individual title the following February. Riddel's team mates M E Anderson, W Hart and J W Stanley brought Shettleston home over 100 yards in front of Garscube and Maryhill.

Hugh Gilchrist (Paisley Harriers) won the National Novice title from 280 runners representing 36 teams at Bothwell Castle grounds. Third placed R Reid led Eglinton Harriers to the team championship, becoming the first provincial club to win the team title in the first seven years of the event, with another Ayrshire club, Doon Harriers, being successful the following year and Eglinton again winning the Bryson Cup in season 1934/35, with Glasgow clubs winning all the other seventeen team titles in the inter war period.

After the championship the need for maintaining order in the athletes dressing room was discussed by General Committee and it was agreed that policemen be engaged in future to assist in maintaining order in the dressing rooms. It was also agreed to drop the previous requirement of four qualifying Saturday runs from club headquarters as an entry requirement for the Novice championship.

J Suttie Smith, narrowly defeated in the 1926 Eastern District Championship, was again involved in a sprint to the finish in the 1927 race but this time won by 2 seconds from M Stewart (Edinburgh Northern). Suttie Smith's victory gave Dundee Thistle Harriers a hat trick of individual titles following wins by T Whitton 1925 and G W Farquharson 1926. Dundee Thistle, anxious to preserve Suttie Smith's "Junior" status, did not enter him in the 1926 National Championship with the intention of him winning the District title the following year. But Smith was ineligible for International selection as he did not compete in the National and, even although he had beaten clubmate Thomas Whitton, who was selected for the International, the selectors would not include him in Scotland's team.

C H Johnston (Glasgow University) won the Western District title at Hamilton Racecourse with Plebian and Motherwell YMCA dead heating for the team championship - the first and only time in the history of the District Championship. Under modern tie breaking rules Plebian would have won the title from Motherwell, but both teams were awarded first team medals.

The Renfrewshire AAA, inaugurated in 1926, received a permit to hold their inaugural cross country championships on 25th December. It seems that Christmas Day was no different from any other Saturday at that time and over 120 runners took part in the seven mile race.

In January 1927 General Committee received a letter from Clydesdale Harriers requesting assistance in gaining the return of the Dunbartonshire Cup from Duncan Wright. Wright, once a member of Clydesdale, had not returned the cup to the club in spite of repeated requests from the cup owners. A letter was received from Wright acknowledging possession of the cup, but stating that "He had inadvertently packed the cup in his luggage for a trip to visit relatives in Australia and had left the cup by mistake in Australia on his return to Scotland". He agreed to contact his relatives in Australia to arrange the return of the cup but, to this day, Clydesdale Harriers have never regained possession of the cup.

The 1927 National Championship was held at Redford Barracks, Edinburgh with 22 teams entered. The race started and finished on the Recreation Grounds at the Barracks with the 10 mile course covering long stretches of heavy ploughed land on each of three laps.

Three times National Champion Wright led from 6 miles followed by Frank Stevenson and West District Champion C H Johnston. On the final lap he opened up a 50 yard gap over Stevenson to win in 60 minutes 23 seconds - the slow time reflecting the heavy going over the tough country which slowed him to one of the slowest winning times over 10 miles since the race was inaugurated. C H Johnston finished third, winning the Junior Championship, but missing the International race due to injury. Maryhill justified their position as favourites, quickly packing at the head of the field and extending their lead as the race progressed. The further the race progressed the greater was the superiority of the Maryhill runners, who eventually finished their six runners inside the first 21 runners home to score 62 points, exactly half the points total of Edinburgh Northern, 124 points, who were the only East Club in the top ten teams. Suttie Smith of Dundee Thistle Harriers finished fifth in his first appearance in the National to gain selection for the International team where he was to become a fixture, gaining ten consecutive International vests between 1927 and 1936.

There were repercussions from the Championship when an irate farmer discovered that the competitors had gone off the marked trail and run through a field of sown wheat, causing damage to the crops. The matter was placed in the hands of the Police Prosecutor in Edinburgh, but the prompt action of the Union President J W Dickson (Heriots CCC) stayed the execution of a writ for damages by agreeing to pay the farmer a sum not exceeding £10. A later account for £8 was reluctantly paid by the Hon Treasurer, as there was no way of denying liability in the matter, although this payment caused the Championships to be run at a loss.

The International Championship was held at Caerleon Racecourse in Newport and, as so often was the case at this Welsh venue, the weather was appalling. Frank Stevenson had the best run of his career when finishing fourth, just beaten by two seconds in the finishing sprint for third place by H Gallet (France). With the rest of the Scottish team performing without merit Scotland took third place behind France and England in the five nation competition.

The growing popularity and spread of cross country was displayed by the Scottish Army Command Championships attracting a record entry with a separate race for new recruits being held in addition to the usual race for trained men. The recruits race proved so popular that area eliminators had to be held at Glencorse, Hamilton, Berwick on Tweed, Perth and Inverness and the Cameronian Regiment won the team title with twelve men to count and recorded a double when also winning the trained mens competition.

At the 1927 A.G.M. a record attendance of 59 delegates from 33 clubs (26 from the West and 7 from the East) expressed keenness to expand the sport and the matter of Schools participation was discussed. It was agreed to proceed with races, no more than 3 miles in distance, on the basis of the Summer Inter Scholastic Sports organised by the SAAA, although there is no record of any races being staged. It was also agreed that new "hall marked" medals with the lion rampant would be provided as follows:- National Individual medals 30/- (£1-50); 25/- (£1-25); 20/- (£1-00). National Team medals 25/- (£1-25); 15/- (75p); 12/6 (52½p). District Individual and Team Medals 20/- (£1-00); 10/- (50p); 7/6 (37½p).

There was indication of a growth of open competition, as distinct from the usual list of club pack runs and inter club events, when permits were granted for an open cross country team race organised by Mauchline Harriers in Ayrshire (January 1st); an open Relay Race organised by Grange Harriers in Edinburgh (January 19th) and Gala Harriers 6 mile Road Race on January 1st at Galashiels.

The 1927/28 season opened with the District Relays in November 1927. The Western District race was held at Thornliebank with 32 teams from 25 clubs taking part, the biggest club entry being from National Champions Maryhill Harriers who fielded three teams. Frank Stevenson put Monkland into the lead on the opening lap with the fastest time of the day ahead of Shettleston and Plebian. At half distance Plebian moved into a lead they were never to lose and won by 120 yards from Shettleston with Garscube third. Maryhill had a disastrous opening, finishing only thirteenth and, despite good runs by International W H Calderwood and SAAA mile champion D McLean, eventually finished fourth.

The rise of Ayrshire athletic clubs continued when Maxie Stobbs of Catrine AAC won the National Novice title at Bothwell Castle and Doon Harriers defeated over thirty clubs to win the team championship. Maryhill proved that their "Junior" runners were every bit as good as their National title winning Seniors when winning the Western District team championships for the second time in three years. The Eastern District title was won by James Wood of Heriots CCC who, like Tom Jack, was born in West Calder. Primarily a track runner Wood nevertheless gained four consecutive International vests between 1928 and 32, but is better known for his track performances which included a 3 miles National record of 14 minutes 44.2 seconds at Glasgow in 1931 to narrowly better the 27 year old record of Johnny McGough (Bellahouston). He finished fourth in the 6 mile race at the inaugural Empire Games at Hamilton, Canada in 1930 and two years later won the AAA 10 mile title in 52 minutes 00.2 seconds, setting an intermediate 6 mile time of 30 minutes 34.0 seconds which was not beaten for twenty years.

Excellent weather with good, fast underfoot conditions welcomed 220 runners from 20 clubs to the 1928 National Championship at Hamilton Racecourse. There were two 1½ mile laps round the button hook race track and two large 3 mile laps sweeping out into the country at Low Park by the River Clyde. The leading group of runners were together until the 6 mile point when Suttie Smith and Frank Stevenson, running together, opened up a 50 yard gap from W H Calderwood (Maryhill). Over the final 3 mile lap the Dundonian raced away to establish a winning 120 yards gap over Stevenson with Calderwood a similar distance behind in third position. Lance Corporal Robert R Sutherland of the Scots Dragoon Guards, running as an individual for Garscube, finished fourth and gained the National Junior title. Sutherland, a Govan man, had won the British Army 10 mile cross country championship just seven days earlier and was to run in the English National a week later for Birchfield Harriers, with whom he was to win many English team honours.

Maryhill Harriers retained the team championship, their counting six runners being in the first sixteen home for a winning total of 55 points, defeating Plebian Harriers, 122 points, with Garscube finishing third with 171 points just four points clear of Monkland Harriers. Maryhill's 67 points margin of victory was a record for the National, bettering by two points Garscube's 1925 margin of victory over Shettleston.

John Suttie Smith's emergence to become National Champion, the first of a record five consecutive individual titles, was a fortunate result of a change of direction from his first sporting interest in gymnastics. A member of the Dundee Gymnastics School, Smith won the District juvenile and junior championships, the Dickie Cup for the best rope climber and was a member of the team which won the Scottish Gymnastic Shield. In 1925 he was persuaded to take part in Invergowrie Sports where his successes in the 880 yards and mile races led to him joining Dundee Thistle Harriers. Short of stature Smith nevertheless utilised an unusually long stride and high knee lift which required much energy. This was provided by a rigorous training schedule and a unique lung capacity which placed him in the top five per cent of distance runners.

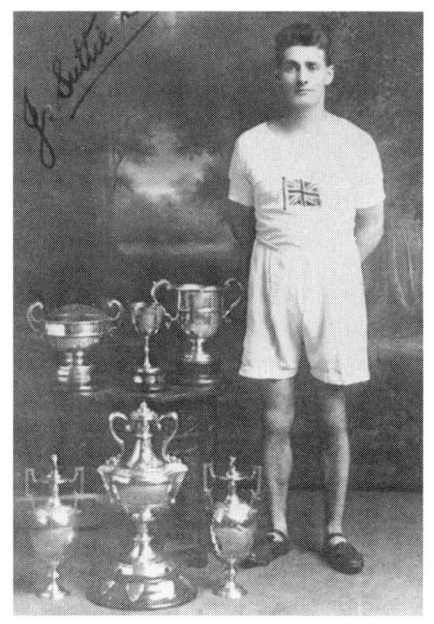

J. Suttie Smith, National Champion on five consecutive occasions between 1928-1932, with collection of athletic trophies.

Suttie Smith had an outstanding number of successes. As well as winning the National title five times he won the SAAA track 10 mile championships four times, the track 4 mile three times and won the Scottish YMCA cross country title for seven consecutive years in addition to representing Great Britain in the YMCA Olympiade meeting at Amsterdam in 1928 where he won the 5,000 metres.

The 1928 International Championship was held at Ayr Racecourse over a flat course covering the grassy racecourse and fields and roads to the east of the enclosure. Lieut - Col Sir Thomas C R Moore Bt., CBE, OBE, MP, who succeeded William Struthers as Union Hon President and was to hold the position for 42 years, started the race. Sir John Gilmour, Secretary of State for Scotland, was among a distinguished gathering of nobility, gentry and politicians in attendance. Running in heavy rain Suttie Smith and Harold Eckersley (England) went to the front of the five country field. The two set a fast pace from the start and by 6 miles led by over 150 yards from two French runners. As they passed the start for the third and last time Smith tried to break clear and establish a lead from Eckersley who hung on grimly to the leader. Try as he did Smith could not get clear of his determined pursuer, and finally Eckersley's strength proved decisive and he won by 30 yards from the Scot who, informed sources said, would have won the title had he exercised better judgement. Although having home advantage none of the other Scots could place in the first ten to finish and Frank Stevenson 14, who had finished fourth in the Welsh championships, and Robert Sutherland 18, were the next counters for the Scottish team which finished third, 104 points, behind France, 45 points, and England 55 points.

The visiting countries were well entertained with a post race reception by Ayr Corporation and a Dinner and Reception at Glasgow City Chambers on the Friday evening. Entertainment at Glasgow was provided by the St Andrews choir and artists from the Pavilion Theatre which included The Sharina Sisters, Bert Denver and Billy Maurice, and Dudley and Stafford who produced an enjoyable evening for teams and officials. Glasgow's Lord Provost Sir David Mason said, in his welcoming speech, "Cross country running was one of the purest forms of amateur sport and was clearly first from a health giving point of view".

Union President JCA Bodie replying, said "Its popularity was probably due to the fact that it was the one sport where the City Fathers were not troubled with the provision of expensive facilities which other sports needed, like sports halls, playing fields and stadiums. For all that cross country runners required was free access to run over the open country".

Although Maryhill recorded their third successive victory in the National Team Championships, the 1928/29 season belonged to Shettleston and Dundee Thistle who dominated the individual and team titles at all the other levels of competition.

The competitive season opened at Bothwell Castle where the National Novice Championship was held for the sixth successive year. The increased interest in cross country was fully demonstrated by the record entry of 40 club teams compared to the entry of 18 teams in the inaugural race 10 years earlier. However a point of concern was that, except from one team from Dundee and four from Edinburgh, the other 35 entries were Western District teams from Glasgow and the West of Scotland. James Hood of Shettleston took command of the $4\frac{1}{2}$ miles race, run over three grassland laps, and won by 60 yards from 19 year old Robert Graham (Motherwell YMCA) with reinstated professional J M Petrie (Dundee Thistle) inches behind in third place. Shettleston won the team championship in the closest finish in the history of the race. Motherwell YMCA, despite having three men home before Shettleston's second finisher crossed the line, had to be content with second place just one point behind the Glasgow club with the previous year's winners, Doon Harriers, in third position.

Robert Graham, who later joined Maryhill Harriers, was to become Scotland's most outstanding middle distance runner of the Thirties. He set Scottish records over 880 yards (1 minute 55.8 seconds), 3/4 mile (3 minutes 04.6 seconds), 1 mile (4 minutes 12.0 seconds - also a British record) and 2 miles (9 minutes 17.3 seconds); winning numerous Scottish and British track titles and competing in the 1934 Empire Games mile and 1936 Olympic Games 1500 metres events with distinction.

Shettleston continued their domination in the West, winning both the District Relay and Team championship titles with Dundee Thistle showing equal supremacy in the East by winning both the Eastern District Relay and Team championships with J M Petrie stepping up from Novice to Senior inside a single season by winning the Eastern District Individual title.

The 1929 National was held at Hamilton Racecourse over a course with tricky underfoot conditions due to an overnight thaw leaving the ground treacherous to runners. Twenty three teams were entered, with four from Edinburgh and one from Dundee comprising the usual small entry from the East. Suttie Smith set off in an emphatic manner, leading from the start at such a pace that no one else could keep up with him. The crimson vested Dundee runner led by 250 yards at half distance from clubmate Tom Whitton who ultimately finished second due to his close challengers Frank Stevenson being forced to retire after a heavy fall and Western District champion C P Wilson (Irvine YMCA) dropping out due to a knee injury. Smith outclassed his rivals to win by 400 yards from Whitton with W J Gunn (Plebian) third, ahead of D T Muir (Maryhill) who, after being called into his club team as a last minute reserve on the morning of the race, won the National Junior title and led his club to their third successive team championship victory. Maryhill Harriers had six in the first twenty six home to total 90 points, and win from Dundee Thistle, 150 points, and Plebian, 167 points.

France staged the 1929 International Championship race at the Hippodrome de Vincennes in Paris with a record entry of ten countries taking part due to the appearance of Italy, Luxembourg, Spain and Switzerland in addition to the usual six ICCU member countries.

Suttie Smith again led home the Scottish team, whose nine athletes came from eight different clubs, but did not run with any of the brilliance he showed at Ayr the previous year. He only finished in sixteenth position, and Scotland had to wait until Tom Whitton 50, closed in the team for a high scoring total of 189 points. The Scottish team eventually finished in fifth position, behind France 31 points, England 74 points with a surprising Spain, 117 points, taking third place ahead of Belgium, 180 points.

Suttie Smith showed that his run in the International was just an unfortunate off day when he smashed the Scottish 10 mile track record with a great run at Celtic Park the following month. The race developed into a tense duel between the Dundee runner and Frank Stevenson, the 1927 champion. Smith led through 6 miles in the fast time of 30 minutes 47.0 seconds (just two seconds outside the

Scottish team for the 1929 International Championships at Paris leaving by train from Edinburgh. The team consisted of J. Suttie Smith, J.F. Woods, D. McLeod Wright, F.L. Stevenson, T. Whitton, W.G. Gunn, C.P. Wilson, R. Allison and J.H. Gardiner. Officials from extreme right, G. Dallas and G. Aithie.

Scottish record) and set a new 7 mile record of 36 minutes 01 seconds. Stevenson then took the lead, setting record times at 8 miles (41 minutes 15 seconds) and 9 miles (46 minutes 30 seconds), only for Smith to sprint past in the final lap to win in the Scottish record time of 51 minutes 37.8 seconds, bettering James Wilson's nine year old record by 26.6 seconds with Stevenson also well inside the old record.

He again won the title in 1934 with an excellent run of 51 minutes 41.4 seconds - the only occasions that the championship was won with sub 52 minute performances in the entire series of championship races up to 1948. Smith's 10 mile record of 51 minutes 37.8 seconds stood for 24 years until Ian Binnie's record run of 50 minutes 11.0 seconds at the 1953 Cowal Games at Dunoon.

It is difficult, in the 1990's, to realise the conditions and difficulties which existed in the early years of this century. Conditions of living and working and concepts of coaching, training and racing were greatly different from modern day ideas.

Athletics training of early eras was entirely different to the training of even club athletes of the modern era, being of a "hit and miss" affair compared to modern, rigorous training schedules. Athletics books of the time advocated training of general endurance work, consisting of walking and running "in the gentle fashion". The most successful distance runners were usually the ones with the greatest natural talent and ability, not as is often the case today, those who are prepared to work hardest. Advice from an athletic book of the day consisted of "plenty of sleep, dumb-bell exercises, a cold douche or tepid bath and sleeping with the windows open" as being beneficial to a successful athletic career. Training consisted of running two, or greatly daring, three times per week in the evenings with a club outing over the country on Saturday afternoons in pack runs or inter club meetings.

There were two main reasons for this lack of emphasis on training. Firstly people did not believe it possible to train every day without causing physical damage to the body. Advice from older runners consisted of "don't overdo it; don't burn yourself out" and other warnings in similar vein. A second influence on training stemmed from the length and nature of work. For many runners their work entailed hard, manual labour with working hours up to 6 or even 7pm on weekday evenings and up to 2pm on Saturdays. In the early years of the sport, championships did not start until after 3 or sometimes 4 pm to allow competitors and officials to arrive at the race venue after working on Saturday mornings.

Athletic clothing remained almost unchanged during the period from the turn of the century to the start of the Second World War. Vest, shorts and shoes were the only items of equipment made especially for the sport. Anything else, such as training shoes (plimsoles) and cold weather clothing (coats and flannels) were purchased in ordinary clothing shops. A 1932 advertisement by sports outfitters listed spiked trackshoes from 12/6 to 25/- (52½p to £1-25p); vests from 2/6 to 4/6 (12½p to 22½p); shorts 2/9 to 6/6 (14p to 32½p) with tracksuits (in white, navy blue or green) costing 15/6 (77½p). The plimsole shoes cost as little as 1/6 (7½p), but gave the runner little or no protection when running on the cobbled road surfaces, and were a factor which gave a lot of truth to the idea that it was not desirable to train every day without incurring injury.

1930 to 1939

The "Thirties" decade was by far Scotland's most successful period in International competition. In the 27 years since the inception of the International championships in 1903 Scotland had won just five medals - one gold from James Wilson (1920); three silvers from George Wallach (1914), J G McIntyre (1923) and J Suttie Smith (1928) and a bronze medal from George Wallach (1911) - together with placing runner up in the team championship on just four occasions, all before the First World War, when no more than five countries took part in the Championships.

The "Thirties" were completely different, with six medals gained - one gold from James Flockhart (1937); three silvers from Robert Sutherland (1930 and 1933) and W C Wylie (1935) and two bronze medals from J Suttie Smith (1933) and Alex Dow (1936). The team race also provided great satisfaction for Scotland, as they finished runners up to England on three occasions and took third place four times, when there was usually seven countries competing in the championship. There were two memorable high spots in the International Championships; in 1933 when Robert Sutherland and J Suttie Smith finished second and third respectively behind Jack Holden (England), and James Flockhart's 1937 win at Brussels over a top class field to become the first (and only) home developed Scot to win the International title.

There were big changes domestically when the 1929 AGM decided that the Western District had grown too large to continue in its present state. As it was then constituted it contained over 80% of the harrier clubs in Scotland and it was agreed to create two new Districts in its place. All clubs from Lanarkshire, Dunbartonshire and the Glasgow area would compete in the new Midland District, and clubs in Renfrewshire, Ayrshire and the South West of Scotland would compete in the South Western District. The Eastern District boundaries remained unchanged and each District held annual Relay Championships and the usual "Junior" District Championship.

This District set up remained unchanged for the next 45 years until the administrative District change in 1975 when the Midland and South Western Districts were combined to form a new Western District, together with the introduction of a Northern District to control cross country running in the Highlands of Scotland, in addition to the unchanged Eastern District.

The District Relay Championships were the first events of the 1929/30 season. The committee of the new South Western District displayed great initiative and enterprise by ensuring their first Relay Championship was a sponsored event - possibly the first in cross country history. The race, started from the North Foreshore of Largs, was under the patronage of the Town Council and attracted 14 teams from 11 clubs. Irvine YMCA, with the brothers CP and R Wilson in their team, led from half distance to win by 27 seconds from Greenock Glenpark with Barleith Harriers third.

Plebian, winners of the last two Western District relay titles, duly won the first Midland title from 25 teams at Bothwell Castle. Very heavy rain and strong winds ensured that the strongest runners would prevail and, after W J Gunn led on the opening lap from Frank Stevenson, the Plebian runners went on for a runaway victory by 53 seconds from Garscube. The Dundee Thistle team of W Slidders, J M Petrie, P McGregor and J Suttie Smith easily won the Eastern District Relay at Corstorphine with James Wood (Heriots) being fastest of the day, 21 seconds clear of J Suttie Smith who made his usual slow start to the season.

The 1929 Novice Championship, held as usual at Bothwell Castle, continued to be very popular and attracted over 250 runners from 40 clubs. Unfortunately the large number of runners caused panic in the officials at the finishing line, and the poor standard of officiating among the finish recorders resulted in mistakes in tabulating all the finishers and errors in the final team scores, which caused uproar from Maryhill Harriers. The initial count of team scores gave Shettleston, the holders, the lowest points total. However Maryhill, who had three runners home in the first twelve to finish, claimed that their fourth counter had finished 42nd and this place would have given them a total two points less than Shettleston and thus victory in the team championship. But no trace of the missing Maryhill fourth counter could be found on the official place scoring sheets, although ample evidence was given by competitors that he had finished somewhere in the forties as claimed.

An emergency meeting of General Committee after the race decided that the Individual result, J Millar (Beith) winning by three seconds from W Fisher (West of Scotland), would stand, but the team race would be rerun over the same course in two weeks time. Only 140 runners from 20 clubs, compared to the original 250 runners from 40 clubs, turned up for the rerun two weeks later. Dundee Thistle, Beith and Edinburgh University, all in the first six teams to finish in the original race, did not appear for the rerun.

Shettleston, determined to prove that they were rightful winners in the first race, overwhelmed the opposition, placing their four counting runners in the first twelve home. W Simpson finished third, with 16 year old Andrew Stevenson finishing second counter in fifth position, D Stevenson ninth and A McKinnon twelfth for a winning total of 29 points. Plebian, led by the winner A Ingram, finished runners up with 44 points ahead of a disappointed Maryhill 48 points who, despite having their first three runners home inside the first seven finishers, had to wait for the final counter in thirty fifth position.

Shettleston's entire team came from a radius of less than a mile from their clubhouse and young Andrew Stevenson, after a successful running career with Shettleston, became Union Secretary for four years between 1960 - 64 and was President in 1966 after earlier being President of the Scottish AAA in 1954.

Two hundred runners from 18 clubs took part in the inaugural Midland Championship at Hamilton Racecourse with Renfrewshire champion James Campbell (Bellahouston) winning by nine seconds from William Gardiner (Motherwell YMCA) whose brother James had finished second the previous year. Springburn, after finishing runners up to Shettleston the previous year, won the team title for the first time since 1898. In the Eastern District race at Kirkcaldy W A Sanderson (Gala) won the individual title with Edinburgh Southern winning the team championship - a repeat of the 1920 event when the same clubs won the individual and team titles. Irvine completed a successful season when, having already won the Ayrshire relay and team championships, they added the South Western team title to the relay title won earlier in the winter.

Club championship day before the National Championship had a large number of clubs, no longer in membership of the Union, staging their club event. These included such defunct clubs as St Peters AAC, Invergowrie Harriers, Barleith Harriers, Glasgow Tramways AC, Greenock Auchmountain Harriers, Glasgow Harriers, Edinburgh Northern Harriers, Plebian Harriers, Olympic Harriers, Roslin Harriers, Paisley Junior Harriers, Eglinton Harriers, Lochwinnoch Harriers, Doon Harriers and Canon ASC, who had staged a 23 mile race from North Berwick to Edinburgh won by J Morrow in 2 hours 38 minutes 15 seconds.

There was an entry of 270 runners from 20 clubs in the National Championship at Hamilton Racecourse, in spite of another 16 clubs including Gala, Falkirk Victoria and Glasgow University having their club championships or inter club runs on the same day. Maryhill, missing two of their top runners W H Calderwood and A H Blair, nevertheless fielded a strong team to meet the challenge of Dundee Thistle. Suttie Smith and Frank Stevenson set the early pace with British Army champion Robert Sutherland close behind. At half distance Sutherland, who had won the National Junior title two years earlier, moved into second place but Suttie Smith had established a lead of 60 yards at 6 miles and extended it to over 100 yards at the finish with Sutherland defeating Stevenson by the same margin. South Western champion Maxi Stobbs (Catrine AAC) won the National Junior title in sixth position.

Maryhill, led by Dunky Wright 5, who was their only finisher in the first ten, eventually won the team championship for a record fourth consecutive year after a close tussle with Dundee Thistle. The Dundee club, with Suttie Smith 1, James Petrie

Medallists in the 1930 National Senior 9 mile Championship at Hamilton Park Racecourse. J. Suttie Smith (Dundee Thistle Harriers) left, recorded the third of five successive individual victories with R.R. Sutherland (Garscube Harriers) centre, finishing runner-up and F.L. Stevenson (Monkland Harriers) right, finishing third.

7 and W Slidders 8 in the first ten, were early team leaders but the superior packing of Maryhill ensured they had their six men home in the first nineteen. Dundee Thistle were actually three points in front with each club having five men home, but lost in the end with Maryhill scoring 86 points to win by just eight points.

Suttie Smith was in a forward position in the English National, just a week later, when forced to retire with a leg injury at the 3 mile point. Robert Sutherland, running for Birchfield Harriers, finished twelfth of the 334 competitors and was in Birchfield's winning team.

A huge crowd of 30,000 spectators watched the International race at Royal Leamington Spa over a very hilly and rough course. Sutherland started slowly and at half distance moved up to join the leaders. At 6 miles the Scot was third, gaining ground over each stretch of plough covered in the race. Over the final mile he moved up to challenge Tom Evenson (England), and the pair sprinted neck and neck over the final 100 yards, with Evenson just getting the verdict by two yards in a close finish, with Sutherland being just ONE second behind the winner, but defeating the National Champions of each of the six competing countries. Suttie Smith, still feeling the effects of his injured leg, finished thirteenth, almost two minutes behind Sutherland, with Scotland scoring 111 points - a great improvement on the 1929 total of 189 points - to finish third of the seven countries competing.

This was Sutherland's year of being the eternal runner up, after an exhausting racing programme which established him as the Iron Man of cross country running. His race sequence was as follows:-
Second to Suttie Smith in the Scottish National 10 miles race on 7th March (Smith finished thirteenth in the International)
Twelth to W Howard in the English National 10 mile race on 14th March (Howard finished fourth in the International)
Second to J Broadley in the Army 10 mile race on 19th March
— (Broadley finished tenth in the International)
Second to T Evenson in the International 10 mile race on 22nd March

After running so well in these high quality 10 mile championship races within the space of just 15 days, Sutherland received an invitation to compete in an International event in Paris on Sunday 30th March. The race, organised by the Petite Parisian newspaper, attracted over 1,600 competitors and was over the shorter distance of 7 miles. Roger Rerolle (France), who finished ninth in the International race, won in a sprint finish from Sutherland who was beaten by just ONE second - the same narrow margin as he lost by in the International Championship.

So ended Sutherland's memorable month of races when he was beaten in four major cross country races, besides the International, but defeated every one of the race winners in the International race - the most important race of the year. It was a daunting programme but one Sutherland regularly repeated in the next few years with great success, but little recognition, as he never won either the Scottish or English Nationals or the International for ultimate fame and inclusion in the record books. However, Sutherland's consistent performances made him the unsung hero of Scottish cross country running, and one who fully deserved greater fame than he received, having the great misfortune to come up against John Suttie Smith and James Flockhart, who were probably the greatest distance runners in Britain at the time.

Sutherland was equally successful on the track as on the country and, the following summer, finished fourth in the Empire Games 3 miles race at Hamilton, Canada. He also won the SAAA 4 mile track title on three occasions, recording the only sub 20 minute winning time in the 46 year history of the event when winning in 19 minutes 59.8 seconds in 1931. At the close of his athletic career in 1937 he won the SAAA 2 mile steeplechase championship, having recorded numerous victories in the triangular international matches against England and Ireland.

He won 14 Army championships, 5 Inter-Service championships as well as 2 silver medals in the ICCU International, and, when running for Birchfield Harriers in the English National, twice finished third and three times fifth on the way to leading Birchfield to the amazing record of seven team championship victories in eight years.

The results recorded in the opening season were representative of the decade as a whole with each of the three Districts having distinctive characteristics.

In the Eastern District championship the team title was shared equally between Dundee and Edinburgh clubs, each city winning five titles each. The Relay championship for the McKenzie trophy was dominated by Edinburgh Northern who won eight of the ten titles with Dundee Thistle winning the remaining two.

Glasgow clubs won all ten individual and team titles in the Midland District Championshiup races with Shettleston and Plebian each winning four titles in the Relay championships. Ayrshire athletes won nine of the ten Individual titles in the South Western District championship, with only future Union President Alex K McDonald of Greenock Auchmountain breaking the pattern with his win in 1935, and Ayrshire clubs taking the team title on six occasions. Beith Harriers won five of the nine District Relay titles won by Ayrshire clubs with Greenock Glenpark's victory in 1933 being the only Renfrewshire club to break the Ayrshire domination of the relays.

The ever popular Novice Championship was the first major event of the 1930-31 season, attracting over 320 competitors from 40 clubs to Bothwell Castle. Robert Simpson of Motherwell YMCA became the first and only member of a Lanarkshire club to win the individual title when defeating A D McDonald who led Garscube to their fourth team victory. The Westerton clubs won by 35 points from Plebian - the largest margin of victory ever recorded in the championship.

"Cross country runners have seldom, if ever, been called upon to face such adverse conditions as prevailed at Hamilton Racecourse" said the contemporary report on the Midland Relays. Snow and sleet, fiercely blown by a driving blizzard, fell throughout the race and the runners ploughed through deep slush. The course was confined to the racecourse enclosure, otherwise it was doubtful if the runners could have remained upright on the exposed country area beside the River Clyde. Despite the difficult conditions only one of the 27 teams failed to finish. Motherwell YMCA led from half distance to win by almost half a minute from Plebian, thanks to fine runs by Robert Graham and Willie Gardiner on the final two laps of the race.

Strong winds spoiled the South Western Relays, held from Barrfield Pavilion at Largs Esplanade. The first two laps were completed successfully with Irvine YMCA leading from Greenock Glenpark and Beith, all three teams well clear of their rivals. However by the third lap the strong winds from the River Clyde had blown the paper away from the official course and the first three runners inadvertently cut a large section from the course.

The race finished with Beith defeating Greenock Glenpark and Irvine YMCA, but the fourth club home Barleith Harriers - who were the first team to cover the full trail - protested at the first three clubs receiving the medals. The organisers decided that the race would be rerun the following Saturday but Barleith, fully believing themselves to be the rightful winners, protested this decision to the General Committee of the NCCU.

An emergency mid week meeting of General Committee over ruled the rerun decision and awarded the title to fourth placed Barleith. A warning from General Committee was given to clubs that, in championship races, flags should be used to mark courses rather than paper trails which could be rendered useless by the elements, as race leaders should be able to follow the course without the necessity of searching for a change in direction of the trail. Well intentioned though the advice was, little action was taken on it, and difficulties with paper trails lasted for a long time in cross country events before the traditional laying of paper trails was finally abandoned for more modern and efficient methods.

J Mercer (Penicuik Harriers) took full advantage of local knowledge when winning the Eastern District championship - held for the first time at Penicuik - from James Brannan (Dundee Hawkhill), who was later to keep cross country alive in Tayside during the Second World War. Donald Urquhart (Garscube) won the Midland 7 mile championship at Hamilton, finishing almost one minute in front of W Fisher (West of Scotland), with Shettleston winning the team championship by 26 points from Plebian with Garscube finishing a distant third.

A biting east wind and treacherous, icy underfoot conditions at Hamilton Racecourse slowed competitors in the 1931 National championships, but Maryhill runners, who had undergone special training from Dunky Wright, won the team title for an unprecedented fifth time. Suttie Smith, running for Dundee YMCA Gymnastic club after a fall out with Dundee Thistle, gave a machine like display of running to win for the fourth successive time, bettering the previous record of three successive wins by James Patterson (Watsonians CCC) 1898/99 and 1900 and Dunky Wright 1923/24/25.

Smith led from the start and finished the 10 mile race in an untroubled 59 minutes 20 seconds, with Robert Sutherland finishing runner up, as in the previous year, a further 22 seconds behind with W J Gunn (Plebian) third almost a further minute behind. Tall, long striding James Addison (Greenock Glenpark) won the National Junior title in eighth place with fourth placed T Muir leading Maryhill's six runners in the first 15 home to victory, with 55 points for a big 59 points margin over Garscube with Plebian, 192 points, finishing third.

The administrative change, which established three Districts, was shown to be successful when the International team contained three members from each District. J Suttie Smith (Dundee YMCA), J F Wood (Heriots CCC) and J M Petrie (Dundee Thistle) were from the East; R R Sutherland (Garscube), W J Gunn (Plebian) and J Gardiner (Motherwell YMCA) from the Midlands and M Stobbs (Catrine AAC), C P Wilson and D Fry (both Irvine YMCA) from the South West.

Despite having run two 10 mile races in the two weeks prior to the International at Dublin, winning the Army Championships and finishing third in the English National at Kettering, Robert Sutherland's impressive running led Scotland to second equal position with France, who had won the team championship on six occasions in the Twenties.

Continuous morning rain had left Baldoyle Racecourse with heavy underfoot conditions, and the Scottish runners started slowly. Sutherland, who seemed to reserve his best running for the big occasions, was only thirty fourth at the end of the first lap but his great strength told as he worked his way through the field to eventually finish eighth, two places in front of National Champion Suttie Smith. With three Frenchmen dropping out of the race due to the cold, wet conditions, and Scotland's tail for once performing well, there was a tie for second place between Scotland and France, each scoring 102 points behind England. Scotland, whose final counter finished twenty eighth compared with the thirty third position of the final French runner, gained the verdict under International tie break rules to record their best team position since 1914. The team did not have long to celebrate their performance as, having sailed from Glasgow on Thursday evening they left Dublin immediately after the race, catching the final Saturday evening steamer to Glasgow.

Domestic competition, previously restricted to NCCU championships, was now providing more opportunities for athletes. Meaningful races were staged compared to the previously universal inter club runs. Counties such as Ayrshire and Renfrewshire staged Relay and team championships, the Scottish YMCA championships attracted over 20 clubs and international class runners, the Edinburgh District league provided three meetings per season and other leagues, covering Tayside and Fife, and Aberdeen and the North East, all helped in developing the standard of runners and encouraging the growth of the sport throughout Scotland.

J K Hewitt won the Novice Championship at the start of the 1931-32 season, the first victory by an Edinburgh University student since W S Moor won ten years earlier, with Shettleston winning the team championship for the sixth time. Hewitt, who led his University team to many successes, continued his excellent form when winning the Eastern District individual title and was selected as reserve for the Scottish team for the International Championship.

Since 1928 every Scottish National Championship at Hamilton Racecourse had the same result - John Suttie Smith winning the individual title and Maryhill Harriers defeating all comers to win the team championship - and it was no different this time.

Two hundred and seventy runners from 23 clubs, despite another 22 clubs holding club championships and inter club runs on the same day, lined up for the start. James Wood (Heriots CCC) surprised his rivals with the fastest start ever seen in a National race, and the SAAA 10 mile champion led for the first 3 miles with Suttie Smith and Henry McIntosh (Edinburgh Northern) closing the gap. Suttie Smith went into the lead at 5 miles with Robert Sutherland chasing Wood who was an isolated second. The Dundee runner strode away from his rivals for a 250 yard victory over Sutherland, to record a record fifth consecutive win. The Army runner held off repeated challenges from Wood over the final 200 yards to take second place for the third successive year by the narrow margin of just one second, with Maxi Stobbs (Catrine) close behind in fourth place.

R Peattie (Monkland) won the National Junior title when finishing eighth ahead of South Western Champion Tom Todd (Kilmarnock Harriers). Maryhill, led by eleventh placed Dunky Wright, placed their six runners in the first twenty three home, to win the team title with 105 points for a record sixth time, defeating

Dundee Thistle 135 points and Plebian 162 points. This was the third time the Dundee club had finished runners up to Maryhill in the National, and their officials were disappointed to discover that if Suttie Smith had still been a member of his old club instead of representing Dundee YMCA, then Thistle would have totalled 93 points and won the team title for the first time in their history - an honour they had to wait for until 1937.

After finishing fifth in the English National 10 mile race at Wolverton and leading Birchfield to the team championship, Sutherland was prevented by Army duties from competing in the International race. A big come through was achieved by another army runner, Corporal James Wilson of Edinburgh Southern Harriers, who exceeded all expectations when finishing eighth in the field of almost 400 runners in the English championship event.

Suttie Smith and James Wood were always up with the leaders in the International Championship at Brussels and, though tiring at the end of the fast run race, finished seventh and eighth respectively. England dominated the race, filling the first six positions for a minimum score of 21 points, and France finished runners up ahead of Scotland who ran well to finish third 45 points clear of Belgium.

The main feature of the 1932-33 season was the rapid emergence of James Flockhart from a novice at the start of the winter to Scottish National Champion and favourite for the International title just six months later. Flockhart was 23 years of age when he took up cross country running in the autumn of 1932, instantly proving himself a "natural" athlete and one of the most amazing discoveries in distance, and especially cross country, running.

Prior to his debut in cross country Flockhart had been an enthusiastic cyclist and, in his own words "simply murdered himself in road racing". He had, however, a solid background of running in his early years. When he was at school it was a common practice for him to run each Saturday afternoon from his Auldhouse home to East Kilbride and back - a distance of $3\frac{1}{2}$ miles - to get the newspaper with the late football results.

His first runs with Shettleston impressed everyone, and his performance in the club trials showed such promise that he went straight into Shettleston's first team for the Midland Relay Championships at Hamilton Racecourse. In the race, running the third fastest lap of the day in his first open race, he led Shettleston to victory for the first time, defeating holders Plebian by 200 yards with Garscube third.

By running in the Midland Relays Flockhart bypassed the Novice stage of an athletes development. The National Novice at Hamilton was won by W Hinde of Edinburgh Northern, a product of the Edinburgh Boys Brigade cross country championships who, little more than a month after joining Northern, defeated over 250 competitors to win the National Novice. He finished well clear of A Austin (Shawfield) with Springburn winning the team championship for the first time in 14 years.

Flockhart fulfilled all expectations when winning the Midland 7 mile title a few months later, defeating 233 runners from 21 clubs. He finished 300 yards in front of Jack Gifford (Victoria Park) with 17 year old J J McDonald (St Peters), soon to be the inaugural National Youth title, in third place. Springburn, runners up in 1932, improved greatly to win the team championship by the large margin of 75 points from Shettleston who finished runners up 3 points in front of Garscube.

The 5' $5\frac{1}{2}$", 8 stone 7lbs Flockhart rapidly improved with regular training. At that

James Flockhart (Shettleston Harriers) right, is congratulated on his first ever victory in the 1933 National Senior 9 mile Championships at Hamilton Park Racecourse by five times winner, James Suttie Smith (Canon ASC) left, James Wilson (Edinburgh Southern Harriers) centre, finished runner-up in the race.

time his training schedule consisted of a fast 3½ mile run on Tuesday, a medium 6 miles on Thursday and a 9 mile cross country run on Saturdays with the fast pack, always finishing with plenty in reserve.

The largest gathering of runners ever seen in Scotland took place at Hamilton Park racecourse for the 1933 Scottish National Championships. Constant demand for a separate Youth Championship resulted in an inaugural race for runners between 16 and 18 years of age, with 162 runners from 25 clubs joining with the Senior entry of 230 competitors to give a total of almost 400 runners.

Suttie Smith, running for Canon ASC after another of his frequent club changes, led for the first 5 miles with Flockhart and Corporal James Wilson (Royal Scots and Edinburgh Southern) in close attendance. At 7½ miles Flockhart had an 80 yard lead from Wilson with Suttie Smith a further 50 yards behind. Over the final lap of the 10 mile race Flockhart drew away in easy fashion to double his lead over Wilson with Suttie Smith, failing in his attempt to record six individual wins in a row, finishing third, ahead of Robert Sutherland (Garscube). Showing vast improvement since the Midland Championship, Shettleston broke Maryhill's long sequence of team triumphs. In a closely contested team race they won with 154 points from Springburn 167 points, with just 10 points covering teams from second to fourth, as Maryhill 175 points and Plebian 177 points, finished close behind.

Flockhart's win at the first attempt earned him both the Senior and Junior National Titles - only the third man to achieve the double in 30 years. These titles, together with the club and Midland District titles earned earlier in the season and his rapid improvement as he gained experience, made him "in Scottish eyes" the

Scottish team at 1933 ICCU International Championships at Caerleon Racecourse, Wales. From left: H. McIntosh (31); J. Girvin (30); S.K. Tombe (29); J. Suttie Smith (27); J.G. Flockhart; W.D. Slidders (33); W. Hinde (32); R. Gatons; R.R. Sutherland (in black jersey); seated J. Wilson.

favourite for the International race at Caerleon racecourse in Newport, Wales. He made a good start to the race and, in company with teammates Suttie Smith and Robert Sutherland, stayed close on the heels of the leader for 6 miles. All three Scots displayed such pace and endurance that hopes of a Scottish victory were high.

Running in heatwave conditions Flockhart suffered an injured foot crossing a section of rough, uneven, stoney ground. As the leading group approached the steep 250 feet high "Heartbreak Hill" at 7 miles he started to drop behind due to his injury. At this point Scotland, in their best ever performance in the International, had their counting 6 men in the first 13 runners and looked to be challenging England for the team title. Heartbreak Hill proved the decisive point in the whole race. For, as Scottish runners faltered and tired to lose precious places, English runners picked up places to finish 6 in 9, to Scotland's 6 in 18, and win the team title with 32 points to Scotlands 62 points with France third with 109 points.

Suttie Smith and Sutherland ran the final 2 miles together and they closed on Jack Holden (England) in the final finishing straight. Robert Sutherland proved the stronger and he repeated his 1930 silver medal position when finishing 9 seconds behind Holden, but 4 seconds clear of Suttie Smith, whose third place was his best run since his silver medal 5 years earlier. Harry McIntosh (Edinburgh Northern) finished eleventh just 3 seconds in front of Flockhart with W D Slidders (Dundee Thistle) 16 and S K Tombe (Plebian) 18 completing Scotlands most successful team in International history.

On their return home from Wales the Scottish team arrived at Crewe Junction Station in the early hours of Sunday morning to find they had a two hour wait for a connecting train to Glasgow. With heavy rain outside, the inevitable ball was produced, and an impromptu game of football was soon in progress on the deserted platform.

Soon a touring party of Theatrical Variety Artistes, who were on their way to fulfill a theatrical booking in Glasgow, arrived on the scene. The party of Englishmen immediately challenged the Scots to a football match. The innate skills of the "tanner ball" Scots prevailed and, in spite of the vocal encouragement from the lady artistes, the harriers won the match. One of the Artistes, fancying himself as a sprinter, challenged the Scots to a race over 100 yards. Quick explanations that everyone was a long distance runner who had completed a gruelling 9 miles cross country race just 24 hours earlier were met with scorn by the confident Englishman. However, George Dallas, Secretary of the NCCU who had won the SAAA 440 yards title 13 years earlier, took up the challenge. The distance was paced out along the deserted platform while George took off his jacket and waistcoat, handing over bundles of paper, handfuls of loose change and his watch and wallet, before rolling up his trousers and taking off his shoes. George's speed had not been lost and he beat his opponent "out of the park" to make the score Scotland 2 England 0.

Somewhat crestfallen by now, the English party produced its trump card when one of their number, an acrobat to trade, challenged the Scots to a race on their hands. Somewhat startled by this strange challenge the Scots were nonplussed for a minute till a quiet voice, with a pronounced Dundee accent said "I'll tak ye lad". This was Suttie Smith, a champion gymnast in his younger days, to whom the venture was a normal happening. The agreed distance of 30 yards was paced out, and the side of the platform was lined by the party of spectators in case either of the competitors strayed off course. The race was on and the little Scot won "hands down" for a final score of Scotland 3 England 0.

Flockhart's remarkably successful season was enthusiastically received in the SAAA book "Fifty Years of Athletics" which stated "This novice of recent discovery has set the whole athletic universe talking; winning the Midland, National Junior and Senior titles in one year - indeed something to be proud of. Veterans predict a brilliant future for the youth who, like many of the veterans of the past, has raised the level of cross country running in Scotland to an International Standard".

Two former National Novice Champions proved successful in the 1934 District Championships with A McGregor (Plebian) winning the Midland title and J Millar (Beith) the South Western title. Alex Dow (Kirkcaldy YMCA) ran away from his rivals to win the Eastern title by almost a minute at Musselburgh racecourse, the first of many successes that included an ICCU International bronze medal just two years later.

Running over the course at Ayr racecourse, which would be used for the International Championship at the end of March, Flockhart retained his individual title in the National Championship. He displayed the fast starting, pace setting characteristics that would become his hallmark in all races, going to the front of the field at the start to establish a lead of 100 yards at half distance from R Sutherland, with the Edinburgh Northern pair, J P Laidlaw and W Hinde a further 50 yards behind. At $7\frac{1}{2}$ miles the Shettleston runner had increased his lead to fully 200 yards, but in the final 2 miles Sutherland reduced the gap to 150 yards as Flockhart eased up to victory in 56-12, with the Army sergeant runner up in 56-41 and Laidlaw third 56-55, 12 seconds in front of his clubmate W Hinde.

The team race resulted in a most unusual tie for first place - unusual in that it was only the second in the history of the race after the 1910 tie between Clydesdale and West of Scotland - and for the fact that the tie breaking rule could not decide the issue. Though Plebian runners finished 4, 8 and 12, Dundee Thistle runners packed so well that their full counting team finished between 15 and 25, well before the fourth Plebian runner finished in thirty third position. Both clubs totalled 126 points, just 16 points in front of Edinburgh Northern, but the tie breaking rule resulted in both clubs again tying with 39 points each. The referee did not apply the final tie breaking method of awarding the team title to the club whose final counting runner finished nearest to the winner - which would have given the verdict to Dundee Thistle whose final counter was 25 to Plebian's 35 - and two sets of gold medals were awarded to the evenly matched clubs. Eastern District champion Alex Dow, after a slow start, finished well to take fifth place and the National Junior title.

With the memory of the secure second place at Wales, together with the advantage of running before a home crowd over a known course at Ayr, the Scots were hoping to challenge England again for the team title and place 4 runners inside the first 10 to finish. But it was not to be. The Scots were run off their feet in a fast run race, where the fast start caught them unawares, and found wanting in strength and stamina at the end of the race. Flockhart worked his way through to sixth position with R Sutherland 11 and A Dow 12, for Scotland to finish third with 105 points, just 3 points behind runners up France.

Tiny 5' 2" Charles Smith of Dundee Hawkhill, who had an early background of gymnastics like his elder brother Suttie, won the Novice title at the start of the 1934-35 season and went on to win the Eastern District title at Galashiels, finishing 200 yards clear of the favourite A W Carfrae (Edinburgh) with Dundee Thistle taking the team championship for the second year in a row ahead of city rivals Hawkhill. Alex K McDonald, the leading light in the war time Scottish Cross Country Association and Union President in 1961, won the South Western title at Beith and led Auchmountain Harriers to the team championship.

The fast striding, stylish Anglo Scot W C Wylie of Darlington Harriers, a native of Coatbridge, was the surprise winner of the National title at Hamilton. Flockhart, as usual, was the early pace setter with Wylie content to run easily in his wake. With a mile to go Wylie struck fiercely as the runners tackled a steep incline on the approach to the racecourse from the countryside by the River Clyde. He quickly broke clear of the tiring Flockhart and strode to victory in 57 minutes 54 seconds with Flockhart second 23 seconds behind and Suttie Smith third a further 18 seconds behind. The lightly built (8stone 4lbs) James Freeland, a baker from Hamilton who was forced to train at odd hours due to his job, surprised everyone by finishing strongly to take the National Junior title in fourth place, ahead of Charles Smith and the other District Junior champions. Freeland was killed in active service with the RAF in the Second World War and his son Lindsay is now an honorary member of the Scottish AAA.

Suttie Smith, running that year for Edinburgh Northern, led his club to the team championship, with 6 in 33, for a 125 points total, ending a 24 year domination (1911 to 1935) of the National team championship by West clubs. The previous year's joint winners Dundee Thistle were runners up with 138 points, ahead of Garscube who took third place with 186 points - just 7 points in front of fourth placed Shettleston. Sixteen year old George Craig (Shettleston) won the first of two National Youth titles, and Springburn, with three of the previous year's winning team still eligible, repeated their team championship victory over Shettleston and Victoria Park AAC.

Wylie, in his first International appearance, ran remarkably well to finish second in the 1935 race at the Hippodrome d'Autevil in Paris. Within the first mile he was spiked from behind, losing his left shoe. He ran for the next 8 miles with a bare foot, taking the lead after 3 miles and leading for much of the race. Holden's strength told in the end, and he broke clear in the final mile to win by 100 yards from the Scot who finished with a cut and bleeding foot to take the silver medal 2 seconds clear of W Eaton (England) who was to win the title the following year at Blackpool.

Good runs by Alex Dow 10; J Suttie Smith 12 and James Flockhart 13 helped Scotland to take an excellent second place behind England, 30 points, in the seven nation team contest with a total of 84 points, well clear of France 102 points. Wylie ran twice again in the International but never reproduced the same form as at Paris. Wylie had an unusual winter training schedule for the country, walking a fast 10 miles on the road four nights per week and 25 miles on Sunday morning. He ran only twice per week - a fast 3 or 4 miles road run on Wednesday evening and steady 9 miles over country every Saturday when not racing.

He was successful over the country in England, winning the Northern Counties and North Eastern Championship titles. His successes carried on to the track in summer where he won the Northumberland and Durham 880 yards, 1 mile and 2 mile track titles on the same afternoon. After finishing runner up in the 1935 SAAA 3 mile championship, he took up steeplechasing and won the Scottish 2 mile steeplechase title in 10 minutes 38.0 seconds - a record which lasted till 1953, and gained third place in the AAA steeplechase title in 10-27.0, with Robert Sutherland finishing just 10 yards behind.

Plebian Harriers, who seemed to record their best performances on the road and in relay events - with excellent records in the Midlands relay and Edinburgh to Glasgow race - overwhelmed the opposition in the National Novice championship at Bothwell Castle at the start of the 1935-36 season. W G Black won the individual title, emulating the achievement of his clubmate S K Tombe who won at his first attempt in 1925, and the Plebian runners packed well to win the team championship for the first time.

A resurgent Dundee Thistle team ended Edinburgh Northern's run of six wins in a row in the Eastern District relay championship, displaying the powers of their youngsters who had won the District "Junior" title for the past two years. Beith Harriers scored their expected third in a row relay win at the South Western event, with Shettleston continuing their series of alternate wins with Plebian in the Midland relays. The Plebian club had won in 1929-31-33-35 and Shettleston had scored their victories in 1932-34 and 36.

J Kelly of Springburn defeated over 200 competitors to win the Midland 7 mile championship at Hamilton despite, as a miner, finding it exceedingly difficult to maintain a regular training schedule. He won by 100 yards from Archie Craig Junior, son of the 1913 National champion and seven times International Archie Craig, who was competing for Shettleston like his young brother George (two time National Youth Champion). The first appearance of John Emmet Farrell (Maryhill) in national competition was notable when finishing fourth 43 seconds behind the winner. Shawfield Harriers, one of the younger Glasgow clubs formed just ten years earlier, surprised the other 18 competing teams when winning a close team contest in which just eleven points covered the first four teams.

William Kennedy (Kilbarchan) won the South Western Junior 7 mile title by eight seconds from P J Alwell (Beith) over a frost bound course at Inchinnan. Kennedy started running with the Army and had his first notable success when winning the Army 10,000 metres championship in Shanghai in 1932. Both he and Alwell gained two Scottish international vests before the war. A W Carfrae (Edinburgh Harriers), who had earlier won three races in the Edinburgh District League, won the Eastern title at Redford Barracks over a heavy 7 mile trail, finishing 37 seconds in front of George Carstairs (Edinburgh University) who was to be Scotlands top 3 miles/5,000 metres runner in the period up to the Second World War.

Carstairs won the SAAA 3 miles title three times, raced internationally for both Scotland and Great Britain and bettered the Scottish 3 mile record with his run of 14 minutes 29.8 seconds on a grass track in Dublin - but gained no recognition for his run as he was born in India where his father was a Church of Scotland missionary at the time. He found Paris a lucky city for there, on two occasions, he recorded wonderful runs finishing runner up in the 1937 International Student Games 5,000 metres race and taking sixth position in the 1938 European Championships 5,000 metres in 14 minutes 48.4 seconds for the fastest ever time by a Scot.

At the end of January 1936 clubs cancelled all races in the cross country programme as a mark of respect and mourning for the death of King George V.

After his surprise defeat by W C Wylie in 1935, Flockhart returned to winning form in the 1936 National Championships at Lanark Racecourse. He took the lead in the early stages of the five lap 9 mile race and, running brilliantly all the way, won for the third time with Guards Sergeant Robert Sutherland again finishing second. Alex Dow (Kirkcaldy YMCA), despite being as far back as thirteenth on the opening lap, recovered well to finish third in front of tiny 5' 2" Charles Smith (Dundee Hawkhill) whose elder brother John Suttie Smith dropped out of the race at half distance.

Tall, long striding Angus McPherson (Airdrie) finished fifth to win the National Junior title, but due to competing in unpermitted athletic meetings as a youngster, with the need for reinstatement to the amateur ranks, he was ineligible for selection for Scotland's team for the International Championships. D T Muir (Maryhill), 1929 National Junior Champion and J M Petrie (Dundee Thistle) 1929 Eastern District Champion, were also reinstated amateurs, but while McPherson and Muir never gained selection, Petrie strangely gained international selection for Scotland in 1930-31-32 - an inexplicable situation when reinstated runners were strictly barred from international honours on both track and cross country.

Springburn Harriers, won the Senior team championship and the accompanying Elkington Shield for the first time, scoring 106 points to defeat Maryhill 142 points who, led by ninth placed John Emmett Farrell, had 38 years old Dunky Wright as their final scorer in forty third position, with Bellahouston close behind with 144 points and the holders Edinburgh Northern only finishing tenth. George Craig (Shettleston) retained the National Youth 3 mile title, showing the free flowing, stylish running action of a natural runner, and led his club to the team title - a success that they were, surprisingly, not to repeat until 1954 - but on this occasion placing their counting four runners in the first nine to finish to score just 17 points, easily defeating Victoria Park 54 points.

Alex Dow, in all his five Scottish International appearances in the Thirties, was never outside the first three scorers for the Scottish team, displaying a natural ability that gained him many victories without any great training schedule or hard work behind him. In the 1936 International at Squires Gate Stadium in Blackpool Dow was at his best over a flat fast course with scattered artificial obstacles. He was part of a team which included three men - John Suttie Smith, Robert Sutherland and W C Wylie - who had all finished runner up in recent years, but the main Scottish hope lay with James Flockhart who was undefeated all season.

The race was run in blazing hot sunshine and Dow, accustomed to the torrid heat from his Army service in the Far East, was more at home with the weather than his colleagues. Starting in tenth position after the opening rush he was eighth at half distance, sixth at 6 miles and a relentless, surging finishing run brought him home third just 6 seconds behind Jack Holden (England), a three times winner, with British 6 and 10 mile record holder William Eaton finishing a clear winner by a 150 yard margin. Robert Sutherland ran his usual consistent race to finish thirteenth but Flockhart had to struggle painfully for twentieth place, finishing an exhausted and perplexed runner with no excuses for his disappointing run except for saying "my limbs would not move fast enough". Scotland 112 points, finished third behind England 41 points and France 66 points when a repeat of the second team position in 1935 had been reasonably expected.

George Hume, who had been Secretary/Treasurer of the International Union from 1921 to 1936, died that year with the French Athletic Association announcing that their government had presented him with a medal of honour for his distinguished services to sport.

Snow fell during the 1937 Midland District championship at Hamilton, but W Donaldson (Shettleston) had little difficulty in winning by 40 yards from W G Black (Plebian) and R Simpson (Motherwell YMCA). Shettleston won the team title from Plebian and Maryhill (Gordon Porteous 14, was second counter in Maryhill team). A young Dundee Hawkhill team, average age of 23 years, revealed tenacity, pace and determination to win the Eastern District team title by 6 points from firm favourites Edinburgh University who were led by the individual winner G Smith.

After a ten year absence the National Championships returned to Redford Barracks in Edinburgh with 20 clubs entered for the 9 mile race. In bitterly cold, unfavourable conditions Flockhart had little difficulty in retaining his title, leading from the start to establish a 200 yard lead from J M Petrie (Dundee Thistle), Robert Sutherland and John Emmett Farrell (Maryhill) at half distance. Flockhart continued on his relentless way, but Farrell finished strongly to take second place 18 seconds behind the winner, with Robert Sutherland finishing third, ahead of J M Petrie who led Dundee Thistle to their first, and only, outright team title with 78 points for a large winning margin of 47 points over Maryhill, with Plebian 198 points, a distant third.

Archie Craig Junior (Shettleston), son of Archie "Baldy" Craig the 1913 National Champion who was SAAA President that year, won the National Junior title when finishing thirteenth in the Senior race. SAAA Junior mile champion Robert Reid (Doon), ran fluently to win his first Youth title, finishing 10 seconds clear of John Muir (West of Scotland) with Carntyne AAC winning the team championship.

After his many disappointments in the International Championships, James Flockhart achieved the victory that everyone knew he was capable of when recording a magnificient win at the Stockel Racecourse, Brussels. Flockhart displayed a great deal of tactical sense, showing more restraint than usual in responding to challenges from other competitors. Unlike the usual Flockhart he was content to stay behind the leaders and not respond to the impetuous Continental runners in their spasmodic bursts to the front. At 7 miles Flockhart moved to the front, making a decisive challenge to the leader, A Siccard (France), and the long striding Scot moved into a decisive lead.

Up the home straight Flockhart's head was slightly back with strain and tiredness, but he maintained his pace to cross the line 65 yards clear of his nearest rival in 49 minutes 50 seconds, to become the second Scot to win the International title - 17 years after Wilson's victory at Belfast. Flockhart's victory was one of the most convincing of the long series, and his magnificient individual triumph was consolation to the Scots who slipped back to fourth in the team championship after their series of forward team places in previous years. After the race Flockhart was escorted to the Royal Box and presented to King Leopold of the Belgians who displayed an excellent knowledge of the sport in his conversation with Flockhart. The King congratulated Flockhart on his victory and presented him with a personal medallion to commemorate his victory. With Alex Dow being the second finisher back in seventeenth place Scotland totalled 122 points behind England 55 points, France 70 points and Belgium 98 points.

The National Novice amply justified its title as the most popular of all the NCCU Championships when over 300 runners from 41 clubs lined up for the start of the 1937 race at Bothwell Castle. The strange rules of the event were demonstrated when 16 year old Robert Reid of Doon Harriers, the National Youth champion, lined up together with rivals twice his age who had been trying for years to win the title. Reid followed A T Peters (Maryhill), the British Territorial Army mile champion, round the early stages of the 5 mile course. He went into the lead at 3 miles and, displaying power and stamina far beyond that expected for a lad of his years, crowded on the pace to win in 24 minutes 36 seconds, 18 seconds in front of Peters who had just 3 seconds to spare from James Morton (Springburn). Springburn, with 3 runners in the first 10 to finish, continued the tradition of team victory by Glasgow clubs who had a greater opportunity to recruit new members from a large population than provincial clubs, winning with 28 points from Maryhill 64 points.

Reid's victory caused great administrative trouble, for it was subsequently revealed that he was a reinstated amateur. A clause in the championship rules stated that "competitors shall be ineligible who have been reinstated to the amateur

Members of Scotland's team at the ICCU International championships at Brussells in 1937. From left to right; R.R. Sutherland, W. Dow, W.H. Wylie, J.C. Flockhart, J. Campbell and C. Smith.

ranks" but this had slipped past the Scrutiny Committee and Reid had been allowed to enter. Reid was disqualified and the Novice title awarded to the runner up A T Peters (Maryhill). As a schoolboy, just a few weeks past his fourteenth birthday, Reid had won a nominal prize of a few shillings in an unpermitted Coronation Sports Meeting when totally unaware of the amateur laws but nevertheless losing his amateur status.

Doon Harriers appealed against his disqualification, and there was a great deal of sympathy for Reid who had been wrongly advised that he was eligible to compete in the Novice Championship. A special meeting of General Committee was called to consider the appeal "whether it was meant that the rule should have specified clearly that it was not applicable to members whose certificate of reinstatement stated that their offences were of a minor nature carrying no extreme penalties". General Committee, by an overwhelming majority, approved an amendment to the rule in question which ensured that Reid, and all other runners whose reinstatement was under the category of minor offences, would be eligible to run in the Novice Championship race. At the Annual General Meeting in September 1938 the rule change was approved, and made retrospective to the start of the 1937/38 season, so that Reid was duly recognised as the National Novice champion almost a year after he actually won the race.

James Flockhart, after his 1937 International victory at Brussels, decided on a late start to the 1937/38 season and had a very low key approach to the early season up to Christmas. He finished 60 yards behind SAAA 6 mile champion W Donaldson in Shettleston's trial race for the Midland relay championship. On the day of the relay race at Garscadden SAAA mile champion Robert Graham, who was sailing to Australia the following week, was ruled out of Maryhill's team because he had not taken part in two qualifying runs from Maryhill Headquarters before the date entries closed for the championship. Donaldson pulled Shettleston from fourth into a big lead at half distance with the fastest lap of the day, 13 minutes 12 seconds, leaving James Flockhart and W Sutherland with an easy task over the final two stages. But John Emmett Farrell recorded a fine run of 13 minutes 16 seconds over the final lap to pull back all but 7 seconds of the 42 second lead Shettleston had at the start of the final stage.

P J Alwell, who left Beith Harriers to join Ardeer Recreation Club (the renamed Eglinton Harriers), recorded the fastest lap in the South Western Relay at Stewarton and led his new club to victory with three times winners Beith in second place. Edinburgh Northern Harriers regained the Eastern Relay title winning for the seventh time in 8 years, but were unplaced in the Junior championship race at Kirkcaldy later in the season. A Archer (Edinburgh Southern) won the 7 mile race from J W Martin who finished runner up for the third consecutive time but led Edinburgh University to the team championship breaking a monopoly by Dundee clubs who had won on five occasions in the past six years.

Bellahouston repeated their 1934 team victory in the Midland championship at Hamilton Racecourse with Tommy Lamb winning the individual title by over half a minute from Gordon Porteous (Maryhill) with Alex Austin (also Bellahouston) finishing third. Bellahouston, in a prelude to their national team success the following year, won the team title by 12 points from Victoria Park with Springburn third. Greenock clubs dominated the South Western race at Johnstone with Glenpark winning by 35 points from close rivals Wellpark with Ardeer third. Hugh

Livingstone (Kilmarnock), an unraced novice at the start of the season, won the individual title by 13 seconds from James Thomson (Glenpark).

With the 1938 National Championships being held at Ayr Racecourse Captain W H Dunlop invited thirty prominent runners to go for a training run over the National course to familiarise themselves with the terrain - an experience which proved valuable to them in the actual race. A record number of 430 runners competed in the Senior and Youth races with 22 clubs fielding teams in the Senior race and 19 in the Youths. The field was rather bare of several top runners with four of the top eight in the 1937 National missing. W C Wylie, winner 3 years earlier, Robert Sutherland (competing in the English National) and the Dundee Thistle international runners J M Petrie and A T Whitecross were all absent.

John Emmett Farrell, who started running four years earlier at the age of 24, had an earlier mixed sporting career as a wrestler and swimmer in which he represented Scotland in the 800 and 1500 metres swimming events at the Tailteann Games in Dublin and competed with distinction in sea swimming distance events. Farrell ran with great strength and determination to win the individual race and lead Maryhill to the team championship in the Diamond Jubilee Anniversary Year of the clubs formation. He won in 52 minutes 26 seconds, racing home 150 yards in front of a fresh looking Alex Dow 52 minutes 55 seconds with P J Alwell third in 53 minutes 18 seconds.

The Maryhill team revived memories of their record six in a row series of team wins in the early Thirties when their experienced team, with an average age of over

John Emmett Farrell, winner of the National Championship at Ayr Racecourse in 1938 being chaired by members of the winning Maryhill Harriers team. From left to right; A.H. Blair (212); R. McPherson (209); W. Nelson; J.E. Farrell (208); P. Hanlon (Maryhill trainer); D. McLean (225) and G. Porteous (210).

30 years, improved throughout the race to win the team championship for the first time in six years (and the last time in this century). Despite close rivals Shettleston having three men in the first nine home, before Maryhill had their second runner across the finishing line, Maryhill won by 26 points. The following details of the team positions emphasise the valid cross country dictum that "the final three men in a team are every bit as important as the first three men to finish". 1. Maryhill Harriers (1 J Farrell; 12 R McPherson; 15 W Nelson; 18 G Porteous; 25 A Blair; 28 D McLean) 99 points. 2. Shettleston Harriers (5 J Flockhart; 7 A Craig; 9 J C Ross; 30 W Sutherland; 36 D Morrison; 38 A Hall) 125 points.

It was a disappointing race for James Flockhart, best in Europe less than a year earlier, who had been passed by Tom Gibson and Tom Lamb (both Bellahouston) in the final half mile, when he was badly tired after a serious lack of training had robbed him of his dream of a fifth individual victory to equal the record total held jointly by Suttie Smith and Andrew Hannah.

Flockhart had started the season with a new training plan which involved only easy running and no serious racing till the New Year. However, from January onwards, his plans were upset by illness on more than one occasion and he was twice beaten in club races by International Archie Craig. The gruelling 9 mile course showed up his lack of fitness and, uncharacteristically, he was only thirty seventh in the International race and the last counter in Scotland's team.

Robert Reid easily won the Youths title for a second time finishing 32 seconds in front of Alan Haddow (West of Scotland) who went on to win the title the following year. This was an expected victory as Reid had finished just a yard behind Alwell in the Ayrshire 7 mile championship a few weeks earlier - and Alwell had gained third place in the Senior race.

The International race at the Balmoral Showgrounds in Belfast was a disappointing one for Scotland with only champion Farrell running well. Though his running action was seen to be laboured on the final lap his grit and determination drove him on for a last effort to take eighth position, over a minute clear of the next Scots runner Archie Craig 24. Scotland totalled 164 points to finish fifth for their worst team performance of the decade with Belgium and Wales finishing in front of Scotland in third and fourth places behind England and France.

One of the features in the 1938/39 season - the final one before the Second World War - was the great strength of the Scottish Universities. Glasgow and Edinburgh Universities both made their first appearances in the Edinburgh to Glasgow Relay race; George Carstairs won the Eastern Junior title at Hawick and led Edinburgh Hares and Hounds to the team title defeating local club Teviotdale Harriers, who repeated their 1937 team victory.

In the British Universities Championships at Liverpool George Carstairs finished runner up to Frank Aaron, a future English National Champion, with J Muir and T McGlynn (both Glasgow) finishing third and fourth to lead Glasgow University to team victory, after finishing third in their first appearance in the championships in 1938, with Edinburgh finishing third. In the first Scottish University Championships at Garscadden Carstairs won the individual title with Glasgow, five in the first nine, easily winning the team championship from Edinburgh and Aberdeen - thus maintaining their unbeaten record in the face of repeated challenges from Universities in England, Scotland and Ireland.

Double National Youth Champion George Craig became the fourth Shettleston

Harrier to win the National Novice title with one of the newest clubs, South Glasgow AAC, winning the team championship.

There were three ex Novice champions in the Midland championships at Pollokshaws - R Simpson (Motherwell), W G Black (Plebian) and D Fyfe (Springburn) - but there was a surprise winner in James Morton of Springburn who was later to become Union President. Morton had defeated D Fyfe by seven seconds when winning Springburn's club championship one week earlier. Running with fine judgement and plenty of spirit he finished with a fine sustained challenge over the final half mile to win the 7 mile race by seven seconds from W G Black. Morton had to that date spread his talents equally between hockey and running, but this win encouraged him to concentrate on cross country, with many rewarding events both competitively and administratively resulting from his choice of cross country as his main sporting interest. Victoria Park AAC, founded in 1930, placed their six runners in the first twenty home to win the team title and record their first ever NCCU honour.

Nineteen year old Robert Reid (Doon), who had the enviable ability to run from the front, setting the pace without thought of what was going on behind him, won the South Western Championship at Beith. He led the 7 mile race from start to finish, winning by 450 yards from J Barr (Beith) with Greenock Wellpark winning the team title from the exceptionally young Doon Harriers team from the tiny Ayrshire mining village of Benwhat near Dalmellington. Reid prepared for the National Championship at Lanark Racecourse adding victory in the Ayrshire championship over P J Alwell (third in the 1938 National) to his club championship win and his fastest lap in the Ayrshire relay race. These performances, together with his two Youth titles and his wins in the National Novice and South Western championships, established him as favourite for the National Junior and Senior titles.

The 19 year old Doon Harrier, in his first 9 mile race, and facing Scotland's top Seniors for the first time, went to the front as was his usual practice. He ran away from the cream of Scottish cross country runners to win by 200 yards from his Ayrshire rival P J Alwell, with the holder John Emmett Farrell finishing third a further 250 yards behind. Bellahouston Harriers, after an absence of 25 years, won the Senior team championship with a team of stalwarts which had no individual stars but packed their six counting runners between tenth and twenty ninth place.

On the other hand the teams they defeated provided six of the first nine runners to finish, but the final counters in their teams finished so far behind that they were defeated. It is interesting to note that with four men home in each team Shettleston had 22 points, Maryhill had 40 points and Bellahouston had 60 points. The full finishing positions of the teams, in one of the most intriguing team contests in the history of the championships, are detailed below:- 1. Bellahouston Harriers (T Gibson 10, G Hunter 14, J Campbell 17, A Kennedy 19, T Lamb 21, A Hamilton 29) total 110 points. 2. Maryhill Harriers (Holders) (J Farrell 2, R McPherson 5, M Robertson 15, G Porteous 18, H Blair 32, A Peters 42) total 114 points. 3. Shettleston Harriers (A Craig 3, J Ross 4, J Flockhart 7, W Sutherland 8, R Thomson 56, J Collins 67) total 145 points.

Reid's victory gained him both the Senior and Junior titles, becoming only the fifth man in the 53 year history of the Championship to win the National race at his first attempt, following the illustrious footsteps of P McCafferty (WSH) in 1903; T

Jack (ESH) in 1907; J Motion (Eglinton) in 1921 and J Flockhart (Shettleston) in 1933.
The victory of Bellahouston Harriers, who became the eighth club in the decade to win the National team title, was a portent of war. For, similarly to their 1914 victory when the First World War started just five months later, their 1939 victory was just six months before the start of hostilities in the Second World War.

The Scottish team at the 1939 ICCU International championships held at Ely Racecourse, Cardiff. From left to right; J.C. Ross (53); W. Sutherland (57); R.C. Reid (49); A.C. Craig, J.E. Farrell (51); J.C. Flockhart (56); W. Kennedy (55) and P. Alwell (50).

The 1939 International race at Ely Racecourse in Cardiff was a big disappointment for the young Scottish champion. Running in his usual fast starting manner he was twelfth at 3 miles, but as the race progressed over a heavy course his stride shortened and he faded to fifteenth at 6 miles, twenty fifth at 8 miles, and eventually dropping back to thirty first at the finish, outside the counting six of the Scottish team, as he found the big occasion too much for him. As at Belfast in 1938, Emmett Farrell was first Scot home, finishing seventh to be second Briton home behind Jack Holden (England) who won for a record fourth time. Flockhart again displayed his ability to prepare himself for an important race, finishing twelth as second Scot and fourth placed Briton in the race. Scotland totalled 120 points to finish fourth team, just 5 points behind Belgium and 25 points behind England who were second a long way behind the winning French team.

The war clouds gathering over Europe made it questionable whether the continental teams of France and Belgium would be allowed to travel to Wales, but the full complement of seven countries gathered for the race. The event ended on an optimistic note with the announcement that the next International race would be held in Scotland in 1940, probably in the week after Easter. Unfortunately the War prevented this and it was to be seven long years before the competing countries assembled at Ayr for the resumption of the International Championships.

1940 to 1949

When the long period of international dissent and trouble was resolved by the declaration of war in September 1939, the National Cross Country Union joined the Scottish AAA in suspending organised athletics in Scotland and setting up Emergency Committees to look after the sport during the War years. The long period of drawn out tension between Germany and Great Britain had given the General Committee time to prepare for the suspension of championships and permitted meetings in a similar manner to the First World War between 1915 and 1919. But the conduct of the War in the early stages was entirely different from the First War as there was no long term fighting on the Continent and after the withdrawal of Allied troops from Dunkirk there were large numbers of servicemen stationed in Scotland.

As well as large numbers of harrier club members being called up to the Forces there were considerable numbers who were still civilians engaged in war work at home. They kept the clubs open and active and made welcome the servicemen stationed in the neighbourhood, engaging them in club runs and inter club competition.

Early in the War the clubrooms of Dundee Thistle Harriers were bombed during a sneak German bombing raid. The destruction occured on a club training night and runners luckily escaped with scratches and shock. The Thistle Harriers then shared the Hawkhill Clubrooms and the two clubs amalgamated to form Dundee Harriers. But the Hawkhill Clubrooms were then requisitioned for use as National Fire Service sleeping quarters, and the club found themselves homeless. However they kept the sport going in Dundee by using football clubrooms, cyclist huts and even tennis pavilions for training, and indeed managed to promote races which secured support from all over Scotland by season 1940/41. Of the 20 or so clubs in membership of the Eastern District, all but the Dundee clubs and Edinburgh and St. Andrews Universities were forced to close down for the duration of the war due to depleted membership, scarcity of recruits and lack of competition.

Edinburgh University entertained various Service Units at their new headquarter sat King's Buildings and during races the steep hill near the finish attracted a wide variety of comments from breathless finishers. The Army runners, who had probably been detailed to run, used appalling language as they struggled over the hill, while Navy runners, only too glad to be ashore on dry land, tackled the steep incline without a murmur.

Former Dundee star Jim Brannan started the Eastern Cross Country League in season 1941/42, involving Dundee Harriers, St. Andrews University, where cross country had a large number of enthusiastic adherents, and teams from various Service Units in the area. Within a short time the League took off and upwards of 100 runners competed in the monthly races during the winter season staged at venues including Dundee, Kirkcaldy, Arbroath, Rosyth and St. Andrews.

In the West, Shettleston Harriers were one of the main clubs still, functioning, and promoted two "unofficial" Scottish Championships at Barrachnie in 1941 and 1942. John Emmett Farrell (Maryhill Harriers), National Champion in 1938, won the

1941 race with Norman Neilson (Springburn Harriers), taking the 1942 race. In 1943 the "unofficial" championship was held at Westerton in Glasgow, the homeof Garscube Harriers who made so many wandering servicemen welcome during the war years. Jim Brannan (Dundee Harriers) won the 5 mile championship race from serviceman George Burdett (Shettleston Harriers), a former Sheffield University runner who won the 1938 British University Cross Country title, with Ron Mulgrew (Springburn Harriers) in third place.

In August 1943, after a meeting between former National Champion Dunky Wright (Maryhill Harriers) and Oliver Hepburn (Bellahouston Harriers), the Secretary of the Midland District before the War, clubs in the Midland and South Western Districts were invited to attend a meeting in Blythswood Masonic Chambers, Glasgow to consider restarting inter club fixtures.

Club delegates gave full support to the proposal and the Scottish Cross Country Association, named after the first ever governing body in the 1880's, was formed with the following aims:-

1. The desire to offer cross country competition to suit current demand for those at home who loved the sport; for Scottish Youth at school and beyond,and for all interested servicemen stationed in Scotland.
2. To preserve cross country running in Scotland and present it in as healthy a state as possible to the post war era.

The S.C.C.A. sprang up naturally as an emergency organisation when operating clubs were left without vital leadership and cohesive organisation. It was born of necessity in difficult circumstances, proving effective and articulate, with growing power in the following years such that it truly carried the banner of Scottish Athletics in the latter years of the War. The office bearers of the Association were President Dunky Wright (Maryhill Harriers), Vice President John Cuthbert (Garscube Harriers) and Secretary/Treasurer Alex K McDonald (Auchmountain Harriers). Just three months after inauguration the Association staged a Ballot Relay race for Seniors and a Youths team race at Glasgow Green with good fields in each race.

The first S.C.C.A. National Championship was staged in Renfrew in March 1944, with almost 100 competitors running in the Senior 7 mile race and 50 runners in the Youths 3 mile event. George Burdett won the Senior title from his Shettleston Harriers clubmate Harry Howard, with Tommy Gibson (Bellahouston Harriers) in third place, and Maryhill Harriers winning the team championship. Ben Bickerton (Shettleston) gave early evidence of his talent, which was to flourish in post war competition, by winning the Youths title, with South Glasgow Harriers being worthy team champions.

Inter club muster runs were hugely popular with the 10 clubs in membership during the first winter, being held at Pollokshaws, Shettleston, Stirling, YMCA buildings in Motherwell and Renfrew and at Auchmountain Harriers headquarters in Greenock. They proved great fun, providing opportunities for city and provincial athletes to really get to know each other. Wise cracks, witticisms, jokes and cross talk with resultant loud laughter echoed over the easier sections of the runs and despite the prevailing difficulties with restricted rations, tea was always served after each run.

In the spring of 1944 the muster runs continued and the Scottish Marathon Club was formed by athletes who met at S.C.C.A. meetings. Dunky Wright, Scotland's foremost marathon runner, who had won two British marathon championships, the marathon gold medal in the inaugural 1930 British Empire Games in Canada, and finished fourth - just 250 yards behind the winner in the 1932 Olympic Games marathon at Los Angeles - became the first President of the Club. Among the founder members were Andy Burnside, Roddy Devon, Alex Donnett, Alex MacDonald, George Pickering, Walter Ross and Joe Walker.

The second season saw an explosion of activity. The season started with the McAndrew relay race, which had been held throughout the war at Scotstoun, followed by the Dundee Kingsway relay race which was started in 1942, the Glasgow Green race and Shettleston Harriers 4 x 2½ miles cross country relay and 3 mile Youth team race at Barrachnie.

The 4½ mile road race at Maryhill for the Nigel Barge Memorial Trophy followed on the first Saturday in the New Year. This trophy, presented to Maryhill Harriers by Colonel Barge, D.S.O., M.C., D.L., from Armadale, Rhu in memory of his son Nigel who was killed at Dunkirk, was first contested in January 1943, when Tommy Gibson (Bellahouston Harriers) won in 24 minutes 56 seconds with Garscube Harriers winning the team race. In 1944 local runner John Emmett Farrell won in 24 minutes 34 seconds, leading Maryhill Harriers to victory in the team race and the 1945 race was won by Harry Howard (Shettleston Harriers) in 24 minutes 12 seconds, a victory he repeated the following year in 24 minutes 4 seconds defeating 107 runners from 29 clubs with Maryhill Harriers completing a hattrick of team victories.

A winter 2 mile track race was staged at Ibrox Stadium, sponsored by the Empire Games Club and Rangers F.C., with the Association's Championships climaxing the winter season in March at Dalziel Estate, Motherwell. John Emmett Farrell defeated 130 competitors to win the Senior 8 mile title from Harry Howard (Shettleston Harriers) and Alex Kidd (Garscube Harriers), with Maryhill Harriers retaining the team championship. D Shevlin (St. Machan's AAC) defeated 75 runners to win the Youth 3 mile title with Shettleston Harriers winning the team championships.

During the second year the number of clubs in membership of the S.C.C.A. grew to 24, with new clubs such as St. Modans F.P's, St Machan's AAC, Castlehill Colliery Youth Club, Vale of Leven AAC and the Lanarkshire Cross Country Association, springing into existence and organising muster runs and races for member clubs throughout the winter. The social side was not neglected and a function was held in the Ca'dora Restuarant, Glasgow in January 1945 which was thoroughly enjoyed by 120 members and guests including representatives from the S.A.A.A. and N.C.C.U.

A difficulty peculiar to the War emerged that winter when most runners found that they had worn through the soles of their running shoes. They were not the sophisticated running shoes currently in use, with cushioned feet and hard wearing soles, but simple plimsoll sandshoes that had been in continual use unchanged for almost 5 years. There was a great shortage of such shoes in the shops and precious clothing coupons had to be surrendered in these days of rationing - even if the shoes could be found in these times of universal shortage. Dunky Wright resolved the shortage. Acting on a hunch he searched around in out of the way districts and ultimately unearthed a supply of pre war sandshoes which were shared out among the runners of S.C.C.A. clubs, thus averting a disaster which could have brought cross country running to a stop. The runners wanted to recommend Dunky for a Knighthood, and another war time problem was overcome by his ingenuity in renewing the runners supplies of "sannies".

Events continued during the summer with an attack on the one hour track record of 10 miles 1027 yards set in 1933 by Dunky Wright. The race, held at Ibrox in April, resulted in John Emmett Farrell setting a new Scottish record of 11 mile 77 yards - adding nearly half a mile to the record with the amazing 48 year old Dunky Wright finishing runner up with 10 miles 1442 yards - almost quarter of a mile better than his 12 year old record. Six competitors in all bettered the old record with each receiving a commemerative medal.

Many "Salute the Soldier" and "Welcome Home" Sports meetings were held during the summer after the end of the War, with Rangers Sports, which had been staged throughout the War Years, being the high spot of the summer. Fourteen heats of the handicap mile, with over 50 runners in each heat, were staged in front of a capacity 50,000 crowd of spectators. The S.C.C.A. staged a Young Athletes gathering at Helenvale Park, Glasgow in July with large entries in each event.

The N.C.C.U. disbanded their Emergency Committee at the start of the cross country season in October 1945, but were content to concentrate their energies on staging the I.C.C.U. International Championships at Ayr Racecourse in March 1946, and did not resume any of the District National or Championship events that winter.

The S.C.C.A. maintained their programme of popular muster runs at various venues in Central and Western Scotland throughout the winter. The final "unofficial" Scottish Championship over 10 miles was held at Hamilton Park Racecourse, acting as a team selection event for Scotland's team for the International at Ayr. Charlie McLelland (Shettleston Harriers) won the individual race by 80 yards from the Maryhill Harriers pair of John Emmett Farrell and Gordon Porteous, with veteran James Flockhart (Shettleston Harriers) in fourth position. Shettleston Harriers, with four runners in the first 10 home, easily won the team championship, scoring 51 points to defeat Maryhill Harriers 78 points and Bellahouston Harriers 92 points. In the Youths 2½ miles championship Victoria Park AAC dominated the race with J Adams winning by 50 yards from R Smith (Garscube Harriers), with R Laing 3 and M Roberts 4 completing the winning Victoria Park team, 8 points, which defeated Shettleston Harriers, 28 points. Having truly achieved its aim "To preserve cross country running in Scotland and present it in as healthy a state as possible to the post war era" the S.C.C.A., in the words of its Secretary A K MacDonald, "died happy and contented and was buried at the command of its own constitution" in August 1946, having handed over cross country as a going concern to the National Cross Country Union of Scotland. The greatness of the Association was its very simplicity and democracy was its working method throughout its existence.

With Scotland having the honour of previously being nominated to stage the ICCU International Championships in 1940, the International rota of venues disregarded the intervening War years and Scotland was agreed as the host country for the event in 1946. The N.C.C.U. General Committee eagerly seized the opportunity and concentrated their efforts on producing a successful race at Ayr Racecourse- the venue when the International Championships were last hosted by Scotland in 1934.

The War years were barren of International competition except for a Junior International match held in March 1940 when France, Belgium and England contested a 5 mile race in the Bois de Boulogne, Paris. The English team sailed across the Channel to France, escorted by destroyers and planes. Leeds University student Frank Aaron gave England individual victory by 50 yards with France, 34 points, winning the team contest from England 60 points and Belguim 102 points. Aaron went on to win the English Senior title in 1949, 50 and 51 and represented his country 4 times in International competition. Another competitor in the race was Belgium's Gaston Reiff, who, though only 14 at Paris, went on to win the 5,000 metres Gold Medal at the 1948 London Olympic Games and set world records at 2,000 metres, 3,000 metres and 2 miles. The return journey to England was delayed by 24 hours while the Royal Navy swept recently laid German mines from the Channel with another naval escort seeing the happy English team safely home.

The International Championships at Ayr were a great success with NCCU Secretary George Dallas, who had attended every International and ICCU Council meeting since 1921, being the guiding light behind the organisation and Tom Fraser acting as Appeal Fund Secretary. The French and Belgian teams had a long and tiring journey by ship and rail to Scotland, and the appearance of England, Ireland and Wales ensured a full turn out of all six member countries. Scottish hospitality was fulsome, with teams and officials being taken to Hampden Park and Rangers Football ground on the day before the race, with Glasgow Corporation entertaining all the teams to dinner in the City Chambers, and a celebratory after race banquet in Ayr Town Hall on Saturday evening. To complete the overwhelming Scottish hospitality the teams and officials each received a bottle of whisky, a beautifully bound volume of Robert Burns poems and a tartan tie.

The race itself was a disappointment for Scotland when, in common with the other Home Countries, they ran well below expected form, leaving the Continentals to win both the Individual and Team honours - a feat they were to repeat for the next five years before the British teams recovered lost form.

Scotland, not helped by their team manager having the team walking miles round the course just hours before the race, finished a distant fifth with 178 points in the team contest, which was won by France 43 points, from Belgium 77 points, with England 96 points, getting the better of Ireland 113 points for 3rd place. Only James Flockhart of Shettleston Harriers, a near veteran at 38 years of age, could be satisfied with his 15 place after finishing fourth in the recent trial race, subsequent to recent "demob" from the Army, and another to disappoint was Robert Reid (Birchfield Harriers) who was only 26 - one place behind the consistent John Emmett Farrell.

Many excuses were advanced for Scotland's disappointing performances at Ayr, and their subsequent failure to improve at Paris in 1947, where they again finished fifth out of six competing teams. These included the severe food rationing in force throughout Britain and the fact that, except for Glasgow and the West of Scotland, there were no International class runners in the North, South or East of Scotland to strengthen the International team. The concentration of International level runners in Glasgow and the West of Scotland was fully evidenced when, in the following 16 years of Scottish team competition in the International Championships, only 6 Eastern District athletes - C D Robertson (Dundee Thistle H), J Sanderson (Gala H), A Ross and W F Lindsay (both Edinburgh Southern H), A S Jackson (Edinburgh University H & H) and S Taylor (Aberdeen AAC) made 12 international appearances between them.

The harsh rationing, necessarily enforced throughout Britain for years after the

War, ensured that runners missed the tremendous value of the regular vitamin diet of fresh eggs and meat, denying them the bonus of a couple of poached eggs or a nicely done point steak at critical periods in the course of training and racing. The Irish and Continental teams had no such worries on this score, having only the trouble involved in the carriage of sufficient quality food when journeying outside their country. Ireland, indeed, carried sufficient supplies of eggs and meat to feed their team for their stay in Scotland which would have fed the Scots team, on rationing standards prevailing at that time, for at least two months. The officials of the Irish team received the gratitude of the British teams by their generous act of providing supplies of food to their competitive rivals without which the British runners would have been insufficiently nourished.

The first Annual General meeting of the Union for seven years was held on 21st September 1946 in the Religious Institute Rooms, Glasgow with 69 delegates attending. The meeting, under the chairmanship of John Fallon (Kilbarchan Harriers), who had served the longest ever Presidential term of office since 1939, was most disappointing and unsatisfactory. What with the long drawn out discussions on changes to the constitution and the election of Office Bearers, conducted with an unfortunate lack of dignity, there was no time for discussion on Other Business - a matter which bitterly disappointed delegates at the first A G M in seven years. Joe Walker (St. Modans AC), a future President of the Scottish AAA, summed up the feeling of many present when asking "that better arrangements be made for the future".

Oliver Hepburn (Bellahouston H) was elected as the first post war President with

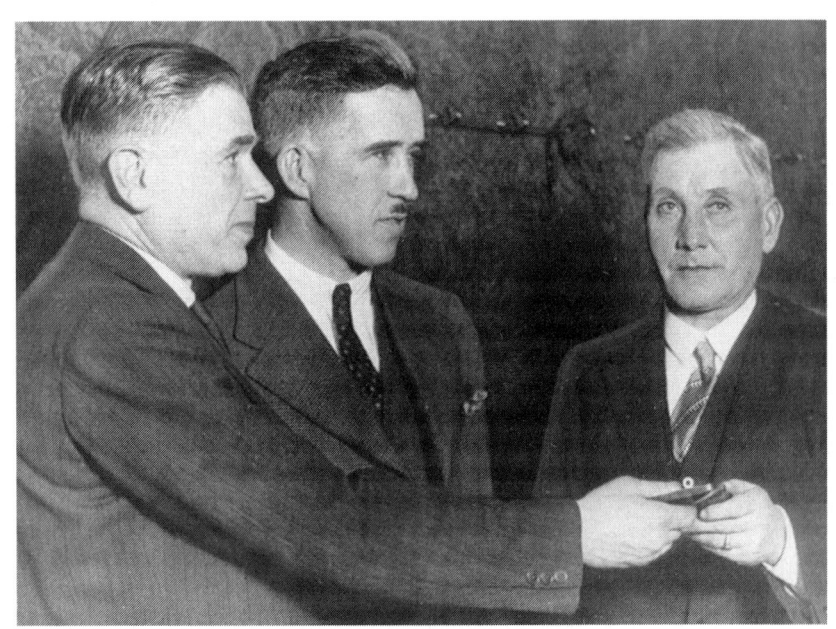

Two of Scotiand's greatest administrators; George Dallas (Maryhill Harriers) left, Hon. General Secretary from 1921-1960; and Duncan McSwein (Greenock Wellpark Harriers) centre, Hon. Treasurer from 1946-1973; John Howieson (Shettleston Harriers), right, Union President 1922-1924 receives a presentation from George Dallas.

Alex Donnett (Dundee Thistle H) being Vice President. For the first time the duties of Secretary and Treasurer were separated, with George Dallas, who had carried out these duties for the past 25 years, retaining the post as Hon Secretary. Duncan McSwein (Greenock Wellpark H), already Treasurer of the Scottish AAA, became the new Hon. Treasurer - a post he was to hold with distinction for the next 27 years until handing over custody of the Unions funds to his son Robert, who is still Treasurer in Centenary year.

The three District Committees were re-constituted with A N Crosbie (Edinburgh Southern H), taking over as Chairman of the Eastern District with M Stewart (Edinburgh Northern H) acting as Secretary. D Scott (Monkland H) and E Taylor (Shettleston H) occupied similar posts in the Midland District and T McKay (Auchmountain H) and G Pickering (Renfrew YMCA H) were the top officials of the South Western District.

The eagerly anticipated 1946/47 season saw Maryhill Harriers, with their great strength in depth of distance runners, win the two opening road relay events. They won the McAndrew Trophy at the Victoria Park AAC race at Scotstoun from the home club and then defeated Bellahouston Harriers in the Kingsway Relay at Dundee.

James Fleming (Motherwell YMCA H) served in the Army during the War and, before his demob in the summer of 1946, competed in the Allied Armies Championship in Cairo. He travelled 400 miles by army truck in three days over sand and rough roads, and was only narrowly beaten in the 1,500 metres by a Turk who won in 4 mins 08 secs. The Turk collapsed on the line, leaving Fleming sure he would have reversed the decision if the race had been over the full mile, having finished second to Sydney Wooderson in the British Army Mile Championship earlier in the war. He also showed good cross country form when winning the Royal Scots Battalion Championship, covering the $4\frac{1}{2}$ mile course in 23 mins 00 secs to defeat 50 rivals and better the course record by over two minutes.

When he entered the National Novice Championships at Pollok Estate in November, one of 280 entrants from 35 clubs in the first official post war National Championship, the victory in the Army race was far from his mind. But it was enough, under the championship rules of a Novice necessarily "not having won honours in a cross country race", to diqualify him from the race. Though changed and ready for the race he was not allowed to start, the Referee's decision leaving him standing on the side lines to watch a race he could have won.

The race, one of the closest in the history of the event, saw James Stuart (Shettleston H) winning narrowly from James Smart (Edinburgh Southern H), with just 17 seconds covering the first six finishers. Stuart, an actor in the Citizens Theatre, had served as a Flying Officer in the R.A.F. during the War and had led Carntyne AAC to victory in the Youths National Team Championship in 1937. The team title went to Vale of Leven AAC, only formed 12 months earlier, who ran as a pack under the coaching of Archie Peters a former Maryhill Harrier. J Getty finished 11, H Coll 12, A Campbell 13 and W Gallacher 15 for team victory with 51 points, defeating Edinburgh Southern H 68 points.

The exceptionally bad winter weather prevented athletes training properly, as the prolonged snow and hard frost resulted in dangerously hard conditions on slippery roads, fields and parkland. The abnormal weather of extreme cold, heavy snowfalls and almost permanent ice underfoot, resulted in rugby in the Glasgow area being unplayable due to frozen grounds for 10 weeks and, on the day the Scottish National Championships were held at Lanark Racecourse, seven of eight Scottish League Football fixtures were cancelled due to frozen grounds. Lanark Racecourse was covered in 18 inches of snow after an overnight snowstorm and the Youths, over 70 strong, set out to blaze a trail and trample down the snow for the Seniors later in the afternoon. It was the strength of Wilfred Young (Victoria Park AAC), already Midland Youth Champion, which overcame Stewart Lawson (Maryhill H) and, with his clubmates filling the next three places, Victoria Park AAC totalled a near "possible score" of 13 points to win easily from St. Modans AC 56 points. Lawson is still running with Maryhill Harriers and, now a physics lecturer at Glasgow College of Technology, is a stalwart of the veterans running scene having recently won the over 50's age group Marathon Championship.

In the Senior Championship almost 230 competitors from 18 clubs contested the 10 mile race. Andrew Forbes (Victoria Park AAC) started favourite, having won the Midland "Junior" Championship and recorded the fastest lap in the Midland Relays. The other "Junior" Champions were James Reid (South West) and Charles Robertson (East), but under the rules of the day many of the top athletes were "Seniors" who were only eligible to compete in the National Championships and open races.

Forbes started slowly, letting his rivals make the pace over the heavy going on the snow covered course. He went into the lead at the 6 mile point and, running with his usual erect action and poise, opened up a gap of over 150 yards by the finish over Alex McGregor (Bellahouston H) and John Emmett Farrell (Maryhill H). Forbes had the distinction of winning the Junior and Senior title double, something only achieved previously in the 56 year history of the event by P J McCafferty (West of Scotland H) 1903, T Jack (Edinburgh Southern H) 1907, J Hill Motion (Eglinton H) 1921, J C Flockhart (Shettleston H) 1933 and R Reid (Doon H) 1939.

Andrew Forbes (Victoria Park AAC) winning the first post war National Championship at Lanark Racecourse in March 1947.

Alex McGregor, 13 years after winning the Midland "Junior" Championship, finished second and led Bellahouston Harriers to victory in the team contest for the Elkington Shield which they had held since 1939. Bellahouston had two members of their 1939 winning team competing - Tommy Lamb 13 and Tommy Gibson 17. With their counting six runners in the first 17 to finish, and their eighth man home before Victoria Park AAC had their fifth man home in 26 place, Bellahouston outclassed their rivals, scoring 59 points to win from Victoria Park AAC 90 points, and Maryhill

Harriers 120 points.

James Flockhart (Shettleston H) had a disasterous run, finishing only 40th, but he had injured his foot on icy roads just 48 hours before the race and was unable to wear spikes. Taking this into account the Scottish selectors showed their faith in his ability, and his talent of bringing himself to peak fitness for important races, by selecting him for the International at the Hippodrome de St. Cloud in Paris. There Flockhart revealed himself worthy of their trust, finishing seventh just 50 seconds behind R Pujazon (France) and being first Scot home and second British athlete behind H Olney (England). This was his best postwar performance and he went on to gain two more International vests in 1948 and 49 to bring his total to 11 - equalling Dunky Wright's record of appearances.

It is only, of course, conjecture, but Flockhart's record of appearances could have been greatly increased by the missing 7 years during the War between 1940 and 1946, and could have exceeded the 12 ICCU International vests achieved by Andrew Brown in the Fifties and Sixties, or the 14 ICCU and IAAF combined international vests accumulated by Jim Alder in the Sixties and Seventies.

In general, cross country quickly recovered its verve and vitality after the War with members returning from the War rejoining clubs whose ranks were swollen by ex-servicemen. These returning soldiers were fit from strenuous life in the services, and keen to retain their physical fitness with regular running rather, than just drifting back to watching sport as spectators.

The "Scots Athlete", a monthly magazine edited by Walter J Ross, which faithfully chronicled the successes and disappointments of Scottish athletics, road and cross country running, started in April 1946. In its early days it carried notices from clubs, including well known, famous clubs such as Shettleston H, Maryhill H, Edinburgh H, Dundee Thistle H and Clydesdale H together with lesser known clubs like Vale of Leven AAC, Aberdeenshire H, Shotts AC, South Glasgow AAC and Monkland H, stating that they were restarting training and inviting former and new members to join the club.

Monkland Harriers in Coatbridge were highly successful, and intimated a record membership of over 100 - the highest total of runners since their inauguration in 1905. Their Secretary David Scott, later to become President of the Union in 1952/53, stated that the club had recently installed a lamp for ultra violet and infra red treatment, together with a radiant heat bath. He believed electrical treatment for athletes would play a big part in keeping runners fit and well in the future, and help cure injuries quickly, and displayed a forward thinking that characterised the spirit that rapidly re-established the sport after the War. Indeed where, even now in this advanced age of electronics gadgetry, do we find clubs that have similar facilities to help injured runners recover fitness? It is a pity that this spirit of initiative was not continued, and spread to the bigger clubs, with equipment provided as a matter of course to aid the physical development and retain the fitness created by training.

The Eastern District Cross Country League was revived after an eight year lapse of competition, with the first match being held at Dr Guthrie's School in November 1947. James Smart (Edinburgh Southern H) won that race and the next one at Musselburgh in January 1948, with Tom Braid (Edinburgh University Hares and Hounds) winning the final event at Kirkcaldy in February. Edinburgh Southern Harriers, celebrating their Golden Anniversary, won all three team contests to retain the Sandilands Shield from their University rivals. This success, added to their victories in the Eastern District "Junior" Team Championship and Relays, made Southern the top team from the East but they only finished eigth inthe National Team Championships behind seven teams from the West.

National Champion Andrew Forbes, named as an Olympic possible at 5,000 and 10,000 metres for the London Olympic Games that summer, had concentrated on short distance track training and was an interested spectator at Ayr Racecourse for the 1948 National Championships.

In Maryhill Harriers' Diamond Jubilee year John Emmett Farrell, at 38 years of age, repeated his victory of 10 years ago at the same venue. He took the lead after covering two of the three laps of 3 miles 300 yards, and went on to win by 70 yards from Frank Sinclair (Greenock Wellpark H), with George Craig finishing just one second behind, and leading Shettleston Harriers to victory in the team contest. When Farrell won the Individual title in 1938 Maryhill Harriers won the team championship - their fourth team title of the 1930's decade. On this occassion they finished fourth, just 8 points behind Garscube Harriers, with Shettleston Harriers, 57 points, winning by 33 points from the holders Bellahouston Harriers. Farrell's individual title in Maryhill's 60th anniversary year was their final appearance in the honours list, as they never again won an Individual or Team title in National competition.

John Emmett Farrell (Maryhill Harriers), winner of the 1948 National Senior title at Ayr Racecourse, 10 years after his first victory in the event at the same venue.

However, as one great club faded away, another took its place. Shettleston Harriers scored the first of three consecutive team victories before Victoria Park AAC broke their sequence, and went on to win themselves for three years in a row. Indeed it was not until 1963, when Motherwell YMCA Harriers won the team championship, that any other club broke the Glasgow pairs domination of the right to hold the Elkington Shield, with Shettleston scoring nine victories and Victoria Park winning six times.

In the Youths race Claude Jones, to be President of the Union in 1983/84, finished in sixth position and led Edinburgh Rover Scouts to the bronze medals behind Kirkcaldy YMCA Harriers and St. Modans AAC. The individual title was won by Harry Fenion (Lochwinnoch AAC), who progressed to win the Senior title in 1957 as a member of Bellahouston Harriers, completing a meritorious double by winning the Scottish Marathon Championship the same year.

The third place of George Craig, Scottish 6 miles champion, which gained him the Scottish Junior title, ensured automatic selection for the Scottish team to compete in the International Championship at Reading. This completed a unique family treble, for his father Archie "Baldy" Craig, National Champion in 1913, had seven Scottish vests and his elder brother Archie Jnr. had two vests in 1938 and 39 before the Second World War. George was to achieve two more International appearances in 1949 and 50 to bring his total to three, giving the Craig family twelve International vests between them. The only other father and son international duo were the Sommervilles from Motherwell, with Willy Sommerville making the International team in 1946 and 47, after his father J A Sommerville had represented Scotland in 1905 at Baldoyle Racecourse, Dublin.

The following season, sparked by the disqualification of Fleming the previous year, saw the Novice qualification rules changed, stating that "those winning a prize in a race of one mile and upwards, or having competed twice in the National Novice Championships are not regarded as Novices". The difficulty of investigating Novice qualifications and the resulting controversies saw the discontinuance of the Novice Championship after season 1948/49, and Tom McNeish of Irvine YMCA Harriers was the final winner of a Championship that had lasted for 30 years.

The 1949 National was again held at Ayr Racecourse, with heavy rain in the 24 hours before the event contributing to the gruelling nature of course conditions which were judged to be the worst for over 30 years. Uncovered barbed wire fences resulted in numerous competitors finishing bleeding profusely, and a stream, out in the country beyond the Racecourse, which had to be crossed three times, was rendered hazardous because it was swollen and in spate. With both banks a sea of mud, from which no correct take off could be achieved, this natural hazard meant icy immersion each time and had an adverse effect on many runners.

On this most trying and difficult course James Fleming (Motherwell YMCA H), Scottish 1 mile champion, displayed tenacity and strength, as well as speed, and fought an exciting battle over the final mile with James Reid (West Kilbride AAC). The lead changed hands many times, with each runner passing the other along the finishing straight, before Fleming brought out reserves of strength Reid could not match to win by 25 yards, with John Emmett Farrell maintaining his remarkable record of finishing in the first three on every occassion since 1937.

In the Youths race ninth placed Ewan S Murray led Garscube Harriers to second place in the Team Championships, just two points behind the winning team of West Kilbride AAC, who were headed by the Individual Champion - Gilbert Adamson. Murray later established himself as a first class administrator, being Hon. Secretary of both the Scottish AAA and the Scottish CCU. He was elected President of the Union in 1972/73 and went on to serve two terms as Chairman of the British Amateur Athletic Board before becoming a member of the European AA and Chairman of the Scottish Commonwealth Games Council.

1950 to 1959

In the three seasons since the War ended, Scottish cross country had continued in the manner in which it had been run for over half a century. The three Disticts - Eastern, Midland and South Western - had held their usual "Junior" District Championships, together with open Relay Championships, and the National Championships had been restricted to "Seniors." The team "Junior" referred to a status of not having won honours in cross country running, and did not refer to any age group classification. Those runners who had represented their country were ineligible, as were counting members of the first and second teams, together with the first three individuals in the annual National "Junior" Championships. The previous individual winners of each District Championship, and the members of the winning team, were rendered ineligible to compete in any further District "Junior" Championships, having graduated to the "Senior" category regardless of their actual age.

The rules also allowed only those in the "Senior" category to compete in the National Championship. This resulted in 1939 in the anomalous situation of Bobby Reid (Doon H), having won the National Youths titles in 1937 and 38, then running in the South Western "Junior" Championship over 7 miles and winning the title to graduate to "Senior" status. Thus, at the age of 18 years, he was eligible to run in the National Senior Championship and astonished his older rivals by winning the title at his first attempt over the 9 mile course.

In 1950, in common with the English Cross Country Union, a radical change of rules introduced a National Junior 6 mile race for runners between 18 and 21 years. The old rules for District Championships were dropped from season 1949/50 onwards. All Juniors were eligible to take part, with no restrictions about not competing again after winning Individual or team titles. Thus runners could win the Individual title more than once, and clubs could field a winning team the following year instead of having their counting runners reclassified as "Seniors" and ineligible for any further District competition. These new rules gave athletes a more comprehensive competitive programme and allowed clubs to use their full manpower resources in their quest for District and National team honours each season.

Athletes immediately took advantage of this new freedom of competition as Charlie "Chick" Robertson (Eastern District) and James Reid (South Western District) won the Individual title they had first gained in 1947. In the Eastern District a strong Edinburgh University team dominated the team championship, winning on six out of the next seven years and also winning the District Relay title on three occasions.

In the Eastern District cross country League the University Hares and Hounds were defeated by Edinburgh Southern Harriers for the first three years of the decade and then won the Sandilands Shield on four consecutive occasions. AdrianJackson was the mainstay of the students team, winning nine individual races, but Tom Braid, George Walker and Robert Sherwin also contributed League victories in the students run of successes.

In the more competitive Midland District, the championship was surprisingly won by Walter Lennie (Vale of Leven AAC), the Dunbartonshire county champion who defeated a number of Internationals in a close run race at Motherwell. Shettleston Harriers won the team title - the first of six successes they recorded in the decade, with their close rivals Victoria Park AAC winning on the other four occasions and not another Midlands club getting a look-in during the Fitfies.

With the new Junior Championship over 6 miles added to the National Championship programme there were three races to be decided. Due to the fact that it was still accepted practice for most men to work on Saturday mornings, cross country meetings did not usually start until 3.00 p.m., to allow competitors time to travel to the venue after finishing work about mid-day.

With this restricting factor in mind the Youths 3 mile Championship was separated from the National Championships in March and held in December 1949 at Kings Park, Stirling - the only occasion on which this championship was not part of the main championship programme. Lanarkshire champion James Finlayson (Hamilton H) won the first of his two National Youths titles from over 160 competitors. Way back in 82 position future Union President Ian Clifton had a poor run, finishing only fourth counter for Edinburgh Southern Harriers, but recovered well to finish runner up to Ian Morrison (Edinburgh Rover Scouts) in the Eastern District Youths Championship just two months later.

The 1950 Championships were held at Hamilton Park Racecourse for the first time since the Thirties and the organisers were so satisfied with the course that they established the venue as a Championship home for the next 19 years until the paucity of changing and the total lack of any washing facilities drove them away in 1969 to new venues.

Bobby Reid (Birchfield Harriers) scored a rare victory, setting his rivals a merry chase as he forced a fast pace from the start, to burn off his rivals and win from Frank Sinclair (Greenock Wellpark H) and Tommy Tracey (Springburn H). Reid's victory came 11 years after his initial win in 1939 and was only his second competitive appearance in the National Championships, having preferred to run each year in the English National, but turning in such good performances in England that the selectors made him an "ever present" in the Scottish International team each year. Indeed this victory gave him a unique record in the Scottish championship - that of having won every race he had contested! He won both the Youth titles in 1937/38 and the two Senior titles in 1939 and 50 - the longest gap that any runner has spanned in winning National Senior titles. This achievement bettered the 10 year gap of Farrell 1938/48 and the 8 years of Wallach between 1914/22. In the future only Jim Alder (victories between 1962 and 71) and Nat Muir (between 1979 and 87) came near the achievement by Reid at Hamilton.

Reid, who initially ran for Doon Harriers, was the first runner whose lifestyle was to benefit from his running ability. A bakers apprentice in Dalmellington, Ayrshire, Reid was just 19 years when, as Scottish champion, he ran in the 1939 International race at Ely Racecourse in Cardiff. Overawed by the occasion he finished outside the Scottish counting six, but his obvious potential attracted the attention and patronage of C.A.J. Emery, the 1938 International winner, who arranged a job for him in the BSA factory at Birmingham. Once settled there he joined Birchfield Harriers, as so many other Scottish athletes did before and after him, and gained athletic honours in Midland and English National Championships.

Gilbert Adamson (West Kilbride) ran a solo race to become the first winner of the

18-21 years Junior title winning by 44 seconds from the pre race favourite Midland Champion Walter Lennie. Future International star Eddie Bannon finished sixth, and led Shettleston Harriers to second place behind Edinburgh University H & H. The Edinburgh students were the surprise of the day, finishing runners up to Shettleston Harries in the Senior team championship ahead of Victoria Park AAC, as well as winning the Junior team title. This was the students best achievement till their all conquering team of 1967 went one better and won both the National Senior and Junior team championships at the same venue.

Belgium hosted the International Championship race at the Hippodrome de Boitsford as a preview to the European Athletic Championships the following August. The event was greatly enlarged with six Continental countries making a record entry of ten teams taking part. Scotland recorded their usual mediocre performance when, led by 29 Andrew Forbes, they finished seventh, defeating only Wales, Holland and Luxembourg. Indeed the most memorable point from Scotland's point of view was their first ever direct flight to Brussels after so many years of tedious, tiring travel by rail and boat to Continental venues. They were accompanied by Bob Lindsay of Paisley Harriers who had travelled with the Scottish International team as an ex official member to all Championships since 1912, missing only the war years.

Lindsay was known as "Mr Pickwick", a nickname he acquired when accompanying the Scottish team to Paris in 1947. When the party arrived at the Gare du Nord Station they were met by an official welcoming party. Struck forcibly by Mr Lindsay's uncommon personality, and the rather unusual combination of dignity and quaintness expressed by his attire, Maurice Maurel, the well known French athletics journalist, featured him in the sports paper L'Equipe the following day.

Maurel wrote of "a character with a florid face who appeared as if he had stepped, not from a train, but from a novel by Charles Dickens. His clothes were of Victorian style, and with his black overcoat he affected a stiff, white wing collar with a tie like contraption and wore a time honoured bowler hat. His left hand held a travelling bag and in his right he held, protected by a moleskin wrapper, the yellow Lion Rampant Flag he was to wave so energetically in support of the Scottish team". A kenspeckle figure at British and Continental internationals Lindsay witnessed many excellent displays by Scottish athletes, including individual victories by James Wilson and James Flockhart, but never achieved his keenest ambition of seeing a Scottish team triumph.

The 1950/51 season was a triumph for Victoria Park AAC who were celebrating their 21st anniversary. They won their own McAndrew Trophy relays at Scotstoun,the Dundee Kingsway Relay, the Midland District Relay title and defeated close rivals Shettleston Harriers in the eight stage Edinburgh to Glasgow race. Andrew Forbes, in leading Victoria Park to all these victories, had vied with Tom Tracey (Springburn H) for the fastest lap on each occasion. In the Nigel Barge road race in early January Forbes scored a decisive victory in 23 mins 41 secs, finishing 50 secs ahead of Tracey, but the tables were turned in the Midland Championships when Tracey won from Junior Edward Bannon (Shettleston H) with Forbes only third. But Forbes had the satisfaction of leading Victoria Park 81 points, to victory over Shettleston H 97 points, with Springburn H 108 points a close up third.

In the National Championships Shettleston lost Bannon from their Senior team and Victoria Park had to do without the services of such top class Juniors as Robert Calderwood, Alex Breckenridge, Syd Ellis and Ian Binnie. The Senior 9 mile race was a duel between Forbes and Tracey, who raced away from the field, with Forbes proving the stronger over the final stretch to snatch victory by five seconds with their nearest challenger "Chick" Robertson (Dundee Thistle H) finishing third, 71 seconds behind Tracey.

It was the rule at this time for individual entrants, and runners whose club did not finish six runners for a counting team, to be excluded from the scoring which determined the final points totals of the clubs in the team championships. Thus third placed C Robertson (Dundee Thistle H) and seventh placed A Gibson (Hamilton H) were excluded from the team scoring and J Stevenson, who actually finished in eighth position, contributed only six points to Springburn's total in the team championship. This rule, which added a great deal of time to the calculation of the team results, and resulted in a number of inconsistencies and anomalies, was scrapped a few years later and the actual finishing position in the race was the points contributed by each athlete to their clubs final score.

Victoria Park, without the help of their four top Juniors, found that the backup of James Ellis 5, James Stirling 9, Ronnie Kane 10, Charles "Chic" Forbes 11 and Duncan McFarlane 14, to the winning Andrew Forbes was sufficient to give them their first ever National Team Championship - a feat they were to accomplish for the next two years and on six occasions in total throughout the Fifties.

Springburn Harriers finished runners up, with Tracey 2nd and Stevenson 6th, well backed up by James C R Morton 8 who resurrected memories of his 1939 victory in the Midland District "Junior" championship. Morton went on to be Union President in 1963/64, and was a highly successful and inspirational manager to the Scottish team for a long number of years. Morton had been, along with his son Forbes, an Assistant Secretary of the Scottish AAA, and was a top class track referee - occupying this position at the 1970 Commonwealth Games at Meadowbank Stadium in Edinburgh. He delighted in telling the story of the 10,000 metres race on the opening day of the Games, won by Lachie Stewart in record time from Ron Clarke (Australia) and Dick Taylor (England). Such was the downpour of rain throughout the race that the recorders lap scoring sheets were soaked and reduced to a mushy pulp. It was only after Morton took them home, and dried them out carefully in his gas oven, that they could be deciphered to determine the finishing order of the runners after the first three medallists and discover the intermediate lap times of all the runners in the race.

Third placed Shettleston, bolstered by the addition of Eddie Bannon who had won the National Junior title by 36 seconds from the holder Gilbert Adamson (West Kilbride), again entered for the English National at Richmond, Yorkshire. An outstandingly brave run by Bannon gave him a close up fourth place in the field of 600 competitors and helped Shettleston to finish second team behind Sutton Harriers - the best ever result by a Scottish team in this highly competitive championship and improving on the fifth team places they had achieved in 1949 and 50.

At Richmond, Bannon was just 10 seconds behind third placed G Saunders who went on to win the 1951 International race at Caerleon Racecourse in Newport, Wales later in the month. There Bannon, celebrating his 21st birthday, foundered on the heavy going. Downpours of rain, for almost the whole 24 hours before the race, had turned the course into a quagmire of mud and, with four water jumps, eight to ten feet wide, to be negotiated on each of the four laps, it was only the strongest of the strong who prevailed.

Bannon finished a disconsolate forty ninth in the International, outside the counting six of the Scottish team, which was led home by Tom Tracey, who ran for over half the distance without a shoe which had been sucked off in the sea of mud. Scotland only finished sixth of the eight competing teams, while England, recovering from their post war slump in form, scored their first team success since 1938 when narrowly defeating France by seven points.

Victoria Park completed a highly successful season when their 10 man team finished fifth in the British Road Relay championship over the London to Brighton course in April. Tom Tracey climaxed his season when finishing a brilliant third in the Festival of Britain 9 mile race in London - ahead of International champion G Saunders - and led Scotland to a surprise second place in the Home Countries International team contest.

Victoria Park AAC started the 1951 season with a record breaking win in their own McAndrew relay at Scotstoun. Showing their ability and liking for road racing, the Victoria Park team of Ian Binnie, Sydney Ellis, Johnny Stirling and Andy Forbes bettered the course record, with Eddie Bannon getting a good start to the season when breaking the lap record by 10 seconds with his first run of 15 minutes 20 seconds ahead of Tom Tracey and Andy Forbes who also bettered the old record.

Edward Bannon (Shettleston Harriers) finishing the 1951 English National Championships at Richmond, Yorkshire, helping his club to second position in the team championship.

Bannon again recorded the fastest lap in the Midland District Relays, but his club was defeated by an enthusiastic young team from Springburn Harriers. The Midland Championships, run in a sleet blizzard with deep snow underfoot, saw Bannon winning easily by almost half a minute from Motherwell's top Junior David Nelson with Andy Forbes a distant third. Shettleston scored a surprise victory, helped greatly by the forward running of 40 year old veteran James C Ross, winner of the Midland "Junior" title in 1932, who was their second counting finisher in twelfth position.

In the South Western District Championships at Paisley, Tom Stevenson (Greenock Wellpark H) won the Individual title, the first of six titles won in eight years by the Stevenson brothers. John, the younger brother, was successful in 1954/55 with Tom winning four titles in 1952/53/56 and 59, and their club taking the team championship on five occasions.

Forty one year old Matt Butler was another grand veteran, displaying remakable consistency to finish in the winning Irvine YMCA team after taking eighth place in the Ayrshire Championships. Butler had previously, as a member of Kilmarnock Harriers in the Thirties, won five team championship medals, with his first success being 20 years earlier in season 1931/32. These two veterans, James Ross and Matt Butler, were the forerunners of the large number of veterans in the Seventies and Eighties who kept on running well past their fortieth birthdays and established a separate level of cross country running with their own National Championship. These fine performances in the District Championships resulted in one of athletics foremost writers commenting "Cross country runners are like Grand National horses in their ability to withstand the onslaught of Anno Domini".

Victoria Park withstood the challenges to their confidence by their defeats in cross country events, and turned out a full strength team in the Edinburgh to Glasgow relay race. They displayed their great strength in depth by placing Ian Binnie on the first lap. Binnie, for any other club, would have been an automatic choice for the "champions lap" on the long seven mile slog on the sixth stage run to Airdrie War Memorial. Running with great style Binnie handed over a 54 second lead, and his team mates were never headed throughout the race to finish up with a winning margin of 3 minutes 26 seconds at the end of the eight stages, with Shettleston Harriers being runners up.

Bannon continued to show good form in the run up to the 1952 National Championships, winning the New Year cross country race at Beith from Andy Forbes who defeated clubmate Ian Binnie in the Nigel Barge Road Race at Maryhill. Bannon's ability to pace himself through the early season, using the County and District Championship events as preliminary tests to get himself into a winning position by the time the National came round, was well proven at Hamilton Racecourse.

There he faced the challenge of Anglo Scot Andrew Ferguson of Highgate Harriers, who had recorded the Scottish record time of 14 minutes 11.6 seconds for 3 miles when finishing runner up in the 1950 AAA Championship. Ferguson had some outstanding cross country runs in England to his credit, but was outclassed by Bannon who ran away with the Individual title, defeating Ferguson by 57 seconds with Tommy Tracey taking third position ahead of Andy Forbes.

Victoria Park runners returned to form with a vengeance to win the Senior team championship with the lowest total of points in modern times. Johnny Stirling ninth, closed in the scoring six runners for the low total of just 36 points, to defeat Springburn Harriers by 54 points, with Shettleston Harriers third with 106 points.

David Nelson (Motherwell YMCA) was a run away winner of the Junior title, finishing 300 yards in front of Donald Henson (Victoria Park) and future cross country great Andrew Brown (also Motherwell YMCA). Victoria Park's youth policy to supplement their senior team paid off with Henson leading home Bobby Calderwood 7, Alex Breckenridge 8 and W. Duncan 13 for an easy team victory over Bellahouston Harriers and Falkirk Victoria Harriers. Nelson's run was enough to convince the selectors to include him in the Senior International team, the first of many great Junior champions who were to be rewarded with selection for the International Championships over the longer 9 mile distance.

Scotland were hosts to the I.C.C.U. Championship at Hamilton Park Racecourse, the first time in almost half a century that the event had returned to the place where it had first been staged in 1903. Admission prices were 2/-(10p) to the ground, with payment of 4/-(20p) for admission to the stand. George Dallas, for 30 years Hon Secretary of the Union, was an appropriate and natural choice as President of the I.C.C.U. He became the first ever National Secretary to be so honoured and ably chaired the annual Congress at their meeting in Glasgow on the morning of the Championship

Alain Mimoun of France was a runaway winner of the Individual title, leading his coloured, North African teammates - who all finished in the first 10 across the line - to an overwhelming team victory over England. In spite of a strong, troublesome wind, not conducive to fast times, Mimoun won by 300 yards in 48 minutes 19 seconds with the next three runners home also bettering Bannon's winning National time of 49 minutes 24 seconds over the same course.

Edward Bannon (Shettleston Harriers), 4 times National Champion 1952-1954 and 1956, clearing a fence in the International Championship at Hamilton Park Racecourse in 1952 when he finished fourteenth.

Bannon was 54 seconds slower than his run in the Scottish National, finishing fourteenth just in front of Jim Peters, the great marathon runner who closed in the English team of six runners. For once there was good back up from the Scottish team, with Tom Tracey 22, Andy Forbes 24, Bobby Reid 26 and Junior champion David Nelson 29 all finishing within 50 yards of each other. This good display of team packing enabled Scotland to finish fourth team, 14 points ahead of Spain, for their best performance since Cardiff in 1939 when they also finished fourth team.

France received the Lumley Shield, the team prize of rich craftmanship and unique design. The trophy was presented by Mr Alan A. Lumley, son of the donor, in the first presentation by a member of the family since it was first presented to England 49 years earlier.

Since Shettleston Harriers had finished runners up in the 1951 English National Championships, after being only second to Victoria Park in the Scottish Team Championship, the Scotstoun club had been busy with their plans to mount their own challenge to the top English clubs. All through the winter the Victoria Park athletes had been busy training and raising funds for their trip to Birmingham. Club members held dances and sold football cards to raise money to send the team of nine athletes; and the selected runners trained at special track sessions on Sunday mornings at Mountblow track in Clydebank. Pre-warned of the extra fast start over the first half mile, which was customary at the English National, captain Andrew Forbes set his team to run fast 880 yards repetitions each Sunday in addition to their longer distance runs for stamina.

For few runners knew the value of spead as well as Forbes. He won the Scottish 3 mile track title in 1947 and 48, after returning from the War where he served in the Royal Artillery for six years. He had improved the Scottish Native record to 14 minutes 32.2 seconds in 1947 and lowered it further to 14 minutes 18.4 seconds when finishing runner up, just inches behind the Irish Olympic representative John Joe Barry. Two further victories came in the 3 miles in 1951 and 52, after his most memorable track achievement in the 1950 Empire Games at Auckland, New Zealand.

Though selected for the Scottish team Forbes, having started a new job, could not afford the time off work for the $2\frac{1}{2}$ months required for the round trip to New Zealand and back by sea. Fortunately a great friend and patron of the sport, Sir Alexander King, came to the rescue and paid for Forbes and his club mate Alan Paterson, the high jumper, to fly to New Zealand - a journey that in those days took almost a week. There was a quick return for the money, as both Victoria Park athletes won silver medals on the opening day of the Games. In a great struggle over the final lap of the 6 mile race Forbes finished second in 30 minutes 31.9 seconds. close behind New Zealander Harold Nelson 30 minutes 29.6 seconds.

The economics of the Glasgow club's trip to the English Championships are illuminating today. Railway travel from Glasgow to Birmingham was £4.8/8 - return (£4.43$\frac{1}{2}$p); an overnight sleeping berth cost 12/6 (52$\frac{1}{2}$p), with seat reservations 1/- (5p) and bed and breakfast accomodation in a Birmingham hotel was £1.1/- (£1.05p) with the total cost of the trip for 12 persons being £65.12/- (£65.60p) for the entire weekend including meals.

In the race Eddie Bannon was first Scot to finish in sixth position, with Andy Forbes finishing 11 to lead home the Scotstoun club. The team championship was closely contested with the forward running of Jimmy Ellis 32 and Ian Binnie 41 who had established leading positions in the "blitz" start proving decisive. They were backed up by the "pack of three"-Chick Forbes 51, Ronnie Kane 52 and Johnny Stirling 54 - to give a final total of 241 points.

There was close competition from two English clubs - Bolton United Harriers (255 points), who had their first four runners home inside 28 position and Manchester AC (288 points) who also had their first four home inside 31 places - all before Victoria Park's second runner Jimmy Ellis crossed the line in position. But the Glasgow club's superior packing was decisive and their final score of 241 points brought them victory by the narrow margin of 14 points to become the first

Victoria Park AAC team which won both the Scottish and English National team championships in 1952. Back row from left; R. Calderwood, R. Kane, I. Binnie, D. McFarlane and A. Breckenbridge; Front row from left; J. Stirling, A. Forbes, C. Forbes and J.Ellis.

"foreign" club to win the English National Team Championship in the 76 year history of the event.

They finished the season with a flourish when taking third position in the London to Brighton road relay race - their best ever performance in the event. The Glasgow club competed in this event for the next six years and only once finished outside the first nine places in the closely contested race.

Victoria Park started the 1952/53 season as they finished the old - winning every thing in sight. They won both the Kingsway and McAndrew road relay races in early season competition, but fell to Shettleston Harriers in the Midland District relay championship where the Barrachnie club started a run of five consecutive victories. Eddie Bannon recorded the fastest lap of the day in both the McAndrew relay and the Midland relay where he was 26 seconds ahead of Hugh Kennedy who led Bellahouston Harriers into third place.

In the South Western District relay championship Greenock Wellpark also started a five year domination of the title with the International Stevenson brothers and marathoner George King providing the backbone of the team which held off the challenges from their Ayrshire and Renfrewshire rivals. Dundee Hawkhill Harriers broke the hold of the Edinburgh clubs on the MacKenzie Trophy when winning the Eastern District relay title, being led home by Alex Black who recorded the fastest lap. The Dundee club also won the Eastern District Championship later in the season at Craigmillar. Black established himself as a possible member of the Scottish International team but, concentrating on an ambitious summer track programme, failed to compete in the National championships and dropped out of the sport with his potential unrealised.

Victoria Park recorded the biggest ever winning margin in the Edinburgh to Glasgow relay when finishing almost six and a half minutes in front of Shettleston Harriers. They fielded a team without weakness in all eight stages of the race, taking the lead on the second stage to establish a lead they were never to lose. Shettleston, after a poor start, were always behind the young Bellahouston team in the first half of the race. They claimed second place on the sixth stage thanks to an excellent run by Bannon; and Clark Wallace and Ben Bickerton brought them home three and a half minutes in front of Bellahouston Harriers.

Alex Breckenridge, with victories in the Beith New Year cross country race and the Nigel Barge road race, finished runner up to Eddie Bannon in the Midland Championship. He led Victoria Park to an overwhelming retention of their team title, with the eighth Victoria Park runner across the line before runners up Bellahouston Harriers had their fourth man home.

John Stevenson led Greenock Wellpark to the team title in the South Western District Championship after an initial tie with Irvine YMCA Harriers on an equal points score. This led to the first implementation of the new tie breaking rule approved by the NCCU which stated "the place numbers of the counting competitors involved in the tie on points will be taken as they would read with only the tieing teams finishing in the race, and the team with the lowest points aggregate thus produced will be declared the winner".

As expected Bannon retained the 1953 National individual title, winning by 47 seconds from Andy Forbes with the Stevenson brothers, 22 year old John and 23 year old Tom, finishing third and fourth respectively. Victoria Park, with their counting team inside the first seventeen runners across the line, won the team title for the third year in a row from Shettleston and Springburn Harriers. Alex Breckenridge, who had shown such outstanding early season form, won the Junior title, with Victoria Park retaining the team championship from Shettleston Harriers with the renamed Braidburn AC in third place. The Braidburn club had previously been known as Edinburgh Rover Scouts, founded and nursed along by former National Champion Tom Jack who was known to all club members as "Pa Jack".

Victoria Park's fame as a family club was fully evidenced when the Ellis brothers, Sydney 3 and Norman 6, gained gold team awards in the Junior Championship with their elder brother Jimmy joining Andy and Chick Forbes in the winning Senior team.

A crowd of over 20,000 spectators watched the 1953 International Championship at the Hippodrome de Vincennes in Paris. The race was celebrating the 50th Anniversary of the first championship in Scotland in 1903, and the French organisers had invited Yugoslavia and Switzerland in addition to the eight member countries of the ICCU.

The growing success of the International race resulted in a letter from the International Amateur Athletic Federation (I.A.A.F.) stating that "in view of the ICCU championships having assumed much bigger international dimensions, it was felt that the race should, in future, come more within the orbit of the I.A.A.F." This ominous and contentious proposal was sidestepped by the International Board, and was set aside without discussion by member countries. But it was the start of a campaign by the I.A.A.F. to take cross country running under its control. The inevitability of this takeover increased with the growing popularity of the Championship race, and the participation of additional European and North

African countries in the next decade. The growth of competing countries, which ultimately spread as far as New Zealand, made it inevitable that the I.A.A.F. would gain control of the Championship and run it under their own rules to the detriment of Scotland and the other Home Countries of Great Britain.

The Paris race was run in intensive heat wave conditions, over a course of dirt track and fast grassland which bore little resemblance to cross country as accepted in Scotland. Twenty three year old Bannon produced the performance on the International stage all Scots had hoped, for with a superb run which gave him fourth place in a keenly contested race. Bannon ran a beautifully judged race to be prominent throughout, and actually led the field for a spell over the final lap. The race was won by 31 year old regular army officer Franc Mihalic, who survived a tiring thirty hour train journey across Europe from Yugoslavia to win the individual title and lead his Yugoslavian team to third place. Scotland did well to finish fifth of the ten competing countries with near veteran Andy Forbes 12, Archie Gibson (Hamilton H) 30 and Clark Wallace (Shettleston H) 33, also returning good performances.

The speed of the Continental competitors, particularly in the first mile, was the feature of the race. Used to flat, fast regular surfaces for their racing, their training was based on producing speed as their main racing ability. British runners favoured country courses with stiff climbs, ploughed fields and plenty of variety. Athletes raised to such varied conditions sacrificed rhythm and speed for a more rugged style of running which produced strength. Limbs so developed became slower in reaction and, except in adverse weather conditions, such a type of "strength" runner was always outpaced by a "speed" runner. If British runners wished for future success in International races against continental opponents there must be a change of ideas. If cross country races in Britain were held more on courses suitable for speedy running they would entice more track runners to take part and widen the base of the sport, thus producing more top runners eligible for the International team.

After their Scottish team championship success Victoria Park made another attempt at the English Championship, finishing in third place in the team championship. In 1958, again competing as Scottish Champions, they finished fifth, but had the consolation of winning the Charles Otway Memorial Cup as the team finishing the full complement of runners with the least number of points - a trophy much valued by competing clubs as it shows the strength of a club over the nine counting runners in the team.

The 1953/54 season saw a change in personnel in Scotland's two top clubs with Victoria Park losing Alex Breckenridge, who emigrated to America to join the U.S. Marines, and Shettleston Harriers gaining the services of Scottish marathon champion Joe McGhee, formerly of St. Modans AAC.

Victoria Park had their usual good start to the season, taking the first two places in the Kingsway relay race, winning their own McAndrew relay where Ian Binnie reduced the course record to 15 minutes 01 second and continued their success when again winning the Edinburgh to Glasgow relay race. They took the lead on the fourth stage and, helped by a sixth stage record by Ian Binnie who bettered Flockharts 1937 record by 11 seconds, eventually won by almost two minutes from Shettleston with Edinburgh Southern Harriers recording the best post war performance by an Eastern District Club when finishing a distant third just four seconds ahead of Springburn Harriers.

However Shettleston again won the Midland relay title thanks to a fine performance by Eddie Bannon, who ran away from Ian Binnie on the final lap to establish almost a minute winning margin over Victoria Park, whose 'B' team took third place.

Greenock Wellpark, with their international trio of John and Tom Stevenson and Frank Sinclair, easily won the South Western District relay title from Beith Harriers, and Edinburgh Southern Harriers took the Eastern Relay title thanks to a good run by W.A. "Sandy" Robertson who recorded the fastest lap of the day. Robertson, now with Troon Tortoises AC, won the Eastern District Championship in a thrilling race with North of England student Adrian Jackson. He finished three seconds in front of Jackson, who was to win the Individual title on three consecutive occasions later in the decade, but on this occasion led Edinburgh University to the first of three consecutive team titles.

Bannon won Beith Harriers New Year cross country race from Harry Fenion (Bellahouston H) who went on, in Bannon's absence, to win the Midland District title at Lenzie. There Fenion was challenged by young John McLaren of Shotts Miners Welfare Club who, with the handicap of a withered left arm tied to his chest, ran a sensational race in his first appearance in open competition. McLaren showed that this disability, due to a childhood attack of polio, was no handicap by cleverly negotiating fences and obstacles without losing ground to his rivals. He made light of the atrocious weather conditions that prevailed on the day to finish runner up, just 15 seconds behind Fenion. Team champions Victoria Park, without Breckenridge, Binnie and Andy Forbes, still had their full team home inside the first 19 to finish, before city rivalsShettleston Harriers had their fourth counter over the line.

In the 1954 National Championships only Bannon, who retained his Senior title for a hat trick of wins, gained his expected victory. John McLaren showed great grit and courage to win the Junior Title at his first attempt, defeating the favourite, Adrian Jackson, by just four seconds in an exciting race. Bannon's individual win, together with Joe McGhee's seventh place, led Shettleston Harriers to the team championship, ending Victoria Park's run of three championship wins.

There was a very close finish in the Youths race as Ian Cloudesly won by just two seconds from W. Hunter Watson (Edinburgh University) with Shettleston having just 6 points to

John McLaren (Shotts Miners Welfare Club), winner of both the Scottish and English National Junior Championships in 1954.

spare over a Springburn Harriers team led by fourth placed Eddie Sinclair who, in later years, was the coach who developed Springburn's youngsters of the Seventies into National team champions. Sinclair had his greatest success with Graham Williamson a 1500 metres and 1 mile runner of the highest International class.

Scotland finished fifth of the seven countries competing in the International Championships at Birmingham, with only Bannon, in fourteenth position, displaying his true form as the rest of the team disappointed badly.

Shettleston Harriers proved themselves the top club in Scotland during the 1954-55 season. They ended Victoria Park's run of five consecutive victories in the McAndrew relay race, winning by 12 seconds, and giving an early display of their impressive strength in depth when their B and C teams finished fourth and fifth in a field of almost 60 teams. Victories for the Barrachnie club followed in the Midland District Relays and Championships where, John McLaren (still a Junior) had a brilliant run to defeat Eddie Bannon with Donald Henson (Victoria Park) in third place.

However the Victoria Park runners, who were better on the road than over the country, proved their resilience and determination when winning the Edinburgh to Glasgow relay for the fifth year in a row in the new record time of 3 hours 46 minutes 43 seconds, knocking more than 2 minutes from the old record. But they had just 34 seconds to spare at the finishing line from Shettleston, who never gave up the fight for the lead, and had the satisfaction of also bettering the old record.

In the early days of 1955 Andrew Brown won the Beith race, having earlier been just nine seconds slower than Bannon in the Midland relays. He was showing the benefit of the extra training he received during his National Service in the Royal Air Force, and was beginning to display the form which was to gain him twelve international vests in the next fourteen years. A very severe spell of snow and frost caused the cancellation of many football and rugby matches, but cross country running continued through the cold spell overcoming the handicap of running in the snow.

Donald Henson, despite finishing third in the Midland Championships and breaking the record for the seventh stage on the Edinburgh to Glasgow relay, became one of the most surprising winners of the Senior title at the National Championships. He ended Bannons series of three victories when winning over a frosty course at Hamilton Racecourse, finishing six seconds in front of John Stevenson with Joe McGhee, fresh from his marathon victory in the Empire Games at Vancouver, finishing third, and leading Shettleston Harriers to the team title.

John McLaren retained the Junior title by over 100 yards from Adrian Jackson who, supported by A. Horne 9, W. Hunter Watson 11 and James Paterson 12 won the team championship for Edinburgh University from Bellahouston Harriers. McLaren later scored a unique double when becoming the first Scot to win the English Junior title from 600 rivals, after travelling overnight in an exhausting 13 hour bus journey from Glasgow. Billy Goodwin (Bellahouston) retained his seasons unbeaten record in Youth competition, adding the National title to his Renfrewshire and Midland titles, defeating John Wright (Clydesdale H) and James Ewing (Victoria Park) who had occupied the same positions in the Midland Championship behind the Bellahouston runner.

The Scottish team had one of its poorest ever peformances in the International Championship at San Sebastian, finishing seventh of the eight competing

Leaders in the Senior 9 mile race at the 1955 Scottish Championships at Hamilton Park Racecourse. From left to right; Ian Binnie (194) 4th; Donald Henson (195) winner; Tom Stevenson (98) 5th and John Stevenson (97) 2nd.

countries, with Wales beating Scotland for only the fourth time in the history of the championships. Bannon, 35, was the first Scot home with National champion Henson finishing 42 in his one and only international appearance for Scotland.

Despite Victoria Park setting a new record of 62 minutes 28 seconds to win their own McAndrew relay race by just five seconds from Shettleston Harriers, the Barrachnie club started off the 1955/56 season as they had finished the previous one. Led by Eddie Bannon, who recorded the fastest lap in the Midland relays at Stepps, Shettleston had an overwhelming victory by over a minute, defeating a surprising Garscube quartet who owed their medals to good runs by Stan Horn and Gordon Dunn. A record breaking victory in the Edinburgh to Glasgow relay followed, with Shettleston including three Juniors George Govan, Ian Cloudesly and Robert Wotherspoon in their strong team which won in 3 hours 46 minutes 13 seconds bettering the old record by 30 seconds. Victoria Park finished runner up 1 minutes 45 seconds behind with Springburn Harriers finishing a distant third.

John McLaren, now a member of Victoria Park after his two National Junior title successes, won the Midland title by 6 seconds from Andrew Brown who, though so near to victory, had to wait until 1962 for his first success in the event. Bannon was third, with Shettleston scoring 56 points to retain the team championship, winning by 83 points from Springburn Harriers and Clydesdale Harriers, with Victoria Park a disconsolate fifth.

It was comeback time for both Individual and Team champions at the National Championships, as both Bannon and Victoria Park overcame early season disappointments. Bannon had run without sparkle throughout the winter and, while everyone was sure that the ability and class to win the National title was still there, it was a pleasant surprise when he won for the fourth time in five years. He crossed the line eleven seconds in front of Andrew Brown, who was to win the title two years later, with brothers Tom and John Stevenson finishing in front of John McLaren.

After finishing behind Shettleston in every cross country race throughout the season Victoria Park scored a surprise victory in the 1956 National Championships. Though without Graham Everett and Joe McGhee, Shettleston's team members ran well below expectation, except for Eddie Bannon. It was the opposite with Victoria Park, where fifth placed McLaren received excellent support from Bobby Calderwood 9, Jim Russell 10, Ian Binnie 11, with Ronnie Kane 22, and Chic Forbes 23, closing in the team for a total of 80 points. Shettleston could only finish third behind Greenock Wellpark Harriers, who had their best ever season having earlier won the Renfrewshire and South Western relay and team championships thanks to the excellent trio of the Stevenson brothers and marathoner George King.

Tom Stevenson, the South Western champion, won his first International vest as a 19 year old in 1949, before the rule was introduced restricting international appearances to those over 21 years (unless specifically voted as exceptional cases by the selection committee). He gained six international vests in the eight years to 1956, with his young brother John having four appearances in the International team.

Billie Goodwin, who started the season with a record breaking win in Clydesdale Harriers popular Youths road race, then reeled off victories in the Renfrewshire and Midland Championships. He retained his National title with an effortless run and later just failed to carry off the double in the English National Championships. Running as an individual, the Bellahouston Youth was boxed in at the start of the race, losing a lot of ground. He had to weave his way through the large field of runners eventually finishing second just 60 yards behind the winner.

Scotland showed welcome improvement in the 1956 International race at Belfast, finishing fourth of eight teams, beating Portugal by 1 point and Spain by 7 points. John McLaren 12, and Pat Moy (Vale of Leven AAC) 14, were both within a minute of the winner Alain Mimoun (France) who was to win the Olympic marathon title later in the year.

In a race of records at the McAndrew relay race - the opening event of the 1956-57 season - Victoria Park bettered their own course record by 74 seconds, but had just 5 seconds to spare from chasing Shettleston, with Bellahouston also inside the old record. Ian Binnie bettered his own lap record by 5 seconds with a time of 14 minutes 53 seconds on the final lap with Scottish mile champion Graham Everett also inside the old record with his run of 14 minutes 57 seconds.

British University champion Adrian Jackson had little difficulty winning the first race of the Eastern District cross country League at Saughton. He went on to complete a clean sweep of all three League races, and lead Edinburgh University to the Sandilands Shield for an overall team victory, as well as winning the Eastern District title from J. Devlin (Edinburgh Eastern Harriers).

A Youths individual and team contest was introduced to the Eastern District league for the first time with the G.K. Aithie Trophy as the prize. James. Messer (Edinburgh Northern Harriers) proved himself Scotlands top Youth, winning all three League races, the Eastern District title and the National Championship.

There was the end of an era in both the Midland and South Western Relay Championships where Shettleston and Greenock Wellpark each won for the final time in a remarkable series of five consecutive victories. Shettleston's win at Stepps was achieved by George Govan, Clark Wallace, Eddie Bannon and Graham Everett who finished 200 yards in front of Victoria Park and Bellahouston. Few present would have realised that it would take eleven years for Shettleston to again win the title, mainly due to a seven year run of successes by Motherwell YMCA Harriers.

Taking the lead on the second stage, Victoria Park went on to record their sixth victory in the Edinburgh to Glasgow relay. Shettleston were only fourth at half distance, almost two minutes behind, and Ian Binnie added another 65 seconds to their lead on the sixth stage with a fine performance of 33 minutes 20 seconds to help Victoria Park to victory in 3 hours 47 minutes 40 seconds over Shettleston Harriers with Edinburgh Eastern Harriers winning the medals for the most meritorious performance of the day.

John McLaren retained his Midland title over a tortuous course at Renton, finishing 40 yards in front of Scottish steeplechase champion Gordon Nelson (Bellahouston H), with Graham Everett a further 150 yards behind, just ahead of National champion Bannon. Shettleston won the team championship by 19 points from Victoria Park and Bellahouston, and looked to be favourites for the 1957 National at Hamilton Racecourse. But it was not to be. Though their long standing policy of developing youngsters through the age group paid off with easy team wins in the Youth and Junior Championships, Shettleston could only finish fourth in the Senior event.

Harry Fenion, nine years after winning the National Youths title, scored a surprise victory in the Senior 9 mile race. With no one willing to take the lead there was a close group all together at six miles until Fenion broke clear and opened a gap. Bannon, the holder, dropped back just when he had previously proved strongest, leaving Fenion to win by 60 yards from clubmate Joe Connolly who outsprinted John McLaren at the finish. McLaren headed a confident Victoria Park team of John Russell 4, Bobby Calderwood 8, Ian Binnie 14, Ronnie Kane 28 with veteran Andy Forbes 36 being the final counter. Bellahouston finished runners up, with Eastern District champions Edinburgh Southern Harriers finishing third.

There were record turnouts in the National Championships, with 18 teams and 64 individuals in the Senior race, 22 teams in the Junior and 20 teams in the Youths races. The welcome spread of cross country running throughout the land was evidenced when newly affiliated Lochaber AC from Fort William, competed in the National for the first ever time.

A fearsome 9 mile course at Waregem in Belgium faced the Scottish team for the 1957 International Championship, with some three dozen natural and artificial obstacles and hazards to be covered on the six lap course, including a 14 foot water jump across a stream. The severe course was difficult for those of small stature, like Scottish champion Harry Fenion, who fell flat on his face at an obstacle on the opening lap and never recovered from the bad fall, eventually finishing fifth counter in 51 position. The best performances came from Pat Moy 28, John McLaren 35 with Bannon 37, and Scotland once again disappointed when finishing in eighth place, beating only Wales and Switzerland, with each team member finishing an average of ten places worse than the previous year.

A theory was put forward that where long distance travelling, and a consequent change in diet, was involved, the form of Scots athletes declined dramatically. This poor performance led the NCCU to appoint a Team Manager for future International races who was to keep in touch with the preparations of top athletes for the big races of the domestic season. Ian Ross of Edinburgh Southern Harriers, Chairman of the Eastern District Committe and a Senior coach, was appointed, and given full control of the International team after the National Championships and their preparations for the International race.

Victoria Park, strengthened by the signings of Gordon Dunn from Garscube and South Western champion Alex Small from Plebian, had their most successful season during 1957-58. A 'flu epidemic cut the entries in the McAndrew relay at the start of the season, but Victoria Park, led by Ian Binnie who again returned the fastest lap time, won by two minutes from Shettleston. The Scotstoun club were in a class of their own in the Edinburgh to Glasgow relay, setting two stage records and breaking the overall course record by over two minutes with their winning time of 3 hours 44 minutes 12 seconds to defeat Bellahouston by over four minutes. Shettleston, without the services of such experienced runners as Eddie Bannon, Graham Everett and Joe McGhee, finished third a further 23 seconds behind.

Victoria Park led from start to finish with John McLaren taking 50 seconds off his own fourth stage record with his run of 29 minutes 14 seconds with Gavin Nelson just nine seconds slower. Alex Breckenridge bettered J. Campbell's (Bellahouston H) 1938 fifth stage record by 29 seconds with a fine run of 27 minutes 28 seconds, and though there was a temporary drop in confidence on the sixth stage, when Ian Binnie was forced to drop to a walk on the run in to Airdrie, a hasty leg massage drove away the cramp and he was able to resume running again.

John McLaren recorded the fastest lap, nine seconds ahead of George Govan, to lead Victoria Park to a 250 yard victory in the Midland relay championship, with Bellahouston second and Clydesdale H a distant third. Edinburgh Southern Harriers, with the consistent quartet of Sandy Robertson, Jack Foster, Willie Lyall and Graham Stark all recording times within 16 seconds of each other, won the Eastern District relay title from Edinburgh Eastern Harriers with Neil Donnachie (Braidburn AC), Scottish AAA President in 1988-90, being second fastest, just one second behind Charles Fraser (Edinburgh Eastern H). Sandy Robertson won the final two races of the Eastern District League defeating Adrian Jackson to lead Edinburgh Southern to victory in the League competition for the Sandilands Shield. But Jackson retained the Eastern title, with Edinburgh Southern scoring a comprehensive victory to retain the team title and show that they were developing into a team that could challenge the top Western clubs.

John McLaren scored his fourth individual victory in the Midland Championship at Renton. He displayed strength, tenacity and fine judgement to come from behind Graham Everett at half distance and eventually win by 40 yards from the Shettleston miler with John Wright (Clydesdale H) in third place. Bellahouston Harriers looked the likely team winners but when Harry Fenion, running in the first six, dropped out at half way their hopes were dashed. D. McAdam finished forty first to complete the Bellahouston team - a difference of about 35 points from Fenion's expected position, and it was coincidental that that was the exact margin by which Victoria Park won the team title.

Beith Harriers won the South Western team title for the first time in 22 years defeating Irvine YMCA Harriers, with former champions Greenock Wellpark finishing in third place.

Shettleston Harriers opened their new clubhouse at Barrachnie in the New Year in the presence of founder member John Howieson, a former Union President.

However on the running side they started the National without the support of Joe McGhee, troubled by back and hip injuries, and Eddie Bannon, whose domestic and business arrangements had prevented him from carrying out an adequate training schedule to prepare for the National. This caused him to miss the race for the first time since he won the Senior title in 1951. Shettleston gained consolation by the presence of newly signed Alastair Wood, an RAF Officer from Elgin.

The largest number of runners ever entered for a National Championship gathered at Hamilton Racecourse. This was due to the introduction of a Boys 1½ mile Championship which attacted a large entry from runners under 15 years of age. The inaugural title was won by J. "Lachie" Stewart of Vale of Leven AAC, competing in only his third race. Stewart only started running the previous autumn, winning a club race and then winning the Boys title in the Dunbartonshire Championship. He arived too late for the Midland race but won the inaugural National title by 20 yards from Mike Ryan (St Modans AAC), a future Olympic marathon bronze medallist when running for New Zealand. George Heriots School won the team title - the first of three consecutive titles at this new age group.

Andrew Brown (Motherwell YMCA Harriers) (164), Scotland's most capped athlete in the ICCU International championships, leading the National Championships at Hamilton Park Racecourse in 1958. From left; J. Kerr (298), A. Brown, W. Robertson (57), J. McLaren (229), J. Connolly (9), G. Everett (behind), G. Nelson (10) and W.J. More (135).

Andrew Brown (Motherwell YMCA) won his first and only National title over a tough test of strength and stamina in which the course was extended to include the rough countryside between the race course and the River Clyde. Brown finished fifteen seconds in front of Graham Everett, with newcomer Alastair Wood finishing in fourth position behind John Russell (Victoria Park), who led his club to a narrow team victory over Bellahouston Harriers. The team contest was very exciting. With three runners in each team home, Victoria Park led by just three points; with four home they were one point behind; with five home they trailed by four points but with Victoria Park's final counter being 24 against Bellahouston's 36, the Scotstoun club scored their sixth team championship title since the war by the narrow margin of just eight points.

The 1958 International championship, held at Pontcanna Field, Cardiff, resulted in the now expected poor performance from Scottish runners. National Champion Andrew Brown and John McLaren failed even to make the counting six for their country, and it was left to John Russell, away back in twenty fifth position, to be the first Scot to finish. Scotland finished sixth of nine countries, defeating Ireland, Spain and Tunisia with Wales, inspired on their home territory, again finishing ahead of Scotland.

Alain Mimoun (France) was beaten by just 1 second by Stan Eldon (England) for the individual title, and just missed out in his bid for a remarkable record. Mimoun had won the International title four times before - in England, Eire, Northern Ireland and Scotland - and had hoped to complete a successful circuit of the British Isles by winning in Wales.

Another step on the road to I.A.A.F. control was taken when the I.C.C.U. Board agreed to affiliate to the I.A.A.F. This decision would lead, despite prolonged negotiations between the two bodies, to the ultimate loss of the International Championship under ICCU rules. Tunisia and Morocco were accepted as member countries, with the decision that a race would be held in North Africa as soon as the arranged rota would permit. This decision, with its financial implications, caused anxiety to Scotland as they had only sent eight competitors to Wales, and next year were to send just seven competitors to Portugal due to the travelling expenses involved.

Bellahouston Harriers, who had been so near success in past years, finally achieved the break through they deserved in season 1958-59. They won the Midland relay title for only the second time in the history of the race as Des Dickson (Bellahouston) and Bill Kerr (Victoria Park) led the field on the opening lap. The Bellahouston runners Bert Irving, Harry Fenion and Joe Connolly ran away from their rivals to win by 250 yards from Victoria Park and Shettleston. Andy Brown, running in the worst of the sleet showers on the final lap, recorded the fastest lap of 12 minutes 45 seconds - just three seconds faster than Pat Moy - with these two runners being the only ones to better 13 minutes for the course at Stepps.

Edinburgh Southern won the Eastern relay title at Hawick and Beith Harriers won their first South Western relay title for 20 years at Paisley. Bellahouston continued their welcome break through when winning the Edinburgh to Glasgow relay in 3 hours 49 minutes 29 seconds, finishing 400 yards in front of Shettleston Harriers with the holders Victoria Park AAC in third place.

Andy Brown won the Nigel Barge road race in 23 minutes 02 seconds with Bill Goodwin (Bellahouston) and Pat Moy (Vale of Leven) following him home in rapid succession. Brown met his match in the Midland Championship when miler Graham Everett won the first of three consecutive titles. Everett went into the lead at half distance and went on to win by 80 yards from Brown with the holder, John McLaren, finishing third a further 120 yards behind. Billy Goodwin was the first Junior to finish in seventh position, and received a special NCCU plaque for the newly instituted District Junior Championship. John Linaker (Pitreavie AAC) and Willie Thomas (Irvine YMCA) were the inaugural Junior champions in the Eastern and South Western Championships respectively.

In a closely contested Midland team championship Shettleston's team finished in the first 23 home to defeat Bellahouston by just 9 points, with Victoria Park a further 12 points behind. Lachie Stewart won the Midland Boys title but had to give best in the National championship race to Eastern champion George Brownlee (Edinburgh Southern H) who won by 6 seconds.

Alastair Wood (RAF and Shettleston H), won the 1959 National Senior 9 mile race after finishing runner up in the RAF 9 miles cross country championship just 24 hours earlier, and travelling overnight to Scotland to compete for Shettleston. He finished 33 seconds in front of John McLaren with Bert Irving (Bellahouston) finishing a close up third, just five yards behind. The feature of the race was the poor form shown by the previous years international team with six of the Internationalists - Andy Brown, Des Dickson, Harry Fenion, Andrew Fleming, Pat Moy and John Russell - all finishing outside the first dozen.

Shettleston, with Wood 1, Graham Everett 4, Joe McGhee 5, and George Govan 10, backed up by Ian Donald 15, and Clark Wallace 20, easily added the National title to the Midland Championship. They totalled just 55 points to win by the huge margin of 82 points from the holders Victoria Park - the second largest winning margin in the history of the championships, just behind the 95 point margin Shettleston established ten years earlier when again defeating Victoria Park and Bellahouston.

Billy Goodwin won the Junior title by 33 seconds from John Linaker, with fourth placed George Brown leading Edinburgh University to the team championship, ahead of St Andrews University who had Donald Macgregor, a future Union President, in their team. Lanarkshire and Midland Youth champion Jim Bogan (Glasgow University), gave up and retired when leading at half distance, leaving Willy Fleming (St. Modans AC) to win the Youths title by 3 seconds from James Johnstone(Monkland Harriers).

National champion Wood was first home in twenty third position in the International race at the Estodium National in Lisbon, with Scotland again disappointing when only taking sixth position in the field of eight competing countries.

1960 to 1969

The decade of the Sixties was for the Union, as in the rest of Britain, a time of change. There were three Honorary Secretaries of the Union during this short period - in contrast to a period of over 60 years between 1898 and 1959 during which the Union had been served by only three Secretaries. George Dallas completed the final year of his 39 year period of office as Secretary, to be followed by Andrew Stevenson for four years and Ewan Murray for the next five years.

A presentation dinner for George Dallas was held in December 1960 at Mores Hotel, Glasgow when the Honorary President Sir Thomas Moore presented him with a gift from the Union to commemorate his long period of service. Although there were two toasts proposed, and entertainment from various artistes throughout the evening, the main item was "Tales of George Dallas". Most of those present at the dinner had their recollections of the actions and achievements of the administrator who had guided the Union for four decades. The anecdotes flowed freely and included tales of his achievements as an athlete over track and cross country, his publicising of the sport as a reporter, and his custody of the Union's affairs and finances. The tales were told with vigour and enthusiasm and heard by the audience with delight and enjoyment as they recalled fond memories of the Maryhill harrier who had meant so much to Scottish Cross Country through the years.

George Dallas, Scotland's top administrator and official, on his retiral after completing 40 years as Honorary Secretary of the Union.

Stevenson started the change gradually and Murray vigorously accelerated the rate of change, overhauling the legislation and organisation of the Union to modernise and stream line its structure. Symptomatic of this change was the renaming of the Union from the rather long winded, clumsy title of "National Cross Country Union of Scotland" to the more snappy "Scottish Cross Country Union" which had been used originally during the early period of 1890 to 1903. This change was decided at the Annual General Meeting of 1964 and the only reason for the name change that can now be traced was that it was more modern and easier to say.

Over the decade the National Senior title was won by seven different athletes with only Fergus Murray (Edinburgh University) and Lachie Stewart (Vale of Leven) winning the title on more than one occasion. There was the emergence of top runners such as Jim Alder, Ian McCafferty, Eddie Knox and Dick Wedlock who climbed through the age groups from being Senior Boy Champion in 1961 to winning the National Senior title eight years later. Shettleston Harriers, Edinburgh University and Edinburgh Southern Harriers all took turns to dominate the Senior team championship, recording three wins each, with only Motherwell YMCA breaking their monopoly of the championship during the decade.

The International team, always a barometer of Scotland's level of success in the sport, grew in stature and achievement in the latter half of the decade, helped and encouraged by innovations in team coaching, get togethers and management. These enlightened changes gave them their greatest successes internationally for over 30 years with both Junior and Senior teams having notable successes in the annual ICCU International Championships.

Graham Everett (Shettleston) retained his Senior title at the Midland Championships held over a good, meadowland course at Renton. He doubled his 60 yard lead at half distance to win easily from Andrew Brown and Joe Connolly with four times winner John McLaren finishing fifth, to lead Victoria Park to a surprise team victory over Bellahouston. In the Eastern Championships at Galashiels, John Linaker (Pitreavie), still a Junior, crowned a successful season when winning the Senior title by 20 seconds from the brothers Alastair and Norman Ross who led Edinburgh Southern to the third of four successive team victories. Brown won the Inter District 9 mile race at Hamilton, finishing 10 seconds clear of teammate Joe Connolly with the Midlands team, who had their counting 6 men in the first 8 to finish, easily winning from the Eastern and South Western Districts. However Brown was surprisingly defeated by an in form Linaker in the Scottish YMCA championships, losing by almost 600 yards in one of his rare defeats at this level of competition.

Shettleston miler Graham Everett won the National Senior title defeating the holder Alastair Wood, who had progressed from the RAF to Oxford University. Everett set a fast pace from the start, with only Wood being able to stay with him, and at half distance, with the pair well clear of the pursuing field, Wood took up the running. Everett then displayed his track speed, which he had carefully honed in the weeks before the race with victories in the 1,000 yards (2 minutes 18.2 seconds) and 3,000 metres (8 minutes 49.0 seconds) at Shettleston's winter track meeting, and drew away to win easily by 30 yards from his clubmate with Andrew Brown finishing a distant third 500 yards behind. With their counting 6 runners in the first 25 to finish, Shettleston retained the team championship by 41 points from Bellahouston.

Jim Alder, representing Morpeth Harriers, made the first of many appearances in the Scottish Championships to finish runner up to John Linaker in the Junior race. James Finn (Monkland) was a surprise winner of the Youths title and Hugh Barrow (Victoria Park), World 1 mile age group record holder, added the National Boys title to the Midland title he won earlier in the year.

The International was held over the same course at Hamilton and Alastair Wood led the Scottish team home to fifth place - one place better than the previous year and, more importantly, with 62 points fewer on the score board. Wood finished seventh, with Everett 22 and Bruce Tulloch, the British 3 mile record holder, taking advantage of his Scots parentage to turn out for Scotland and finish twenty third in a race won by A Rhadi, the Morrocan who was to win the Olympic Games Marathon Silver Medal in Rome six months later.

Although Scottish cross country champion, three times Midland champion and four times cappped for Scotland, Graham Everett, like so many other track stars, considered the winter season competitions mainly as preparation for the track races in the summer. Everett was Scotland's most successful miler of the post war period, winning the SAAA mile title on seven successive occasions between 1955 and 1961 - an unequalled achievement - with his best year being in 1960. That year he won the AAA title in 4 minutes 02.8 seconds and the Scottish title in the National record time of 4 minutes 03.9 seconds - his third mile record during which he improved the Scottish best from 4 minutes 11.2 seconds. He also showed impressive form at the 2 mile distance between 1959 and 1961, reducing the Scottish record from 8 minutes 57.2 seconds to 8 minutes 38.2 seconds (the third best time ever run by a British athlete).

The following season Everett, who had failed in his intention to better the four minute mile barrier and gain Olympic selection for 1500 metres, despite clocking a personal best of 3 minutes 45.7 seconds for 1500 metres, started off the winter season with some fine performances. He won the Nigel Barge road race, scored a third successive victory in the Midland championship with a convincing 250 yards win over Andrew Brown and Joe Connolly and led Shettleston to the team championship over the holders, Victoria Park. He finished fifteenth, and leading Scot, ahead of John Linaker 16 in the Martini international race at Brussels, with Scotland finishing seventh of fifteen competing countries. This was the first of many international races on the continent to which the SCCU would receive invitations to send teams due to the rising standard of Scottish runners.

In the National Championship at Hamilton Racecourse Everett did not run with his usual free flowing action, turning in a below par performance on the day that Joe Connolly produced his best ever running to win the National title in relaxed and confident style. Everett finished runner up 300 yards behind Connolly with Andrew Brown finishing strongly to take third place ahead of Steve Taylor

National Champion Graham Everett (Shettleston Harriers), a member of Shettleston's 4 time winning National championship team 1959-1962, and top Scottish 1500 metres/ 1 mile track runner.

(Aberdeen) and Alastair Wood. Two future Scottish champions were to the fore in the age group races, with Jim Alder finishing third behind Jim McLatchie and Mike Ryan in the Junior race and Dick Wedlock (Shettleston) winning his first National honour when adding the Boys Championship to the Midland title he had won earlier in the winter.

Everett narrowly defeated Connolly for the honour of being the first Scot to finish in the International championship at Nantes, France the following month, finishing eighteenth with the National champion three places behind. In a race won by Basil Heatley (England), his teammate Martin Hyman, who was to win the New Year "Round the Houses" race in Sao Paulo, Brazil the following year, finished third. Hyman now lives and teaches in Livingston, is a member of the local club, Livingston and District AC, and is still an active competitor, together with his wife, in many races and especially veterans races. Scotland finished sixth of nine countries in the International race.

Left: Two Scottish National champions competing on the track. Alastair Wood (RAF, Shettleston Harriers and Aberdeen AAC), champion in 1959, leading from Joe Connolly (Bellahouston Harriers), champion in 1961.

Although Andrew Brown had won the National title in 1958, season 1961-62 was definitely the Motherwell harrier's finest year in his long and distinguished career in Scottish and International athletics. He led Motherwell YMCA to victory in the Midland relay championship, the first of seven consecutive victories; won the Nigel Barge New Year race and the Midland championship at Renton, which had previously been dominated by John McLaren (4 wins) and Graham Everett (3 wins), and led his club to the team championship - a title they were to hold on four consecutive occasions and win five times in six years. Brown's happiness was enhanced when his young brother Alec won the Youth titles in the Midlands and Scottish National championships.

Brown was out on his own at Renton and, although challenged in the early stages by John Linaker - a new Motherwell recruit, he forged ahead before half distance to win by over 100 yards. Linaker, who had a bad accident clearing a fence in the final stages of the race, was overtaken by Bert McKay but held on for third place ahead of the holder, Graham Everett, to ensure that Motherwell became the first club in the history of the race to have the first three athletes home.

At the start of the season Alec Brown, on finding that Motherwell YMCA were short of a full Youths team, coerced his friend Ian McCafferty to join the club to make up the team. Such was the rough and ready entry of McCafferty, later to become one of the greatest talents in Scottish, British, European, Commonwealth and World middle distance running, to athletics. McCafferty, within a few short weeks, was to display his ability for running, finishing runner up to Brown in the Midland, Scottish YMCA and National championships races, and the rapid flowering of the unique talent was underway.

Alastair Wood, who had joined Aberdeen AAC on his move to the North East, won the Eastern District title at Dundee, defeating clubmate Steve Taylor. R K Harley, who had finished fourth in the National Junior championship the previous year when leading Teviotdale to their first ever National team title, was again in fine form. He finished third to lead Teviotdale to the team championship, their first title in 63 years, and end the run of five consecutive team titles by Edinburgh Southern. Craig Douglas, in the winning team, gained the District Junior title - an honour he was to retain the following year when he won the Senior title becoming only the third Teviotdale man to win the title after A J Grieve (1907) and J Grierson (1913).

Although suffering a temporary upset in the Inter District 8 mile race at Cleland Estate, Motherwell, when he suffered a surprise 14 second defeat by Bert McKay, Brown started the National championship as favourite with two former champions Graham Everett and Alastair Wood also in the field of 300 runners. The pace was set by 24 year old agricultural student Callum Laing, a son of the manse from the North of Scotland studying at Glasgow University, who was the best distance runner produced by any Scottish University to date. At the 2½ mile marker Jim Alder, who had previously competed in the Youth and Junior championship, displayed the great improvement in form he had made and went into the lead. He held off an attempt by Brown to take the lead at half distance and raced away to win his first Scottish title by 70 yards from Brown, with Laing taking a surprising, but well deserved, third place having already gained second place in the British Universities championships. Shettleston, led by Joe McGhee 10, retained the team championship for their fourth consecutive title, defeating Aberdeen (led by A Wood 4 and S Taylor 5). Motherwell, despite having three runners in the first nine home, did not have sufficient depth at this top level, and finished fifth team.

Brown gained his revenge over Alder in the British YMCA championships two weeks later at Manchester, winning by the large margin of 400 yards from the Geordie Anglo Scot, and leading the Scottish team to a resounding victory. Seemingly getting better as the season progressed, Brown kept his best performance for the International championship at Graves Park, Sheffield. After a bad patch during the middle of the race, Brown was back in twenty fourth position at the start of the final 1½ mile lap of the race. With a strong finishing surge he tore his way through the field, gaining fifteen places to eventually finish ninth, just 29 seconds behind the winner, Gaston Roelants (Belgium). Scotland finished fifth, just 8 points behind fourth placed Morocco. The Junior team did better, gaining the team bronze medals behind England and Morocco, with Lachie Stewart 10, leading home Alastair Heron 11 and James Finn 16.

Motherwell were again the top club the

Andrew Brown
(Motherwell YMCA Harriers)
National Champion in 1958

following season 1962-63, retaining the Midland relay and team championships and winning the National team championship for the first time in 55 years. Andy Brown and John Linaker led all the way in the Midland 6 mile race until Linaker fell in the closing stages, letting Brown away for a 3 second victory with Lachie Stewart winning the Junior title when finishing a close-up third. With six runners in the first twenty Motherwell retained the team title from Glasgow University and Shettleston.

The Motherwell pair Brown and Linaker, together with Alastair Wood (Aberdeen), went into an early lead in the National championship, drawing well clear of the field. Running together as a group they were out on their own with just a mile to the finish when Brown, hoping to retain his title, broke clear with a strong burst. But his rivals were faster finishers than him, Linaker being SAAA Steeplechase champion and Wood 3 mile champion, and they overtook him with half a mile to go. Linaker timed his finishing sprint to perfection, winning by 10 yards from Wood with Brown third a further 10 yards behind. With the great start of having three runners in the first four home (Bert McKay was fourth), Motherwell won the team championship for the first time since 1908. But it was no walkover, for the Motherwell club had to wait anxiously for their final counter John Poulton to finish in forty fourth position, with Kenny Ballantyne 24 being the sixth and final counter for Edinburgh Southern. Motherwell's top three finishers decided the issue and they totalled 106 points to win by just 9 points from Southern.

Fergus Murray, a first year student at Edinburgh University who had previously won the Nigel Barge road race from a record field of 157 runners, won the Junior title as he liked - winning by over a minute from Mike Ryan (St Modans) with Lachie Stewart finishing fourth behind Alec Brown. Murray led Edinburgh University to the Junior team title, the first of 3 consecutive Junior team wins (1963-65) and 3 Senior team wins (1966-68) in a six year period when Edinburgh University runners dominated Scottish cross country and road running with a staggering series of wins thanks to punishing training schedules that developed talent to its fullest potential. Ian McCafferty won the Youths title by 11 seconds from Ian Young (Springburn) and his achievement of later winning National titles in the Junior and Senior categories was equalled only by Nat Muir.

Due to financial difficulties Scotland sent only 7 Seniors and 4 Juniors to compete in the International Championships at the Hippodrome de Lasarte in San Sebastian. Missing from the Senior team was Jim Alder who had dropped out of the National championship before reaching half distance. The Morpeth runner's absence was the only time between 1962-76 that he was not in Scotland's International team during his record sequence of 14 International appearances. Andrew Brown was once again the first Scot home in eleventh position, with the two who beat him in the National championship race, A Wood 31 and J Linaker 36, being the next counters in the Scottish team which finished eighth of eleven countries. Lachie Stewart finished third in the Junior race and led the Scottish team to bronze medals in the team race.

The first Scottish Schools Cross Country Championships were held at Newcraighall in Edinburgh, and these Championships, so often the birth place of emerging athletes who would go on to International honours for Scotland, have grown in stature and size such that approximately 2,000 competitors take part in the excellently organised championships every year.

A new club Edinburgh Athletic Club, graced the Scottish scene at the start of the 1962-63 season. Formed by the amalgamation of five clubs of Edinburgh Harriers, Edinburgh Eastern and Northern, Octavians AC and Braidburn AC, the new powerful club would balance the growing strength of rival Edinburgh Southern in the capital city. Their first successes came in the younger age group events in District and National competition, and it was not until 1973 that they won their first National Senior team title when they started their glorious run of four consecutive team championship wins with five titles inside six years. Their first administrative honour came when Alastair Falconer became Union President at the start of the 1962-63 season.

With Teviotdale winning the second of three consecutive Eastern relay titles, and Motherwell retaining the Midland relay title, the District championships loomed large in the target of both clubs. Fergus Murray, having won the SAAA 3 mile track title the previous summer and set to gain 5000 metres selection for the 1964 Olympic Games at Tokyo the following summer, scored an easy win in the Eastern District race at Hawick. He finished 200 yards in front of his former clubmate, Rob Coleman (Dundee Hawkhill), with Mel Edwards (Aberdeen University), later to become National Junior champion, finishing third another 100 yards behind. Edinburgh Southern won the team title from Teviotdale, but the Hawick club gained consolation when winning the Youth team championship led by Joe Raeburn who won from John Fairgreive (Edinburgh AC), later to become SAAA Hon Secretary and Scotland's first athletic administrator.

First year Junior Ian McCafferty won his first Midland District title, finishing 27 seconds in front of clubmate Alec Brown with Lachie Stewart, competing over his home course at Renton, finishing third. Motherwell's team of 1, I McCafferty; 2, Alec Brown; 5, R McKay; 6, D Simpson; 7, Andrew Brown and 9, G Henderson totalled just 30 points, one of the lowest aggregate scores ever recorded in the championship, to defeat Shettleston 103 points.

Greenock Glenpark, led by fourth placed Willy Murray, won the South Western Senior team championship for the first time since 1950, with Ian Harris winning the individual title from his Beith clubmate, Tom Cochrane, who was to win for the next five years in a row.

Fergus Murray, after winning the British Universities championship at Nottingham and finishing a close up third in the Martini International 6 mile race at Brussels, behind Gaston Roelants and Derek Graham (N. Ireland), lined up with confidence for the National championship race. Racing over a heavy $7\frac{1}{2}$ mile of racecourse turf Murray trounced three former National champions. His great strength and speed proved decisive, giving him a 39 second margin of victory over Jim Alder with Alastair Wood third, a further 22 seconds behind, but 4 seconds in front of Andrew Brown.

Ending the long domination of the National team title by West of Scotland clubs for the previous 27 years, Edinburgh Southern followed their Eastern District team championship win with their first ever team victory in the National championship. Not since Dundee Thistle's win in 1937 had an East of Scotland club won the National team title. But this win was a turning point in the distribution of National honours for, from that date onwards, Edinburgh clubs won 21 of the 27 team championship titles. Only Shettleston (1971,72 and 77) and Cambuslang (1988-90) have since broken the East domination of National team honours. Indeed, the breakthrough by East clubs was evident throughout the 4 age group races. Fergus Murray was joined on the honour roll of individual champions by Mel Edwards (Junior) and W G Kerr (Boys) with only Edward Knox of Springburn winning the Youth title and breaking the East monopoly. In the team championships the East had no rivals, with Edinburgh AC winning both the Boys and Youth team honours and Edinburgh University taking the Junior team title. Indeed, of the 12 team championship places at stake in the 4 races, East clubs won 8 to the West's 4.

Even at this early stage Ian McCafferty combined speed training and distance racing throughout the winter cross country season. The week after the National he took part in a 2 mile race at half time at a match at Ibrox Stadium and, despite having to swerve to avoid a policeman in the home straight and losing ground, finished second to Lachie Stewart, with both sharing the winning time of 9 minutes 02 seconds. In the International Championship at Leopardstown Racecourse, Dublin, McCafferty displayed his sharpness when winning the Junior title. He went into the lead from the start and dictated the pace throughout the race to win by 25 seconds - the largest winning margin in the history of the race - and become the first of three Scots to win the title, being followed by Eddie Knox (Springburn) and Jim Brown (Monkland). Backed by Alec Brown 7, and Joe Reilly 9, McCafferty led Scotland, 17 points, to second place in the team contest, finishing just 1 point behind England in what was to be our best ever attempt to win the International Junior team championship.

For the third year in succession Andrew Brown was the first Scot home in the Senior race finishing twenty ninth, just one place in front of Jim Alder. The big disappointment of the day was the performance of Fergus Murray. He started well, being up with the leaders in the early stages, but drifted back as he ran without conviction or determination, and eventually finished fourth team counter in fortieth position - the first of many poor races in the International where he never ran to his full potential. Scotland finished seventh of nine countries with only Holland and Wales behind them.

The District relay championships at the start of the 1964-65 season saw Teviotdale win the East race for the third year in a row and Motherwell YMCA record their fourth successive win in the Midland event. The Nigel Barge road race at Maryhill, at the start of 1965, resulted in a runaway victory by Ian McCafferty who won in the course record time of 22 minutes 29 seconds from Fergus Murray.

Both these runners proved successful in their respective District championship races retaining their titles with excellent performances. Throughout McCafferty's run at Renton he never looked like being beaten, establishing a 120 yard lead at half distance and doubling it over the second lap with a powerful run that left such eminent rivals as Andrew Brown and Lachie Stewart trailing far behind. Motherwell, aided by their new recruit, first year Junior Dick Wedlock finishing sixth, won the team championship for the fourth year in a row to better Shettleston's previous best series of three in a row between 1955-57. Eddie Knox (Springburn), with 30 wins in the past nine months through a long, exhausting, racing programme on track, road and cross country, won the Youths title by the remarkable margin of 41 seconds. Murray lived up to all expectations when winning the East title at Newcraighall by 80 yards from his much improved teammate Roger Young, with former winner Craig Douglas third. The Edinburgh students won the team title for the first time since 1956, easily defeating Teviotdale and Edinburgh Southern.

The National championships at Hamilton Racecourse continued to grow in size and stature, with 21 clubs finishing teams in the senior race, a record for the event, and 7 former champions - J Emmett Farrell, Andy Forbes, Andy Brown, Alastair Wood, Jim Alder, John Linaker and the holder Fergus Murray - lining up in the field of 350 runners. Murray retained his title with a solo run throughout the $7\frac{1}{2}$ mile race. In an unrelenting mood Murray set off at a gallop from the start, and by 2 miles had opened up a gap from the following group of Andrew Brown, Lachie Stewart and Jim Alder. Alder set off in pursuit of the leader at 3 miles but made no impression on the flying Murray who eventually won by 24 seconds from Alder, with Stewart third, a further 11 seconds behind and Brown fourth. Edinburgh Southern, led by fifth placed Donald Macgregor, retained the team championship with their final man finishing fortieth for a winning margin of 106 points over Aberdeen, who were led home by A Wood 8 and S Taylor 9, but had to wait until ninety fifth place for their last scorer.

Ian McCafferty won the Junior title, sharing the lead with Roger Young (Edinburgh University) for most of the way, but displaying his experience and will to win in the final stages for a 15 second victory over the Edinburgh student. Backed up by Alec Brown 3, and Dick Wedlock 4, Motherwell had to wait until R Darroch 37, finished, and lost the team title to Edinburgh University, whose team of R Young 2, I Young 6, A Blamire 9 and J Wight 11 totalled 28 points for victory. Eddie Knox recorded an easy victory in the Youths race, winning by 34 seconds from John Fairgreive (Edinburgh AC), the Scottish Schools champion, and gained selection for the Scottish Junior team in the International Championships at Ostend. Edinburgh clubs again showed that their city was becoming a stronghold of the sport in Scotland when they won three of the four team championships with Paisley Harriers, coached by Robert McSwein, breaking the East monopoly by winning the Boys team title after wins in the Renfrewshire and South Western District championships.

Although beaten by Murray in the Scottish National Jim Alder had displayed top form in other races. He won the English North East Counties race by 1 minute 21 seconds from Olympic Steeplechaser Ernie Pomfret; finished third in an International race at Brussels just 11 seconds behind Olympic 10,000 metres champion Mohammed Gammoudi (Tunisia), and took fourth place in the Hannut International race in Belgium, with A Brown 8 and I McCafferty 11, to give Scotland second team prize behind England, beating Belgium and West Germany among others.

Alder ran true to form in the International at Wellington Racecourse, Ostend, giving 100% effort and displaying great determination, as he did every time he donned a Scottish vest. He was seventh in the record field of 125 competitors at half distance but slipped back eight places to eventually be first Scot in fifteenth position - 40 seconds behind the winner - but 54 seconds in front of champion Fergus Murray 39 who had another disappointing run when it mattered most. The Scottish team finished sixth of the fifteen countries participating, and the growing international reputation of the race was confirmed when New Zealand, competing for the first time, finished third behind England and France. Scotland defeated 1963 team champions Belgium and Morocco, West Germany, Ireland, Italy and Algeria among others. Youth champion Eddie Knox finished fifth in the junior race, just 4 seconds behind third place, and the Junior team, which in preceeding years had finished third in both 1962 and 1963 and runner up in 1964 finished a close up fifth just 10 points behind bronze medallists Morocco.

The Boys championship race, for runners under 15 years of age, which started in 1958, was altered in season 1965-66 into two races. This change was confined initially to District championship level and it was to be a further two years before the split into Senior Boys (13 to 15 years) and Junior Boys (11 to 13 years) was adopted at National Championship level.

Motherwell YMCA continued their domination of the Midland relay championship when winning for the fifth year in a row, Edinburgh Southern recorded a lone victory in the East race, splitting two 3 year series of wins by Teviotdale and Edinburgh University, and Beith retained the South Western title.

Lachie Stewart, who won the inaugural National Boys title in 1958, had been busy studying dentistry at evening classes in the intervening years as a Youth and Junior. With studies successfully completed the Vale of Leven athlete had time to train, and he blossomed forth, with the resultant hard work producing startling performances in track, road and cross country races. Undefeated since the start of the season, except for his second place in the long Morpeth to Newcastle race at New Year, Stewart won the shorter Nigel Barge race in the record time of 22 minutes 05 seconds, a time that would still win the race more than a quarter of a century later. First year Junior Eddie Knox finished runner up in 22 minutes 26 seconds, 3 seconds inside the old record, with brothers Andrew and Alec Brown close behind.

Stewart continued his strong running when winning the Midland title at Renton. He led by 80 yards at half distance and doubled his lead by the finish to defeat Knox, one of the youngest runners in the race, who won the District Junior title. The strong whipcord frame and sharp features of Knox would become familiar in championship events as his talent and strength gained him many successes. Motherwell, trying for their fifth successive title, placed their six men in forty two - to be beaten by 11 points by Victoria Park (6 in 27), who had been defeated by Motherwell the previous year by exactly the margin they won by in 1966.

Fergus Murray, hoping to equal the record of three Eastern District consecutive wins by fellow student Adrian Jackson between 1957-59, had one of his periodical inexplicable, indifferent performances, running well below expected form to captain his team to victory from the rear instead of leading by example. In a race won by Bill Ewing (Aberdeen University), by 10 yards from Chris Elson (Edinburgh University), the Edinburgh students placed their counting six runners inside the first twelve, with Murray 13, shepherding them home in front of him.

Edinburgh Southern were the first Scottish club to compete in the European Club Champions Cup at Arlons, Belgium. In a morass of mud over the entire course Donald Macgregor lost his shoe and had to retire from the race, leaving Southern to make an unprepossessing debut when finishing in seventh place, just one place in front of tail enders Luxembourg.

Murray and his Edinburgh University teammates were in impressive form at the National Championships at Hamilton Racecourse where the trail was now, of necessity, confined to the actual race track inside the boundaries of the ground, with no entry to the rough country by the riverside. Murray, Stewart and Linaker ran together for 4 miles, but then Murray turned on the pressure, increasing his pace and found little reaction from his rivals. He established a lead and, with an impressive display of stamina on a heavy, muddy course, proved he was at his best when running on his own. He won by 70 yards from Stewart, the Inter Counties winner, with Jim Alder (now representing Edinburgh AC) who made a late run for the tape which took him into third position ahead of John Linaker (Pitreavie). Edinburgh University, who had been so successful throughout the season, packed their six men into the first twenty one home to win the National Team Championship for the first ever time. Such was the enormous margin of their victory that they had their entire team home before runners up Victoria Park had their first man finishing in twenty second position. This outstanding performance allowed the students to record a 109 points margin of victory - the largest ever recorded in the history of the event.

Murray's third triumph in a row was only the fifth time that an athlete had achieved this success in the 81 year history of the championship. John Paterson (Watsonians) 1898-1900, Duncan Wright (Clydesdale/Shettleston) 1923-25 and John Suttie Smith (Dundee Thistle/YMCA) 1928-30 had achieved their successes before the Second World War and Edward Bannon (Shettleston) 1952-54 was the sole athlete to accomplish it after the War. However since Bannon recorded his last win there had been 9 different winners of the National title in the period 1955- 63 until Murray started his run of victories. It was no coincidence that, in this period of time without a dominant champion who could act as an inspiration, the Scottish team suffered one of their poorest spells in international competition.

Two of Scotland's top runners in the Sixties. Fergus Murray (131) (Edinburgh University Hares and Hounds) running in bare feet in the 1966 National Senior 7½ mile Championship at Hamilton Park Racecourse which he won from Lachie Stewart (Vale of Leven AAC) on the left.

Ian McCafferty, with a prior victory in an International race at Madrid to his credit, was in majestic form when retaining his Junior title by 49 seconds from Knox, with Edinburgh student Alastair Blamire third. Shettleston's youth policy proved successful when they won the Youths and Boys team championships and took third team place in the Youths race at the English National at Sheffield where Lachie Stewart finished fifth in the Senior race won by Ron Hill.

Finances again dictated that Scotland was represented by only seven Seniors and four Juniors in the International championships at Rabat, Morocco. Ian McCafferty, still a Junior, displayed the true, world beating talent everyone knew he had when he finished fourteenth in the Senior race. He was only second Scot to finish behind Lachie Stewart 12, but that was only part of the story, for it was the breath taking confidence and ability that McCafferty displayed during the race that marked him out as a potential world beater. From the start McCafferty was in the leading group and, running strongly and confidently, the self assured young Scot went into the lead at 2½ miles. Still in the lead at 4 miles, misfortune struck, and he had to stop to take a stone out of his shoe. The stop cost him over 20 places, and he carried on in bare feet catching up six places in the remainder of the race to finish two places behind Stewart and two in front of Jim Alder who ran his usual competent race.

Scotland totalled 202 points, over 100 points better than the previous year, but still finished sixth of thirteen countries. It was galling for the Scots to discover that they were just 18 points behind third place Morocco, especially when National Champion Murray had a poor run to finish in ninetieth place and did not even count in the team of six instead of possibly leading the team home as might have been expected. If Murray had run true to form he would have been up with Stewart, McCafferty and Alder inside the first twenty and the resultant gain of over 50 points from the final counting Scot, J Johnston 78, would have ensured an easy third place for Scotland behind England and France for their first set of medals in over 30 years. Eddie Knox showed his ability in the Junior race when finishing third, just 5 seconds outside the silver medal position, with the Scottish team continuing their good record when finishing third of eight countries, behind England and Belgium.

Since 1926 it had been the custom for Scots athletes to have their first competitive race of the New Year at Beith, and many famous names had won the race up to 1967, when the quality of the field was outstanding. Ian McCafferty won in record time, finishing 32 seconds in front of Lachie Stewart, with the brothers Andrew and Alec Brown finishing third and fourth respectively. The quality of Scottish runners was also evident the next day in the prestigious Morpeth to Newcastle road race where Dick Taylor (Coventry Godiva) won, with Scots runners filling the next 5 places through the efforts of Jim Alder, Lachie Stewart, Mel Edwards, Martin Craven and Donald Macgregor, with Edinburgh University winning the team contest.

McCafferty's winning sequence continued with three victories on successive Saturdays. He won the Nigel Barge race at Maryhill, becoming the first athlete to cover the 4½ mile course in under 22 minutes, with his record time of 21 minutes 58 seconds beating Lachie Stewart by 17 seconds, and then defeated Eddie Knox by over half a minute when he won the Springburn Cup road race at Bishopbriggs a week later. A switch of the Midland Championships from the long time venue at Renton to the rolling grassland of Bellahouston Park suited McCafferty down to the ground, as he proved when defeating over 200 competitors from 16 clubs to win by 68 seconds from the holder Lachie Stewart, with Alec Brown beating older brother Andrew for third place. With their spearhead, leading three runners in the first four home, Motherwell recorded their fifth District team title in six years. Mel Edwards won the East title, and led Aberdeen AAC to their first victory in the team championship, with Irishman David Logue, who was to gain many honours and successes with Edinburgh University and Edinburgh Southern in the future, winning the Junior title.

McCafferty, who regarded the winter season purely as a time to prepare for the summer track season, when the meaningful and important races in International matches and major championships were held, devised a varied, yet interlocking, system of races. He competed on road and cross country to develop strength and took part in shorter indoor track races to retain and sharpen his speed. This arduous and testing schedule was copied by few athletes with any success, and only Ian Stewart, who carried out the same formula of race preparation a few years later, was able to equal McCafferty's success at indoor and outdoor competition.

At the beginning of February he had a busy and successful weekend when he won the AAA Indoor 2 mile title at Cosford in the European and United Kingdom record time of 8 minutes 36.4 seconds, running the final 880 yards in 2 minutes 4 seconds. Twenty four hours later he ran for Scotland in the International cross country race at Hannut, Belgium where he finished second, just 5 seconds behind Gaston Roelants, with Lachie Stewart 4 and Jim Alder 15, giving Scotland second place in the team contest. McCafferty missed the Scottish National Championships at the end of February, preferring to run for Britain against France in an indoor International at Lyons, where he won the 3,000 metres in the British record time of 7 minutes 56.6 seconds. He later finished a disappointing fifth in the European Championship Indoor 3,000 metres race at Prague, clocking only 8 minutes 10 seconds.

The New Zealand team, who had finished third in their first appearance in the 1966 International Championship at Ostend, arranged a European tour of races as acclimatisation for the International race at Barry in Wales. It was agreed they would compete as non counting guests in the Scottish National and, just 48 hours after flying into Scotland from New York, they lined up at Hamilton Racecourse. Eddie Gray finished first in the race, breaking clear at 2 miles and going on to win from Lachie Stewart who was the only Scot to finish in the first seven runners across the line, with New Zealand scoring a comprehensive victory in the International contest by 26 points to the Scottish total of 58 points.

Mike Ryan, formerly of St Modans before emigrating to New Zealand, was still eligible for the Scottish championship and finished second 24 seconds behind Stewart, with Andrew Brown just 1 second behind in third position. Ryan thus became the first athlete to win medals in all four age group races in the Scottish championships, having started his unique collection back in 1958 when again finishing second to Lachie Stewart in the inaugural Boys championship race. Ryan, representing New Zealand, gained marathon bronze medals in the 1966 Commonwealth Games in Jamaica and the 1968 Olympic Games at Mexico.

Edinburgh University, led home by Jim Wight 10, had their full team of 6 runners home in the first 28 across the line to total 109 points. Their winning margin of 144 points over Edinburgh Southern was another record, with Victoria Park finishing third with 260 points. The Junior race, where the age category was changed from 18 to 21 years to 17 to 20 years, was the closest of the day with Eddie Knox and Alastair Blamire locked together throughout the 5 mile race. Neither would give way, whatever the pressure applied by the other until, in the final 100 yards, Knox forced his way ahead for a narrow 1 second victory over Blamire. The Edinburgh student, however, had the satisfaction of leading his teammates to the team title over Shettleston and Springburn to give Edinburgh University a double team triumph only ever achieved in modern time by Victoria Park. Edinburgh became the first Scottish University to win the BUSF team championship when defeating Cambridge and London Universities at London later in the season. Shettleston's

Youth policy successfully continued when they won the Boys team title and finished runners up in the Youth and Junior team contests. Many of these youngsters would be in the Shettleston team which won the Scottish Senior team championship in 1971 and 1972 and went on to win the English National team title.

One week after the Scottish National, Lachie Stewart became the first Scottish athlete since James Flockhart in 1937 to win an individual medal in the English National Championship. Competing at Norwich Stewart finished second in the Senior 9 mile race to Dick Taylor (Coventry Godiva) who had beaten Ian McCafferty in the Junior race 2 years earlier. Stewart outsprinted Barry Rose (New Zealand) with Eddie Gray, winner of the Scottish race 7 days earlier, finishing sixth. However in the International race at Barry, Stewart was in turn outsprinted by Rose for third place and the Scot finished in fourth position, just out of the medals, with Jim Alder 24, being the next Scots finisher in a team which finished fifth of ten countries. Eddie Knox followed McCafferty as Junior International champion in an exciting race. He was in the leading group throughout and edged his way into the lead 400 yards from the line, holding on for a 2 second victory over a Belgian. Scotland finished third in the team championship.

Edward Knox (Springburn Harriers) who won both the Scottish National and International Junior titles in 1967.

Soon after the start of the 1967-68 season there was a widespread outbreak of foot and mouth disease in Scotland and the Union, to stop the spread of the disease by runners, banned all cross country races on grass fields or ploughed land. This ban lasted for 3 months from November 1967 to January 1968 when it was lifted, and permits granted on condition that agreement was obtained from the land owner, or farmer of the land, over which the race would be run. The District Relays were satisfactorily completed before the ban came into force. Motherwell, who were in a class of their own when four men counted but were highly vulnerable when six or eight men were required as in team championships or the Edinburgh to Glasgow race, won the Midland relay title for the seventh and final time and Edinburgh University outclassed their rivals when retaining the East title.

Scottish athletes again were to the fore in the New Year Morpeth to Newcastle race won by Fergus Murray by 40 yards from Jim Alder, with Alastair Blamire fourth ahead of Donald Macgregor. In Scotland, Gareth Bryan - Jones (Edinburgh University) won the Nigel Barge race and Dick Wedlock defeated Jim Brennan (Maryhill) and Pat McLagan (Victoria Park) in the Springburn Cup race. Maryhill Harriers, one of the first clubs to present prizes to veterans over 40 years of age, extended the prize list even further when giving prizes to super veterans over 50 years of age in their Nigel Barge race.

Gareth Bryan-Jones, another of the stream of star runners emerging from Edinburgh University as a result of the tough training routine that all student cross country runners tackled as a matter of course, won the East District title at Dundee. The University team had their six runners home in the first nine to finish for a total of 32 points to defeat Aberdeen 77 points. With Ian McCafferty winning an 8,000 metres race in Minove, Belgium and Lachie Stewart finishing second to Mamo Wolde (Ethiopia) in the International event at Elgoibar the way was open for a new winner in the Midland Championship at Bellahouston Park. Pat McLagan seized his opportunity and won by 60 yards from Jim Brennan, with Shettleston regaining the team championship after a lapse of seven years. In the South Western District there was the emergence of Laurence Spence who won the Senior Boys title - the first of seven District age group titles which he won in the period 1968-73. Spence represented Greenock Glenpark during that period and, after engineering studies at Strathclyde University, went on to compete for Shettleston and Spango Valley AC in the new Western District Championships. There he gained three further District Individual titles, together with many team honours, as well as gaining 8 Scottish International vests in the period 1976-84.

The 1968 National Championships were the last to be held at Hamilton Racecourse, as the lack of suitable changing facilities and the total absence of any washing facilities finally caused the Union to take the annual championships to more suitable venues throughout Scotland. With not a single shower or any running water, hot or cold, in the entire area used for changing, competitors had to let the mud dry on their arms and legs before dressing for the return journey and a welcome wash once they had arrived home.

With Ian McCafferty's wedding being held on the day of the National Championship, Lachie Stewart started favourite to score a repeat victory in the Senior race. But he did not have it all his own way, for Alastair Blamire, runner up in the 1967 Junior championship and one of the most improved runners of the year, gave him a determined challenge throughout the race. The pair were neck and neck throughout the entire $7\frac{1}{2}$ mile race, with Stewart gaining his expected win only in the last few strides to finish one second clear of the gallant Blamire. Running in his first National, Anglo Scot Jim Wright, (Tipton/Edinburgh AC), finished third a further 10 seconds behind. Andrew Brown finished seventh to gain International selection and his twelfth Scottish vest to better the record of eleven held jointly by Dunky Wright and James Flockhart.

Edinburgh University, who had finished second team in the BUSF Championship, won their third team championship in a row by the narrowest possible margin of one point from Aberdeen. This was the closest margin of victory in the National since West of Scotland won in 1901 and 1909 and Bellahouston in 1914. The places of the two teams were as follows:-

1) Edinburgh University H & H (A Blamire 2; G Bryan-Jones 10; D Logue 13; I Hathorn 19; A Wight 24; J Wight 25) Total 93 points.

2) Aberdeen AAC (M Edwards 9; W Ewing 14; P Stewart 16; A Wood 17; S Taylor 18; J Clare 20) Total 94 points.

Another race was added to the championship programme when the Junior Boys race was decided for the first time. The winner of the inaugural event was James Mulvey (Shettleston) with Springburn, already Midland District team champions, winning the National team championship.

The preparations for the ICCU International Championships at Tunis were the most methodical and carefully organised that the Union had ever carried out. Monthly training sessions were held under the supervision of team manager Jim Morton at Cleland Estate, Motherwell where a mock up course, shaped like the one the runners would encounter at Tunis, was available for practice. Arrangements were so precise that, on the day of travel, a training run was arranged for the team at a sports ground near London Airport to alleviate a 2 hour delay between planes. The careful preparations were fully rewarded when the Scottish team returned their best performance in 32 years by finishing a close up fourth of thirteen competing countries. The Scots were not to the fore at the start and the first 5 counters were scattered up to fortieth position at half distance. In the final 3 miles of the race the Scots improved greatly, and Ian McCafferty, who had achieved two International wins in Belgium during a severely restricted competitive season, again showed his great ability when he charged through the field to gain seven places to be first Scot home in tenth place. His achievement was matched by 35 year old team captain Andrew Brown who, after placing 48 in 1966 and 43 in 1967, drove the team onwards while pushing himself into the first 20 finishers. From a team score of 172 points at half distance the Scots gained an average of 6 places per man for a final total of 137 points, just 8 points behind Spain who gained the bronze medals with 129 points. The individual performances in this excellent Scottish team result were:- I McCafferty 10; L Stewart 18; A Brown 19; J Wright 20; J Alder 23; G Bryan-Jones 47. Total 137 points. Brown finished his season when he won the Scottish YMCA title at Cleland Estate, for the twelfth time in 14 years, defeating George Skinner (Bellshill).

Shettleston, with Dick Wedlock back in the fold after his sojurn with Motherwell YMCA, won the Midland Relay title at the beginning of the 1968-69 season, starting a run of five successive wins. Edinburgh University continued their domination when they scored their third consecutive win in the East Relay race. Lachie Stewart won the Nigel Barge race in a personal best of 22 minutes 01 seconds, just 3 seconds outside McCafferty's record, and 15 seconds ahead of Dick Wedlock who went on to win the Springburn race the following week.

It was the end of an era in the South Western championship, with Tom Cochrane (Beith) winning the Senior title for the fifth time in a row and his seventh title in total. He defeated John Ferguson (Ayr Seaforth) and Dick Hodelet, who led Greenock Glenpark to the team championship defeating Beith. Fergus Murray, in his first cross country race of the winter, finished third in the East District championship behind Adrian Weatherhead (Heriot Watt University) and Donald Macgregor, who led Edinburgh Southern to team victory in the absence of the top Edinburgh University runners. The students, as Scottish champions, were competing in Belgium where they finished fifth in the European Champion Clubs event at Arlons led by seventh placed Dave Logue.

With the international success over track and cross country of Scottish runners like Ian McCafferty, Lachie Stewart, Jim Alder and Dick Wedlock and the excellent showing of the Scottish team in the International Championship, invitations rolled in to the Union for Scottish runners to compete in International races throughout the Continent. At the end of January the quality and strength of Scottish cross country was fully evidenced by the fact that two Scottish teams competed on the Continent on the same weekend - at Hannut in Belgium and Tunis in North Africa. Lachie Stewart, Jim Alder and Dick Wedlock ran at Hannut and Alastair Blamire, Donald MacGregor and Jim Wright ran at Tunis. When it is considered that Ian McCafferty, Fergus Murray, Gareth Bryan-Jones and Bill Mullett stayed at home the great Scottish array of talent at that time is fully realised.

Lachie Stewart defeated Marianno Haro (Spain) in the Elgoibar International race before being struck down by 'flu. He had barely recovered by the time of the National Championships at Duddingston Park in Edinburgh where the ground was icy, rutted and rock hard after a bad spell of weather. Still suffering from the after effects of the 'flu Stewart had no chance of achieving his third successive win, and finished a disappointing tenth. Dick Wedlock shared the lead with Alder for three of the five laps before striking out on his own over the final 3 miles to score a well deserved victory. His only other National win had been in the Boys race 8 years earlier and, in the intervening years he had the misfortune to record good performances, which would have won races in any other era, behind such illustrious names as McCafferty, Murray and Stewart. Alder faded in the last couple of miles and Fergus Murray sped through to take second place 8 seconds behind the winner, with Anglo Scot steeplechaser Bill Mullett (Shettleston) finishing third, a further 4 seconds behind.

Shettleston gained another two individual titles when Norman Morrison and James Mulvey won the Junior and Senior Boys events respectively. The Shettleston successes continued with wins in the Junior and Youths team championships and second places in the Senior (behind Edinburgh) and the Junior Boys (behind Law and District) team championship events.

The International championships, for the first time since 1960, were staged in Scotland and the Union, in conjunction with Clydebank Town Council, staged them at Clydebank. A hilly, picturesque course was laid out around Dalmuir Park and the adjacent golf course, that was acclaimed as the most testing course over which the championship had been held for a good number of years. Without any of the bad luck that had affected his performance in previous International championships, Ian McCafferty finished third for the best individual performance by a Scot since Flockhart's 1937 victory in Brussels. Always up with the leaders he surprised everyone with his lion-hearted approach to the event, refusing to give way to anyone throughout the race, resisting every challenge to his forward position and finishing strongly to take the bronze medal ahead of England's Mike Tagg, a future International champion. England won the team championship from France and Belgium, with New Zealand fourth ahead of Scotland in the field of 13 countries. Lachie Stewart 20 was closely followed home by Fergus Murray 23 who made a remarkable comeback as third Scottish counter in a race where he had previously disappointed with a series of dreadful runs in the past.

Ian McCafferty (Motherwell YMCA Harriers and Law and District AC) leading Tijou of France in the 1969 International championship at Clydebank, where he gained the Individual bronze medal.

1970 to 1979

There were many momentous happenings during the decade which affected Scottish Cross Country, both domestically and internationally, and the effect of these changes is still felt today. Domestically it was a decade of change in the National Championship programme and in the format of District administration. For 45 years the sport had been administered at District level by three District Committees - the East, Midlands and South Western Committees. This lasted until 1975, when the Midlands and the South Western Districts amalgamated to form the new Western District and the Northern District was created from the old North of Scotland AAA, greatly extending and improving opportunities for the control and development of the sport.

The Fifties and Sixties had seen the inauguration of the Senior and Junior Boys Championships, in a National Championship programme where the last innovation had been the introduction of the National Youths Championship race in 1933. Three new relay championships were created in the Seventies - the National Senior and Young Athletes Cross Country Relay Championships and the National Six Stage road relay championship - in innovative moves which greatly increased the championship racing programme.

Internationally the change of control of the International Championship, from the International Cross Country Union to the International Amateur Athletic Federation, was a take over which had been a long time in preparation and long been dreaded by the Union. It opened up the cosy, restricted ICCU International Championship, contested by teams from the four Home Countries, a few European and North African teams and the adventurous New Zealanders, into an I.A.A.F. World Championship event which rapidly encompassed teams from all the continents. The new, enlarged World Championship came to Scotland in 1978 and, after a great deal of dissent and trouble, was eventually staged successfully in Bellahouston Park, Glasgow.

The numbers of competing athletes and clubs grew throughout the decade, and veteran athletics, for those runners over 40 years of age and also for those of a much greater age, also developed through the efforts of the Scottish Veteran Harriers Club. The club promoted age group running, and encouraged promoters of both road and cross country races to include age category classes in open competition for the growing band of runners who did not let advancing age drive them from the sport, but continued enjoying running in their own age group races.

The National Senior team championship was dominated by Edinburgh clubs, with only Shettleston, who won two titles at the start of the decade and another one in 1977 (stopping Edinburgh AC's attempt to equal the record of six successive titles), interrupting the successes of Edinburgh AC and Edinburgh Southern. Individually the brilliance of star runners, such as Ian McCafferty, Lachie Stewart and Fergus Murray, faded from the scene. But the emergence of Edinburgh architect Andy McKean, who won the National Individual title four times, compensated to some degree and his strong leadership of Edinburgh AC to numerous team triumphs was one of the highlights of the era.

The flow of talent through the age group championships continued with such talented youngsters as Ronnie MacDonald, Jim Brown, Lawrie Reilly, Allister Hutton, Nat Muir, John Graham and Graham Williamson all winning National titles in Youth and Junior championships.

In the 1969/70 season Edinburgh Southern scored a convincing victory in the Eastern District relay championships, recording the first of seven consecutive wins to better the series of six wins by Edinburgh Northern Harriers between 1930 and 1935. Shettleston scored their expected win in the Midland relay for the second of a run of five in a row victories, and Beith Harriers retained the South Western relay title for the last of 11 titles they won in the 46 year history of the District.

Scots runners again dominated the annual New Year race from Morpeth to Newcastle with Jim Alder, showing the form that was to lead to the Marathon silver medal in the 1970 Commonwealth Games at Edinburgh that summer, winning from Fergus Murray and Jim Wright. Dick Wedlock won the Beith New Year cross country race, but finished runner up to Lachie Stewart in the Nigel Barge road race at Maryhill the following Saturday. Stewart raced round the $4\frac{1}{2}$ mile course to win in 21 minutes 54 seconds - 4 seconds faster than the course record held by Ian McCafferty, who on this occasion finished eighth, almost a minute behind the winner. Adrian Weatherhead, who had earlier won the annual SCCU v Scottish Universities contest, finished in third position. In the 1970 Midland championships at Lenzie Ian McCafferty, in one of his rare outings over the country, ran away from a field of over 200 competitors to win his fourth District title in seven years. He raced into the lead at the start and, with just a mile gone, had a lead of almost 100 yards. He increased his lead on every lap and eventually won by the wide margin of 72 seconds from a stunned Eddie Knox, with third placed John Myatt leading Strathclyde University to their first ever team victory. In the Youth race future cross country stars were in action, with Ronnie MacDonald (Monkland) winning by 5 seconds from Jim Brown (Bellshill). Alastair Blamire won the Eastern District title to become the sixth Edinburgh University student since the Second World War to win the race. He finished 80 yards in front of Fergus Murray (Edinburgh Southern), winner 5 years earlier, who led his club to the first of six consecutive team victories - bettering their own record of five wins in a row between 1957 and 1961. Bill Stoddart of Greenock Wellpark won his first South Western title and led his club to the team championship.

In the early Seventies Scottish distance runners were among the best in Britain and Europe, and the Union received many invitations for teams to compete in International cross country races throughout Europe. These races allowed our top runners to test themselves against the best runners in Europe and prepare properly for the National and International championship events. The glamour, that was once the exclusive property of track and field stars in the summer International matches, was now available in the winter, and the resulting trips to compete in foreign countries encouraged the best distance runners to take cross country running seriously throughout the winter. Running for Scotland at that time were such Olympic and Commonwealth Games internationals as Lachie Stewart, Ian McCafferty, Jim Alder, Fergus Murray, Dick Wedlock, Donald Macgregor and Gareth Bryan - Jones with other fine runners such as Alastair Blamire, Norman Morrison, Bill Mullett, Eddie Knox, Adrian Weatherhead and Jim Wright all strong enough to gain selection for Scottish teams competing on the Continent. Lachie

Stewart was the most successful and consistent Scots runner on the Continent with numerous wins, especially in Spain, where the Spanish spectators nicknamed him "El Lachie". Stewart won two International races in Spain that winter, at Madrid and the Juan Muguerza race at Elgoibar in Northern Spain, and finished fourth at San Sebastian with Dick Wedlock in sixth place. Such was the depth of top class talent in Scottish Cross Country at that time that, on the same day, two Scottish teams competed with success on the Continent. Alastair Blamire finished second at Bilbao with a Scots win in the team contest and Jim Alder finished fifth in a high class international race at Hannut, Belgium with the Scots team finishing third.

The 1970 National Championships, now back to a routine of being held alternately in the East and West of Scotland after their long sojurn at Hamilton Park Racecourse, were held at a misty, wet Ayr Racecourse. Jim Alder, undoubtedly the most patriotic Anglo Scot to run for, and compete in, Scotland, while living outside the country, was at his best in this race. Always in the leading group over the heavy, tiring racecourse turf he went into the lead at half distance, shadowed by steeplechaser Bill Mullett and his Shettleston teammate Dick Wedlock. Alder's strength and will to win proved decisive and he forged ahead of the Shettleston pair to win by 50 yards for his second National title, 8 years after his first success in 1962. Wedlock finished strongly to take second place, 3 seconds ahead of Mullett, with Edinburgh Southern winning the team title from city rivals Edinburgh AC and Shettleston.

Former triple champion Fergus Murray finished fourteenth, good enough to be included in Southern's winning team but not to gain selection for Scotland's team for the International Championship at Vichy. His speed had been blunted by a fast marathon at Kobe, Japan, where, after travelling half way across the world at just 5 days notice, he improved his personal best by 26 seconds with an excellent run of 2 hours 18 minutes 04 seconds for second position in a top class International field.

In a closely contested Youths race Ronnie MacDonald confirmed his Midland District win by taking the title 4 seconds in front of Jim Brown, who just held off a late challenge from South Western champion Lawrie Spence (Greenock Glenpark), with both runners sharing the same time.

Public Transport strikes disrupted the Scots team travel to the International Championships at Vichy, necessitating three separate flights and two bus journeys in a tiring journey to France which did much to cause the disappointing Scots performances in the actual race. Ian McCafferty did not finish, leaving Lachie Stewart to be first Scot home in twelfth place - well ahead of Bill Mullett 25, Jim Alder 31 with Adrian Weatherhead 42, Dick Wedlock 45 and Norman Morrison 46 finishing in a bunch to close in the scoring six and give Scotland a total of 201 points for fifth position out of the thirteen competing countries.

Scotland's fifth place was another example of the "so near, yet so far" syndrome which had affected the National team in the past few years in the International championship. The expected high finishing position from McCafferty, lost because he dropped out, was symptomatic of the bad fortune which always seemed to affect the Scottish team in the International. The scoring six runners required to finish in the top 25 or 30 runners home to guarantee a medal winning team score, but, time and time again, something always happened to one of the stars which prevented the team getting in the first 3 teams to finish. The previous team positions show how close Scotland came to gaining that elusive team medal: 1966

(6); 1967 (5); 1968 (4); 1969 (5) and fifth again in 1970.

The 1970/71 season was a triumph for Shettleston Harriers who swept the board in domestic competition and also became the first club since Victoria Park (1952) to win the English National team championship. The Commonwealth Games, held at Meadowbank Stadium the previous summer, overshadowed the winter season long after they were over. The Games cast their shadow of success on cross country races, with track medallists Lachie Stewart (10,000 metres gold medal) and Ian McCafferty (5,000 metres silver medal) not having their usual successful winter season.

After Edinburgh Southern, Shettleston and Greenock Wellpark had retained their respective District relay titles, Shettleston won the Edinburgh to Glasgow relay race despite Stewart performing below his usual high level. Stewart, who became Scotland's national hero after his 10,000 metres victory on the opening day of the Games, ran out of mental drive and competitive spirit due to the aftermath celebrations of the Games. His fame led him to appear in anti-smoking adverts and television commercials, attend banquets and receptions, make public appearances and give numerous newspaper and magazine interviews, generally leaving little time for the hard training he required to maintain race fitness.

However new young stars were rising to the fore, with schoolboys Ronnie MacDonald and Jim Brown mixing with Scotland's top seniors and trouncing them in important races. 18 year old Ron MacDonald, Scottish and English Junior 1500 metres champion, won the Nigel Barge Road Race in 22 minutes 04 seconds, beating Commonwealth Games 10,000 metres representative Dick Wedlock by 3 seconds, and he also won the National Junior title. His constant rival, Jim Brown from Bellshill, was discovered by cross country enthusiast John Waddell at a local school sports meeting and encouraged to join the local Bellshill Harriers club where his talent was encouraged and brought to fruition.

The precocious Brown startled his senior rivals when winning the Midland Championship race at Stirling University in his first year as a Junior. While older, heavier rivals sank in the thick, clinging mud the lightweight Brown skimmed over the surface to win by 60 yards from Norman Morrison, who led Shettleston (5 in the first 11 home) to the team title. Brown won both the Senior and Junior titles, a feat he was to repeat for the next 2 years in which he was eligible for Junior honours. In the Junior Boys race Nat Muir (Shettleston) recorded his first title-winning victory, and a report of the race noted that "Muir scampered over the line as if he could have kept going all day" and forecast for the Shettleston youngster " a number of victories in future years".

Adrian Weatherhead (Octavians) won the Eastern Championship from former winners Fergus Murray and Gareth Bryan-Jones (both Edinburgh Southern) who, with 5 in the first 9 runners home, retained the team championship. Bill Stoddart, who became the oldest runner to gain a first time cap for Scotland when he ran in the 1970 International Championship, won the South Western title for the second time at Beith and led Greenock Wellpark to team victory.

The 1971 Postal Strike disrupted entries to the National Championships. The Union decreed that telephone entries would be accepted by the convener, in place of the usual official entry forms, and that entries would also be accepted on the day at a cost of 2/6 (12½p) for each individual runner and £1 for a team of 12 runners with 6 to count. In spite of all the difficulties, entries were 300 up on the previous year, with a total of 1524 entries in the 5 championship races. The championships at Bellahouston Park, which were the first ones staged in Glasgow for almost 50 years, were held over metric distances for the first ever time, with the Senior 7½ miles race becoming 12,000 metres in distance. The Union made another breakthrough when obtaining the first commercial sponsorship from confectionery manufacturer Lees of Coatbridge, who produced macaroon bars and snowballs for distribution among competitors and officials.

Defending champion Jim Alder, who had recently finished second to English International Trevor Wright in the E.C.C.U. Northern championship race, was confident at the start, but received a surprise challenge from Edinburgh University student Alastair Blamire. Alder went into the lead after 2 miles, shadowed by Blamire, and the two leaders were together until the last lap, when Alder opened a 10 yard gap which he widened to 40 yards at the finish. Dick Wedlock finished third, over 200 yards behind, but led Shettleston, 5 runners in the first 15 home, to a clear team victory over Edinburgh Southern.

Monkland clubmates Ronnie MacDonald and Jim Brown disputed the lead throughout the Junior 10,000 metres race, with MacDonald just gaining the verdict from Brown, who shared the winning time, with Ian Gilmour (Birmingham University) third a further 11 seconds behind. Nat Muir finished third in the Junior Boys race, just 2 seconds behind Sam Elder (Victoria Park) and Shettleston proved the top club in the championship, providing the winning team in the Senior, Junior and Senior Boys races and third in the Youths team contest.

After their Scottish National team championship victory Shettleston felt strong enough to challenge for the English National team title at Norwich. Competing in a field of over 1800 runners the Shettleston men ran brilliantly to win the title - the first Scottish club victory since Victoria Park AAC won 19 years earlier. With a splendid spearhead of Alastair Blamire 11; Lachie Stewart 19; Dick Wedlock 24 and Norman Morrison 32, Shettleston supporters saw Henry Summerhill cross the line 65 and then had an agonising wait for Tom Grubb 131, to close in the team for a total of 282 points, with Tipton Harriers finishing a close up second with 289 points. Jim Brown, who had earlier finished runner up in two International Junior races in Spain, finished third in the Youths race.

Ian McCafferty, selected for Scotland's team for the International championship on past performances, dropped out of the party at the last minute due to illness. The team had a very tiring and delay ridden journey to Spain and this, together with stomach upsets which struck various runners, ensured that the potential and the actuality of performance of the Scots were poles apart. Rail, hailstones and gales spoiled the International championship at San Sebastian and heavy, sticky mud slowed the runners throughout the race. Commonwealth 5,000 metres gold medalist Ian Stewart, in his first appearance for Scotland, finished ninth to lead the Scottish team to seventh position in the team contest. Stewart was followed home by Dick Wedlock 24 and Norman Morrison 25 with Scottish Champion Jim Alder, who had been the most consistent Scot throughout the winter when winning both SCCU matches against the Northern Counties, and the British Army and the North Eastern Counties, finishing 38, ahead of Alastair Blamire 58 and a despondent Lachie Stewart 60.

In the Junior International Jim Brown, after leading for most of the race, was overtaken by Nick Rose and Ray Smedley (both England) in the final straight and

Shettleston Harriers team which won both the Scottish and English National team championships in 1971. Back row from left; W. Scally, H. Summerhill, R. Wedlock, N. Morrison and A. Blamire. Front row from left; L. Meneely, T. Patterson, L. Stewart and T. Grubbs.

won the bronze medal. With backing from Ian Gilmour 13 and Ronnie MacDonald 14, Scotland finished second to England in the team championship for the best Junior performance in 7 years. Brown also won the Scottish Schools Senior title at Cleland Estate, defeating Ronnie MacDonald and Paul Bannon - two Scottish International athletes of the future.

Another great International of the future Allister Hutton, who became the first Scot to win the London Marathon, finished third in the Scottish Boys Brigade championship behind Sam Alexander (Glasgow) and Lawrie Spence (Greenock). Hutton, who had earlier won the Eastern District Youth title, started running after discovering that athletics was one of the challenges in the Duke of Edinburgh's Award Scheme, and quickly joined Edinburgh Southern after his initial success in Boys Brigade competition.

Scotland's strength in international cross country was probably at its highest in season 1971/72, with regular victories in Continental races; Ian McCafferty winning his first (and only) National title; the youthful Jim Brown at his most commanding over the country and the two Commonwealth gold medal Stewarts, Ian at 5,000 metres and Lachie at 10,000 metres, concentrating on the winter sport as preparation for the Olympic Games in Munich in the summer.

In the early season District relay championships, Edinburgh Southern and Shettleston retained their titles, winning for the fourth and fifth consecutive times respectively, with Ayr Seaforth AC winning the South Western title for the first time in 9 years. Dick Wedlock had one of his best country runs when finishing second in the European champion clubs race at Arlon in Belgium. In a race won by European

Marathon champion Karl Lismont (Liege AC), Wedlock finished runner up 15 seconds behind. He was backed up by Lachie Stewart - recovering from his annual bout of flu in fifth place - 17 year old Paul Bannon 11 (the youngest runner in the race) and Henry Summerhill 23, for Shettleston to record the best ever Scottish performance in this prestigious event with second place behind Liege AC, but ahead of Darmstadt AC (West Germany). At this time the top ranked Scottish athletes were among the most sought after in Europe, with the Union receiving invitations to send teams to all the important International events on the Continent. In the early weeks of 1972 Scotland gained three international wins with Ian Stewart winning at Chartres, France, after finishing runner up to Roelants at Hannut, Belgium, and Lachie Stewart gaining two victories in Spain.

The first race for "El Lachie" was the Juan Muguerza at Elgoibar in Northern Spain to which there was a nightmare prelude of travelling. The plane was rerouted to Madrid due to storms, instead of landing at Bilbao, and the team then had a horrendous 6 hour car journey over snow covered mountain roads, arriving at their destination at 4-30am, allowing little sleep before the race. Stewart displayed little evidence of his tiring journey when winning with his usual fighting finish, with Dick Wedlock in fourth place. The following weekend Stewart made another 2,000 mile round trip to San Sebastian to win the 8,000 metres race over a sea of mud, finishing inches in from of Jack Lane (England). Jim Brown won the Junior race at San Sebastian from top Continental and North African rivals to establish himself as one of the favourites for the International Junior title.

Domestically the District Championships were an important prelude to the National Championships. Sam Downie (Falkirk Victoria) won the Eastern title, after winning the Junior title the previous year, and John Ferguson (Ayr Seaforth) won the South Western event, with first year Junior Lawrie Spence winning his fifth age group title when becoming the Junior Champion. The Midland title, in the absence of L Stewart, R Wedlock and R MacDonald on International duty in Spain, became a two man race between defending champion Jim Brown and Ian McCafferty. After the first mile the two were out on their own. McCafferty forged ahead on the flat, fast sections of the course at Bellshill and Brown made it up on the hilly ground. Brown eventually proved the stronger to win by 30 yards from McCafferty, with Alastair Blamire finishing a distant third over 300 yards behind, leading Shettleston to retain the team title ahead of Clydesdale, who were led home by sixth placed Allan Faulds.

The National Championship, held for the first time at Currie, was the occasion for McCafferty to display that he was a world class cross country runner in addition to his exploits on indoor and outdoor tracks. He did not, as so often in the past, start favourite for the title. He had dead heated for first place with Jim Alder in the inaugural Carnethy Hill race at Penicuik just 7 days earlier, in a surprising display of strength and agility over the tough course. At that time hill running was regarded as simply an extension of cross country and not the specialist sport it has developed into nowadays.

As so often happened with McCafferty, his indifferent, disappointing early season form was no pointer to his true potential, and he recorded a brilliant performance when it was least expected. Faced with Jim Alder, out for his third successive Senior title, McCafferty made a determined effort from the start, and built up a 50 yard lead by half distance. Over the next 3 miles Alder made up the gap and, with 1 mile to go, had established a 40 yard lead. A big ploughed field had to be crossed just half a mile from the finish and here, contrary to all expectations, McCafferty proved the stronger. He closed the gap on a tiring Alder, and opened up on the flat, grassy surface of the finishing straight to sprint home to a 6 second victory over the defending champion in one of the best and most exciting finishes seen in the championship for many years. Led by A Blamire 3, and L Stewart 5, Shettleston placed their six counters in the first 37 home to win by 91 points from Edinburgh AC. Jim Brown, now a member of Monkland Harriers and coached, like clubmate Ronnie MacDonald, by Tom Callaghan, won the Junior title by 29 seconds from Paul Bannon (Shettleston).

This performance gained McCafferty his seventh International vest for Scotland inside eight years, and this consistency of performance is often overlooked by many who principally regarded him as purely a track runner. His cross country achievements included his international Junior championship victory at Dublin and gaining the individual bronze medal at Clydebank - the only individual medal won by a Scot in post war international competition to that date. But it is really for his performances on the track that McCafferty will be remembered.

Although becoming the first home Scot to break the four minute mile barrier at the age of 24 with his run of 3 minutes 56.8 seconds at Reading, setting a Scottish record which lasted for 6 years until broken by Frank Clement (3 minutes 55.0 seconds at Stockholm in 1975), McCafferty was at his best over the longer distances of 3,000 metres/2 miles and 5,000 metres/3miles. He was just 21 years old when setting his first Scottish 3 mile record at the 1966 Commonwealth Games in the sweltering heat of Kingston, Jamaica. There he finished fifth in 13 minutes 12.2 seconds, after sharing the lead with Kenyan Kipchoge Keino and Australian world record holder Ron Clarke for most of the race. He was a race winner, as well as adept at recording super fast times, and in international matches for Scotland and Great Britain between 1966 and 1972, McCafferty had an undefeated record.

With his eyes always on the wider International horizon he did not give great importance to mere Scottish track titles, yet won 3 titles at 1 mile between 1965 and 1967 and gained his only 5,000 metres title in 1971. In 1967 he blossomed to full world class with a series of record breaking runs over 2 and 3 miles. He twice broke his own Scottish 3 mile record with runs of 13 minutes 09.8 seconds behind Ron Clarke in the AAA Championships and 13 minutes 06.4 seconds, again behind the Australian at Dublin, which was also a United Kingdom record. Over 2 miles McCafferty set a United Kingdom and European Indoor record of 8 minutes 36.4 seconds at Cosford in 1967, and improved to 8 minutes 33.2 seconds outdoors at the British Games at White City, London.

The 1970 Commonwealth Games at Meadowbank Stadium, Edinburgh included the 5,000 metres race, for which McCafferty is best remembered, where he came closest to fulfilling his immense potential. Earlier that summer the Law runner became the first Scot and only the second Briton, to better 13 minutes 30 seconds for 5,000 metres, when finishing runner up in 13 minutes 29.6 seconds to Dick Taylor (UK record of 13 minutes 26.2 seconds) in the British Games at Meadowbank. In the Games 5,000 metres the race was fast throughout and with 2 laps to go McCafferty went into the lead, forcing the pace such that only fellow Scot Ian Stewart and defending champion Kipchoge Keino (Kenya) could stay with him. Stewart went into the lead at the start of the final lap and McCafferty shadowed him until the 200 metres point where he tried to take the lead. Stewart held off the challenge, and although McCafferty surged again unsuccessfully in the finishing straight, he could only finish second to take the silver medal behind Stewart. Stewart's winning time of 13 minutes 22.8 seconds was a new European, United Kingdom and Scottish National record, while McCafferty's run of 13 minutes 23.4 seconds - in spite of being the fourth fastest time ever run at that time - gained him only a Scottish Native record, which still stands 20 years later.

The Olympic year of 1972 was to be McCafferty's last big year. In the Olympic Trials at the AAA Championships at Crystal Palace David Bedford front ran his way to victory in the magnificent time of 13 minutes 17.2 seconds - just 0.6 seconds outside Ron Clarke's world record. Ian McCafferty recorded 13 minutes 19.8 seconds for a new National record and the third fastest time ever. The Olympic Games at Munich were a total disappointment to McCafferty. Qualifying easily in his 5,000 metres heat in 13 minutes 38.2 seconds, after a swift last lap sprint of 54.7 seconds, McCafferty had too much time to think and doubt between the heat and race final. Always a worrier about his races, he had anxiety and sleeplessness to contend with in the run up to the final. Running without the confidence that his fitness and proven ability should have inspired, he was a shadow of his true self and finished only thirteenth in a race he was fully capable of winning.

He never raced again as an amateur, either on the track or over cross country, and turned professional in January 1973. This was a total failure and a decision he bitterly regretted, but he was to remain in the athletic wilderness for more than $3\frac{1}{2}$ years before applying for reinstatement as an amateur in 1976. His request, which the SAAA approved upon receiving his application, restored him to the amateur sport, and he now coaches his daughter.

After the Scottish Championships at Currie, Shettleston travelled to Sutton Coldfield to defend their English National Senior team title. A freak snow blizzard, which raged throughout the championship, was of such severity that one of the race officials collapsed and died on arrival at the hospital. The conditions ruined the race as a contest, with runners collapsing from exposure and exhaustion. In dreadful conditions of snow, hail and extreme cold, Lachie Stewart and other Shettleston runners dropped out, requiring medical attention, and Shettleston did not finish a team of 6 runners in the event. Conditions were totally different at the International Championship at Coldham's Common in Cambridge. Bright sunshine and dry, firm underfoot conditions on a rolling parkland course, with just one stretch of ploughed land, made it ideal terrain for Scotland's team. The team, unusually, ran as selected, with no drop outs from illness or injury, and was quoted as being one of the favoured countries to win the International team title in the last race held under ICCU control.

After many years of discussion and negotiation, the opposition by the four Home Countries had been overcome. The recommendation by the IAAF cross country committee that "the championship become a true world championship race open to all the countries in the world" had been approved by the IAAF Council. Consequently the existing set up, whereby a core of ICCU member countries competed as a right and invited other countries to compete in their race, was abandoned after the 1972 race in England, with the IAAF taking control thereafter.

The Scots position as favourites was fully justified. They included two 1970 Commonwealth Gold medallists in Ian and Lachie Stewart, two silver medallists Ian

McCafferty and Jim Alder, Dick Wedlock (a sub 29 minute Commonwealth Games 10,000 metres runner) and Alastair Blamire (a G B International steeplechaser). The team was completed by University runners Andy McKean and John Myatt and Anglo Scot Jim Wright. With the knowledgeable, impartial "Athletics Weekly" tipping the Scottish team as medallists, the national fervour of acclaim at home, where they were regarded as sure winners, was fully understandable. However it seemed that the higher that a Scottish team was built up as favourites for success, the greater was their fall on their actual performance. Just as 6 years later, when the Scottish national football team was frenetically acclaimed on their departure to the World Cup Finals in Argentina, so was the cross country team ever hopefully sent forth across the border to their race in England.

And the results were the same on each sporting occasion! Just as the Scots failed dismally in Argentina, so did the runners disappoint the high hopes placed in them at Cambridge. Scotland, with strong teams, occasionally ventured near the brink of greatness, but too often they turned away from grasping their opportunities. The experienced star runners usually buckled under the weight of expectations and produced performances well below their capabilities, such that Scotland's post war team position never bettered fourth place, even in the restricted competition of the ICCU championship.

Ian Stewart finished third at Cambridge, just 37 seconds behind the winner Gaston Roelants of Belgium, to gain the bronze medal and equal the best ever post war position recorded by McCafferty 3 years earlier. However the back up anticipated from Ian McCafferty and Lachie Stewart - both expected to be placed in the first 10 runners home - failed to materialise. Ever reliable, steady Jim Alder was the next man to finish in twentieth position, followed by L Stewart 27, A Blamire 36, A McKean 44, and R Wedlock 71 for a team total of 201 points. Ian McCafferty, way back in 79 position, was not even a team counter! England won the team championship with 84 points, followed by Morocco 94 points and Belgium 140 points with Scotland 201 points, finishing fourth ahead of Spain, France and Finland.

Team manager Jim Morton, who had hoped for so much with his star studded team, and still fallen short even of a bronze medal, said "This should have been Scotland's year. It can only be called a bloody disaster. When the established men let you down, and can give no explanation afterwards, then there's something far wrong. It's time for a major rethink on the Senior men's team".

One consolation for Scotland was the running of Jim Brown in the Junior Championship. He progressed from his 1971 bronze medal position to gain a well deserved silver medal. After leading for much of the race in his usual impetuous, forward running style, he was in third position approaching the finish. However, when Francesco Fava (Italy) staggered and fell with exhaustion in the final 50 yards, Brown sprinted home into second place and led the Scottish team to fifth place in the team contest.

This was Scotland's last real chance to win the International team title as, with the IAAF championship being open to the world, the number of competitors grew larger each year and Scottish finishing positions - both individual and team - grew progressively worse. New countries, from Eastern Europe and Africa, took the race seriously, and although the individual genius of Ian Stewart gained a Scottish individual victory at Rabat, Morocco in 1974, within a decade the best Scots finishing position was to deteriorate to outside the first 100 finishers.

The following season, 1972/73, was a momentous one for Scottish Cross Country. Scotland competed for the first time in the IAAF World championship, Ian McCafferty abandoned amateur sport to become a professional runner, Jim Brown won the International Junior title, Norman Morrison won the European champion clubs race and a major new sponsor, Coatbridge Town Council, was found to back the National championships.

Early season competition saw Edinburgh Southern winning their fifth consecutive District relay title in their record run of seven successes, Victoria Park ending Shettleston's long run of victories in the Midland event and Ayr Seaforth retaining the South Western title.

Norman Morrison of Shettleston, a 1500 metres/1 mile track runner who, like Ian Stewart and Ian McCafferty, used the winter season principally as preparation for his summer track competition, had his best ever year. He won the Nigel Barge road race in the record time of 21 minutes 51 seconds, followed home at 5 second intervals by Paul Bannon, Douglas Gunstone and Dick Wedlock. He followed this success by becoming the first Scot to win the European champion clubs race at Arlon with Lachie Stewart finishing third. Shettleston showed their great strength when again finishing second, just 2 points behind the holders Liege AC, and 20 points in front of English champions Tipton Harriers.

Jim Brown achieved the Junior/Senior title double for the third year in a row when winning the Midland championship in a solo run at Bellshill. After the first lap Brown assumed complete control of the race and won by 17 seconds from Alan Partridge (East Kilbride), with SAAA 800 metres champion David McMeekin (Victoria Park) in third place. A resurgent Clydesdale Harriers, led by fourth placed Douglas Gemmell, won the team title from Victoria Park to record their first ever District victory, and their first important senior team success since winning the National Senior team championship 66 years earlier. Lawrie Spence (Greenock Glenpark) won the South Western title at Kilmarnock, defeating elder brother Cameron who represented Greenock Wellpark, with the Glenpark club winning three of the four team titles. Edinburgh University architectural student Andy McKean, who had won two of the three Eastern District League races, won the East District title at Currie by 24 seconds from Ian Elliot who led Edinburgh Southern to the Senior team championship.

Over a snow covered course at Drumpellier Park in Coatbridge, 1200 runners competed in the National Championships. Pre-race favourite Andy McKean, with a big build up of Eastern District title, Scottish and British Universities wins and impressive runs in International races throughout the Continent, was in fine form over the open, rolling course broken only by a short, steep hill at the end of each lap. McKean took the lead on the third of the five laps, with only the surprising Adrian Weatherhead challenging him. He eventually won the first of his four National titles by 100 yards from Weatherhead who had 9 seconds to spare from Lachie Stewart, suffering from post influenza effects, with Norman Morrison and former English National Youth champion Colin Falconer (Springburn) finishing at one second intervals behind Stewart. Edinburgh AC, led by sixth placed Jim Alder, packed their first 4 finishers in 12 to win their first ever National team title defeating Shettleston, the holders, by 44 points. After promising so much, without ever winning the team championship, Edinburgh AC won for the four consecutive years the Championships were held at Drumpellier Park and on 5 occasions in the period from 1973 to 1978.

Jim Brown, after falling on slushy snow at the start, recovered well to retain the Junior title by 60 yards from Lawrie Spence, and lead Monkland to the team title. Mark Watt (Shettleston) became the first person to win individual titles in three age groups consecutively. After his 1970 Junior Boys win, he won the Senior Boys title in 1971 and 72, and his victory in the Youths race at Coatbridge gave him his fourth consecutive title. Nat Muir, still growing in stature and strength, finished runner up in the Senior Boys race behind Alan Adams (Clydesdale).

The first World Cross Country Championships under the control of the IAAF were held at Waregem Racecourse outside Ghent, Belgium, with 20 countries taking part. The event was a personal triumph for Jim Brown, who had considered his second place at Cambridge to be a failure, and was bitterly disappointed that it had been his final appearace in the International Junior race. However the IAAF changed the qualifying conditions, such that runners "had to be under 21 years of age on the day of the race"; giving Brown at 20 years and 5 months, a third and final chance to win the elusive title. Brown went into the lead at the start of the second of three laps of the 7,000 metres course, running with his head tilted back in his familiar fashion and with that toothy grin resulting from his usual practice of removing his false teeth and handing them to the team manager with the words "hold these for me till the race is over".

Brown opened up a 10 yard gap over Leon Schots (Belgium) on the second lap and, on the final lap, he was away - running free to increase his lead to a winning 40 yards at the finish with fast finishing Cianeros Haro (Spain), whose older brother Mariano finished runner up in the Senior race, running into second place ahead of Schots. Brown thus became the oldest ever World Junior Champion, and achieved a full set of individual medals - bronze, silver and gold - in successive years. The IAAF, in 1974, changed the ruling on Junior age qualification, requiring athletes to "be under 20 years of age in the year of competition." This meant that the oldest a Junior winner could be in future was 19 years 3 months as the race was always held each year in March.

Norman Morrison, despite losing a shoe early in the race, pluckily ran in the Senior race to finish thirteenth - first Scot and third Briton home - and lead Scotland to eighth place. The team title was won by new entrants Russia, who finished 10 points ahead of Belgium, with New Zealand third and Finland fourth. Scotland's drop to eighth team position was the start of a long, downhill slide to mediocrity as more and more countries entered the World Championship.

Although the sport in Scotland was to grow in numbers due to the running boom of the early eighties, the stars, who could hold their own in any race with the world's best, were lost to cross country. From 1973 onwards the lure of the International World Championships disappeared and the top runners gradually lost interest as the inevitability of Scotland losing her right to continue to appear in the race as a separate country became a reality. Although it took another 14 years for the four Home Countries - the founders of the ICCU and the International race - to be forcibly amalgamated into a joint United Kingdom team, it was apparent that the guarantees of the IAAF for Scotland's autonomy would not last far into the future.

The 1973 World Championship at Waregem was Lachie Stewart's tenth and final appearance in a Scottish vest after a long and distinguished career since his first appearance in 1964. However his athletic successes had been just as great on the track where he was Scotland's most successful post war distance runner, winning 13 Scottish National track titles between 1965 and 1973. He won 3 titles at 3 miles; 1 at 5,000 metres; 2 at 6 miles; 3 at 10,000 metres and 4 at 10 miles, in the face of tough opposition when Scotland was at her strongest in distance running, and also set 11 Scottish National and Native records.

An early rivalry with John Linaker in the mid Sixties resulted in Stewart setting a Native record of 8 minutes 49.4 seconds behind Linaker (8 minutes 48.8 seconds) in the 1966 National 3,000 metres Steeplechase. Stewart went on to set a National record of 8 minutes 44.8 seconds and to represent Scotland in the 1966 Commonwealth Games at Kingston, Jamaica, and Great Britain in the European Championships at Budapest.

In 1967 and 68 he displayed his great versatility as a distance runner when winning the National 3,6 and 10 miles titles each season, a feat only once before accomplished by John Emmett Farrell (Maryhill) in 1946. Although he represented Great Britain in the 1972 Olympic Games 10,000 metres in Munich, Stewart's finest performance came 2 years earlier in the Commonwealth Games at Meadowbank Stadium in Edinburgh.

There, running on the opening day of the Games, he won the 10,000 metres Gold medal in his finest ever victory and set the Games alight. Running in pouring rain throughout the race he defeated Ron Clarke (Australia), the World record holder, and Dick Taylor (England), the United Kingdom record holder, winning with a searing last lap sprint down the home straight. His winning time of 28 minutes 11.8 seconds was a Games, Scottish All Comers, National and Native record which, 20 years later, still stands as the fastest time ever recorded by a Scots athlete on a Scottish track.

In season 1973/74 an invigorated Victoria Park team broke Shettleston's five year hold of the Midland relay title with Edinburgh Southern (Eastern District) and Ayr Seaforth (South Western District) retaining their titles. The record in the Nigel Barge road race was beaten for the second year in a row when Ronnie MacDonald won in 21 minutes 50 seconds, with Lachie Stewart equalling the old record when finishing one second behind, with Jim Brown in third place.

David Logue, engaged on post graduate veterinary studies at Glasgow University, won the Midland District title at Cleland Estate. He broke clear of Lawrie Spence (Strathclyde University) at 2 miles, and won by almost half a minute, with Stuart Easton (Shettleston) in third place. Nat Muir, one of the most improved youngsters in the country, won the Youths title by 20 yards from John Graham (Motherwell), runner up in the National Youth Championship. Springburn Harriers displayed great strength in depth with team victories in all four age group races with future track star, Graham Williamson, taking their only individual title in the Junior Boys event.

Jim Brown, studying physical education at Borough Road College in London, won the Senior title in his first year of eligibility at the National Championships at Drumpellier Park, Coatbridge. 21 year old Brown and defending champion Andy McKean ran together at the head of the 400 strong field, setting a fierce pace for the first two of the five laps of the 12,000 metres course. Brown proved the stronger, breaking clear at half distance with a determined display of aggressive running that carried him to a 150 yard victory over McKean, with Ronnie MacDonald finishing third a further 40 yards behind. Lawrie Reilly (Victoria Park) easily won the Junior title by 21 seconds from Allister Hutton (Edinburgh Southern), and John Graham reversed the Midland District verdict when winning the Youth title by inches from Nat Muir in the most exciting finish of the day.

Edinburgh AC, led by second placed McKean who had good backing from J Alder 5, D Gunstone 8, J Patton 15, J Milne 18 and P Hay 27, easily won the Senior team title from Edinburgh Southern and Aberdeen. However, the other 4 championship team titles were won by Springburn Harriers in an unprecedented display of team strength to confirm the display when they "swept the board" in the Midland District Championships. The coaching, encouragement and attention of Jack Crawford and Eddie Sinclair, together with the close liaison between Springburn Harriers and local schools such as Lenzie Academy, whose headmaster was Billy Williamson (a former Glasgow Rangers player), finally paid off the well deserved dividends. Stewart Gillespie 6, led the Junior team to victory over Glasgow University; Graham Crawford 4, was first home for the Youth team which beat Shettleston; Ian Murray took the Senior Boys individual title with Springburn defeating Edinburgh AC and Graham Williamson 3, just 2 seconds behind Jim Egan (Larkhall YMCA), led his team to victory over Victoria Park AAC.

Andy McKean finished third in the English National, just 8 seconds behind future Olympians David Black and Bernie Ford, with Jim Brown, after leading the 1,000 strong field for 6 of the 9 miles of the race, fading to ninth position in the final stages after having earlier finished runner up in the British Universities Championship. Lenzie Academy, whose teams consisted of members of Springburn Harriers, dominated the Scottish Schools Championships at Clydebank, winning all three team titles with Nat Muir, winner of the Union's Junior/Youth trial race, winning the 15-17 individual title.

The IAAF World Championships were held at Monza and the Scottish party of 19 (9 Seniors, 6 Juniors and 4 Officials) travelled to Italy at a cost of £2,000, averaging £100 per person for 3 nights hotel accomodation and return flight from Scotland to Italy. Grants from the Scottish Sports Council and Ushers Brewery Trust helped with the travelling costs. Brown, in his first appearance, dominated the Senior race. He went into the lead from the start, setting a fierce pace which the others were content to follow throughout the race. With just half a lap to go Brown surrendered his lead to Erik de Beck (Belgium) and Mariano Haro (Spain) who took the first two places, with Brown fading in the finishing straight to be passed by Karel Lismont (Belgium), the European marathon champion, in the last few strides. The Scot finished fourth, just out of the medals, but only 5.4 seconds behind the winner in the closest finish ever seen in the championship.

Brown's Monkland clubmate Ronnie MacDonald finished 31, ahead of Andy McKean 46 and Colin Falconer 47 with the team totalling 273 points for seventh position in the 15 country contest. Scotland's Junior runners redeemed their pride with a good display as Bill Sheridan 12, Paul Kennedy 13 and 15 year old Nat Muir 19, the youngest ever athlete to represent Scotland in the World Championships, were the first United Kingdom Juniors to finish the race and lead Scotland, 93 points, to fourth place in the team championship - just 3 points behind bronze medallists Italy. The IAAF announced that Scotland would be the venue of the Championships in 1978, successfully crowning the Union's promotional campaign to host the event.

The 1974 Annual General Meeting decided to institute a National Cross Country Relay Championship for Juniors and Seniors over the classic 4 x 2½ miles distance already used in the District relay championships. The 1974/75 season saw the creation of two new clubs, with the amalgamation of all the small clubs in Ayrshire to form Ayrshire AAC, and those in Lanarkshire to form Clyde Valley AC. These two clubs were formed to offset the power of the existing top clubs such as Shettleston, Edinburgh AC and Edinburgh Southern during the winter season and to compete in league meetings during the summer track and field season. The strength of the newly formed Clyde Valley AC was immediately apparent in the inaugural National Relay Championship at Bellahouston Park. With the backbone of Jim Brown and Ronnie MacDonald from the former Monkland Harriers, they won an exciting race to gain the first title by 9 seconds from Edinburgh AC, with Edinburgh Southern third a further 23 seconds behind.

Lifted by a new found wave of confidence Scottish runners recorded a series of individual victories in International races in Britain and the Continent. Ronnie MacDonald won the annual Inter Area match, with his teammates packing well to win the team contest from North, South and Midlands, and Jim Brown won an 8,000 metres race to mark the 75 Anniversary of Barcelona FC with Scotland (A McKean 4 and L Reilly 5) winning the team race from England, Spain and Belgium. Ian Stewart made a successful return to running after his temporary retirement after his disappointing performance in the 1974 Christchurch Commonwealth Games and a foray into cycling as an alternative. He won an International race at Gateshead and defeated a strong field in the Madrid "Round the Houses" road race on New Years Eve and, with the backing of R MacDonald 4, W Mullett 6 and N Muir 7, led Scotland to a clear team victory over Portugal and Spain. Andy McKean was outpaced by European Steeplechase champion Bronislaw Malinowski (Poland) at Barcelona, finishing second, just 2 seconds behind the winner.

With Edinburgh AC's top runners competing in the European champion clubs race at Arlon, where they finished fourth, Edinburgh Southern had it all their own way in the Eastern District Championships at Fernieside. Led by Allister Hutton, who won the individual title by 80 yards from Paul Kenney (Dundee University), with Nigel Barge race winner Jim Dingwall (EAC) third, Southern had 6 runners in the first 11 home, to win their record sixth team title by 77 points from Falkirk Victoria. In the Midland Championships, held in freezing fog at Drumpellier Park, Stuart Easton (Shettleston) scored a surprise victory in the Senior race, with Nat Muir showing unbeatable form when winning the Youths title by the massive margin of 70 seconds.

The National Championships returned to Coatbridge where Andy McKean scored a runaway victory. He established a 17 second lead by half distance and extended it to 46 seconds at the finish to defeat Edinburgh AC clubmate Adrian Weatherhead, who finished runner up 6 seconds ahead of Ian Gilmour (Clyde Valley), in only his second race of the winter. Edinburgh AC won the Senior team title for the third year in a row, displaying awesome strength in depth with their 6 counting runners finishing inside the first 11 runners home. They totalled only 37 points, one of the lowest winning scores in the history of the championships. Such was their strength in depth that their second group of 6 runners (essentially their 'B' team) totalled 282 points, which would have been good for fourth place in the team championship behind Edinburgh Southern 101 points and Shettleston 199 points, if they had been accepted as a counting team. It is well worth recording this amazing team performance which dominated the championships and has never been approached since:- A McKean 1; A Weatherhead 2; J Alder 5; A Wight 8; D Gunstone 10; J Wight 11. Such was the Edinburgh dominance that Jim Dingwall, who finished thirteenth, did not count in their team, and this great disappointment was one of the reasons that caused him to join Falkirk Victoria the following year.

Allister Hutton reversed the previous year's placings in the Junior race, setting a fast pace from the start to win by 9 seconds from a tired Lawrie Reilly. Nat Muir won the Youths title, finishing 17 seconds in front of Charlie Haskett (Dundee Hawkhill), and recording the first National title in an unbroken series of victories which lasted for another 6 years to 1981 through the Junior and Senior championship races. Indeed, after 1982, when he was beaten by Allister Hutton, Muir won the National Senior title for a record equalling 5 years from 1983 to 1987 to give him a total of 12 National titles in the Youth, Junior and Senior races.

The World Championship event was staged in far away Rabat in Morocco and the Union had earlier made a public appeal for financial assistance to send the International team to North Africa. The Union stated in their appeal "In a sport where so much work is carried out voluntarily and unpaid, and where athletes work so very hard for their success, your help would be doubly appreciated".

The Championships were a personal triumph for Anglo Scot Ian Stewart, who once again displayed his unique ability to successfully combine speedy Indoor competition with longer distances over gruelling cross country courses. Stewart displayed all his former ruthlessness, being as ferocious a competitor as ever, but with a more relaxed attitude from his year out of competition which stood him in good stead in the heat of international competition. After winning an International 3,000 metres indoor race at Orleans in 7 minutes 56.8 seconds, he won the European Indoor 3,000 metres Championship race at Katowice, Poland, in the most exciting race of the Championship in 7 minutes 58.6 seconds.

Just 7 days later Stewart competed a formidable and unprecedented double when winning the Individual World Cross Country title. With such a short space of time between the two dissimilar events in distance and conditions, few athletes in the past had ever attempted it, let alone achieved it. But Stewart confirmed his reputation as one of the most competitive runners in the world with an accomplished performance in difficult conditions. Over a flat, fast course, with stretches of sand and artificial mounds, Stewart overcame an early attack of stitch to follow the fast early pace set by Bill Rogers (USA) and Mariano Haro (Spain). These three runners split the field and remained together, until Stewart launched his bid with 1,000 metres remaining, to record Scotland's first victory since Jim Flockhart won in 1937. Haro had to be content with his fourth consecutive silver medal in the race - just 1 second behind the jubilant Scot. Juniors Allister Hutton 38, and Lawrie Reilly 43, displayed excellent form when finishing ahead of all the Seniors, of whom National champion Andy McKean 53, was the leader. Scotland totalled 292 points in the Senior team championship to finish sixth in the entry of 23 countries. Scottish schools champion Jim Burns finished eleventh in the Junior race, 4 seconds in front of Nat Muir and Scotland, with 95 points, finished fifth in the team championship ahead of England.

Anglo Scot Ian Stewart, born in Birmingham in 1949, first excelled at 1500

Scotland's only two post-war medallists in the International cross country championships. Ian Stewart (left), gold medallist at Rabat, Morocco in 1975 and Ian McCafferty (right), bronze medallist at Clydebank in 1969.

metres/1 mile, being the third Scot to better the 4 minute mile barrier at Reading in 1969 with his run of 3 minutes 57.4 seconds behind Ian McCafferty 3 minutes 56.8 seconds, and went on to set a United Kingdom 1500 metres record of 3 minutes 39.0 seconds later the same year.

However it was at 3,000 metres/5,000 metres (and later at 10,000 metres at the end of his career) that Stewart displayed his world class talents. In 1969 he had a European Championship double, winning the Indoor 3,000 metres title in 7 minutes 55.4 seconds and the outdoor 5,000 metres at Athen in 13 minutes 44.8 seconds. The following year Stewart recorded the victory that will live forever in the memories of Scottish athletic fans when winning the Commonwealth Games 5,000 metres title in an enthralling race at Edinburgh. He displayed outstanding reserves of strength, speed, determination and sheer fighting spirit in a sustained surge over the final lap to win in the new European, United Kingdom, Scottish All Comers and National record times of 13 minutes 22.8 seconds with fellow Scot Ian McCafferty racing to the silver medal behind him.

The Anglo Scot was selected for the Olympic 5,000 metres at Munich in 1972 after a qualifying run of 13 minutes 24.2 seconds at Crystal Palace behind David Bedford and Ian McCafferty and won the bronze medal in 13 minutes 27.6 seconds behind Lasse Viren (Finland). In 1976 he finished seventh in the Olympic 5,000 metres final at Montreal, which was again won by Viren, recording his seasons best time of 13 minutes 27.8 seconds. After that he turned to the longer distance of 10,000 metres on the track and became the first Scottish runner to better 28 minutes for the distance. In 1977 he won the United Kingdom 10,000 metres title in 27 minutes 51.3 seconds, and later improved the Scottish record to 27 minutes 43.0

seconds - a time which still stands to this day.

Stewart's performances did much to improve the respectability and standing of Scottish distance running, but his contribution to Scotland was never seen as being whole hearted. In accepting Scottish athletic eligibility, through his father's birth in Scotland, rather than compete for England, Stewart seemed keener to run for Scotland to spite and annoy the English athletic authorities rather than to help the Scots in International competition.

The April Annual General Meeting at Meadowbank Stadium agreed a reorganisation of the District set up in Scotland. The North of Scotland AAA, which had controlled and organised athletics and cross country in the Highlands, was disbanded and reformed as the Northern Districts of the SAAA and SCCU. The South Western District, with the amalgamation of all the Ayrshire clubs into Ayrshire AAC, had too few clubs remaining to continue as a separate District and was joined with the Midland District to form the new Western District. This administrative reorganisation reconstituted the boundaries of the old Western District which had been broken up in 1929 to form the two Districts - Midland and South Western - in the West of Scotland, which had lasted for 45 years.

In the preceeding year, since the IAAF announced that Scotland would host the 1978 World Championships in Scotland, the Union General Committee had recommended that the event be held in Glasgow. Controversy erupted at this announcement and Tom Callaghan (Clyde Valley AC) astonished the Annual General Meeting when he read from a letter sent to Coatbridge Town Council in 1973 by SCCU Hon Secretary Robert Dalgleish. The letter stated "It is indeed with pleasure that my Committee accepts the very kind offer from Coatbridge Town Council to sponsor the International Championships should Scotland be invited to act as host nation in the near future". Somehow this committment had not been made known to the General Committee during the debate on where the Championships were to be held, and the decision on Glasgow as host venue was taken in ignorance of the agreement made by the Hon Secretary with Coatbridge just a year earlier.

The Hon Treasurer Robert McSwein stated that Glasgow's sponsorship terms came nowhere near the offer from Coatbridge, and the Union stood to lose about £3,000 by accepting Glasgow's offer which put nothing in the SCCU kitty, but simply covered the costs of staging the championships. After criticisms of political manoeuvering and statements of the Union's credibility being put under great strain, a timely reminder was made that Coatbridge had provided generous sponsorship for the National Championships for the past 3 years while Glasgow had no record of helping or promoting the sport. Incoming President Donald Duncan gave guarantees that an Inquiry would be held into the choice of venue and the competing claims of both Glasgow and Coatbridge would be thoroughly investigated.

The 1975/76 season started with the District Relay Championships, and first year Junior Nat Muir recorded the fastest lap of the day at the first Western District championship at Bellahouston Park to anchor Shettleston to victory, 29 seconds ahead of Clyde Valley. Edinburgh Southern completed a seven year run of successes in the Eastern District relay championships when winning at the Jack Kane Centre, Edinburgh. Their team of Ian Elliott, Allister Hutton, Alastair Blamire and Gareth Bryan-Jones won by 100 yards from Edinburgh AC, and went on to win the

National relay title at the same venue, defeating Shettleston who had Nat Muir recording the fastest lap on the final stage.

The high standard of Scottish cross country running was displayed in the Inter Area match at Lichfield where Ian Stewart won, and, even without top stars such as Jim Brown, Andy McKean, Ron MacDonald and Lawrie Spence, Scotland finished second - just 6 points behind the North team. Scots again ran well at Gateshead in an International event won by Brendan Foster with A McKean 7, and J Brown 11, just ahead of 17 year old Nat Muir 12, who was being successfully blooded for future International events. The Scottish team, although beaten by England, defeated the Rest of Europe Select.

With Nat Muir in San Sebastian winning a Junior International race, Lawrie Reilly (Victoria Park), the slim, pale, scholarly looking athlete who nevertheless had bettered 29 minutes for 10,000 metres on the track the previous summer, won the Senior title at the Western District Championships at Drumpellier Park, Coatbridge. He won the 6 mile race by 23 seconds from Frank Clement (Bellahouston), with Phil Dolan (Clydesdale) in third place. Springburn Harriers provided the winners of the other three races, with Ian Murray (Youth), Graham Williamson (Senior Boys) and Robert Barr (Junior Boys) all winning Individual titles. Adrian Weatherhead, a consistently under rated athlete in cross country running, despite many splendid performances including finishing National Championship runner up more than once, won the Eastern District Senior race at Cupar. He defeated University champion Paul Kenney (Dundee University), with Donald Macgregor (Fife AC) finishing third over his home course. Edinburgh AC halted a run of seven consecutive team championship victories by Edinburgh Southern when winning the Senior team title to add to their first ever team success in the Eastern District League. Ian MacKenzie (Forres), who had won the North of Scotland AAA Senior Championship 6 times between 1966 and 1975, won the inaugural Northern District title.

There was a record entry of 1,600 competitors in the 5 races of the National Championships held for the fourth time at Drumpellier Park, Coatbridge. Andy McKean and his Edinburgh AC clubmates obviously enjoyed the course at Coatbridge, for the Edinburgh architect won the Senior title for the third time in four years and Edinburgh easily won the team championship for the fourth consecutive time. McKean and Weatherhead went into the lead early in the race and stayed together until the final lap, where McKean

A mud splattered Andrew McKean competes for Scotland in the IAAF World Championships at Bellahouston Park, Glasgow in March 1978.

established a winning 80 yard lead from his clubmate, with A Hutton winning the battle for third place from Lawrie Reilly and Royal Navy Lieutenant Rees Ward (Shettleston). Nat Muir started a three year domination of the Junior title when winning from Paul Kenney.

The British University Championships were staged by Stirling University over a picturesque course around the loch in the University grounds, and Scottish runners dominated the race, filling 4 of the first 6 places. Jim Brown finished runner up to Olympic 1,500 metres runner Ray Smedley and Lawrie Reilly 3, Ian Gilmour 4 and Lawrie Spence 6 all ran brilliantly.

Chepstow Racecourse in Wales was the venue for the 1976 World Championships, and Scottish hopes fell in the week before the race when 3 of the selected National team had to withdraw due to an attack of influenza. Carlos Lopes of Portugal, later to win the marathon gold medal at the 1984 Los Angeles Olympic Games, won the individual title with Jim Brown 24, being the first Scot to finish - 20 places further back than his run in Monza two years earlier. The team finished tenth with 347 points, with team captain Jim Alder, in his fourteenth international appearance for Scotland in fifteen years, finishing as the final team counter in 96 position. This total of 14 international vests in the period 1962 to 1976 was a Scottish record for appearances in both the ICCU and IAAF cross country championships and Alder, in his biography "Marathon and Chips" states "On the bus coming back the late Jim Morton, who was team manager, presented me with a silver salver to commemorate the past fifteen years....... I knew the end of my era had come". Although he finished eighth at 41 years of age in the 1980 National Championships at Callendar Park, Falkirk, shouting his famous war cry "Geronimo" as he crossed the finishing line, he was not selected for the International team as the selectors preferred to pin their faith on younger men for the future rather than select the veteran Alder.

Nat Muir confirmed his early promise, finishing third to take the bronze medal behind two American runners in the Junior race, but the other Scots ran disappointingly with National Youth Champion A Smith (Shettleston) 35, being the next Scot to finish.

Born in Govan in 1940 James Alder was fostered by the Alder family of Morpeth and grew up in the North of England to become one of Scotland's greatest ever distance runners. Three years after his first Scottish cross country title in 1962, Alder achieved his first notable track success when finishing a close up second to Ron Hill in the AAA 10 mile track championship, with both runners sharing the winning time of 48 minutes 56.0 seconds. He showed excellent form in the shorter 6 mile/10,000 metres distance the following year when finishing ninth in the 1966 European Championship race and winning the bronze medal in the Commonwealth Games 6 mile race. He also achieved a best time of 27 minutes 28.6 seconds for 6 miles and became the first Scot to run more than 12 miles within 1 hour at Walton in 1965, ending up with a Scottish record distance of 12 miles 972 yards at Leicester in 1968 that still stands today.

But it was at the marathon that Alder excelled. In 1964 he became the first Scot to better 2 hours 20 minutes for the marathon distance of 26 miles 385 yards with his run of 2 hours 17 minutes 46 seconds in the AAA Championship race behind Basil Heatley. He won the 1966 Commonwealth Games title at Kingston, running in blistering conditions where the temperature never fell below 80° to pass Bill

James Alder (Morpeth Harriers and Edinburgh AC); three times National Champion in 1962 and 1970-71. Alder, who gained 14 International vests, was one of Scotland's most successful and consistent runners over track, road and cross country.

Adcocks (England) on the final circuit of the stadium track, and win in 2 hours 22 minutes 07 seconds, after being misdirected at the entrance to the stadium and losing valuable ground.

He followed this gold medal triumph with a bronze medal in the 1969 European Games at Athens, after failing to finish in the 1968 Olympic Marathon at high altitude Mexico City. He then won his only SAAA championship title when, running over the course for the Commonwealth Games, he scored a narrow 3 second victory over Donald Macgregor in the 1970 marathon race at Edinburgh in the fast time of 2 hours 17 minutes 11 seconds. Over the same course he recorded his fastest ever time of 2 hours 12 minutes 04 seconds to win the silver medal in the Commonwealth Games behind Ron Hill, 2 hours 09 minutes 28 seconds.

The controversial matter of the venue for the 1978 World Championships was finally settled during the season. General Committee, early in the season, decided not to hold the Championships in Coatbridge and confirmed Glasgow as the championship venue. Clyde Valley AC, outraged at this decision, received the support of 18 member clubs and called a Special General Meeting in Springburn Sports Centre on the morning of the National Championships. Spokesman Tom Callaghan claimed at the meeting that Coatbridge had never been given a fair deal or a realistic opportunity to state details of their proposals for sponsorship of the World Championships at the Coatbridge venue.

Inverness solicitor Donald Duncan, President in 1975/76, presented his Inquiry report on the factors leading to the choice between Glasgow and Coatbridge, and the presidential report was exhaustively discussed for over 2½ hours. The report received approval by the narrowest of margins, being passed by 28 votes to 27, although Glasgow as the official venue was later approved by the greater margin of 31 votes to 23. Duncan chaired the meeting with courtesy, tact and firmness, requiring all his professional skills to control the meeting which, at times, grew angry with intense, heated discussion and argument over the issues at stake. Duncan's year in office was one of the most troublesome and rumbustious periods in modern SCCU history, and he overcame difficulties and tensions which no other Union President had ever experienced due to the bitterness and controversy existing during the year.

Shettleston, inspired by the running of Nat Muir, and strengthened by the recruitment of Strathclyde University student Lawrie Spence, started the 1976/77 season with a win in the Western District Relay Championships by over a minute from Clyde Valley. They then won the National Relay title at Kings Park, Glasgow by 34 seconds from Edinburgh AC, with Falkirk Victoria finishing in third place.

Andy McKean confirmed his superiority in the East when he won a record twelfth Eastern District League race and gained his third Senior title in the Eastern District Championships to lead Edinburgh AC to a repeat team victory. A fascinatingly close race occurred in the Western District Championships at Galston between Clyde Valley clubmates John Graham and Jim Brown. The two raced together in the lead throughout the race until the extra four years racing experience that Brown enjoyed over 20 year old Graham proved decisive. In the final half mile he outpaced Graham to win by 9 seconds, with Phil Dolan (Clydesdale) finishing a distant third over 200 yards behind. Shettleston retained the Senior team title, scoring just 47 points to win by the huge margin of 163 points from Springburn, who did well in the younger age group races with individual wins from Graham Williamson (Youths) and Stuart McPherson (Junior Boys) and second place in the Senior Boys race, when Graham Band finished behind Ian Doole (Clyde Valley).

Andy McKean became the sixth athlete to win the National title three times in a row when he defeated over 400 entrants in the Senior race at the 1977 National Championships at Glenrothes golf course. Running in 6 inches of snow McKean won by 21 seconds from Allister Hutton with a superb display of front running. Edinburgh AC, who had won the Senior team title for the past 4 years in a row, and were hoping to win in their attempt to equal Maryhill Harriers record of 6 consecutive wins between 1927 and 1932, found Shettleston in unbeatable form. Having already won the Western District Relay and Team titles, the National Cross Country and Edinburgh to Glasgow relay races, they completed their clean sweep of team honours with a narrow win in the Senior team championship. Led by L Spence 4 and R Ward 5, they totalled 117 points to win by 8 points from Edinburgh Southern with the holders Edinburgh AC another 3 points behind in third place.

Shettleston won another team title in the Junior race where Nat Muir won by almost a minute from John Graham with John Robson (ESH) in third place. Tom McKean of Clyde Valley, later to gain 800 metres fame with silver medals in the 1986 European and Commonwealth Games and three consecutive wins in the

Europa Cup, finished third in the Junior Boys race just 6 seconds behind the winner Stuart McPherson (Springburn).

Scotland had slipped from fifth to tenth in the past few years in the World Championship team competition and, with over 20 countries competing at Dusseldorf, West Germany, the slide downwards from their position among the top nations continued. Allister Hutton proved his continuing maturity into a strong, confident runner, being the first Scot in fourteenth position, ahead of J Brown 36, L Reilly 41 and A McKean 49. Nat Muir dropped from the previous years bronze medal position to a lowly eighth in the Junior race with the Junior team finishing only seventh.

Following the success of the Young Athletes relay championships introduced in 1975 at District level, a National Championship was introduced in season 1977/78. The District running order of Junior Boy, Senior Boy followed by a Youth was retained, and used in the National Championship event at Callendar Park, Falkirk. Earlier the Western District Relay championships had been held at Beach Park, Irvine, later to become one of the best known venues for District and National championship events. The race was held on undulating grassland over sand dunes which ensured that the surface was well drained and dry, whatever the weather. The seaside course was laid with crystal clear markings which ensured that no runner could go off the correct trail as laid by Jim Young and Willy Fulton of Ayrshire AAC. Shettleston retained the Senior title, winning by almost half a minute from Law and District AC, with Springburn recording the second of five successive Young Athletes Relay wins. Edinburgh Southern scored a narrow victory at Livingston, winning the Eastern District Relay title by 5 seconds from Edinburgh AC and completing a double with victory in the Young Athletes race.

Thanks to excellent runs by Ian Gilmour and Jim Brown, who recorded the two fastest lap times of the day, Clyde Valley regained the National Relay title they had first won 4 years earlier. They won by 100 yards from Edinburgh AC with Falkirk Victoria third, a further 100 yards behind. Springburn renowned for the strength of their younger age group teams, added the inaugural Young Athletes title to their Western District title defeating Eastern District champions Edinburgh Southern.

Nat Muir won an International race at Gateshead over a tough, hilly $4\frac{1}{2}$ mile course to soundly defeat David Black (England) and Steve Jones (Wales) and later finished second to Steve Ovett in a 5 mile International race in Belfast. National champion Andy McKean finished fourth in a high class race at Elgoibar, Spain proving he was to be reckoned with in both the National and International races. Jim Dingwall, who always fell short of International selection over cross country courses, displayed his road racing talents when he scored a record fourth successive win in the New Year Nigel Barge race at Maryhill.

Bitterly cold weather created a dangerously icy, rutted surface for the Western District championships at East Kilbride. Nat Muir and Jim Brown decided, on safety grounds, not to compete, and John Graham and Frank Clement found the underfoot conditions too dangerous to continue past the first mile. Lawrie Spence persevered to win his first District title, despite falling into a burn and losing much of his lead to second placed Phil Dolan, who eventually finished 20 seconds behind. Shettleston retained the team championship, winning for the third year in a row from a much improved Cambuslang Harriers. Andy McKean won his fourth Eastern District title in six years, overcoming treacherous mud over a hard ice base to win

Three Scottish Internationalists (left to right); Lawrie Spence, Scottish team captain, Lachie Stewart and Alastair Blamire, all members of Shettleston Harriers National team title winning teams of the Seventies.

and lead Edinburgh AC to a team victory over Falkirk Victoria.

The 1978 National Championships, held at Bellahouston Park, Glasgow, utilised the 5 lap trail to be used for the World Championships at the same venue later in the month. Allister Hutton ran away from his rivals with a determined display to win his first ever Senior title. He took the lead on the second lap to open a 10 second gap on Rees Ward and Andy McKean. Running with great determination and strength on the steep ascents, and letting loose with his flying stride on the downhill sections of the course, Hutton eventually won by 38 seconds from Ward, with McKean finishing a distant third a further 28 seconds behind. Edinburgh AC succeeded Shettleston as winners of both the Senior and Junior team titles, winning the Senior championship for the fifth time in six years. Nat Muir had applied to run in the Senior 7½ mile race as practice for the World Championship but was turned down as being too young. He was forced to compete in the Junior 6 mile event, which he duly won for the third time by 61 seconds from Doug Hunter (Edinburgh AC). Scottish Schools champion David McShane (Cambuslang) won the Junior Boys race, to gain the first of 4 National titles he would win over the next 5 years in Junior Boy, Senior Boy and Youth competition.

Once Glasgow had been finally settled as the venue for the World Championship a series of specialist sub committees were set up to organise the event. These committees covered such subjects as Venue, Accommodation, Travel, Catering, Police and Press and ensured the meticulous organisation of the event over a long lead-in period up to the staging of the race in March 1978. The championship was estimated to cost £25,000 - being the most expensive cross country event staged in Great Britain - and last minute sponsorship from Rotary Watches ensured the success of the meeting. On the day B.B.C. Television sent 9 cameras - 2 full outside broadcast units - to cover the championship in preference to televising the Premier League football match between Celtic and Rangers at Parkhead. The television race coverage was transmitted live to 12 European countries with an audience of 250,000,000 viewers. Close attention to detail was displayed when 3,000 crocus bulbs, planted on the hillside in the shape of the championship motif, came into full bloom in the week of the race, giving a colourful display. A thick hedge at the start of the finishing straight was required to be preserved without damage and a unique solution was found. Sir William Lithgow, a patron and Honorary Vice President of the Union, had a bridge constructed in his Greenock Shipyard and erected on site, allowing runners to run over the hedge and enter the finishing straight without damaging the greenery.

Jim Morton's high hopes for success in his tenth and final year as Scottish team manager were quashed when Ian Stewart, who had finished second in the English National championship, caught 'flu and was forced to drop out of Scotland's team, joining Rees Ward who had earlier withdrawn due to injury. On race day the weather deteriorated badly and appalling conditions of rain, hail and sleet were blown by strong winds horizontally into the face of runners and spectators. Twenty year old Nat Muir, judged too young to compete in the Senior National race, was selected for the World Championship Senior team. He started slowly in the race, and worked his way through from the mid twenties to fourth place at one stage of the race, before slipping back to finally finish seventh, in a race won by John Treacy of Ireland, and receive the Walter Lawn Memorial Trophy as the first Scot to finish. He was backed up by A McKean 19, and A Hutton 24, for the senior team to finish ninth of twenty countries in the team contest won by France. Ian Brown (Falkirk Victoria) finished a meritorious seventh in the Junior contest to become the first winner of the John D Semple Trophy for the first Scot to finish in the Junior race. The Junior team slipped back to ninth position after some good team performances in earlier years.

There was a reorganisation of relay fixtures in season 1978/79 to give a logical start to the winter season. Since the introduction of the National Relay championships four years earlier it had been held after the Edinburgh to Glasgow relay at the end of November. This resulted in a mixture of road and cross country relays over varying distances. The Union rearranged the fixture list such that the season opened with County, District and National 4 x 2½ mile Cross Country Relay Championships on successive weeks in October as a start to the winter season and a lead in to longer distance races later in the season.

West of Scotland Harriers, the third oldest club in Scotland having originated in 1886, resigned from membership of the Union due to lack of support and the small number of running members. They just missed the start of the running boom in the early Eighties which would have helped them continue in existence, and were sadly missed by other clubs in the Union.

Shettleston won the Western District Relay championship for the third year in a row at Bearsden, led home by Nat Muir who recorded the fastest lap of the day by 4 seconds from Jim Brown. They won by 17 seconds from the Greenock club, Spango Valley AC, who had shown rapid improvement over the previous two years. Allister Hutton recorded the fastest lap time in the Eastern District Relays at Tullibody to help Edinburgh Southern retain the Senior title from Edinburgh AC, with their Young Athletes team also retaining their title for a double win.

Ten clubs were excluded from the National Relay Championships held at the Beach Park, Irvine due to their team entries being received too late by the championship convener. They included the holders Clyde Valley AC, Victoria Park and East Kilbride and warnings were issued to club secretaries to observe closing dates for entries in future races. With Allister Hutton and Ian Elliot recording the two fastest laps of the day in ideal conditions at the seaside course, Edinburgh Southern easily won the Senior title by 40 seconds from Spango Valley with Edinburgh AC third.

The Western District Championships became a survival of the fittest as a biting wind, blowing sleet and rain across Bellahouston Park, caused runners to drop out of the race suffering from cold and exposure. Brian McSloy followed in the footsteps of his Clyde Valley clubmate Jim Brown by winning both the Senior and Junior titles with a surprise 40 yard victory over Graham Clark (Spango Valley), with Victoria Park winning the team championship.

The National championships, which in their long history had survived snow, hail, fog, blizzards, floods and many other hazards, were put at serious risk by a janitors disruption of services to schools at Livingston New Town, West Lothian. The Union was given a special dispensation by the National Union of Public Employees, which allowed the janitor at Deans Community High School to waive the overtime ban and open up the school on the Saturday for changing facilities for the 1,800 entrants in the 5 championship races.

The races were held in bitter, arctic conditions over a tough course made difficult by ice hard, rutted underfoot terrain. Nat Muir, competing in his first Senior championships, scored his expected victory, winning by 26 seconds from his Shettleston teammate Lawrie Spence with Jim Brown finishing third, a further 23 seconds behind. The unusual conditions allowed 30 year old Jim Dingwall to finish fourth, and gain his first Scottish International vest after many years of unsuccessful effort on soft surfaces. His achievement was recognised by being made International team captain for Limerick. Clyde Valley runners Brian McSloy and Peter Fox repeated their Western District successes when winning the National Junior and Youth titles respectively.

Under the team managership of John Hamilton, who succeeded Jim Morton, and controlled the Scottish team for the next decade, Scotland travelled to Limerick, Ireland for the World championship. Ireland's 22 year old John Treacy repeated his individual win over his home course, running away from a large field from 23 countries to win by over 50 yards from Bronislaw Malinowski, the Polish

Leading group in 1979 National Championships at Livingston. Left to right — John Graham, Lawrie Spence, Gordon Rimmer, Ian Elliot, Jim Brown and Nat Muir (the winner).

steeplechaser, who had a Scottish mother. Nat Muir was the leading Scot in tenth position, with John Robson, who had earlier won the 1,500 metres bronze medal in the European Indoor Championships, finishing second Scot far back in fifty second position. The Senior team finished in a disastrous fourteenth position in the team contest - their worst ever performance in the World Championships. The Juniors performed better, with Ian Campbell (East Kilbride) running in third place for much of the race, but tiring in the final stages to slip back to tenth at the finish. He was just ahead of Alastair Douglas (Victoria Park) 11, with Scotland improving three places on their team performance in Glasgow the previous year.

Much discussion about the gap between the 4 man National Cross Country Relay Championship and the 8 man relay race from Edinburgh to Glasgow was resolved by the introduction of a 6 Stage National Road Relay Championship. The race was held on the last Saturday of March, as a climax to the winter season, and this date has been reserved for the Relay Championship ever since. Open to all clubs, the event attracted 58 teams at Strathclyde Park where a traffic free course around Strathclyde Loch was used. Clyde Valley, brought into the lead on the second stage by John Graham, held first place for the next three stages, and started the final 6 mile stage with a lead of almost half a minute. Ian Gilmour ran the final 6 mile stage for the Lanarkshire club but was overtaken before the 3 mile marker by Allister Hutton. He went on to record the fastest 6 mile lap - 25 seconds faster than Nat Muir achieved - and bring Edinburgh Southern home to a 95 second victory over Clyde Valley with Shettleston third. The Edinburgh Southern team of Colin Hume, Colin Youngson, Martin Craven, Dave Logue, Alex Robertson and Allister Hutton won the first title and the club continued to dominate the new championship with 5 consecutive victories up to 1983.

1980 to 1989

The Eighties, the final decade of the Union's centenary, were notable for many factors, chief of which was the great surge of interest from the general public in running. It first started as a craze imported from the United States of America, where running for health had caught the public imagination in a big way. The first running of the London Marathon gave a competitive focus to many adherents, and marathon races were instituted in many towns and cities throughout Britain, with Glasgow holding the first People's marathon in 1982. This growth of competitors in long distance road running resulted in a consequent influx of runners into clubs affiliated to the Union, and an increase in competitors in road and cross country events during the winter season.

Another growth area was in the veteran category of running. With ever increasing numbers of veteran runners competing, the Union instituted Individual and team National Championships in 1985, and 4 years later added another six age group categories to the initial over 40 years championship race. The loss of Scotland's identity as a seperate country, with the right to compete in the annual World Championship, had long been feared and finally happened in 1987. The IAAF decreed that the four Home Countries had to combine and field just a single United Kingdom team in the Championships from 1988 onwards.

The final notable factors were the individual dominance achieved in the National Championships by Nat Muir of Shettleston Harriers, and Edinburgh Southern's hold on the Senior team championship which they won seven times in the first eight years of the decade. Muir also won the Individual title seven times, with his five wins between 1983 and 1987 equalling Suttie Smith's record set between 1928 and 1932. Edinburgh Southern produced a group of top class runners in the period between 1982 and 1987, which dominated the Scottish cross country scene, and equalled Maryhill Harriers 55 year old record of six consecutive National team championship victories.

Season 1979/80 saw the sixth National cross country Relay championship being held at the north eastern venue of Aberdeen, with Clyde Valley winning for the third time over a fast course at Tullos Playing Fields. Their success was largely due to the excellent running of Jim Brown and Brian McSloy, who recorded the two fastest laps of the day. Host club Aberdeen AAC, who had earlier won the Eastern Relay title at Cupar for the first time in 20 years, finished runners up 11 seconds behind with Falkirk Victoria finishing third another 8 seconds behind, but gaining the Young Athletes relay title from Springburn and Edinburgh Southern.

The Eighties decade started well for Scotland when they won the team contest in the International "Round the Houses" road race at Madrid on Hogmanay. Nat Muir finished runner up to Carlos Lopes (Portugal), future World cross country champion and Olympic marathon gold medalist, with Jim Dingwall 4, and Graham Laing 8, completing the Scottish team. Dingwall, on his return to Scotland, just missed his sixth successive win in the Nigel Barge road race at Maryhill, finishing a close up second - just 2 seconds behind Gordon Rimmer (Cambuslang and RAF) who recorded his first major success. Muir won the Belfast International race and

Aberdeen AAC team (from left); Graham Milne, Mel Edwards, Fraser Clyne and Graham Laing, which won the 1979 Eastern District cross country relay championship at Cupar.

then finished sixth in the Villamoura event in Portugal, with Jim Brown close behind. Muir stayed training for a week in the sun after the Villamoura race, and the benefits showed when he won the San Sebastian race in Northern Spain with Brown 5, and Lawrie Spence 15, for Scotland to finish second to England in the team contest.

Home runners had to deal with Scotland's icy winter, and the January District championships were run over hard, rutted ground which made competition very difficult for runners. John Robson successfully switched from international indoor track running to the winter conditions of Callendar Park in Falkirk and won his first East District title, defeating holder and clubmate Ian Elliot by 50 yards, and leading Edinburgh Southern to victory in the team championship over Falkirk Victoria. Brian McSloy (Clyde Valley) retained his Western District Senior title at Dalmuir Park, Clydebank, defeating Graham Clark (Spango Valley) by 15 yards with Clydesdale Harriers, running on home ground, winning the team title from 23 other clubs.

The National Championships were held over the level, well drained grassland course at Beach Park, Irvine and were sponsored, as so often in the future, by A.T. Mays, the travel agents, with financial assistance from Cunninghame District Council and Irvine Development Corporation. The course, which received fulsome praise from competitors as the best championship trail for over a decade, was conducive to fast running except for the final 600 yards of each of the three laps in the Senior race. A long, sweeping downhill stretch led to a 150 metres stretch of strength sapping sandy beach, and this was closely followed by a 1 in 5 sandhill that had the fittest athletes walking up with their hands on their knees by the final lap.

Nat Muir (Shettleston Harriers), the winner, leads from Jim Brown (Clyde Valley AC) and John Robson (Edinburgh Southern Harriers) on a hilly section of the course in the 1980 National Championships at the Beach Park, Irvine.

Defending champion Nat Muir recorded his usual outstanding performance, turning in a decisive mid race surge that brought him home 17 seconds clear of John Robson, with 1978 champion Allister Hutton finishing third a further 29 seconds behind. Edinburgh Southern, with their counting six runners in the first 32 home, retained the team title by 19 points from Clyde Valley. Cambuslang Harriers, led by the Rimmer brothers (Gordon 6, and Steven 18), finished in third position to gain their first ever set of Senior team medals and give portent of further team successes at all age groups in National competition. World Student Games 1500 metres champion Graham Williamson (Springburn), won the Junior title with Edinburgh Southern, led by sixth placed Colin Hume, taking the team championship. David McShane (Cambuslang) won the Senior Boys title to add to his two Junior Boys wins.

The 1980 World Championships attracted 35,000 spectators to the Longchamp Racecourse in Paris, where John Robson emerged as a world class cross country runner. Better known for his success over 1500 metres and 1 mile on both indoor and outdoor tracks, Robson ran a courageous race. The Kelso runner suffered a spiked left knee, only one of the injuries which dogged the Scottish team. The most serious injury was suffered by Nat Muir, who hit the first hurdle in the race, injuring his right heel and dropping out soon afterwards to be taken to hospital for treatment to his injured Achilles tendon. Robson bravely raced home in fifth position, for what was to be the highest Scottish placing in the World Championship in the 12 year period between Ian Stewart winnning at Rabat in

Scottish cross country internationals from left; Frank Clement (Bellahouston Harriers); John Robson (Edinburgh Southern Harriers) and Graham Williamson (Springburn Harriers). All three athletes were Scottish 1500 metres / 1 mile record holders.

1975, and the final team appearance at Warsaw in 1987. He was second Briton to finish, just 19.5 seconds behind the winner Craig Virgin (USA), and over 37 seconds in front of Allister Hutton 29, and Jim Brown 31. In a team contest won by England from USA., Scotland finished seventh - much better than the fourteenth place gained in Ireland the previous year - and this team position was to prove their best achievement in the World Championship.

The National Road Relay Championship returned to the scenic Strathclyde Park venue where Edinburgh Southern retained the title. Clyde Valley went into the lead on stage 4 when John Graham moved from ninth to first and Jim Brown raced to a 46 seconds lead on the next lap, handing over to Brian McSloy for the final 5.7 mile stage round Strathclyde Loch. However Hutton proved the ideal anchor man for Southern, closing remorselessly as McSloy tired, and went on to bring Southern home to a 35 second win with the fastest lap of the day.

The 1980/81 season opened with Law and District AC recording their first ever victory in the Western District relay championship at East Kilbride. Shettleston looked likely winners, with a lead of more than a minute at half distance, but over the final two stages veterans Henry Summerhill and Bill Scally were pulled in by their Law rivals, with Jim Thomson passing Scally with less than half a mile to go for the Law club to win by 200 yards from Shettleston. Cambuslang finished third, ahead of Springburn who won the Young Athletes title from Shettleston. Edinburgh AC won the East District title - only their second Senior title since their formation.

The National Relay championshps were held in the Highlands for the first ever time, staged at Charleston Academy, Kinmylies, in Inverness. The event, organised by North District Secretary Walter Banks with sponsorship from the Highland Regional Council and the North of Scotland Milk Marketing Board, was the stage for Cambuslang's display of growing strength and power as a club of National standing. Holders Clyde Valley lost the title due to the absence of John Graham who was competing in the New York Marathon. There, at his first attempt at the distance, he finished third in a field of over 16,000 finishers, setting a new Scottish record of 2 hours 11 minutes 46 seconds in a race won by Alberto Salazar (USA) in 2 hours 09 minutes 41 seconds. Clyde Valley had a 1 second lead at the final change over, with Ron MacDonald setting off ahead of Gordon Rimmer (Cambuslang), who had narrowly missed Olympic selection the previous summer despite setting a Scottish record of 8 minutes 26.6 seconds for the 3,000 metres Steeplechase. After a neck and neck struggle over the final lap, Rimmer anchored the Cambuslang team of Eddie Stewart, Rod Stone and Alec Gilmour to a 4 second victory over Clyde Valley, with Law in third place, for Western District clubs to score their first ever clean sweep of the medals. Cambuslang finished runners up in the Young Athletes race behind Livingston and District AC.

In open domestic competition the Helen Corbett Trophy race for Youths, organised by Bellahouston Harriers since 1955, celebrated its Silver Jubilee as an event which had helped to develop many of Scotland's youngsters. The race was won by Stewart McPherson of Springburn. His clubmate Graham Williamson won the Springburn Cup race in record time, finishing 20 seconds clear of Frank Clement (Bellahouston) who had earlier won the Nigel Barge road race by 5 seconds from Jim Brown. The annual Senior International match at Stirling University between the Union, Combined Scottish Universities and Northern Ireland had the added attraction of the inaugural Inter District match for the younger age groups of Youths, Senior and Junior Boys. This event gave the youngsters from the East, West and North of Scotland the opportunity of representative competition and a chance to meet rivals for National age group honours. Strong West District teams dominated the contests, winning all the team contests with Garvin McMillan (Youths), and David Russell (Senior Boys), adding individual honours to the West successes with only victory in the Junior Boys race going to the Eastern District.

The West District Championship was held over a snow covered course at Bellahouston Park, with Jim Brown repeating his 1977 victory thanks to a strong, forcing run which brought him home to a 40 yard victory over Cameron Spence (Spango Valley) who defeated his young brother Lawrie (Shettleston). Clydesdale Harriers were the only club to retain their team title, winning the Senior team championship with a sound display of team packing for their best display for over 60 years, defeating by 26 points Cambuslang, who were rapidly emerging as challengers for team honours at District and National level. Fraser Clyne (Aberdeen AAC) won the Eastern District Senior title at Livingston, outsprinting former marathon champion Colin Youngson who, with strong backing from clubmates Evan Cameron 3, and John Gladwin 4, led Edinburgh Southern to an easy victory in the team championship for the third consecutive time. Southern later finished eleventh of 18 clubs in the European Champion Clubs race at Milan with Youngson 29, being the first Scot to finish.

Nat Muir, after the disappointment of his forced retiral from the World

Championships at Paris, set out to redeem himself at the 1981 Championships at Madrid. After a successful summer's track running, during which he set a Scottish record of 13 minutes 17.9 seconds for 5,000 metres (which still stands 10 years later), but failed to make Britain's team for the Moscow Olympic Games, he established a gruelling programme of Continental races throughout the winter. At Denderhouten, Belgium he finished ahead of many of the worlds top cross country runners, winning over a snow covered course by 4 seconds from Emil de Beck (Belgium), after multi world record holder Henry Rono (Kenya) had dropped out due to the bad weather conditions. Muir continued his good form when finishing a close runner up in the "Almonds in Blossom" race in Portugal, and the San Sebastian race in Spain on successive weekends and also defeated a top class field in Chartres, France.

Muir showed the benefits of this tough preparation when retaining his National title, scoring his third successive win at Callendar Park in Falkirk. Miserable conditions of sleet and snow, driven horizontally into the face of runners, turned a fast, bone hard course into a clinging quagmire that made it the survival of the fittest on the day of the race. By 4 miles Muir and Jim Brown were out on their own, and they raced each other to the finish with Muir proving the stronger by just 2 seconds over Brown, with Allister Hutton finishing third a further 14 seconds behind. Edinburgh AC scored a narrow team victory, finishing 12 points in front of city rivals Edinburgh Southern who, except for this defeat, won the Senior team championship on every occasion between 1979 and 1987.

A notable finisher in the Youths race, won by Garvin McMillan (Ayrshire AAC), was Tom McKean of Clyde Valley AAC. McKean, who was to develop into a world class 800 metres runner with silver medals in the 1986 European Championships and Commonwealth Games, three victories in the Europa Cup Final and a World Cup victory in 1989, finished eleventh, 42 seconds behind the winner. The previous year Brian Whittle (Ayr Seaforth AC), another Scot destined for track fame over 400 metres, with a European Championship 4 x 400 metres relay Gold medal at Stuttgart in 1986, finished thirty sixth in the Senior Boys National behind David McShane (Cambuslang).

A mystery illnes struck the Scottish team at the World Championships held at the Zorzuela Racecourse in Madrid, with only six runners actually finishing the race, and Fraser Clyne, Jim Brown and Graham Williamson all dropping out with respiratory problems. Water samples were brought back to Scotland for testing but no cause was discovered to explain the illness, and although the symptoms seemed similar to altitude sickness, the fact that Madrid was only 2,000 feet above sea level discounted that possibility.

After his successful preparations on the continent Muir suffered another disappointment when finishing in twenty sixth position to be second Briton home. In a close packed field Muir finished only 45 seconds behind the winner, Craig Virgin (USA), with Allister Hutton being only 15 seconds behind Muir when finishing another 22 places behind in forty eighth position. The Scots had to wait for Junior champion Alastair Douglas 192, to finish, to complete a team which eventually finished fifteenth and maintain Scotland's record of competing, and finishing a team, in every International Championship since 1903. Ethiopia won the team championship for the first time, starting a run of five consecutive team victories - to be followed by Kenya, with another five wins in a row, for an African domination of the Senior team title between 1981 and 1990 which shows no sign of being broken by any other nation.

The IAAF cross country committee, meeting at Madrid after the Championships, confirmed that the four separate British teams could continue to run independently in the World Championships in future years. This promise, which buoyed up the hopes and confidence of the Union for Scotland's continued independence, was broken within six years by the IAAF.

The National 6 stage Road Relay championship was again staged at Strathclyde Park with Edinburgh Southern winning for the third time thanks to Allister Hutton recording his usual reliable run over the anchor stage of the race.

After defeating over 100 teams in the McAndrew relay race at Scotstoun at the start of the 1981/82 season, Falkirk Victoria won the Eastern District relay title for the first time. This started a run of successes over the next 4 years, ending in 1984 when they also won the Eastern District team championship, and the Edinburgh to Glasgow relay race. Cambuslang won the Western District relay title at Port Glasgow in an exciting race with Spango Valley. The final lap started with Eddie Stewart (Cambuslang) setting off equal with Cameron Spence (Spango Valley) and, in a close fought race, Stewart went on to bring Cambuslang home 27 seconds clear for their first ever title. Clydesdale won the Young Athletes relay title, ending the 5 year run of successes by Springburn, who had dominated the event since its inauguration in 1976.

In the National relay championship at Torrance House Golf Course in East Kilbride, Edinburgh Southern fielded an all international team to win for the third time. Their team of Colin Hume, Evan Cameron, Allister Hutton and Ian Elliot won by 23 seconds from Aberdeen, with the holders Cambuslang in third place, but gaining consolation when winning the Young Athletes title for the first time.

Nat Muir was hit by a car in the San Sylvester "Round the Houses" New Year road race in Madrid and was forced to miss all competition up to the National Championships in an effort to regain top fitness. Ron MacDonald defeated over 200 competitors when winning the Nigel Barge race at Maryhill, finishing 5 yards in front of Alastair Douglas. Douglas went on to win the Scottish Universities title at Edinburgh, defeating Callum Henderson who led Edinburgh University to victory in the team championship, ending a run of six Glasgow wins.

Lawrie Spence won the Springburn Cup road race and went on to win the Western District championship at Coatbridge by 10 yards from former champion Jim Brown. Anglo Scot Neil Black from Morpeth finished third, and led Bellahouston Harriers to the Senior team title. In the Eastern District Championships at Caird Park, Dundee, Fraser Clyne and Graham Laing (both Aberdeen) outclassed their rivals to such an extent that they linked hands and crossed the finishing line in a staged dead heat. Alastair Falconer, the referee, who did not believe in dead heats, declared Laing the winner by inches over Clyne, the defending champion, who was placed second in the same time as the winner. With such a good start Aberdeen won the team championship for the first time since 1967, defeating Edinburgh AC and Falkirk Victoria.

Allister Hutton had been in good form throughout the season, winning the Presto International race at Gateshead and preparing for the National Championships by winning the final East District league race at Dalkeith by 100 yards from clubmate Evan Cameron, with Edinburgh Southern regaining the overall

League title. In a fast run National championship race over the firm, dry grasslands of Beach Park at Irvine, Muir found that his lack of racing fitness was too much of a handicap in his contest with the Southern pair of Allister Hutton and John Robson. These three runners had a splendid struggle over the final 2 miles, with Hutton drawing away to repeat his 1978 win, and Robson taking second place ahead of a disconsolate Muir. David McShane (Cambuslang), after winning individual titles in the Junior and Senior Boys age group races, impressively won the Youths title. Though he did not win individual titles in the Junior or Senior National races he won gold medals with Cambuslang teams on more than one occasion in the Junior and Senior championship races.

Allister Hutton (Edinburgh Southern Harriers) winning his second National Championship at Beach Park, Irvine in 1982. To the left are officials Ian Ross and George Kopelle, both former Union Presidents from Edinburgh Southern Harriers.

The World Championships, originally intended to be staged in Portugal, were switched to Rome when the Portugese decided that they could not properly stage the event. Allister Hutton confirmed his National Championship victory when finishing first Scot in thirtieth position, with only two other Scottish runners John Robson 85, and Ronnie MacDonald 95, finishing inside the first hundred home. With a total of 610 points Scotland finished fifteenth of 19 competing countries and the Juniors, led by Robert Cameron 30, finished in ninth position in their team race.

Edinburgh Southern won the National 6 Stage Road Relay championship at Strathclyde Park for the fourth year in a row. They recorded the easiest of wins and, even without Hutton requiring to turn on his usual last lap histrionics, won by 600 yards from Falkirk Victoria with Edinburgh AC in third place. This victory gave Southern a clean sweep of all the National team titles, having earlier won the National cross country and Edinburgh to Glasgow relay events and the National team championship, a feat they were to repeat the following season in an unprecedented display of team strength.

The 1982/83 season opened with Falkirk Victoria retaining the Senior title at the Eastern District relay championship at Cupar. They won by 8 seconds from Edinburgh Southern, with Aberdeen third, a further 4 seconds behind. Edinburgh Southern won the Young Athletes race and placed their 'B' team third behind Edinburgh AC. The Western District relays at Ayr saw the holders, Cambuslang, out of the medals, with Law & District winning for the second time in three years, 13 seconds ahead of Spango Valley with Springburn third. Cambuslang won the Young Athletes title for the first time, defeating St. Columba's High School from Clydebank and Greenock Glenpark.

Strengthened by the addition of Allister Hutton and John Robson, Edinburgh Southern competed in the National relays which were held for the first time in the Scottish Borders at Hawick Moor Racecourse. The very rugged countryside provided a tough course for competitors, with Ross Copestake and Charlie Haskett combining well to give Dundee Hawkhill a 16 second lead at half distance. John Robson established a 45 second lead for Southern on the third lap, and Allister Hutton trotted home to a 200 yard victory, with George Braidwood bringing Bellahouston through to second place, just 1 second in front of Spango Valley. Edinburgh AC won the Young Athletes title for the first time, after the holders, Cambuslang, had recovered from a lowly twentieth place on the opening lap, through good runs by Martin Hughes (Senior Boys) and David McShane (Youth), to finish runner up just 7 seconds behind.

Edinburgh Southern's team proved as equally adept on the road as on the country, winning both the Allan Scally and the Edinburgh to Glasgow relay races. Shortly after returning from the heat of Brisbane, where he finished sixth in 13 minutes 40.84 seconds in the Commonwealth Games 5000 metres, Nat Muir won the Glasgow University 5 mile race from 639 runners for the fifth time in six years. He also won the Bellahouston 6 mile cross country race, finishing 47 seconds in front of George Braidwood, but could only finish third in the Presto International cross country race at Gateshead. After leading for five laps in the Riverside Bowl course, he faded, and finished third behind David Lewis (England) and Steve Jones (Wales), with Allister Hutton finishing a lowly twenty fifth, after winning the race the previous year. Muir had a successful start to the New Year, setting a record of 21 minutes 46 seconds when winning the Nigel Barge race and then, just 24 hours later, won Shettleston's James Flockhart Memorial 7½ mile race at Drumpellier Park, Coatbridge. He won by 44 seconds from Douglas Frame (Law) and received the richest prize in Scottish athletics - a solid silver trophy dating back to 1760 and valued at £2,000. This trophy, formerly the property of a Scottish Duke, had been donated by the Flockhart family in memory of James Flockhart, the International Champion in 1937. Muir's winning series continued when he took the Springburn Cup race, defeating Lawrie Spence who had earlier won the Beith New Year race.

He continued his 100% record of victories in 1983 when he won the Home Countries International 10,000 metres race at Cumbernauld. He led from the start, stretching his lead over each of the three laps to win by 250 yards from Mike Chorlton (England) who led his team to a one point victory over Scotland, who had Lawrie Spence 4, and Douglas Frame 6, backing Muir.

With Muir resting before the National Championships George Braidwood (Bellahouston) confirmed his excellent early season form to win the Senior title at the Western District Championships over a rugged, hilly course at Lenzie. He finished 4 seconds clear of Lawrie Spence with fifth placed Eddie Stewart leading Cambuslang to their first Senior team title - the first of 5 District team championships won during the decade. Scottish University champion Callum Henderson (Tayside AAC), won the East District Senior title at Livingston by 7 seconds from Terry Mitchell (Fife), with Aberdeen, led by Graham Laing 3 and Fraser Clyne 4, retaining the Senior team championship by just 5 points from Edinburgh AC.

In a closely contested Senior race at the National Championships, at the Jack Kane Centre in Edinburgh, Muir won by 6 seconds from George Braidwood with Fraser Clyne a further 12 seconds behind. Evan Cameron, better known as a marathon runner, finished ninth and led Edinburgh Southern to team victory over Edinburgh AC and Aberdeen.

The English Cross Country Union organised the IAAF World Championships at Gateshead as the centre piece of their centenary celebrations. Resentful of the flat, fast racecourse trails the event had been held on when the event had been staged on the Continent, England laid on a true cross country test at the Riverside Bowl. A muddy course, full of twists and turns with two steep, testing hills per lap, was ideal for spectators, and extracted the best from the runners of 24 countries. In an exciting race, dominated by Kenyans and Ethiopians, Muir finished eleventh, second Briton behind seventh placed Dave Clarke (England). Fraser Clyne, 1 minute 40 seconds behind Muir, finished 97, and was the only other Scot inside the first hundred runners to finish. The team, whose final counter was Graham Crawford 182, totalled a dismal 751 points for a shocking eighteenth place of the 24 competing countries for Scotland's worst ever performance. The Junior's performed even worse, with Robert Cameron 48, leading the team to finish fifteenth of 17 countries, with only Northern Ireland and Kuwait finishing behind them.

Edinburgh Southern completed a successful season when again winning the National 6 stage relay championship at Strathclyde Park. They recorded their fifth consecutive win to again score a remarkable clean sweep of National team honours.

In season 1983/84 Lachie Stewart, whose name evoked so many great memories of wins over track and cross country, was living and working in Greenock and turned out competitively for his new club Spango Valley AC. Officially a veteran, having turned 40 years of age the previous June, Stewart ran the opening lap of the McAndrew relay race at Scotstoun and finished seventh in a field of 131 runners. His good start enabled the remaining Spango runners Chris Leck and the International Spence brothers, Cameron and Lawrie, to win the event for the first time, finishing 15 seconds in front of Falkirk Victoria with Bellahouston third.

Competing over a tough course at Linwood, which included many ploughed fields, Bellahouston defeated over 100 teams to win the Western District relay title for the first time. A strong challenge by Douglas Frame (Law) on the final lap was the feature of the race, as he chased the Bellahouston runner to the closest of finishes. Despite Frame recording the fastest lap of the day, his club just failed by 1 second to retain the title, with former winners Spango Valley finishing a distant third almost a minute behind. Competing on home ground at Callendar Park, Falkirk Victoria won the Eastern District relay for the third year in a row, finishing 7 seconds clear of Aberdeen with Dundee University third a further 4 seconds behind.

Alex Gilmour, out of action for the previous 12 months due to injury, was the hero of Cambuslang's winning team at the National relay championships at Edinburgh. Taking over in fifth place for the final lap, he swept past the runners in front of him, recording the fastest lap time to win by 10 seconds from Edinburgh Southern with Bellahouston third. In the Young Athletes race, teams who were strangers to National honours were successful, with Ayr Seaforth AC winning the title by 14 seconds from Eastern District champions Teviotdale Harriers.

A Home Countries International match at Cumbernauld, started 3 years earlier as part of the Silver Jubilee celebrations of Cumbernauld New Town, was held in the most difficult of conditions in January. Snow covered hillsides, with runners mixing with skiers descending the slopes, made a travesty of known form. Alan Puckrin (Kilbarchan AC), who finished runner up behind Peter Jenkins (Wales), overcame the knee deep snow in masterly style, and led Scotland to a team victory over Wales.

In order to satisfy a demand for a greater number of races over the International distance the District Senior championships were increased from 6 to $7\frac{1}{2}$ miles, with a separate Junior race over 6 miles including a new team championship. The Western District championships were held over Leverndale Golf Course in South Glasgow, and Nat Muir found the firm grass surface to his taste, winning by 30 yards from the Cambuslang pair Alex Gilmour and Eddie Stewart who led their club to team victory, retaining the impressive Maley Trophy. Cambuslang also won the Junior and Youth team titles but Robert Quinn (Kilbarchan) won the inaugural Junior championship race receiving the MacKenzie Medal for his victory. This trophy consisted of one of the gold National championship team medals won by George MacKenzie in the pre First World War period, donated by the MacKenzie family, and mounted on a plaque for presentation to the Western District Junior champion. Terry Mitchell (Fife AC), a former professional runner reinstated to the amateur ranks, won the Eastern District championships at Beveridge Park, Kirkcaldy, with Falkirk Victoria winning the team championship for the first time in 73 years. They defeated the holders Aberdeen, who gained consolation when winning three team titles in the Junior, and Senior and Junior Boys events.

The National Championships returned to the Beach Park, Irvine on their bi-annual visit to the West of Scotland, and conveners Jim and Betty Young received almost 2000 entrants for the five championship races. Nat Muir, who had been defeated by Allister Hutton the last time the championships had been held at this venue, had prepared well for the race. He had competed only twice in Scotland throughout the season, winning both times, preferring to compete in high quality races in England and the Continent where he recorded 2 wins and finished runner up 5 times in 8 races.

Nat Muir (Shettleston Harriers) leads Allister Hutton and John Robson (both Edinburgh Southern Harriers) in the 1984 National cross country championships at Beach Park, Irvine.

Right from the start the Shettleston runner set the pace and, the first time he climbed the sharp, steep hill from the sandy beach, he opened a decisive gap which he stretched to a winning margin of 43 seconds over Hutton with Fraser Clyne third a further 16 seconds behind. This victory, his fifth Senior title in six years, equalled the record of wins jointly held by Andrew Hannah 1890- 1896 and J Suttie Smith 1928-32. The previous years Youth Champion, Robert Quinn, won the Junior title at his first attempt, the first runner since Nat Muir in 1975 to achieve this - with his Kilbarchan clubmate Alan Puckrin finishing runner up 50 yards behind. Edinburgh Southern, with their 6 runners in the first 31 home, retained the Senior team championship by 83 points from Cambuslang, who won both the Junior and Youth team championships in a display of age group strength in depth.

The World Championships were held in the United States of America. This was the first time, other than a brief foray across the Mediterranean Sea to North Africa, that the event had been held outside Europe, and the venue at Meadowlands Racecourse, New York displayed the intention of the IAAF to make it a true world wide event. British runners did well, with Tim Hutchings (England) and Steve Jones (Wales) finishing second and third respectively behind Carlos Lopes (Portugal), who was to win the Olympic marathon at Los Angeles later in the year. Scottish champion Nat Muir had been matching strides with these athletes throughout the season and had been hopeful of a medal. However he never started in the race, being confined to bed with a bronchial virus and a temperature of 103°, able only to watch the race in frustration on his bedside T.V. set. Such was the poor quality of the Scottish runners that team captain, Lawrie Spence, was able to gain the Walter Lawn Memorial Trophy as the first Scot to finish, way back in 112 position. Robert Quinn finished twentieth in the Junior race with a good run, and seemed to be the exception to a general lassitude and loss of form which struck the entire Scottish team.

Edinburgh Southern's 5 year hold on the National 6 Stage relay championship came to an ignominious end when their runner did not appear at the start of the sixth and final stage of the race, and they lost the title by default as they failed to finish a team. Edinburgh AC, who had so often languished in the shadow of their more successful city rivals, seized their chance, and won the race by 300 yards from Cambuslang with Bellahouston a distant third.

The Annual General Meeting at the end of the season approved the recommendation from General Committee that a National Veterans (over 40 years) championship be held, together with a team championship, from 1985 onwards. There had been a great growth in numbers of Veterans competing and an 8 stage relay race from Alloa to Bishopbriggs for veterans only was staged for the first time in March. This race, which has developed into the veterans "Edinburgh to Glasgow" with teams from all over Scotland and the North of England, was organised by Danny Wilmoth, Union Vice President, an enthusiastic organiser of veteran races who has done much to make veterans athletics the success it is.

The District relays started the 1984/85 season. There was a record entry of 118 teams in the Western District event at Bearsden, where Shettleston recorded their first win since 1978 with a 250 yard victory. The tussle for the minor placings was exciting on the final lap with just 2 seconds covering the next three teams to finish behind Shettleston. George Braidwood anchored Bellahouston, the holders and pre race favourites, to second place, just 1 second ahead of Kilbarchan (Robert Quinn), with Spango Valley (Chris Leck) third, just another second behind. Falkirk Victoria led from start to finish in the Eastern District relays at Penicuik to win for the fourth and final time in their winning streak which started in 1981. Their team of Donald Bain, John Pentecost, Peter Faulds and Gordon Mitchell finished 81 seconds in front of Dundee Hawkhill.

The National relays, over a flat course at Linwood, attracted a record entry of 175 teams. John Robson recorded the fastest time of the day on the third lap, lifting Edinburgh Southern from fifth to a 25 second lead. Scottish University champion, Callum Henderson, added another 10 seconds to the lead on the final lap, to finish 200 yards in front of Spango Valley. Bellahouston, whose runners performed better on the road than the country with wins in the McAndrew and Allan Scally Relays to their credit, finished in third position. In a close run Young Athletes race Clydebank won for the first time, narrowly defeating Law & District and Edinburgh Southern.

George Braidwood started 1985 in winning form, defeating 450 competitors in the Nigel Barge road race with Graham Laing 1 second behind and then, one week later, winning the Springburn Cup race by 16 seconds from Lawrie Spence, first Scot home in the Glasgow marathon the previous September.

Spence rounded into form by the time of the Western District championships at Bellshill, winning the Senior $7\frac{1}{2}$ mile title for the third time when he defeated over 300 rivals. Cambuslang, placing their six counting runners in the first 24 home, won the team title for the third successive year, and also won the Junior team championship, with Clydebank winning the Senior and Junior Boys team titles. Colin Hume (Edinburgh Southern) won the Senior title at the Eastern District Championship at Livingston, pulling away from Fraser Clyne in the final stages of the race to win by 100 yards. Gordon Mitchell, in third place, led Falkirk Victoria to retain the Senior team championship.

Callum Henderson, who lost many Scottish International honours due to his refusal to compete on Sundays because of his religious beliefs, won the Home Countries International race at Cumbernauld. He finished 3 seconds in front of George Braidwood, and led Scotland to victory in the team contest, defeating Wales, Ireland and the RAF. Scotland found a new source of representative competition when, competing as guests for the first time, they competed in the English Inter Counties Championships at Leicester. Ian Steel was first home in nineteenth position in the field of 440 Senior runners, followed two places later by Charlie Haskett. The Scottish team would have finished fourth in the team contest behind North Eastern Counties, Yorkshire and Lanarkshire, and this result convinced the Union that the championship, as tough as any International race, would be beneficial to Scottish runners. Moves were initiated for the three Scottish Districts to affiliate to the Inter Counties Union and compete in future years in the Senior, Junior and Youth age group races.

After a long period of sub standard performances due to a respiratory viral infection Nat Muir returned to form with a series of good runs in Continental races. By the time of the National Championships at the Jack Kane Centre in Edinburgh, Muir was back to title winning form. The blustery conditions, with gusting winds and heavy showers throughout the afternoon, were not conducive to good performances. However Muir was not afraid of a solo run, heading a group of five runners for just 1 mile before breaking clear at the top of a hill to take a lead he was never to lose. He eventually finished 23 seconds in front of John Robson, with Ross Copestake (Dundee Hawkhill) third, a further 12 seconds behind. Lawrie Spence, not fully recovered from illness, finished thirty first and failed to gain selection for the International team for only the second time in 11 years. Robert Quinn, who finished fourth in the British Univerisities cross country championships to lead Glasgow to their first British team title in 50 years, retained the Junior title, with Cambuslang winning the Junior team title for the third year in a row - a feat only achieved before by Edinburgh University between 1963 and 1965.

After passing a drug test at the Championships, Muir was off again on his Continental travels and, just 24 hours later, finished a close up second in an International race at Birbeck, Belgium. Running in sticky mud throughout the race, he finished just 2 seconds behind Vincent Rosseau (Belgium), but in front of world class runners Emile Puttemans (Belgium) and Carlos Lopes (Portugal). This run was one of six major races Muir participated in between New Year and the World Championships at Lisbon, winning two, being second three times and finishing fifth in the other race.

Nevertheless, in spite of his careful preparations, the World Championship was again a disaster for Muir. Running in fourth place in the leading group after a mile, one of his spiked shoes was ripped off. He lost time and positions stopping to retrieve the shoe, but finally took off the remaining shoe and ran in just his socks. However a 300 yard stretch of gravel and stones proved to be his undoing as, having to cross it on each of the three laps of the race, he finished with lacerated, bleeding feet back in forty ninth position. John Robson was the first Scot to finish seven places in front of Muir, 66 seconds behind the winner Carlos Lopes, who became the first runner to win the IAAF World Championship three times. Tom Hanlon, a future steeplechasing international and record holder, was first Junior to finish in forty seventh position.

Scotland's international identity was again under attack, with Italy raising the issue of four separate British teams competing in the Championships, wishing only a single United Kingdom team for the future. The matter was not included on the IAAF cross country committee agenda and the British delegate, Robert Dalgleish (former SCCU Secretary) stated "I see no further problems". This reassuring statement fell rather flat, when, 24 months later, Scotland was banned from competing in the World Championships after the same IAAF committee had successfully recommended to the IAAF Council that only a single United Kingdom team be allowed to compete in the Championships. This decision was taken despite an IAAF assurance at Gateshead in 1983 that the matter was settled for the meantime and would not be raised again until 1989 or 1992. Even an agreement by the four Home Countries that they would each accept only a quarter of the travelling expenses subsidy paid by the IAAF, so that the final cost would be the same as just one United Kingdom team, was unsuccessful in its aim of retaining the four Home Countries as separate teams in the Championships.

The inaugural National Veterans championship was held at Drumpellier Park, Coatbridge with former SAAA 880 yards champion Dick Hodelet (Greenock Glenpark), recording a popular victory, with Shettleston winning the first team championship. The National 6 Stage relay championship was held away from Strathclyde Park for the first time in 6 years with a record entry of 107 teams competing at Pollok Park, Glasgow. Bellahouston Harriers climaxed a successful season when, running on home territory, their strong team won for the first time, defeating former winners Edinburgh Southern by almost 2 minutes.

The McAndrew relay race, which started the 1985/86 season, was affected by roadworks at Anniesland Cross, which necessitated competitors running over a lengthened trail of 3 miles 500 yards. The fiftieth running of the event, started in 1935 shortly after the promoting club Victoria Park AAC was founded and run throughout the War years of 1939 to 1945, was won by Edinburgh Southern, for whom Allister Hutton recorded the new lap record of 14 minutes 50 seconds. The Edinburgh club won by 38 seconds from Spango Valley and Motherwell YMCA.

Edinburgh Southern won the Eastern District relay championship at Galashiels, defeating the holders Falkirk Victoria by just 3 seconds, with Teviotdale in third position. Spango Valley led from the start to win the Western District relay at Kilmarnock. Peter Connoghan established a lead on the opening lap and this was extended on the second lap to 45 seconds by Chris Robison, an English International who had competed in the World Championships. A Royal Navy Lieutenant, based at Prestwick as a navigator/observer on Sea King helicopters, Robison had joined the Greenock club on his arrival for a 2 year term of duty in Scotland and was to have a big influence on the Scottish cross country scene during his stay in Scotland. Internationals Cameron and Lawrie Spence brought Spango Valley home to victory over Springburn and Kilbarchan, with Clydebank outclassing their rivals in the Young Athletes race when winning the title by 65 seconds from their 'B' team with Bellahouston third.

The Clydebank youngsters again displayed their outstanding form when retaining the Young Athletes title at the National relay championships at St Andrews. With Glen Stewart, son of 1970 Commonwealth Games 10,000 metres gold medallist Lachie, recording the fastest lap time on the Senior Boys stage, the Clydebank club won by 40 seconds from Victoria Park and Pitreavie. Over a testing grassland course Spango Valley, founded in 1973, won the Senior race to become the first Greenock club to win the National relay title and record the first Greenock victory in a National Championship since Greenock Glenpark won the National team championship in 1923. Chris Robison continued his fine running with the fastest lap of the day on the third stage to hand over a 10 second lead to Lawrie Spence at the start of the final lap. Spence held on to bring Spango Valley home to victory, with Edinburgh Southern finishing runners up 70 yards behind, and third placed Kilbarchan winning their first ever set of senior SCCU medals.

The effect of the distance running boom in Scotland was shown in the entry to the District championships in January 1986. Many runners, who had started only as joggers for health reasons, had been caught up with the enjoyment of competition in marathons and half marathons, and joined athletic clubs to train seriously and compete more frequently at shorter races over road and cross country. This influx of runners, keen to run in the friendly and welcoming atmosphere of cross country events, resulted in an entry of 830 competitors in the Eastern District championships at Denny and 1,139 in the Western championships at Rouken Glen Park, Glasgow. The figure for the Western event alone, exceeded the entry for the National Championship just 5 years earlier.

The Western District venue of Rouken Glen Park was the first time in 66 years that a major championships had been held there, since the National cross country championships had been staged there in 1920 on the resumption of competition after the First World War. Peter Fox (Motherwell), an athlete who had never realised his potential as a District and National Youth Champion due to tough medical studies at Dundee University, came into his own on the ideal rolling, grass lands course. Fox broke clear of the large field at 2 miles and went on to win by 200 yards from Chris Robison, with the holder Lawrie Spence third. These two forward placings allowed Spango Valley to add the District Senior team championships to the District and National relay titles, winning with 93 points from the holders, Cambuslang, 185 points. John Robson won the Eastern District Championships at Denny, finishing 100 yards clear of John Pentecost (Falkirk Victoria), with Simon Axon (Aberdeen) third. The Falkirk club won the Senior team title for the third year in a row when defeating Edinburgh Southern by 27 points.

The Edinburgh club then travelled to Aceotais in Portugal for the European Champion Clubs race. There, in a race won by Alberto Cova (Italy), the World,

Olympic and European 10,000 metres champion, John Robson 11, and Neil Tennant 12, led Edinburgh Southern to ninth place in the team contest for their best ever placing in their 11 appearances as Scottish champions.

Nat Muir had again prepared assiduously for the National Championships at Irvine, finishing third or better in six of the eight International races he had competed in during the first half of the winter season. After a rest in the period before the National, Muir was in a confident mood, and was content to follow the early pace set by Neil Tennant over the undulating grass and sand of the Beach Park. After 6 miles, on the steep sand hill leading from the beach, Muir struck swiftly, and opened up a gap of 30 yards which he maintained to the finish. Tennant, who later finished ninth in the English National championship, finished runner up and, with teammates Callum Henderson 3, and John Robson 4, following him home, Edinburgh Southern had their 6 runners in 28 home, to total 70 points, and finish 66 points in front of Cambuslang. 15 year old Glen Stewart maintained his unbeaten record, stretching back over more than a year, to win the Senior Boys title by 28 seconds - the largest winning margin of the day. This victory came 28 years after his father Lachie Stewart had won the inaugural Boys title at Hamilton Park Racecourse in 1958.

Muir withdrew from the Scottish team for the World Championships at Neuchatel, Switzerland suffering from 'flu - the third time in five years that injury or illness stopped him competing in, or finishing, the World Championship race. With Neil Tennant not finishing the race, it was left to John Robson to receive the Walter Lawn Memorial Trophy as the first Scot to finish in an ignominious 122 position - the worst ever placing for the first Scot in the World Championship. The Championships were dominated by Africans, who filled 7 of the first 8 places in the Senior race, and 9 of the first 10 places in the Junior race, with Kenya and Ethiopia winning the Senior and Junior team titles respectively.

Brian Scobie of Maryhill, an expatriate Scot from Leeds, where he successfully trained women marathon runners, recorded a 300 yard runaway victory in the National Veterans championship at Bishopbriggs. Third placed Ken Duncan led Pitreavie to their first team title, defeating Aberdeen by 11 points, with Victoria Park in third place. The National 6 Stage Relay Championship returned to Strathclyde Park after an absence of one year, being held on the last Sunday in March instead of the traditional Saturday. Even without top runners A Hutton, J Robson, N Tennant and C Henderson, Edinburgh Southern seemed assured of victory when they led from stage 3, starting the final 6 mile stage with a substantial lead of 66 seconds. Alex Gilmour started off for Cambuslang, after his club had worked their way through the field after a disappointing tenth place on the opening lap. He passed Keith Lyall (Southern) before half distance, and raced home to a 41 second victory over Southern, with Spango Valley third a further 27 seconds behind. Sixth placed Kilbarchan were anchored by Rev Bill Hewitt, a keen runner who, after conducting morning service at Elderslie Parish Church, was driven to Strathclyde Park, changing into his running kit in the back seat of the car, and arrived just in time to run the last lap.

The 1986/87 season commenced with the knowledge that the team competing in the World Championships at Warsaw, Poland would be the last Scottish team to compete as an independent country. This reality overhung the entire season, casting a cloud of gloom that from 1988 onwards there would be no Scottish team in the Championships, with Scots restricted to competing in a Trial race which would be used to select the members of the United Kingdom team which would take part instead of the four Home Countries.

Spango Valley won the McAndrew relay race from Cambuslang and then retained the Western District relay title at Clydebank from 139 teams, taking the lead on the third lap to win by 14 seconds from Law & District. Clydebank retained the Young Athletes relay title, winning by 10 seconds from Motherwell with their 'B' team third. An all international quartet from Edinburgh Southern retained the Eastern District relay title at Galashiels. After Ian Steel had established a lead on the first lap, Allister Hutton, who had a disappointing summer representing Scotland in the Commonwealth Games 10,000 metres and Great Britain in the European Championship marathon race, extended the lead on the second lap. Tom Hanlon and John Robson brought Southern home to an easy victory, 76 seconds in front of Teviotdale with Falkirk Victoria third a further 10 seconds behind.

Cambuslang dominated the early stages of the National Relay championships at Kilmarnock, leading from the start to the final changeover. Alex Gilmour set off on the final 2½ mile stage with a 1 second lead from John Robson, with Lawrie Spence third, a further 4 seconds behind. The three athletes, running into the teeth of a strong autumn wind, quickly closed up until Robson broke clear on a hill half-way round. He maintained his lead to the finish for Southern to win by 3 seconds from Cambuslang with Spango Valley a distant third, a further 20 seconds behind. This victory gave Southern their sixth success in the thirteen year history of the championship, a record far in advance of the defunct Clyde Valley (3 wins) and Cambuslang (2 wins). Eastern District champions Pitreavie won the Young Athletes relay title for the first time, thanks to an excellent final lap by Youth Clark Murphy, with Western District champions Clydebank finishing second.

Apprehension as to the declining standards of Scottish cross country running led the Union, with the assistance and advice of International coaching adviser Alex Naylor, to formulate a comprehensive "Plan for the Future". This plan was intended to develop youngsters, and give them international experience and opportunities to race against other athletes at a similar stage of development. The first aim of the plan was the staging of a Celtic Countries International match against Wales, Ireland and Northern Ireland with three races for Young Seniors under 23 years of age, Juniors and Youths. The inaugural match was staged at Irvine with sponsorship from Irvine Development Corporation and Cunninghame District Council which continued in future years. The declining standard of Scottish competitors was revealed when Scotland's solitary success came in the Youths race, won by Clark Murphy, who led Scotland to team victory in the race. Ireland won the team contests in the under 23 and Junior races.

Deep snow, in the weeks prior to the District Championships in January 1987, had caused difficulties in training but Chris Robison showed little effects when winning his first major title in Scottish athletics at the Western District championships at Kirkintilloch. Challenged all the way by Tommy Murray (Greenock Glenpark), Robison went into the lead in the final stages, to win by 40 yards from his Greenock rival, and lead his club to the team title, defeating Bellahouston and Cambuslang. Teviotdale Harriers, preparing for the celebration of their centenary year in season 1988/89, won the Senior team championship at the Eastern District Championships for the first time since 1962. Over a difficult course at Beveridge Park, Kirkcaldy, Terry Mitchell (Fife) won by more than 100 yards from Paul Dugdale (Dundee University), with third placed David Cavers leading the Hawick club to their biggest success in a quarter of a century. Teviotdale, 6 runners in the first 36 home, totalled 104 points to win the title by 7 points from Aberdeen with Pitreavie, 201 points, third.

The National Championships at Callendar Park, Falkirk were one for the record books, as Nat Muir and Edinburgh Southern equalled the record of consecutive victories in the Individual and Team Championships respectively. Muir equalled the record of five consecutive wins set by John Suttie Smith between 1928 and 1932, and Edinburgh Southern equalled the record of six consecutive team wins set by Maryhill Harriers between 1927 and 1932. The Senior $7\frac{1}{2}$ mile contest was a two man race between Muir and Chris Robison, until Muir broke clear to establish a winning margin of 22 seconds over Robison, with Allister Hutton, making a late challenge over the final mile to overhaul Tommy Murray and Terry Mitchell, taking third place a further 11 seconds behind Robison. Hutton led Southern to victory in the team championship with their team comprising 3, A Hutton; 6, J Robson; 26, G Grindlay; 28, N Tennant; 32, I Steel and 38, A Robson.

Clydebank dominated the younger age group races, winning three team titles in the Youth, Senior and Junior Boys championship races by comprehensive margins. These achievements were a tribute to the hard work, encouragement and coaching from stalwarts John Tonner and Alan Marshall who controlled the youngsters development. Alastair Russell (Law & District) won the Junior race, continuing the series of individual titles he had won in the National Championships with earlier victories in the Senior Boys race in 1984, and the Youths race in 1985 and 86.

Although it was not known at the time, Muir's victory was his final appearance in the National Championships, as injury prevented him competing again. Except for Allister Hutton's win in 1982, when Muir was injured after being knocked down by a car in a New Years race on the Continent, Muir had won eight of the nine National Senior titles between 1979 and 1987. These honours, together with his 3 wins in the Junior championships 1976-78 and his 1975 Youth win, gave him a total of 12 National titles - a performance which is unlikely ever to be equalled, let alone beaten in the future. He dominated cross country in Scotland as comprehensively as his list of championship honours indicated, and his love of cross country running, and his consequent concentration on the winter sport, could have been the reason for his lack of success on the track in the summer that his talent indicated he might have achieved.

His track distance running talent flowered early when he won the 1977 European Junior 5,000 metres title in Russia, clocking the excellent time of 13 minutes 49.1 seconds at 19 years of age. The following year he recorded a personal best of 13 minutes 34.9 seconds when finishing sixth in the Commonwealth Games 5,000 metres at Edmonton. His outstanding International success came in 1980, when he defeated a top class 5,000 metres field at Oslo in the Scottish National record time of 13 minutes 17.9 seconds - a time which was third fastest in the world that year - but was recorded too late to gain him a place in Britain's team for the Olympic Games in Moscow. In a track career, which never flowered to the same extent as his cross country one, he never gained a medal in any of the Commonwealth Games he competed in, or gained selection for the Olympic

Games or European championships in the Eighties. He won Scottish titles at both 1,500 and 5,000 metres but never achieved the high honours that Ian McCafferty or Ian and Lachie Stewart won in the Seventies.

The Scottish team made its final appearance in the World Championships at Sluzewiec Racecourse in Warsaw, competing in dreadful conditions on a slippery muddy surface in sub zero weather. Perhaps disspirited by their final appearance in the Championships, Scottish runners ran poorly throughout, and were shown up by Liz Lynch from Dundee, who finished a close second in the Womens Championship, being beaten by just 2 seconds by Annette Sergeant of France. In races again dominated by African runners, with Kenya and Ethiopia winning both the individual and team titles, Nat Muir was first Scot to finish - 1 minute 43 seconds behind John Ngugi of Kenya. Muir finished in fortieth position - the only Scot in the first hundred - with Terry Mitchell the next Scot to finish 97 places behind him. The Senior team finished a disastrous twenty second of 34 competing countries and the Juniors fared no better, finishing twenty fourth team, good enough to beat only Northern Ireland and Kuwait of the 26 competing countries. The positions of the final Scottish teams to compete in the World Championships are recorded below: Seniors -- 40, N Muir; 137, T Mitchell; 146, J Robson; 149, C Robison; 152, T Murray and 180, N Tennant. Total 804 team points; with 181, C Haskett; 192, R Copestake and 196, A Hutton, also finishing. Juniors - 84, A Russell; 103, C McFadzean; 124, M Wallace and 138, D Donnett. Total 449 team points; with 140, D Arnott and 145, J Quinn, also finishing.

Scotland's poor performance on their departure from the World Championship scene was not a proud moment, and nobody could say that Scotland deserved to remain as a competing country with the standard of performance shown at Warsaw. However, the serious manner that other countries treated the championships was exemplified by the preparations of the winning Kenyan team. A selected squad of runners had a one month competitive tour of Spain and Portugal in January. The touring party then returned to Kenya for their National Championships, the results of which determined the leading 15 Seniors and 9 Juniors, who spent a further month together training at high altitude. The final party of 9 Seniors and 6 Juniors were then selected to travel to Warsaw to compete in the World Championships.

It is well worth questioning whether Scotland could ever match these preparations now deemed necessary for success at World Championship level. It is very unlikely, even if the necessary financial resources were made available, that Scotland could find athletes of sufficient talent, ability and determination to make the sacrifices to become full time athletes and give up the security of a career in future life after their competitive days were over.

Brian Scobie of Maryhill recorded his second win in the National Veterans Championship at Musselburgh Racecourse with Pitreavie retaining their team title. Edinburgh Southern won the National 6 Stage relay championship at East Kilbride, scoring their sixth victory in the nine year history of the event. The race was closely contested throughout, with the lead changing regularly. Sam Wallace put the holders Cambuslang into the lead on the opening lap, only for John Graham, who had finished fourth in both the 1982 and 86 Commonwealth Games marathons, to open up a minute lead on stage 2. His Motherwell clubmate Peter Fox extended the lead on stage 3, then Chris Robison recorded the fastest time for the long lap to bring Spango Valley into the lead on stage 4. Edinburgh Southern then brought out their stars and Allister Hutton and John Robson brought them home to a 79 second victory over Spango Valley with Cambuslang in third place.

The 1987/88 season started with Nat Muir out of competition for 3 months with his ankle in plaster, in an attempt to cure his recurring Achilles tendon trouble. The early season District relay championships were notable for exciting final laps which decided the winners, with Allister Hutton bringing Edinburgh Southern their third successive victory in the Eastern District race at St Andrews. After Teviotdale had led all the way, Hutton took over in second position, 11 seconds behind, for the final lap. He then recorded the fastest lap of the day, taking the lead in just the final 400 yards, to win by 8 seconds from Teviotdale, with the host club, Fife AC, in third place. Spango Valley had repeated their win in the McAndrew road relay at Scotstoun on the first Saturday of the season, but played no major part in the Western District relays. Cambuslang, who had only once before won the title in 1981, set off on the final lap with a decisive lead. Adrian Callan (Springburn), equalled the fastest lap time set by Alastair Douglas (Victoria Park) on the opening lap, and lifted his team from fourth to second, failing by just 10 seconds to catch Eddie Stewart who brought Cambuslang home to a narrow victory. Clydebank won the Young Athletes title for the third year in a row, defeating Dumfries AAC by 4 seconds.

Galashiels, the venue of the Eastern District relays for the previous 3 years, hosted the National Relay Championships which attracted 190 Senior and 127 Young Athletes teams. The gruelling course laid by the Border stewards included a steep descent to a burn, swollen by heavy rain and sandbagged to reduce its depth to reasonable proportions. The large number of competitors turned the take off and landing areas into a treacherous quagmire throughout the race, and successful clearance of this hazard on the final lap helped decide the destination of the medals. Alex Gilmour, the ever dependable runner who so greatly contributed to many Cambuslang victories, overtook Lawrie Spence (Spango Valley) on the final lap and led his club to their third victory in the championships. Spence was also overtaken by Adrian Callan, who recorded the fastest lap of the day when bringing Springburn into second place, but he kept third place, holding off a strong challenge from John Robson, to give Western District clubs only their second ever clean sweep of the medals. Clydebank won the Young Athletes race for the third time in four years, defeating Eastern District champions, Pitreavie.

The annual representative match between the Union, Nothern Ireland and the Combined Scottish Universities was held at St Andrews, instead of the usual Stirling venue, and the Inter District contest was extended to include a Senior race for the first time. Chris Robison repeated the previous years race verdict when winning by just 1 second from Terry Mitchell, and Robert Quinn finished sixth to lead the Western District to victory in the inaugural Senior Inter District match. The Western District runners repeated this team victory in the Youth and Senior Boys races with the Eastern District winning the Junior Boys contest.

The Celtic Countries International match at Irvine was a gruelling test in the hardest of harrier traditions, with strong winds and driving rain sweeping across the Beach Park throughout the afternoon. Scotland won the Junior and Youth team contests, with Clark Murphy winning the Junior race from teammate Ian Tierney, and Ian White finishing second in the Youth race. However the Under 23 race was not so successful, with fifth placed David Donnett being the first Scot home in a team which could only finish last behind Wales, Ireland and Northern Ireland.

With so many International racing commitments, as preparation for the National and International championships, Nat Muir was usually competing on the Continent at the time of the District Championships in January. He had, therefore, only one previous win in the Western District Championship, but added another title to his long string of championship honours when winning at Houston. In his first cross country race of the season in Scotland he won in a sprint finish, after being spiked half way through the $7\frac{1}{2}$ mile race. He finished just 2 seconds in front of Tommy Murray with Adrian Callan finishing third a further 16 seconds behind. Cambuslang won the team title, starting a 3 year run of successes up to Centenary year, and Clydebank won the Senior and Junior Boys team championships and took second place behind Victoria Park in the Youths contest. Alastair Russell (Law & District) won the Junior 6 mile race for his fifth District Individual title, having previously won the Senior Boys title in 1983-84 and the Youths title in 1985-86. Northern Ireland steeplechase champion and record holder, Peter McColgan (Dundee Hawkhill Harriers), scored his first major success in Scotland when winning the Eastern District Senior title at Wilton Lodge Park, Hawick. He outsprinted Terry Mitchell to win by 2 seconds, with Teviotdale, competing on their home course, retaining the Senior team title by 10 points from Aberdeen with Dundee Hawkhill in third position.

For the first time since 1979 Nat Muir did not contest the National Championships - forced to withdraw due to a virus illness - and therefore not being able to better the record of five consecutive championship titles he had equalled the previous year. Neil Tennant, second two years ago to Nat Muir over the same Beach Park venue at Irvine, showed full recovery from a persistent back injury to win his first National title. Not deterred by the strong wind sweeping in from the sea, Tennant went into the lead after the first mile, tracked by Chris Robison who, in the previous two months, had won the Royal Navy, Inter Services and English Southern Counties championships, and was to finish fifth in both the English National and the UK World Championship trial race. Tennant ran the final 6 miles on his own, steadily drawing away from the tiring Robison, to win eventually by 33 seconds, with Tommy Murray finishing strongly to take third place just 4 seconds behind Robison. With a spearhead of Alex Gilmour 5, Colin Donnelly 6, and Eddie Stewart 7, well backed up by Ross Arbuckle 13, Jim Orr 14, and Charlie Thomson 18, Cambuslang easily won the team championship with the low score of just 63 points - 99 points in front of Edinburgh Southern, who had the misfortune to have Allister Hutton and Alan Robson drop out of the race. This team victory climaxed a highly successful season for Cambuslang, who had earlier won the Western District relay and team championships, the National cross country relay title and the Edinburgh to Glasgow relay event. Clydebank continued their successes in the younger age group races, with Malcolm Campbell (Youths) and Nick Freer (Senior Boys), winning Individual titles, and the club winning team titles in the Junior Boys and Youths races and finishing runners up to Dunbartonshire rivals Victoria Park in the Senior Boys race. With the Scottish International team having lost much of its raison d'etre, due to its enforced withdrawal from the World Cross Country Championships by dictate of the IAAF, the Trial race for the United Kingdom team to compete in the World Championships became one of the highlights of the season. The first Trial, organised by the British Amateur Athletic Board, for the UK team to compete in New Zealand, was held at the Riverside Bowl, Gateshead. Running in sticky, gluey mud only two Scots, Chris Robison - fifth in the Senior, and Clark Murphy - sixth in the Junior, earned selection for the British team. Only three other Scots, Nat Muir 12, Adrian Callan 17 and Terry Mitchell 19, were in the first twenty finishers home in a disappointing display by Scottish runners. The Walter Lawn Memorial Trophy and the John D Semple Trophy had been reassigned as trophies to be awarded to the first Scots finishers in the UK Trials, and were awarded to C Robison and C Murphy respectively.

Former Scottish marathon champion Colin Youngson (Aberdeen), who had qualified as a Veteran (over 40 years) just 3 months earlier, won the National Veterans championship at his first attempt. Competing at Dalmuir Park, Clydebank, heavy snow, which started to fall as the starters gun sounded and stopped virtually as the last man crossed the finishing line, proved a deterrent to the field of 240 competitors. Youngson set a fast pace no one could stay with and won by 120 yards from Ken Duncan (Pitreavie) and Graham Milne (Aberdeen). Aberdeen won the team championship, defeating Dumbarton and Cambuslang. The oldest competitor in the race, 78 year old John Emmett Farrell, who had won the National title 50 years earlier, received a special award from the Union in recognition of his services to the sport.

In the British Veterans championships at Irvine, Youngson finished runner up to Alan Roper (Swansea), with Scottish wins coming in the older age categories from Willie Marshall (over 60); David Morrison (over 70) and John Emmett Farrell (over 75).

The National 6 Stage road relay championships, sponsored by Royal Mail Letters, were held for the first time in the East of Scotland over an excellent course at Livingston. Springburn, after being successful for many years in the younger age group races on the championship programme, finally won the first National Senior team championship in the 95 year history of the club. They went into the lead on the fourth stage, thanks to Adrian Callan recording the fastest time of the day for the long 6 mile stage, and established a 92 second lead with just two stages to go. Ian Hamer (Edinburgh AC), who was to win the bronze medal in the 1990 Commonwealth Games 5,000 metres race at Auckland, just a few feet behind the winner, pulled back the big lead and handed over a 3

John Emmett Farrell (Maryhill Harriers), National champion in 1938 and 1948. Forty years after his last National title he is placed first in the 1988 British Veterans over 75 years age group division at Irvine.

second lead at the final change over. George Braidwood, who had switched clubs from Bellahouston to Springburn a few months earlier, ran strongly to bring Springburn to victory 37 seconds ahead of Edinburgh with Bellahouston third.

Greenock Glenpark Harriers, who had been quietly developing a strong team, blossomed fourth with a clean sweep of all the relay titles at the start of the 1988/89 season. After winning the McAndrew relay race for the first time, defeating Bellahouston by 4 seconds after an exciting last lap, and winning the Renfrewshire County relay title, the Greenock club lined up as one of the favourites for the Western District relay championship at Drumpellier Park, Coatbridge. Competing in brilliant sunshine, a poor start of twentieth position was overcome by the International trio of Hammy Cox, Alan Puckrin and Tommy Murray - who contributed to all Glenpark's victories, and they worked their way through the field to win by 150 yards for their first District relay title in 22 years. Aberdeen were surprise winners of the Eastern District relay title at Musselburgh Racecourse, recording their first win in 9 years. After Teviotdale had led for most of the race, Welsh International Chris Hall brought Aberdeen into the lead on the final lap to win by 100 yards from the Hawick club with Dundee Hawkhill third.

Greenock Glenpark completed their series of relay titles when winning the National relay championship at Bellahouston Park for the first time in the 14 year history of the event, becoming only the sixth club to win the title. After finishing fifteenth at the end of the first lap, H Cox, A Puckrin and T Murray overcame the deficit to such an extent that Tommy Murray romped home to a big welcome, 33 seconds in front of Springburn, with Dundee Hawkhill third. Victoria Park AAC won the Young Athletes race for the first ever time with an all round team of youthful talent.

After Peter Fleming (Bellahouston) had won the Nigel Barge road race from Brian Scally (Shettleston), after finishing third in the Morpeth to Newcastle road race on New Years Day, and Alex Gilmour had won the Springburn road race, it was the turn of Scotland's youngsters to take the International stage. Competing in the Celtic Countries International match at Irvine they did not run with much success, and only Alastair Russell, who won the Under 23 race and led his team to victory over Ireland, ran with any distinction. Irish runners won the Junior and Youths contests with Scotland finishing fourth and third respectively.

Tommy Murray, runner up in the Western District Championship race on the previous two occasions, continued Glenpark's year of success when winning the Senior title at Kilmarnock. Competing over a hilly course Murray successfully negotiated the muddy surface to win by 53 seconds from Alastair Russell, with clubmate Alan Puckrin third. Murray led Greenock Glenpark to second place in the team championship behind Cambuslang with Steve Ovett, the 1980 Olympic 800 metres champion and former 1 mile and 1,500 metres world record holder, leading Annan and District AC to their first ever set of District team medals in third place. Ovett, who had moved from the South of England a few months earlier to live outside Annan, had joined his local club and, on just 6 weeks training, finished in seventh position in the race. British orienteering international Steve Hale (Perth Strathtay Harriers), surprised everyone when winning the Senior title at the Eastern District Championships at Galashiels. He outpaced John Robson to win by 19 seconds, with Peter Fox (Dundee Hawkhill) in third place. Edinburgh AC won the

Senior team title for the first time since 1978 and also won the Junior Boys team title.

The National Championships were held at Wilton Lodge Park in Hawick as the high spot of Teviotdale Harriers Centenary year - the first time the championships had been held in the Scottish Borders. Five inches of snow had fallen overnight in the worst weather experienced during the entire winter, and the snow continued to fall throughout the day, leaving a covering of slippery snow over an underfoot morass of mud. This resulted in one of the steepest hills on the course - 150 yards in length with a 1 in 9 gradient - becoming a tough test of strength, balance and agility. The testing conditions did not worry Tommy Murray, who became the first Glenpark runner since George Wallace in 1922 to win a National title . At just 8½ stone, with size 10 feet, Murray had suffered from anorexia in his early years and at one time weighed just 3½ stone before recovering the will to live. He floated over the ground, being unchallenged over the second half of the race, to win by 23 seconds from Anglo Scot Paul Evans (Springburn), with Peter Fox third. Steve Ovett, who had won the Stewartry 5 mile cross country race by almost 2 minutes just a week earlier, finished fourth and stated that he had never run in worse conditions but nevertheless enjoyed the race. Cambuslang, led by British hill running champion Colin Donnelly 12, retained the team championships by 34 points from the local club Teviotdale, with Shettleston third.

Scottish runners seemed to have lost incentive, class and quality, being good only for the tail end of the field in top class fields as they proved in the World Championship Trials at Gateshead. In a race won by Tim Hutchings, who went on to finish second to John Ngugi in the World Championship at

Tommy Murray (Greenock Glenpark Harriers), 1989 National champion and two times Western District champion 1989-90.

Stavanger, Norway, Murray was the first Scot to finish in twenty second position - almost 1½ minutes behind Hutchings, followed by C Robison 27, and A Callan 29. The Juniors fared even worse with Anglo Scot Ian Gillespie 17, finishing 78 seconds behind the winner, and the first home Scot Alastair Russell 37, being another minute further behind. Nat Muir sounded the end to a very successful cross country career when he dropped out of the race due to Achilles tendon trouble, stating he was in pain whenever he ran over an uneven surface, and announced he would confine his competition in future to road and track running.

The Union decided, after numerous representations at Annual General Meetings, to extend the National Veterans Championship from a race for Veteran runners over 40 years, by the recognition of 5 year age group bands. This transformed the event, with individual champions being recognised in 6 additional age groups from over 45 years to over 70 years. Scottish championship medals would be awarded to each age group winner, with a second place award being given if 5 or more athletes competed, and a third place award if 10 or more athletes competed. Thus a total of 21 championship medals would be due to be presented if there were a minimum of 10 competitors in each of the 7 recognised age group categories i.e. if 70 runners took part equally distributed through the age groups. This distribution of medals can be compared to the total of just 3 medals awarded in the National Senior championship race where upwards of 500 runners take part.

Cambuslang Harriers team which competed at the European Champion Clubs Cup at Acoteias, Portugal in 1989. From left to right; (Back); E. Stewart, J. Orr, A. Beattie, R. Arbuckle; (Front); C. Donnelly and C. Thomson.

Colin Youngson had little difficulty retaining his title when the National Veterans Championship, under the new rules, was held at Aberdeen. Running over home ground at Balgownie Playing Fields, Youngson recorded an easy victory, finishing 120 yards in front of Charlie McDougall (Calderglen) with Peter Marshall (Haddington) in third place. He led Aberdeen to retain their National team title. Edinburgh Southern rescued a disappointing season when they won the final National championship of the season - the National 6 stage road relay championship at East Kilbride. After a see saw change of positions in the early stages of the race, Allister Hutton continued his proud record of having been a member of every Southern winning team since the championship was first held in 1979. He took over a 1 second lead at the final changeover, and raced to the third fastest time over the long 6 mile lap behind Nat Muir and Alan Puckrin, to bring Southern home with a 53 second margin of victory. Peter McColgan, who had been caught unawares at the final changeover, and lost over 10 seconds donning his vest before starting on the last lap, brought Dundee Hawkhill into second place, 18 seconds in front of Edinburgh to Glasgow winners, Aberdeen AAC.

1990 — Centenary Year

The Centenary celebrations of the Union had been long awaited, assiduously prepared and well enjoyed during season 1989/90. It had initially been planned to recognize 1987/88 as the Centenary season, as the first National championship outside the jurisdiction of the SAAA Sub Committee was held in 1888. However, with further information coming to the attention of the Union regarding the administrative conflict between the Scottish Cross Country Association and the Scottish Harriers Union, and the fact that two rival Championships were held in Scotland at that time, the date was correctly changed to season 1989/90. The Scottish Cross Country Union was established as the sole governing body of Cross Country running in Scotland, following the dissolution of the rival Scottish Cross Country Association and the Scottish Harriers Union, and the first meeting of the Union was held in Glasgow on 1st February 1890.

The initial meeting of the Centenary Committee was held in Glasgow on 1st February 1984 - exactly 94 years to the day after the founding of the Union - under the chairmanship of John Hamilton, who continued in that position for the next 30 meetings of the Committee which ended with a final meeting in April 1990 at the conclusion of the Centenary celebrations. Various sub committees were formed with responsibility for the Centenary Raffle, Souvenirs, Mobile Historical Display, Opening and Closing Events and the Centenary History Book, and the intensive work of these sub committees contributed to making the Centenary season a success.

The Centenary celebrations covered the whole country. The decision was taken that the four main National championships would be staged at venues in the North, South, East and West of Scotland and they were held as follows:- National Cross Country Relay Championships at Inverness on 28th October 1989; National Veterans Cross Country Championships at Dumfries on 4th February 1990; National Cross Country Championships at Irvine on 24th February 1990; National 6 Stage Road Relay Championships at Livingston on 24th March 1990.

Weather has always played an important part in any Harrier cross country race throughout the past 100 years as intimated by the old dictum "Runs will take place whatever the weather". Frequent references have been made in previous chapters to the weather conditions experienced at previous championships. The rain, hailstones, snow, sleet, ice, fog, cold and occasionally, sunshine, that affected races and competitors performances have all been mentioned and, unfortunately, the Centenary season was no different. The Weather Gods had saved up some of the worst weather imaginable and unleashed it on competitors, officials and spectators on the days of the various National Championships when the current fear of the "Greenhouse Effect" seemed very far away.

Right from the first National Championship in the Autumn - the cross country Relays at Inverness - which had frequently been held in sunshine in past years, the weather was poor, described by convener Walter Banks as "dreich and windy". From there on, throughout the winter months, it got worse and worse. The Veterans championships at Dumfries and the National Championships at Irvine were held in dreadful conditions, on wet and windy days, and even the 6 Stage Road Relay Championship at Livingston, at the birth of Spring, was run in a snow blizzard which left runners shivering and numb with cold. In an otherwise normal winter, with no outstanding spells of bad weather, the worst winter days seemed to be reserved for the Saturdays of National Championships throughout the country.

The Centenary season celebrations were split into social and competitive events. Both aspects were covered by the events organised by the Union and the social side was supplemented by events staged by Central and Local Government Authorities, who assisted in celebrating the Union's centenary with civic receptions throughout the country.

The season opened on 1st October with an old style pack outing from Huntershill Outdoor Centre in Bishopbriggs, looking back at past traditions with a "Fun for All" run over the surrounding country. Competitors and officials wore Victorian style clothes, with Sandy Cameron, Ian Clifton, Roddy Devon, Bob Dalgleish, John Hamilton, Alex Johnston, Duncan McLaren, Robin Thomas and James Young dressed like Victorian gentlemen with Robert McSwein attired as an old style club trainer complete with a towel slung round his neck. Runners also entered into the spirit of the event and some weird and wonderful running costumes, with false beards and moustaches, were worn by the "old style harriers". The best attired were Brian Emmerson, David Geddes, Steve Cullen, Brian Collie, Stuart Bennett and Hugh Barrow who all received prizes from the Union for their imaginative dress. Runners from George Heriots School wore shorts in the Victorian fashion, designed and made by girls from the school's home economics class, but their traditional long sleeved singlets were purchased from Marks and Spencer - showing that all fashions come back into style if one waits long enough!

Runners at the Centenary Opening Run at Huntershill Sports Centre, Bishopbriggs. From left to right; John Hamilton (starter), Brian Emmerson, David Geddes, Steve Cullen, Brian Collie, Stewart Bennett, Hugh Barrow, Alex Johnston (Timekeeper) and James Young.

The runners, who represented most of the clubs in Union membership, were alloted to three packs, "slow, medium and fast", which left at appropriate time intervals in the old harrier tradition with a "pace" and "whip" controlling the running of each pack for an enjoyable social run. The fast pack was whipped by Alastair Douglas who indicated changes in pace by a whistle to speed up or slow down as appropriate to the needs of the members of the pack during the run. First home in a racing finish were Internationals Adrian Callan and Robert Quinn, who covered the interesting, testing course laid by Danny Wilmoth in 48 minutes 11 seconds.

Recognition by various Civic Authorities was a feature of the season, and just over a week later a prestigious reception by the Secretary of State for Scotland took place in the Great Hall of Edinburgh Castle. Lord James Douglas Hamilton presided at the enjoyable reception and, in a guided tour of the Castle and attractions afterwards, Past President Harry Quinn astonished the guide and the other members of his party, by holding a mock auction of the Scottish Crown Jewels.

A civic luncheon by the Lord Provost and Council of the City of Edinburgh was held in Edinburgh on 1st February - exactly 100 years to the day after the founding of the Union, and attended by many famous athletes of former years. Later in the month an evening reception for the Union in Dundee by the City of Dundee District Council was also attended by representatives of the local Dundee Hawkhill Harriers, who were also celebrating their centenary season, together with members of other clubs in the Tayside and Fife Regions. The Lord Provost and City of Glasgow District Council celebrated in grand style with a civic dinner and musical entertainment in the magnificent Glasgow City Chambers in March. A birthday cake, decorated with the SCCU Centenary logo, was enjoyed that evening, having been presented by Thomas Tunnock Ltd, who were also celebrating their centenary year.

The Centenary Dinner, held in April in the Central Hotel, Glasgow, was a splendidly nostalgic affair. As usual, toasts were made after the meal, and the toast to the Union on its Centenary was made by Past President Donald Macgregor, a distinguished marathon runner who had competed in both the Commonwealth and Olympic Games. In a most enthralling, informative and entertaining speech, Macgregor detailed the comic, dramatic and sporting highlights of the past 100 years of Union history. He drew comparisons between the harrier traditions and other aspects of life and recounted tales of championship races from the recent, and the dim and distant, past which amused and entranced his audience. Other guests of honour included Sir Arthur Gold and Marea Hartman who also made witty speeches to the assembled company.

The season was not without its tragedies as former Presidents George Kapelle (Edinburgh Southern Harriers), Andrew Stevenson (Shettleston Harriers) and Ian Ross (Edinburgh Southern Harriers) all died throughout the year.

Dundee Hawkhill started their Centenary season with their first victory in the Eastern District relay championship since 1953. Running over home ground at Caird Park, Dundee they led from half distance to win by 70 seconds from Teviotdale with their 'B' team in third place. Peter McColgan recorded the fastest lap of the day with his Dundee teammates David Beattie, Peter Fox and Charlie Haskett all included in the top five times of the day. Springburn, after winning the Lanarkshire county relay title the previous week, gained the Struthers Shield for the first time when winning the Western District relay championship at Dalmuir Park, Clydebank. Leading from

Union General Committee in Centenary Year. Front Row: (left to right); R.L. McSwein (Hon. Treasurer), H. Quinn (Immediate Past President), R.M. Dalgleish MBE (President), D.V. McLaren (Vice President), J.E. Clifton (Hon. General Secretary). Back Row: (left to right); W. Banks MBE, R. Thomas, J.M. Hamilton, A. Smith, F. McCluskie, G. Spence, A. Jackson, W. Robertson, J. McI. Young, J.A. Innes, J. Cherry, I. Aird, D. Wilmoth. Insert (left to right); Mr Scarbrough, Professor Morrison, Mr Cameron.

half distance, good runs by Adrian Callan and George Braidwood brought them home to a 60 yards victory over Clydebank AC, who fielded four first year Juniors all under 19 years, with Cambuslang finishing third a further 100 yards behind.

The first National championships of the season were held at Inverness, with the Relay championships held over rough grassland and stubble fields at Kinmylies, high above the town. Inverness presented a wintry aspect to competitors and spectators with early winter snow on the surrounding hills. Inverness District Council staged the first reception of the season before the championships sponsored by the North of Scotland Milk Marketing Board. Teviotdale Harriers, who left Hawick at 6am, showed they had fully recovered from their tiring drive north when they got off to a good start. After Keith Logan had finished a close up fourth on the first lap, Rob Hall quickly overhauled the three runners in front of him to hand over a 6 second lead to Alastair Walker who, with a splendid run on the third lap, established a 41 second lead over their main rivals - fifth placed Dundee Hawkhill. Dundee's anchor man, Peter McColgan, recorded the fastest time of the day but failed to catch David Cavers, who held on for a 17 second victory for Teviotdale's first National title in their 101st year. Dundee Hawkhill were second, 17 seconds in front of Springburn, with Victoria Park retaining the Young Athletes relay title, defeating Cambuslang by 3 seconds with Pitreavie a distant third.

Dundee Hawkhill's strong road running squad, after finishing second to Edinburgh Southern in the Allan Scally road relay race, scored their long awaited victory in the Edinburgh to Glasgow relay race. Although their former city rivals Dundee Thistle Harriers had won the race in 1937, Hawkhill had never finished in the first three teams prior to their centenary year victory. They won by 90 seconds from Cambuslang, with Aberdeen third, a further 70 seconds behind, and Calderglen gaining the award for the most meritorious performance of the day.

The annual representative match between the Union, Northern Ireland and the Combined Scottish Universities was held over a new course at Cumbernauld, with sponsorship from Cumbernauld and Kilsyth District Council. Robert Quinn won the 10,000 metres race from Union teammates David Cavers and Charlie Haskett and led the Union to an easy team victory. Allan Reid (North) had an excellent race to win the Inter District Senior race by 22 seconds from Neil Thin (East). The Western District dominated the Inter District contest winning two individual and three team titles, losing only the Junior Boys team contest to the Eastern District.

Tommy Murray finished fourteenth in the Mallusk Park International race at Belfast in the New Year, one of the few International races that Scotland is still invited to send teams to. Murray finished 63 seconds behind the winner Craig Mochrie (England), with the final finisher in the Scots team of four finishing twenty sixth, another 24 seconds behind Murray.

The annual Celtic Countries International at Beach Park, Irvine was expanded, in the Senior race, to a full Centenary International with the inclusion of England and Sweden in addition to Scotland, Ireland, Northern Ireland and Wales who competed in the usual Junior and Youths races. Alastair Douglas, who had earlier won the Nigel Barge race in 21 minutes 48 seconds — just 2 seconds outside the 7 year old record held by Nat Muir, went off course in the final stages of the Senior 10,000 metres race. He eventually finished third, just 6 seconds behind Mark King, who led England, 14 points, to a narrow team victory over Scotland, 17 points, with Robert Quinn 5, and David Cavers 9, completing the Scottish team. In the other events of the Celtic International Scotland fared badly, with Ireland providing the Individual winner in both the Junior and Youths races, and Ireland and Northern Ireland winning the respective team contests. The International will rotate between the four competing countries, with the first meeting held as part of Limerick's tercentenary celebrations in Ireland in 1991.

Dundee Hawkhill continued their winning ways at the Eastern District championships at Galashiels, where they won the Senior team title for the first time since 1937, and scored only their third victory in their 100 year history. The Dundee club, led by Charlie Haskett who finished runner up 17 seconds behind defending champion Steve Hale (Perth Strathtay), totalled 83 points to defeat Edinburgh SPC 122 points and Edinburgh Southern 213 points. Tommy Murray easily retained his Senior title in the Western District championships at Troon where he won by 200 yards from Eddie Stewart. Stewart led Cambuslang, 58 points, to one of the most comprehensive team victories ever recorded in the championships, placing their counting 6 runners in the first 15 to finish, before runners up Kilbarchan 254 points, had their first counting runner home.

Adopted Scot Peter McColgan, whose wife Liz had successfully retained the Commonwealth Games 10,000 metres title at Auckland the previous month, became only the second foreigner to win the Senior title at the National championships. His fellow Irishman, P J McCafferty, had won the title 87 years earlier in 1903, and McColgan completed a double victory, having won the Northern Irish championship just 7 days earlier. Run in dreadful weather conditions of sleet, hail and snow, the usually fine surface of the Beach Park at Irvine was churned up into a sea of mud. McColgan, however, negotiated the difficult terrain to win by 24 seconds from Neil Tennant (Edinburgh Southern) with Robert Quinn third, a further 4 seconds behind. Cambuslang retained the Senior team title, winning for the third year in a row, with their team of C Donnelly 15; J Orr 17; E Stewart 19; A Gilmour 20; C Thomson 27 and D Runcieman 28, totalling 126 points, to defeat Edinburgh Southern 159 points, with Dundee Hawkhill, in their best National team performance for over half a century, finishing third with 183 points. All 1200 finishers in the five championship races received a special centenary commemorative medal.

The National Veterans Championships were held at Dumfries, which was judged by officials, spectators and runners to be the wettest place in Scotland on the day of the race. It poured with rain throughout the race, accompanied by a bitterly cold wind in the face of competitors. It says much for the fitness of the veterans that 185 runners completed the event with Cambridge based George Meredith (Victoria Park) winning by 6 seconds from Colin Youngson, who led Aberdeen, 4 in the first 11 runners home, to retain the team title from Teviotdale and Cambuslang.

The United Kingdom Trial races for the World Championships at Aix-les-Bains, France, were held in Scotland by decision of the British Amateur Athletics Board in recognition of the Union's Centenary. Held in Gateshead for the previous two years, the Trials were staged at Bellahouston Park, Glasgow, over part of the trail used for the World Championships in 1978. Due to three weeks of almost continual rainfall prior to the race, the course was muddy, dotted with deep pools of water, and tiring to runners who finished spattered from head to toe in mud. Chris Robison finished fourth, 18 seconds behind the winner Adrian Passey (England), to again gain selection for the World Championships where he finished ninety first. John Robson 15, was the first home Scot to finish, followed by Robert Quinn 20, and Tommy Murray 21. Malcolm Campbell, who runs for Clydebank when competing in Scotland, chose to represent England rather than Scotland and finished second, gaining selection for the UK team for the championships. Mark McBeth 15, was the first home Scot to finish, with Mike McCartney 16, and Steven Wylie 19, finishing inside the first 20 runners home. Union Secretary Ian Clifton was appointed as the Team Manager of the British team for France.

The weather jinx struck again at the National 6 Stage road relay Championship at Livingston, held on the traditional final Saturday of March. On the eve of Spring, snow blizzards raged at both the start and finish of the race, with frozen competitors running well below their normal capabilities. Dundee Hawkhill, third at half distance, moved into second place just 9 seconds behind Teviotdale on stage 4, and former Junior star, Ian Campbell, moved into a 12 second lead on the penultimate stage. Running the final 6 mile stage with the snow blizzard at its height Charlie Haskett increased Hawkhill's winning margin to 47 seconds over Cambuslang, with Edinburgh Southern a distant third, a further 57 seconds behind. The Dundee team of B Cook; C Hall; P McCormack; P Fox; I Campbell and C Haskett gained the club's first 6 Stage relay title and climaxed a successful year in which they won four titles - the Eastern District relay and team championships, the Edinburgh to Glasgow and the 6 Stage road relay championships.

Youth was the focus for the closing event of the Centenary celebrations at Edinburgh. For, just as the season started with a backward look at the early days of cross country running, the final meeting at Holyrood Park was the opportunity for the athletes of the future to participate in the Centenary celebrations. Derek Slythe

(ESPC), formerly Edinburgh AC, won the Youths 2½ mile race and his clubmate Kevin Daley, National Junior Boys champion, won his age group event. Geoff Browitt (Penicuik), who had recorded a rare Scottish victory in the British Schools cross country international, won the Senior Boys event. All athletes received Centenary souvenirs as prizes and centenary mugs were in common usage in many Edinburgh homes after the prize giving.

Souvenirs were a large part of the celebrations and the range and variety of souvenirs was astonishing. The Union offered ties, tee shirts and sweatshirts, pennants, pens and key rings, lapel and blazer badges, mugs and ladies scarves. Many athletes and officials purchased a selection of the available products and tee shirts, one of the most popular items, were known to be worn throughout the countries of Europe, in Zimbabwe and South Africa, in New Zealand and Australia, in the Persian Gulf and in Canada and the USA. Specially engraved commemorative Edinburgh Crystal vases were produced and presented by the Union to sponsors, other athletic governing bodies and local councils.

The Union starts its second hundred years in changing circumstances, with proposals under discussion for amalgamation with the Womens cross country governing body, for the creation of a British Athletics Federation and changes in the existing set up in Scotland for the control of athletics, road and cross country running. United Kingdom Commissions have been established for the control of road running and cross country competition, with the Union in membership of both from their initial establishment. Competition standards are getting higher, travel and accommodation costs to representative and international events are rising rapidly, international competition for Scotland's athletes is getting harder every year and the number of youngsters coming into the sport is falling due to the lower birth rate in the country. All these problems have to be faced and overcome so that cross country at club, national and international levels will be as successful in its second hundred, as it was in its first hundred, years.

Edinburgh to Glasgow Relay Race
1930 to 1939

Road running gradually emerged as a separate rival entity to the established track and cross country running in the thirties. It was headed by the relay race from Edinburgh to Glasgow which was part of a glorious triumvirate of relays sponsored by the News of the World. The others, in England, were the Manchester to Blackpool for Midland and Northern clubs, and the London to Brighton for Southern clubs. The London to Brighton course was used for a National Relay Championship with Scots clubs qualifying to travel South to compete by virtue of their performance in the Scottish race.

The two English races disappeared in the Sixties at the insistence of the police, falling victim to the vast increase in traffic of private cars and lorries, but the Scottish race from Edinburgh to Glasgow, by way of the old A8 route, survived to the immense relief of all who enjoyed competing in and watching the exciting races between the top invited clubs. The main factor in its survival was the construction of the M8 motorway between Edinburgh and Glasgow which bypassed the old A8, thus removing the main volume of traffic on the race route. Other vital decisions such as changing the race day from Saturday to Sunday, altering the starting venue from Edinburgh City Centre to Inverleith Park in the Southern suburbs, and an earlier start time in the morning, all convinced the various Police and Traffic authorities along the 45 mile course to allow the popular race to continue.

The race was conceived as an attraction to serve the needs of distance runners in the interlude between the end of the cross country season and the start of the Summer track season. In 1930, jointly organised by the Scottish AAA and the National Cross Country Union of Scotland, the race was held on 26th April for the first time.

This new race roused the following reaction from one correspondent :-

"In the old days runners eased off at the end of March after completion of the Winter's cross country fixtures and restarted serious training at the beginning of May, and there were fewer cases of staleness round about the time of the SAAA Championships. The increase of competitions may be quite a good thing for some athletes, but in others it is quite the reverse, with the latter unfortunately in the majority. A real interval between the cross country and track seasons is necessary to allow athletes to rest and produce the best results for the Summer season".

In spite of this unfavourable review the race was an instant success with the participating clubs. The first race was run over the following course :-

Stage	St Andrews Square, Edinburgh to :	Distance
1	Maybury Cross (now a roundabout)	5 miles
2	Broxburn	5 ½ miles
3	Wester Dechmont Farm	4 ½ miles
4	Armadale	5 ¼ miles
5	Forrestfield Inn	6 ¼ miles
6	Airdrie War Memorial	7 miles
7	Barrachnie	5 ½ miles
8	Royal Exchange Square, Glasgow	5 miles
	TOTAL DISTANCE	44 ¼ miles

In the sixty years that have elapsed since the first race the above stages have hardly been altered, with the changeover points becoming fixed, except that the starting point has changed, and the finish line is now outside the Glasgow City Chambers in George Square.

Of the seventeen clubs who completed the course in the first race fourteen were from the West of Scotland and only three (Dundee Thistle Harriers and Edinburgh Southern and Northern Harriers) were from the East. The pre-race favourites were Maryhill Harriers who, the previous month, had set up a record of four consecutive victories in the National Cross Country Team Championships, beating the previous record of three wins held jointly by Clydesdale Harriers and Shettleston Harriers. But, on the day, cross country form was no guide and Plebian Harriers won easily in 3 hours 54 mins 07 sec, finishing 300 yards in front of Dundee Thistle Harriers with Maryhill Harriers trailing in a distant third place over half a mile behind.

The tradition was started of clubs placing their strongest runner on the long sixth stage between the Forrestfield Inn, 700 feet above sea level, and the Airdrie War Memorial. On this occasion multi Scottish Champion John Suttie Smith ran 34 min 07 sec for the 7 mile stage which brought Dundee Thistle to within a few yards of Plebian Harriers and set an inaugural stage record which would be highly acceptable to many runners sixty years later.

The following year 22 clubs entered the race — the conversion to an invitation event for the top 20 clubs in Scotland was still in the future — but 21 clubs faced the starter and with Irvine YMCA and Kilbarchan AC dropping out during the race, there were 19 finishers. Leading from start to finish Plebian Harriers repeated their inaugural victory in 3 hours 50 min 39 sec to finish 1 min 28 sec in front of Maryhill Harriers with Garscube Harriers a distant third.

Victoria Park AAC, later to establish a record of five successive wins in the early fifties, were surprise entrants less than a year after being formed at a meeting in Partick Burgh Hall. They finished a lowly 14th in 4 hours 13 min 15 sec with Paisley Harriers finishing 19th, and last, in 4 hours 21 min 08 sec - a difference of 30 min 29 sec between first and last ! Six stage records were set during the race, only the sixth and last lap times surviving. Suttie Smith's 7 mile time was 36 seconds faster than the 34 min 47 sec set by four times National Champion, Dunky Wright (Maryhill Harriers).

No race was held in 1932 but the event resumed the following year, to be held continuously except for the necessary break due to the Second World War. Plebian Harriers completed their hat-trick of victories but were slowed by a head wind to 3 hours 59 min 17 sec with only one stage record — 29 min 48 sec set by A T Armstrong (Plebian) on the seventh stage. Thirteen clubs entered and finished the race with Shettleston Harriers, the new National Team Champions, finishing fourth behind Dundee Thistle Harriers and Maryhill Harriers. Shettleston had Andrew S Stevenson, a future President and Secretary of the Union, on the second stage, with National Champion James C Flockhart running the long sixth stage in the fastest time of the day.

The most notable event in the 1933 race was the fact that it was the first time that the News of the World newspaper sponsored the race. This valuable sponsorship enabled the race to establish glamour and mystique and create the traditions and folklore that makes it one of a clubs main ambitions each season to gain the valuable invitation to compete in the "Edinburgh to Glasgow Relay".

The next two races switched into the cross country season, being held in early January each year, and the poor weather conditions contributed to winning times over four hours on each occasion.

Strong headwinds, accompanied by intermittent heavy showers of rain and sleet, slowed the competitors at some stages to little faster than walking pace in the 1934 race. Dundee Thistle Harriers, who were also to win the Eastern District and National team titles that year, improved from their two previous second place positions to win by almost a minute from Edinburgh Northern Harriers in 4 hours 20 min 47 sec - the slowest ever winning time !

The habit of winning the National team title and the "Edinburgh to Glasgow" Relay in the same year, begun by Dundee Thistle Harriers the previous year, was continued by Edinburgh Northern in 1935. After a slow start, a good run by J Suttie Smith (formerly of Dundee Thistle Harriers and Dundee YMCA Harriers) when recording the fastest lap on the fifth stage, brought them near to the leaders and they moved into the lead over the final two stages to win by 300 yards from Garscube Harriers.

The race reverted to an April start in 1936 with the fine weather contributing to five new stage records. Outstanding among these was the run by R B McIntosh of Greenock Glenpark Harriers on the opening stage where he set a record of 26 min 05 sec that was to last for just short of a quarter of a century until Alastair Wood (Shettleston Harriers) finally bettered it in 1960. Bellahouston Harriers won in 3 hours 51 min 15 sec, the second fastest time on record, with eleventh placed Hamilton Harriers receiving the first set of special team medals for the "Best Improved Performance" which is now termed the "Most Meritorious Award".

All the races to date had started at 2.30 p.m., possibly to allow for the then universal habit of Saturday morning working. In 1937 the start time changed to 11.00 a.m. but most clubs still fielded their strongest team. Dundee Thistle Harriers, already National Team Champions, recorded their second victory when lowering the course record by 25 seconds to 3 hours 50 min 14 sec. Three stage records were set with James Flockhart lowering the 7 miles sixth stage by over half a minute with an excellent run of 33 min 32 sec.

The record fell again when Bellahouston Harriers recorded 3 hours 49 min 47 sec in 1938, beating Maryhill Harriers (who were also inside the old record) by just 18 seconds, though no stage records were set. Two race traditions were innovated that year with Baillie Coltart of Edinburgh Corporation starting the race at St Andrews Square - a responsibility retained by Edinburgh Corporation and latterly Edinburgh District Council to this date. The other innovation was the rule that runners must keep to the left hand side of the road over the entire route. This has stopped the habit that runners previously had of taking the shortest way round bends, and was brought into effect for athletes safety after a fatal accident to a runner in a relay race in the South of England.

In the final race of the pre-war series Maryhill Harriers, after 3 silver and 3 bronze medal performances, climaxed their consistent series with a longed for, and well deserved, victory. Of the winning team, it is incredible to realise, there are two members still actively running over fifty years later. John Emmet Farrell, who made his first appearance in 1938 - the year he was Scottish National Champion - and Gordon Porteous, who first ran in the relay a year earlier, are both active participants in veteran cross country and road running more than a half century further on.

John Emmett Farrel (B1) handing over to Archie Peters after running the fastest time in the sixth stage from Forestfield Inn to Airdrie War Memorial in the 1939 Edinburgh to Glasgow relay race in which Maryhill Harriers recorded their only victory in the event.

Post War 1949 to 1959 Races

It was to be exactly ten years and one day later, on 23rd April 1949, that the event resumed after the interval of the Second World War and the subsequent period of re-establishment of running in the post war years. Financial sponsorship and support from the News of the World newspaper was again established and Shettleston Harriers, winners of the National Championships for the two previous years, recorded their expected victory. They were slowed by gale force headwinds, to a winning time of 4 hours 15 min 25 sec but after leading from gun to tape finished 5½ minutes ahead of Victoria Park AAC who, though best known for their sprinters at that time, were fast developing a team of top class distance runners that would dominate Scottish Cross Country. A notable feature was that Edinburgh Southern Harriers, who finished ninth, were the only club in the 15 strong entry not from the West of Scotland. Although the number of East of Scotland clubs increased to six in 1950 it was to be a long time before they exceeded 50% of the invited clubs in the race. West of Scotland Harriers, only a shadow of the once great club due to recruitment difficulties and troubles after the War, were the first club to be withdrawn from the race by the rule which called for any club falling thirty minutes behind the leaders to be removed from the race.

Just seven months later, on 21st November 1949, Shettleston Harriers achieved the unique record of winning the race for the second time inside the same year. With the previous April date the race was held during the Scottish AAA summer season. With agreement between the two bodies the race date was changed to November, inside the cross country season, and firmly under the jurisdiction of the SCCU where it has been an important and valued fixture ever since. The Shettleston team of Clark Wallace, veteran James Flockhart, John Burton, Harry Howard, Ben Bickerton, George Craig, Eddie Bannon and Alex Maxwell (who replaced Jimmy Ross from the April squad) had a much tougher time winning from Victoria Park. Shettleston runners led for the first five laps with fastest stage times coming from Clark Wallace (stage 1) and Harry Howard (stage 4). But the Forbes brothers, "Chick" on stage 5 and Andrew on stage 6, brought Victoria Park into a 56 second lead with just 2 stages to the tape. However a stirring seventh stage run by Ben Bickerton regained the lead for Shettleston and Eddie Bannon brought the Glasgow club home to their second victory, but the last for a period of five years, during which Victoria Park AAC would record an unprecedented period of race domination including two course records.

Running illegally on the seventh stage for Edinburgh Southern Harriers was young Ian Clifton, still a Youth and ineligible to compete in the race. He later became one of the few men to be President of both the Scottish AAA and Scottish Cross Country Union, being SCCU President in 1978 on the occasion of the last World Championships to be held in Scotland and eight years later being SAAA President in the year of the Commonwealth Games at Meadowbank Stadium in Edinburgh.

Although Shettleston won the Western District and National team titles in 1950 they could not hold off the developing challenge from their Glasgow rivals, Victoria Park AAC, who won after an engrossing struggle. They took the lead on the final stage for a narrow 32 second victory over Shettleston. Greenock Glenpark Harriers, after finishing fourth in both the 1949 races, finished in third place to gain their only set of medals in the history of the race.

Victoria Park won again in 1951, romping home to victory after Ian Binnie established a 54 second lead on the opening lap which was stretched to 3 min 26 sec over Shettleston at the finish in Royal Exchange Square. Their team of Ian Binnie, John and Sid Ellis, Chick and Andy Forbes, Ronnie Kane, John Stirling and Alex Breckenridge was the mainstay of the club in the run of successes over road and country in the Fifties. They were supplemented by Donald Henson, Ronnie Calderwood, John Russell, John McLaren, Gordon Dunn and Norman Ellis.

Victoria Park continued their winning ways in 1952 when, despite setting only one stage record through Andy Forbes on the seventh stage taking two seconds from Donald Urquhart's 15 year old record of 29 min 03 sec, they smashed the overall course record by almost a minute through a sound display of consistent team running that amply displayed their great strength in depth over other clubs. Edinburgh Southern Harriers, sparked by excellent runs on the opening two stages from the diminutive Jim Paterson (later Scottish 440 yard, 880 yards and 2 mile Steeplechase Champion and Scottish 880 yard and 800 metres record holder) and Willie Robertson (now running with Troon Tortoises AC in Ayrshire), finished third behind Victoria Park and Shettleston who filled the first two places in the 1953 race. These bronze medals were the first won by an East of Scotland club since 1938, and although they ruled the roost in Eastern District competition together with Edinburgh University, it was to be a further eight years before Edinburgh Southern gained another set of medals in 1961.

Having lost the National team title to Shettleston, after a run of three consecutive victories, Victoria Park started the 1954 race in apprehension of three times National Champion Eddie Bannon and his Shettleston team-mates. The Shettleston team included marathoners Hugo Fox and RAF Flight Lieutenant Joe McGhee, who had won the marathon title at the British Empire Games in Vancouver the previous summer.

Having lost the National team title to Shettleston, after a run of three consecutive victories, Victoria Park started the 1954 race in apprehension of three times National Champion Eddie Bannon and his Shettleston team-mates. The Shettleston team included marathoners Hugo Fox and RAF Flight Lieutenant Joe McGhee, who had won the marathon title at the British Empire Games in Vancouver the previous summer. Their fears were fully justified for, after Bobby Calderwood finished first home on the opening stage four seconds in the front of Clark Wallace, Shettleston runners led for the next four laps. Marathon champion, Joe McGhee, took over for the 7 mile "champions lap"on the sixth stage with an advantage of 1 min 16 sec over Ian Binnie. But well though McGhee ran, and his time of 33 min 51 sec was only 30 seconds outside the stage record, Binnie had an inspired day on this lonely road through open, exposed countryside.

Displaying the brilliance everyone knew he was capable of producing, the multi Scottish 3 and 6 mile champion steadily eroded the quarter mile advantage his rival had started with. Passing through the crowded shopping streets of Airdrie, Binnie was within striking distance of McGhee and overtook him on the long downhill finish to Airdie War Memorial to establish a narrow three second lead. His new record of 32 min 32 sec, which bettered the previous record by no less than 49 seconds, was to last for the next seven years. From there on it was an assured victory with Donald Henson taking three seconds from clubmate Andy Forbes' seventh stage record and Johnny Stirling setting the fastest time on the final lap through Glasgow city streets, nine seconds faster than Scotland's top miler Graham Everett.

Victoria Park claimed their fifth successive victory, a feat never equalled before or since that year, in the course record time of 3 hours 46 min 43 sec, with Shettleston 34 secs behind also well inside the old record. Club records were improved by third and fourth placed Springburn Harriers and Edinburgh University Hares and Hounds with Falkirk Victoria Harriers, Vale of Leven AC, Clydesdale Harriers and Braidburn Harriers (for whom current SAAA President Neil Donnachie ran the final stage) also improving their club's best ever time in the race.

Shettleston came into their own the following year when, with victories in the Midland District Relay and Team championships and the National Team championships behind them, they took ample revenge for their five successive defeats. Strengthened by the addition of Ian Cloudsley, former National Youth Champion, and George Govan, Shettleston led from the second stage to win by over 500 yards from Victoria Park. They bettered the old record by 1 min 30 sec with seven other clubs also setting best times.

The pendulum effect continued in 1956 with Victoria Park, strengthened by their new recruit John McLaren, the double National Junior Champion from Shotts

Miners Welfare Club, winning by a two and a half minute margin from Shettleston.

Victoria Park 60's great team reached their peak of achievement in 1957, the only time the author competed in the race, running the third lap for Greenock Glenpark Harriers. They displayed the form which won them the National team title when they led from start to finish to set the new record time of 3 hours 44 min 12 sec -over four minutes clear of Bellahouston Harriers who pushed Shettleston into third position for their worst placing since the restart of the race after the war.

Bellahouston Harriers, whose young team had finished second and third in the preceeding years, completed their full set of medals when upsetting the post-war monopoly set up by Victoria Park and Shettleston Harriers. Their first victory since 1938 was not achieved easily, as Victoria Park and Shettleston exchanged the lead over the first half of the race. Once Dick Penman took the lead on the fifth stage and Joe Connolly kept Bellahouston's lead after a struggle with Alistair Wood (Shettleston) and Ian Binnie (Victoria Park) on the long sixth stage, good runs by Des Dickson and Ramsay Black brought Bellahouston home to victory in 3 hours 49 min 29 sec, fully 250 yards in front of Shettleston Harriers. Cambuslang Harriers, who finished 11th, were awarded the medals for the most improved performance, but it was not to be until 22 years later in 1980 when they finished runners up to Clyde Valley AC that they were again medal winners.

Fourth placed Edinburgh Southern Harriers, who to date had just one bronze medal from 1953 to their credit, showed the basis of the team they were building which would win three successive silver medals in the early Sixties. Of the six Eastern District teams in the invited twenty, Edinburgh University (9) were the only other club to figure in the top ten home with Edinburgh Eastern Harriers 14 and Teviotdale Harriers 17, Braidburn Harriers 19 and Falkirk Victoria Harriers 20 (over 36 minutes behind the winners).

The Bellahouston team showed amazing consistency over the next two years, finishing within just six seconds of their 1958 winning time on each occasion, but having to give best each time to a resurgent Shettleston team who had started a run of four successive National Team Championship wins.

The next nine years would be dominated by three clubs who each recorded three successive wins. Shettleston Harriers won from 1959 - 1961, Motherwell YMCA Harriers then dominated from 1962 - 1964 and Edinburgh University, with an amazing bunch of runners, became the first University ever to win the race in 1965 and won for a further two years in the period ending in 1967.

The twenty first race in 1959 was the closest on record. Shettleston led for the first four stages but the tenacious Bellahouston runners closed to 11 seconds on the sixth stage (Joe Connolly), 15 secs on the seventh stage (Bob Gordon), and only W Gorman, running the fastest stage through the busy city streets 3 seconds faster than Freddy Cowan (Bellahouston), kept Shettleston ahead by 18 seconds. Teviotdale Harriers from Hawick received the special medals for their improvement from 17th to 7th position and with Edinburgh Southern Harriers fourth, and St Andrews University seventh it was the best showing by Eastern District clubs in the history of the race.

1960 to 1969 Races

Although fog over Edinburgh hampered the first stage runners in 1960 Alastair Wood shot into the lead from the gun and built up a 100 yard lead by half distance. Running on his own he went on to better R B McIntosh's 24 year old record by the amazing margin of 43 seconds with his record run of 25 min 22 sec. From there on Shettleston runners were out on their own, unopposed in any real sense of the word by their rivals. Graham Everett turned in a record breaking run on the fifth stage, taking 1 min 15 sec from the 29 year old record with his time of 26 min 38 sec. Eddie Bannon brought Shettleston into an unassailable lead on the seventh stage with the fastest time, but the challenge from Edinburgh Southern Harriers, who had held second place since stage two, ended when miler Ken Ballantyne slipped on the greasy road and was struck by a passing car. He was taken to hospital but found not to be seriously injured.

The final time of 3 hours 44 min 32 sec was just 20 seconds outside Victoria Park's four year old record. Bellahouston again finished runners up ahead of Glasgow University who, with good runs from David Gifford and Callum Laing, finished a surprise third — the highest placing ever achieved by a University team. Aberdeen AAC, taking part in the race for the first ever time, finished sixth and received the medals for the most meritorious performance.

Fog again handicapped the runners in the middle stages of the 1961 race, but it did not stop Shettleston capping their third successive victory with a new record of 3 hours 43 min 47 sec. Stage records fell on five occasions. The first record came from John Linaker (Motherwell YMCA) on the second stage (28 min 54 sec) when raising his club from 13th to 2nd; James Campbell, the Dennistoun postman, in his first season for Shettleston, went into the lead with his record of 21 min 33 sec; Andy Brown (Motherwell) set a record of 32 min 27 sec on the "Champions stage" which was bettered almost immediately by Bill Kerr (Victoria Park) who was 2 seconds faster, and Tommy Malone (Shettleston) beat clubmate Eddie Bannon's seventh stage record by 1 second with his run of 28 min 33 sec.

The record breaking was concluded by Ken Ballantyne who took 12 seconds from the final stage record set by F L Stevenson of Monkland Harriers in the opening race way back in 1930. R Wotherspoon brought Shettleston home to a new record of 3 hours 43 min 47 sec over two minutes ahead of Edinburgh Southern Harriers with the next club to dominate the race, Motherwell YMCA, finishing a close up third.

The drawbacks of a November race date were fully illustrated in 1962 when polar conditions of thick snowdrifts stopped the bus carrying runners from Glasgow getting through to the start at Inverleith Park in Edinburgh. The pre-race favourites Motherwell YMCA Harriers could not get their designated first stage runner to the start line and reserve Brian Hodgson stepped in to save the day. Running over a new first stage necessitated by new traffic arrangements Graham Everett (Shettleston) set a new record of 27 min 28 sec with Hodgson finishing 10th a further 55 seconds behind the leader. Running in bitterly cold conditions Motherwell improved from then on. Moving up to sixth on stage three they were behind Teviotdale Harriers for whom John M Hamilton (future SAAA and SCCU President and Scottish International team manager) recorded the third fastest stage time of 21 min 57 sec. Andy Brown improved 23 seconds on the 1957 fourth stage record to finish third, and his young brother Alec and John Linaker gained further places, to bring Motherwell into a 40 second lead by the end of the sixth stage. Bert McKay equalled the seventh stage record to open a gap of more than 2 minutes over Edinburgh Southern Harriers and it was left to John Poulton to bring Motherwell home to their first ever victory in 3 hours 44 min 25 sec.

Motherwell won for the next two years but continued to do it the hard way. The following year it was again as late as the sixth stage when John Linaker went into the lead from Aberdeen AAC, for whom Alastair Wood was now running after his sojurn with Shettleston. Bert McKay, having equalled the seventh stage record the previous year, bettered it by 24 seconds to establish a 2 minute lead and G Henderson brought them home easy winners just 41 seconds slower than the previous year. Aberdeen AAC won their first ever medals in third place and Edinburgh University, in fifth place, received the special set of medals. In a reversal of roles Eastern District clubs filled six of the first ten places in the race confirming a vast improvement in standards in the East of Scotland.

Motherwell's final victory in 1964 was achieved with the addition of Ian McCafferty and Dick Wedlock to their already strong team. They helped Alex and Andy Brown, Bert McKay, Willie Marshall, David Simpson and John Poulton to victory in their slowest winning time of 3 hours 46 min 01 sec. Edinburgh University, with the basis of their remarkable team now in place, but still lacking the final competitive polish they were soon to acquire, finished runners up with the East of Scotland again displaying their growing strength in depth with seven clubs in the first eleven home.

Edinburgh University, facing the fact that never, since the first race in 1930, had a University team won the event, were still quietly confident. They had good reason, for a month earlier they had filled the first two places in the Eastern District Cross Country Relay Championships with Fergus Murray being fastest at 13 min 03 sec and the slowest runner in their 'B' team recording 13 mins 52 secs. This gave them the incentive for success in the event, where a full complement of eight top runners is needed with no weaknesses. The 1965 race was a remarkable one, with stage records set in seven of the eight stages, and an incredible course record of 3 hours 36 min 32 sec resulted for the University team. The improvement of 7 min 15 sec on the previous time was the largest reduction of the course record in the history of the race. The University runners recorded three of the stage records with Alastair Blamire setting a new time of 27 min 01 sec on the opening stage; Olympic 5000 metres runner Fergus Murray running an outstanding sixth stage in 31 min 07 sec taking 1 min 18 secs off the previous record and covering the 7 mile stage at an average speed of 13.4 mph and Jim Wight took 39 seconds off the seventh stage record with his time of 27 min 30 sec. The standard of the race was tremendous with Motherwell YMCA 3 hours 37 min 52 sec and Victoria Park 3 hours 38 min 02 sec also bettering the 3 hour 40 min barrier and the next five teams being under 3 hours 50 min.

With Fergus Murray graduating from Edinburgh University it looked to be a difficult task for the University team to repeat their previous win. However with Alec and Jim Wight, Alastair Blamire, Chris Elson and Ian Hathorn still available, and the emergence of David Logue, Gareth Bryan-Jones and Ian Young, the University looked well capable of defeating their rivals. The students ran as if they knew they would win, never looking round at their pursuing rivals, their sole aim the next

1965 Edinburgh University Hares and Hounds Team. Left to right; Gareth Evans, Fergus Murray, Frank Gamwell, Chris Elson, Roger Young, Ian Young, Alistair Matson and Jim Wight.

changeover point and displaying a zealous professionalism in the best sense of the word.

They achieved their second win with another wonderful display of consistent team running in a time of 3 hours 36 min 53 sec — just 21 seconds outside their own record. They produced four of the eight fastest stage times with three of the runs being in record time. Alastair Blamire equalled his own first stage record; Ian Hathorn set a new record of 21 min 05 sec on the hilly third stage; Jim Wight was fastest on the seventh stage with his run of 28 min 10 sec and Chris Elson took 9 seconds from the final stage record with his run of 23 min 21 sec to bring Edinburgh home to a clear victory. They finished almost three quarters of a mile ahead of Victoria Park AAC, with Motherwell YMCA finishing third just 4 seconds ahead of Aberdeen AAC who had finished sixteenth on the opening stage, but improved steadily to be in second place at the start of the final stage, only to lose two places in the chase through Glasgow's streets to the finish line.

The students' 1967 victory came in less assured style, being much the slowest of their three wins. Jim Alder (Edinburgh AC) set a new opening stage record of 26 min 54 sec with the University 1 min 39 sec behind in eighth place. After Aberdeen AAC led for the next two stages Dave Logue finished the fourth stage 13 seconds in front of Bill Scally (Shettleston Harriers) and the students held the lead to the end. At the start of the final stage the University team were almost two minutes clear of the

209

field and Chris Elson brought them home to victory in 3 hours 44 min 30 sec. Behind him an engrossing struggle was unfolding as Terry Baker, one of two servicemen recruited by Aberdeen AAC from Lossiemouth Air Station, was steadily making up a 12 second deficit on Henry Summerhill (Shettleston Harriers). The two runners were equal with a mile to go and ran shoulder to shoulder along Ingram Street towards the finish.

Baker, who recorded the fastest time of 23 min 17 sec, looked to have the momentum for victory when, in the final 20 yards, a taxi pulled out in front of the runners and Summerhill was quick to seize an advantage. But the judges were unsighted by the vehicle at the finish and awarded a dead heat for second place in spite of Shettleston's protest at the decision.

In the following year, 1968, Shettleston Harriers won and, but for an intervening win by Edinburgh Southern Harriers in 1969, held their superiority over their rivals until 1972. As must be expected in University life, graduation took runners away to the outside world, and the students had the galling experience of seeing former captain, Gareth Bryan-Jones, setting the fastest time on stage six when representing Edinburgh Southern Harriers.

The bright, crisp weather was ideal for competition and John Myatt (Strathclyde University) set a record of 26 min 50 sec for the opening stage, with Alastair Wood (Aberdeen) taking eight seconds off the second stage record. The Aberdeen club unveiled their surprise package on stage three when sub four minute miler Peter Stewart from Birmingham increased their lead to 200 yards over Shettleston Harriers. Dick Wedlock took Shettleston into a 300 yard lead on the fourth stage that was increased to 700 yards at the final changeover, after Lachie Stewart and Les Meneely had been fastest over the sixth and seventh stages respectively. They coasted home in 3 hours 36 min 34 sec — just 2 seconds outside Edinburgh University's seemingly impregnable record set three years earlier. Aberdeen AAC, in finishing runners up in 3 hours 38 min 40 sec improved their best time by over 3 minutes.

In 1969 Edinburgh Southern Harriers scored a surprise win, taking the lead at half distance thanks to a fine run by Gareth Bryan-Jones. On the next stage John Bryant who, sixteen years later won vicarious fame as coach to Zola Budd after her experiences in the 1984 Olympic Games, kept Southern in front of Bill Scally (Shettleston). Good runs by Fergus Murray and Craig Douglas kept the Edinburgh club in front and Jim White brought them home to victory in 3 hours 44 min 57 sec with Shettleston 3 min 09 sec further behind.

1970 to 1979 Races

During the decade honours were shared between Edinburgh Southern and Shettleston, with only the newly formed Clyde Valley AC, in 1979 - the final year of the decade - breaking the monopoly of wins by the two top clubs. Shettleston started off with three wins in a row, to be followed by Edinburgh Southern who repeated the achievement, climaxing in 1975 with an excellent course record of 3 hours 33 minutes 52 seconds which still stands today. Edinburgh AC must be termed as the unluckiest club in the race, for they finished runners up no less than six times without the consolation of a single victory.

Strong headwinds ensured that no records would be broken in the 1970 race, but the runners of Shettleston and Edinburgh Southern, evenly balanced in talent and experience, were locked together throughout the eight stages in a classic duel. It was a cliffhanger from start to finish, with no more than 8 seconds between the teams over the first half of the race, and just a 13 second margin of victory for Shettleston at the finish. This was the closest finish in the 32 races run to date, bettering the 18 second margin of victory that Shettleston had won by in 1959 from Bellahouston Harriers.

After the evenly run first half Henry Summerhill ran a decisive fifth stage to open a gap of almost $1\frac{1}{2}$ minutes for Shettleston. Far from being discouraged by this setback, the Edinburgh runners Donald Macgregor and Martin Craven pulled back all but 16 seconds of the lead, and the stage was set for a stirring finish. Ken Ballantyne, a former SAAA mile champion, started fast and caught Bill Scally within the first 2 miles. But Scally, a member of the well known Glasgow running family, who is still running as a successful veteran competitor with a son and daughter also doing well in athletics, was not worried. He saved his strength for the finish and burst clear of the tired Ballantyne to win by 80 yards. The battle for victory was duplicated in another East/West struggle for third place. Victoria Park AAC had established a lead of a minute at the start of the long 7 mile, sixth stage, only for Jim Alder to run the fastest time of the day and bring Edinburgh AC into the lead for the first time. Good runs by David McMeekin and George Meredith, over the final two stages, gave Victoria Park a narrow 14 second victory in the battle of the two cities.

In 1971 the Shettleston team, with Paul Bannon replacing Bill Scally, repeated their win with city rivals Victoria Park AAC replacing Edinburgh Southern as runners up. After a see-saw exchange of positions over the first three stages Victoria Park had an 11 second lead at the start of the fourth stage. Colin Youngson, a former Aberdeen University student, then teaching in Glasgow and running for Victoria Park (the second of four clubs he would represent in the Edinburgh to Glasgow race), went off course at the turning to Bathgate. This mistake allowed Paul Bannon to catch him and go on to establish a 20 second lead.

An excellent run by Dick Wedlock on the long sixth stage, where he recorded 31 minutes 57 seconds in the face of strong winds and driving sleet - just 21 seconds outside the fastest time recorded by Edinburgh University student Andrew McKean, restored Shettleston to a narrow lead. With Tom Grubb and Henry Summerhill setting new records over the final two stages, Shettleston had almost a minute to spare at the finish in Royal Exchange Square over their Glasgow rivals with Edinburgh Southern third, ahead of Springburn.

After Graham Milne brought Aberdeen AAC into third place, behind Dick Hodelet (Greenock Glenpark) and Allister Hutton (Edinburgh Southern), on the opening lap of the 1972 race, the Aberdeen club unveiled their secret weapon. Ian Stewart, Commonwealth and European 5,000 metres champion and winner of the 5,000 metres bronze medal at the Munich Olympic Games the previous summer, set out on his magnificent run over the second stage which was to smash not only the course record, but the demoralised opposition. Stewart, in his first appearance in the race, was quickly into the lead. His electrifying run of 27 minutes 14 seconds was a new record, bettering Alastair Wood's four year old performance by 78 seconds, with Norman Morrison (Shettleston) being next fastest with his run of 27 minutes 54 seconds. Stewart's run was probably the best performance in the sixty year history of the race and many enthusiasts retain the picture of Stewart, his feet barely skimming the ground, charging up the hill to the changeover with no one else in sight.

Stewart's appearance caused a long running controversy about the inclusion of Anglo-Scots in the race. A sharp distinction was made between exiles who came back from England to represent their club of origin and those top class Anglo runners whose tenuous connection to a Scottish club was subsequent to their emergence as top performers. This, and other subsequent occasions when clubs pulled top Anglo -Scots runners out of the hat to run in the Edinburgh to Glasgow relay and other important events, caused the formulation of a rule for the race which limited the number of first claim Anglos who could compete in the race. The number of athletes, who were first claim, living outwith Scotland but not competing regularly for their club in team competition in Scotland, was limited to just two, and this resulted in better competition in the race.

Despite being over $2\frac{1}{2}$ minutes behind Aberdeen at the end of the third stage, good runs by Alastair Blamire, Dick Wedlock and Lachie Stewart brought Shettleston into a lead of $1\frac{1}{2}$ minutes by the end of the sixth stage at Airdrie. By the time Bill Scally completed the glory leg through the busy streets of Glasgow, Shettleston had a winning margin of 2 minutes 11 seconds over Aberdeen with Edinburgh Southern, having closed to within just 8 seconds, taking third position.

Edinburgh Southern, who had finished second and twice third in Shettleston's 3 year run of victories, turned the tables in 1973 with a team that contained 4 former Edinburgh University stars. They started a 3 year run of wins, pursued on every occasion by city rivals Edinburgh AC, that clearly showed the balance of power was shifting eastwards. Southern had a poor start on the opening stage of the 1973 race, finishing only 12th behind Jim Alder who led for Edinburgh AC from Gerry Price of Achilles AC from Belfast, the first foreign club to be invited to compete in the relay classic. It took another four stages for Southern runners to close the 1 minute 45 second gap and go into the lead on stage 5, where Martin Craven's sharp cadence style of running changed a 57 second deficit from Victoria Park AAC into a 58 second lead.

The champions lap lived up to its name as Olympians Ian Stewart and Donald Macgregor vied with National champion Andy McKean and Dave Logue for the fastest time on the 7 mile sixth stage. Although Stewart (31 minutes 21 seconds) was over a minute faster than Macgregor (32-22) to gain a narrow lead for Aberdeen, McKean took 7 seconds off Fergus Murray's outstanding 1965 record with his run of 31 minutes 00 seconds to move into third place and Irish steeplechaser Dave Logue (Glasgow University) also was faster than Stewart with his run of 31 minutes 16 seconds. With fastest times from Allister Hutton and Gareth Bryan-Jones on the last two stages, Southern finished comfortable winners in 3 hours 39 minutes 14 seconds - over 2 minutes in front of Edinburgh AC, for whom Danny Knowles overtook Aberdeen on the final stage to take second place by 10 seconds.

Aberdeen had fielded Ian McKenzie, the North of Scotland AAA cross country champion, on the short stage 3 but later investigation by the SCCU, on receiving a protest from Victoria Park AAC as to the eligibility of McKenzie, revealed that McKenzie was a first claim member of Forres Harriers and not of Aberdeen AAC. There was, at that time, no rule allowing secondary first claim membership of other clubs in Union membership for runners of Northern Clubs. This change of rules came at a later date and allowed Aberdeen AAC, and other central belt clubs, to utilise Northern athletes in their teams. However, on this occasion the protest was upheld, and the Aberdeen club forfeited their third place medals to the protesting club Victoria Park AAC who had finished in fourth position. Aberdeen also included the ineligible McKenzie in their team in the National championships at Coatbridge later in the season, and again forfeited bronze medals to fourth placed Shettleston Harriers under a General Committee decision which resulted in Aberdeen threatening legal action against the SCCU.

Southern fielded five cross country internationals in the 1974 race, even without naming Fergus Murray, and gained an immediate psychological advantage over their rivals who would have been pleased to make room in their teams for any of the Southern "reject" runners. Due to a strong headwind throughout the race no records were broken, despite the quality of runners taking part. Southern led from the start with Colin Youngson, one of the all time greats of the inter city relay who seemed to reserve his best performance of the year for this race, establishing a narrow lead over Willie Day (Falkirk Victoria) on the first stage.

Good runs by Donald Macgregor, Craig Douglas and Alastair Blamire stretched Southern's lead at half distance to 1 minute 51 seconds over the newly formed Clyde Valley AC, with Edinburgh AC in third place over 2 minutes behind the leaders. Edinburgh AC fought back with fastest laps from Doug Gunstone (stage 5) and Andy McKean (stage 6), but Allister Hutton clawed back 22 seconds from Joe Patton and, despite Jim Dingwall recording the fastest time on the final stage, Southern won by 32 seconds from their city rivals. This was the last time that Donald Macgregor and Jim Dingwall ran for ESH and EAC respectively. They joined Fife AC and Falkirk Victoria respectively, and the subsequent rapid rise to success of these clubs owed much to their inspiration and leadership.

The 10 year old course record of 3 hours 36 minutes 32 seconds, set by the famous Edinburgh University team in 1965, was smashed the following year by an all International Southern team by the massive margin of 2 minutes 40 seconds. Despite heavy rain throughout the 1975 race they set four stage records leading from start to finish after a good start from Colin Youngson, who bettered the first stage record by 47 seconds with his time of 26 minutes 00 seconds, a record that still stands 15 years later on. Further stage records by Martin Craven (stage 3), Allister Hutton (stage 5) and Gareth Bryan-Jones (stage 8), brought them home in the new record time of 3 hours 33 minutes 52 seconds. This fabulous performance by a team with no weaknesses was approached only by Aberdeen in 1983 when their winning time approached to within 1 minute 38 seconds of Southern's record. Indeed in the next 14 races only three teams (Aberdeen 1983, Edinburgh Southern 1985 and Dundee Hawkhill in 1989) managed to win the race in a time which bettered the 3 hour 40 minute barrier.

Edinburgh AC, with the necessary replacement of four of the previous year's team, again finished runners up - just 4 seconds outside the old course record. Their second place was the third of six occasions they would finish runners up during the 1970-80 decade, without a single victory to break their run of silver medals. Belfast Achilles AC, with the help of the Price and Hannon brothers, finished fourth behind Clyde Valley AC who bettered their best race time by no less than 13 minutes 27 seconds with their run of 3 hours 39 minutes 46 seconds. Falkirk Victoria, sparked by Jim Dingwall, improved from 18th to 7th to gain the most meritorious performance medals.

The 1976 race was looked on as a sure thing by Southern supporters who expected their club to win for the fourth time in a row. This had only been achieved once before in the history of the race when, just one year after the race restarted after the Second World War, Victoria Park had five consecutive wins in the period 1950-54. Clubs with three consecutive wins were Plebian 1930-33; Shettleston (twice) 1959-61 and 1970-72; Motherwell YMCA 1962-64; Edinburgh University 1965-67 and Edinburgh Southern 1973-75. The race was held for the first time on a Sunday, a necessary and long overdue innovation to aid the safety of runners in competition, and avoid the congested traffic and crowded footpaths in the busy shopping areas of Airdrie, Coatbridge and Glasgow on a Saturday afternoon.

The race will be remembered as "The John Robson race," but one which the young Edinburgh Southern runner would much rather have forgotten. Later to develop into a world class middle distance runner on the track, take fifth position in the World Cross Country Championship and become a fine performer in road individual and relay races, Robson was comparatively inexperienced at that time and making his first appearance in the Blue Riband of Scottish road relay racing. He took over on stage 3 in second position when, just $1\frac{1}{2}$ miles from the change over point and challenging Paul Forbes (Edinburgh AC) for the lead, he stopped suddenly, threw away the baton over a fence and started to walk back the way he had come. Uproar broke out amongst Southern officials and supporters who were following their team along the course. They made frantic efforts to get him to restart, but their passionate pleading, cajoling and threatening had no effect on Robson who seemed to be suffering both mental agony and physical distress.

However the calmer approaches of club secretary Hamish Robertson and president Ken Ballantyne, who urged him to complete his stage and give the other runners in his team a chance of competition, proved successful. Robson retreived the baton and jogged to the change over, having lost fully 10 minutes during the inexplicable incident during which all but one of the rival teams had raced by. Alastair Blamire took over the baton for stage 4 and led a gallant fight back by Southern runners that saw them gain eleven places to eventually finish eighth, 10 minutes 38 seconds behind Shettleston who won in 3 hours 46 minutes 20 seconds. From the start of stage 4 to the finishing line Shettleston and Southern were equally matched in time, but the prospect of a thrilling head to head struggle had been destroyed by the Robson incident and the total 10 minutes lost on stage 3.

Shettleston, greatly strengthened by the addition of Internationals Laurie Spence, Rees Ward, Bill Mullet and first year Junior Nat Muir, won for the first time in four years. Lachie Stewart moved from sixth to second on stage 3, Nat Muir, Bill Mullet and Rees Ward returned excellent performances to establish a lead that their final two runners held to the finish to win by 74 seconds from Edinburgh AC. Falkirk Victoria gained their first ever medals in third place. Fife AC, in their first appearance in the race, with future Union Presidents Donald Macgregor and Ron Morrison in their team, received the medals for the most meritorious performance.

The hazards of holding the event in November were again evident when bitter cold, together with snow and sleet showers, slowed runners throughout the 1977 race. What an improvement in weather conditions, and consequent better performances and times, would result if the event was switched with the National 6 stage Relay championship and held in March instead of wintery November!

The race was one of the most exciting and competitive ever staged, with three evenly matched teams being within 27 seconds of each other at the final changeover with just 6 miles to the finish. After Frank Clement (Bellahouston) and Nat Muir (Shettleston) had led on stages 1 and 2 respectively with the fastest times on their lap, Edinburgh AC went into the lead on stage 3 thanks to first year Junior Colin Keir. Good runs by Doug Gunstone and Alec Wight kept Edinburgh AC in the lead at the end of stage 5, though John Robson showed complete recovery in confidence, after his disastrous run the previous year, when recording the fastest time on stage 5 to lift Southern into second place.

Dave Logue, nicknamed "Arkle" after the famous Irish steeplechaser, took Southern into the lead on stage 6 where Jim Dingwall equalled the record of 31 minutes 00 seconds for the 7 mile stage. Although Edinburgh AC established a 12 second lead on stage 7, Martin Craven raced home for a 37 second Southern victory with the fastest time over the final stage. There were two foreign teams in the race, Duncaim Harriers from Northern Ireland, and FKALG Stavanger AC from Norway. The appearance of the Stavanger team resulted from Norwegian students who had competed in the race for Strathclyde University, and enjoyed it so much that they raised sponsorship for their home club's appearance in the race on their return to Norway.

The weather again struck its usual icy blast in the next two years with the 1978 race starting in the face of an icy headwind which deteriorated into hail and sleet and the final stages were run in a genuine blizzard of driving snow. After Alistair Douglas (Victoria Park) had finished just 1 second in front of Fraser Clyne (Glasgow University) on the opening stage, with Martin Craven bringing Southern home in fifth position, the Edinburgh club went into the lead on stage 2 through Borderer Ian Elliot. John Robson recorded the only "fastest time" by a Southern runner on stage 4, amply establishing his reputation as a reliable runner in road racing. From then on the Southern team raced away from their rivals to win for the fifth time in six years, finishing almost 3 minutes in front of Victoria Park AAC, who moved into an unchallenged second place on stage 3 and finished almost a minute clear of Shettleston.

Over the previous few years changing fashions in sports sponsorship had given the SCCU grounds for apprehension that the valuable financial sponsorship from the News of the World newspaper was in jeopardy. The enthusiastic support over a period of more than 40 years had given the race an enviable reputation as the glamour event of the season. There were buses to transport West of Scotland clubs from Glasgow to the start in Edinburgh and similar transport for the Eastern clubs back to Edinburgh after the post race meal and prize giving at the Ca'dora restaurant in Glasgow. The sponsors provided an athletes bus for every stage of the race, cars to transport recorders and timekeepers to each relay change over point, and well illustrated and informative programmes issued free to spectators along the race route.

The sponsorship ended with the 1978 race but, thanks to the intervention of race convener Des Yuill of Cambuslang Harriers, a new sponsor Barr's Soft Drinks - makers of the famous Irn Bru - were enrolled to support the race. The 1979 race, the first under their sponsorship which is still going strong 11 years later, was an engrossing one. It was, however, spoilt by a cloud of gloom that hung over the event due to the death, just 48 hours earlier, of 90 year old George Dallas - one of the founders of the race back in 1930. He had been a spectator of every one of the races since its inception, holding court with his many friends in athletics in the Forestfield Inn at the end of stage 5, where he entertained them with reminiscences of earlier race. On a bitterly cold day with icy winds, there were many drams consumed at Forestfield and farewell toasts made to the absent George, who had been such a loyal and faithful official to the Union.

Clyde Valley, after finishing only seventh the previous year, fielded 5 new runners in their team and scored their first ever victory in the event. The previous year's top two clubs, Edinburgh Southern and Victoria Park, finished third and fourth behind the seemingly inevitable runners up Edinburgh AC, who occupied this position for the sixth time in seven years. The Lanarkshire club went into the lead on stage 2 through John Graham's fastest time and, though slipping to second on the next stage, regained the lead at half distance when Brian McSloy recorded the fastest time on stage 4. With Jim Brown being fastest on stage 6, fully 1¼ minutes faster than Allister Hutton - his nearest challenger - the race was won by Clyde Valley, who finished almost 2 minutes in front of Southern in 3 hours 52 minutes 53 seconds - the slowest winning time for 26 years.

1980-1989 Races

After finishing seventh on stage 1 of the 1980 race, Clyde Valley gradually improved up to stage 5, where Jim Brown recorded the fastest time in the face of a cold opposing wind that, at times, was almost gale force in the face of the struggling runners. Brown handed over a lead of 53 seconds to John Graham on the exposed 7 mile sixth stage, where steeplechaser Gordon Rimmer gained 4 places for Cambuslang to finish second, 1 minute 13 seconds behind Graham. Eddie Devlin had the fastest run on stage 7 and young Peter Fox brought Clyde Valley home for his second winners medal - a feat he was not to repeat until running for Dundee Hawkhill in 1989 when they won the race in their Centenary season.

The winning time of 3 hours 57 minutes 19 seconds was the slowest since Shettleston had clocked 4 hours 15 minutes 25 seconds when winning the race on its resumption in April 1949 after the War. Only the first two clubs bettered the 4 hour barrier, with the surprise team of the day, Cambuslang Harriers, finishing runners up in 3 hours 58 minutes 43 seconds. The last team to finish, Spango Valley AC, was still heading for the final changeover at the end of stage 7 when Clyde Valley had crossed the winning line.

Cambuslang, who along with Aberdeen AAC were to prove the top teams of the next decade in Edinburgh to Glasgow competition, had improved rapidly over the previous 5 years. After finishing 13th (1976) and 11th (1977) they gained the services of the Rimmer twins, Gordon and Steven, both serving in the RAF, and their success owed much to these two runners and the improved form shown by Alex Gilmour and Eddie Stewart. In 1978 they finished sixth, improved to fifth the following year, and then gained their first ever medals with the surprise second place in 1980.

With their star runners from Edinburgh University past their best, and out of the first team, Southern fielded many new faces in their team in the 1981 race. Clyde Valley were virtually at full strength, with six internationals, Ian Gilmour, Jim Brown, Ronnie Macdonald, Brian McSloy, John Graham and Peter Fox in their team which hoped for a third successive win.

Allister Hutton took Southern into the lead on stage 2, and from there on they were out on their own. Ian Elliot broke the record by 18 seconds on stage 2, John Robson was fastest on stage 5, and with Evan Cameron and Colin Hume also fastest on stages 6 and 7 respectively, Alex Robertson came home to victory in 3 hours 43 minutes 59 seconds - over $1\frac{1}{2}$ minutes in front of Clyde Valley, who went into second place on stage 4, when Ronnie Macdonald recorded the fastest time, and held that place all the way to the finish at Royal Exchange Square in Glasgow.

Colin Youngson, teaching in Kemnay near Aberdeen, competed for Aberdeen AAC - the fourth club he had represented in the race. He had previously competed for Aberdeen University and gained medals in his outings for both Victoria Park and Edinburgh Southern. His vast experience on the final lap was vital as, facing Alastair Johnston (Victoria Park), it was a case of "two old heads and four old legs fighting to get to the line". Youngson proved to have the two strongest legs, and took Aberdeen into third place by the narrow margin of just three seconds. Sparked by Lachie Stewart, living and working in Greenock, more than 10 years after his Commonwealth 10,000 metres victory, Spango Valley advanced from 20th place to finish seventh and gain the medals for the most meritorious performance of the day.

The following year saw the appearance of a Northern District Select team. Anxious to help the development of the top runners in the North of Scotland, and conscious that no individual club was strong enough to qualify for the race on its own, the SCCU invited a composite team from the North to take part. The team finished 16th and a similar team has taken part in the race every year since.

Allister Hutton again turned in his usual good performance on stage 2, gaining eight places with the fastest time to establish a narrow 3 second lead over Clyde Valley. A record run by Ian Elliot, bettering his own stage record by no less than 47 seconds, gave Southern a 77 second lead over Bellahouston, for whom Andy Daly then caught up 46 seconds. Neil Black recorded the fastest lap to give Bellahouston a 31 second lead which was extended on stage 6 by Peter Fleming to 47 seconds. The positions were drastically revised on stage 7. Craig Hunter ran a storming lap for Southern to hand over a 43 second lead over Edinburgh AC with Bellahouston another 13 seconds behind in third place. The two Edinburgh clubs retained their positions on the final stage with marathon star Graham Laing gaining another set of bronze medals for Aberdeen when making up almost three minutes on Bellahouston over the final stage.

Aberdeen, after threatening the leaders over the previous two years, scored their first ever victory in 1983. After a solid start they were in second place behind Bellahouston on stages 2 and 3 when Craig Ross, taking 30 seconds off the stage 4 record, took them into a lead they were never again to lose. This was Aberdeen's only fastest stage time of the day, but in good running conditions Hammy Cox (Bellahouston)(stage 3); Allister Hutton (Edinburgh Southern) (stage 6) and Peter Fleming (Bellahouston) (stage 8) all broke or equalled stage records.

Between stages 5 and 7 Peter Wilson, Fraser Clyne and Mike Murray added another 7 seconds to Aberdeen's lead, such that Colin Youngson, running in the event for the eighteenth time, took off with a lead of 34 seconds from Southern and 53 seconds from Bellahouston. In spite of a determined chase by Peter Fleming, winner of the Glasgow Marathon just a month earlier, who closed to within 20 seconds at one point, Youngson held on to bring Aberdeen to victory. They recorded 3 hours 35 minutes 30 seconds - the second fastest time on the race all time rankings, and over 20 minutes faster than the Aberdeen club would record on their next victory in three years time.

Bellahouston finished 40 seconds behind in 3 hours 36 minutes 10 seconds for third fastest of all time, but good only for the silver medals. There was a solid backbone of youngsters in their team who had been in the club since young boys - Tony Coyne, Andy Daly, Graham Getty, George Braidwood, Alastair McAngus and Peter Fleming - and it says much for the Glasgow club that they achieved such a good result with home reared talent.

Falkirk Victoria, having three times finished seventh in the past four years since 1980, gained a popular victory in the 1984 race, after having often promised so much but failing to deliver the goods in previous years. They got off to a good start when Donald Bain finished second to Adrian Callan of Springburn on the opening stage and, despite falling back to seventh at half distance, moved to fourth on Stage 5 when Derek Easton recorded the second fastest time on the stage. Jim Dingwall, who is at his best on the road and always reacts well to pressure situations in important races, brought Falkirk into a 39 second lead over Edinburgh Southern on Stage 6. Good runs by John Pentecost and Stuart Easton gave them a decisive victory in 3 hours 40minutes 16 seconds - over 500 yards in front of Cambuslang, who held off a fast closing Spango Valley, who gained their first set of place medals in the race.

The best performance of the day came from Nat Muir of Shettleston on Stage 6 - the champions lap - when he broke the record of 31 min. 00 secs. jointly held by Andy McKean and Jim Dingwall. Muir, Scotland's top distance runner over track, road and country, ran a solo race to gain six places with his excellent run of 30 min. 51 secs - ;the first time the 31 minute barrier had been broken in the long history of the race.

A.G. Barr, who had proved interested and helpful sponsors of the race over the previous six years, displayed the intention of their firm commitment to the future of the inter city relay when announcing a sponsorship for the next six years up to 1990. They also provided club subvention prizes for the first time, with a value of £250 for the winners and £150 for second and third teams.

The Kangeroos AC from Manhattan U.S.A. were invited to compete in the 1985 race, having won an 8 stage relay race over the 50 miles from Manhattan to Mahopac, which had been started by Harry Nelson, (formerly of Vale of Leven AAC) in imitation of the Edinburgh to Glasgow race. This club was an assortment of star athletes, consisting of four separate nationalities, with Olympic athletes Joseph Nzan (Kenya), John Tuttle (USA) and Mike Feurtrado (Jamaica), together with Briton Adrian Leek (3-34.5 for 1500 metres and 2 hours 14 min 52 sec for the marathon) and assorted USA champions over track and cross country.

The Americans took the lead on Stage 3, and with record runs by John Glidewell (Stage 3) and John Tuttle (Stage 4), had established a lead of almost $2\frac{1}{2}$ minutes at half distance over Cambuslang with Southern in fifth position almost another minute behind. Neil Tennant started a Southern revival when recording the fastest time on Stage 6, John Robson did the same when moving to second position on Stage 7, breaking by 9 seconds the Gareth Bryan-Jones record which had stood since 1972. Peter Wilson gained another 14 seconds on the final stage, for Southern to finish runners up to the American team in 3 hours 38 min. 23 sec. - their fastest time in 10 years.

Aberdeen AAC, despite not having won a medal in the three year period since their 1983 win, fielded a powerful team to win the 1986 race. They included two Welsh internationals Chris Hall and Simon Axon, four Scottish marathon internationals Fraser Clyne, Jim Doig, Graham Laing and Colin Youngson together with club stalwarts Ray Creswell and Mike Murray. Running into cold, opposing winds that gusted, at times, to gale force in the face of the runners, Aberdeen went into the lead on Stage 3, dropped back on Stage 4 to third, and Graham Laing took the club into second position on stage 5, just 2 seconds behind Spango Valley from Greenock. Fraser Clyne established an 8 second lead on Stage 6 which was extended to 21 seconds by Mike Murray. Colin Youngson showed his vast experience on the final stage he had run so often by recording the fastest time, to bring Aberdeen home to a 66 second victory over Cambuslang, with Southern third, another 50 seconds behind.

Cambuslang Harriers, who were to win place medals in seven of the ten years of the Eighties decade - an achievement equalled by Aberdeen AAC - finally achieved victory in 1987, after finishing second, third and second in preceeding years. Throughout the race it was a battle between Cambuslang and Edinburgh AC, with the latter club taking the lead on Stage 2 and holding it for three stages before Eddie Stewart recorded the fastest lap on Stage 5 to take Cambuslang into a 30 second lead they were to hold to the finish. Cambuslang's victory was assured when Jim Orr, taking over a 36 second lead, proved easily the fastest over the run in through Glasgow's congested streets to the finish at George Square for an 88 second victory in 3 hours 46 min. 07 secs.

The following year, as Scottish veteran cross country champion, 41 year old Colin Youngson, competing in the race for the twenty second time, anchored Aberdeen AAC to their third victory in five years. Taking the lead on Stage 3, when Ray Creswell recorded the clubs only fastest time of the day, Aberdeen led the field for the next five stages. Their lead varied from 7 seconds on Stage 3 to a maximum of 1 min. 32 secs. on Stage 7. Youngson brought them home in 3 hours 49 min. 08 sec, 21 sec in front of Southern, with Andy Beattie recording the fastest time on the run through the busy streets of Glasgow,to overtake Edinburgh AC and lift Cambuslang into third place.

Edinburgh AC were unlucky throughout the race. Ian Hamer, who was to win the Commonwealth Games 5,000 metres bronze medal at Auckland just 14 months later, developed stomach cramp and dropped from fifth to twelfth on Stage 2. A gradual fight back, aided by fastest stage times from Ian Archibald (Stage 5) and Graham Harker (Stage 7), saw them poised in second place at the start of the final stage. But their final runner was missing at the changeover, and reserve Adam Ward, who stepped into the breach at the last moment, dropped them back to fourth place and out of the medals.

Dundee Hawkhill Harriers had never won the Edinburgh to Glasgow relay though a Dundee club, Thistle Harriers, had won twice in 1934 and 37 in pre war

Aberdeen AAC team which won the 1988 Barrs Inn Bru relay race from Edinburgh to Glasgow. Back row (left to right); Colin Youngson, Ray Creswell, Chris Hall, Fraser Clyne and Ian Matheson. Front row (left to right); Graham Laing, Simon Axon and David Duguid.

days. How appropriate it was therefore for Hawkhill to reserve their first victory for one of the main highlights of their centenary season. Northern Ireland International Peter McColgan went into the lead on Stage 2 and handed over a 41 second advantage to Terry Reid. The lead narrowed considerably when Craig Ross took over on Stage 4 and, when Ross went off course at an unstewarded roundabout at the approaches to Bathgate, the Dundee club dropped to fourth, just 14 seconds behind Shettleston for whom Nat Muir had recorded the fastest stage time.

Ian Campbell, who had finished tenth in the World Junior Cross Country Championship 10 years earlier, quickly regained the lead on Stage 5 and handed over a 53 second advantage. Good performances by Charlie Haskett and Richie Barrie saw Peter Fox start Stage 8 out on his own, and go on to anchor Hawkhill to victory, and gain a winners medal nine years after helping Clyde Valley to victory in 1980. The Dundee club finished in 3 hours 39 min 03 secs, 90 seconds ahead of 1987 winners Cambuslang with 1988 winners Aberdeen in third place.

Staunch Aberdonian and fanatical Edinburgh to Glasgow competitor Colin Youngson, competing in his twenty third race, gained his thirteenth medal. After starting in 1966, with five appearances for Aberdeen University without success, he ran in 1971-72 for Victoria Park AAC, gaining 1 silver medal. He then turned out for Edinburgh Southern from 1974 to 1980 gaining 4 gold and 1 bronze medals. In 1981 he returned to his home club and, between 1981 and 89, gained another 7 medals with Aberdeen AAC, adding another 3 gold and 4 bronze to his collection.

Youngson definitely holds the record for the most medals won in the race with his closest challengers being brothers Chick and Andy Forbes of the successful Victoria AAC. He is also the probable record holder in two other categories. He has competed in the event 23 times to date, his only rival being Brian McAusland who ran on 21 consecutive occasions for Clydesdale Harriers and his appearance for four different clubs (Aberdeen University, Victoria Park AAC, Edinburgh Southern H and Aberdeen AAC) is not known to be exceeded by any other runner.

In its sixty year history the race has acquired a mystery, a magic, a charisma that is unequalled by any other event promoted by the S.C.C.U. Perhaps it is because a club has to be invited to compete in the inter city relay, and can enter of right in the National and Six Stage Relay Championships, that the race is so highly regarded. Some clubs have the ambition of winning or gaining place medals, while for the vast majority it is their season's target simply to gain entry to the race each year.

Stories and tales of the race abound in clubs and are told and retold by old members to new recruits who, after competing in or following the event, become firm believers in the race traditions and legends. The preceeding chapter has detailed the factual story of the race; the triumphs and tragedies, the successes and failures of both individuals and clubs. To end the story of a most unique and enjoyable race the following anecdotes are related which give the comical background to the stern racing in each of the eight stages of the race.

Colin Youngson (Aberdeen AAC), one of the personalities of the Edinburgh to Glasgow relay race, who has the greatest number of race appearances and medals.

One year Ian Binnie of Victoria Park collected the baton from the incoming runner and, out of sight of the changeover officials, handed it to a boy on a bike who cycled alongside him for the length of his run. Just before the changeover he collected the baton and passed it to the next runner. The rules of the race were changed next year to read "a baton shall be carried at all times." While the organisers intended that it be carried "in the hand", Binnie's ingenuity was equal to the occasion. On receiving the baton he slipped it into a loop that had been carefully sewn onto the front of his vest, thus leaving his hands free as desired. Needless to say the rules were changed again the following year!

Another Binnie story, related by Andy Forbes, is of the year Victoria Park won the race trophy and Binnie was the last member of the team to have custody of it before the race. He was told to be sure to get the trophy engraved and bring it to the start at Edinburgh. He did as requested, but his shocked teammates found the runner on the trophy lid clothed in a knitted blue and white stripped vest and Victoria Park's name engraved on the trophy, not only for the previous year, but also for the forthcoming year. When this was pointed out to Binnie he smiled and said "Well we'll just have to win the race because we can't get the engraving off the trophy". And he and his seven clubmates promptly went out and won it as required!

In 1980 Colin Youngson ran the short Stage 3 to set a course record and arrived so far in the lead that he caught his surprised Southern teammate attending to the call of nature in a nearby field and in no position to take over the baton for the next stage. Furious at the delay he expressed himself in graphic terms that displayed an outstanding range of vocabulary far beyond the normal language expected from a teacher of English.

With clubs having the responsibility of getting their runner to the changeover point at the appointed time, many are the speeding cars seen charging along the road with runners changing into running kit on the back seat. Forestfield Inn, at the start of Stage 6, has been the venue of many surprising changeovers. Jim Keenan of Springburn once completed Stage 5, handed over the baton to outgoing Eddie Knox, and veered off, without losing speed, into the adjacent Inn where his clubmates had a drink waiting for him. It has also been done the other way round, with incoming runners looking despairingly for their partner to receive the baton and see him suddenly appearing from the door of the Inn, grabbing the baton and going on his merry way.

Supporters are an important part of the race, lining the roadside to shout and encourage their club runners on their way. Club buses used to be the order of the day but, in modern times individual cars are mostly used, causing parking problems at changeovers which are sometimes the despair of the police. One of the most noticeable supporters is Jackie White (a member of Southern's winning 1969 team) who regularly deafens clubmates, and infuriates and terrifies rival runners and supporters by loudly playing his trumpet at points along the course. Another regular is Claude Jones; always to be seen along the route vociferously encouraging his Edinburgh AC runners and, stopwatch in hand, telling them how much of a lead they have or what time they must make up on the runner in front.

There's also the story of Andy Brown encouraging his clubmate Ian McCafferty and shouting at pedestrians to get out of the runner's way - in Airdrie's busy Main Street on a Saturday afternoon. Tom O'Reilly, standing shivering in thick snow in the early '60s when motorists were abandoning their cars due to impassable streets, said it was not so much dedication that competitors were displaying as "sheer bloody stupidity." It is also worth mentioning the Edinburgh AC supporter loudly cheering, and being asked which of the Knowles twins he was urging on, replied that he wasn't sure but either would do.

In the words of a self confessed race enthusiast "It is an event that must go on; it simply can't be replaced. Run it at the dead of night if you can't get permission for daytime running, run it on Christmas Day if it is the only day you can get; run it illegally if necessary; run it on a time trial basis with two teams a week; run it any way you like

"BUT RUN IT AND NEVER STOP RUNNING IT"

Edinburgh to Glasgow 8 Stage Relay Race

Races from 1930 to 1939 all held in April

1930	1. Plebian H.	3.54.07(rec)	2. Dundee Thistle H.	3.55.00	3. Maryhill H.	3.58.13
1931	1. Plebian H.	3.50.39(rec)	2. Maryhill H.	3.52.07	3. Garscube H.	3.58.30
1932	No race held.					
1933	1. Plebian H.	3.59.17	2. Dundee Thistle H.	4.02.02	3. Maryhill H.	4.02.18
1934	1. Dundee Thistle. H.	4.20.47	2. Edinburgh North H.	4.21.43	3. Maryhill H.	4.22.35
1935	1. Edinburgh Nth. H.	4.03.23	2. Garscube H.	4.04.18	3. Plebian H.	4.04.32
1936	1. Bellahouston H.	3.51. 15	2. Shettleston H.	3.52.51	3. Plebian H.	3.53.57
1937	1. Dundee Th. H.	3.50.14(rec)	2. Maryhill H.	3.52.11	3. Bellahouston H.	3.52.57
1938	1. Bellahouston H.	3.49.47(rec)	2. Maryhill H.	3.50.05	3. Dundee Thistle. H.	3.56.20
1939	1. Maryhill H.	4.06.03	2. Bellahouston H.	4.06.36	3. Shettleston H.	4.08.17
1949	1. Shettleston H.	4.15.25	2. Vic. Park AAC	4.20.56	3. Bellahouston H.	4.21.16

Races from 1949 to date all held in November.

1949	1. Shettleston H.	3.56.57	2. Vic. Park AAC	3.58.07	3. Bellahouston H.	4.02.02
1950	1. Vic. Park AAC	3.52.43	2. Shettleston H.	3.53.15	3. Greenock Glnprk. H	3.59.00
1951	1. Vic. Park AAC	3.56.04	2. Shettleston H.	3.59.30	3. Springburn H.	4.01.09
1952	1. Vic. Park AAC	3.48.44(rec)	2. Shettleston H.	3.55.10	3. Bellahouston H.	3.58.45
1953	1. Vic. Park AAC	3.52.56	2. Shettleston H.	3.54.52	3. Edinburgh Sth. H.	4.01.21
1954	1. Vic. Park AAC	3.46.43(rec)	2. Shettleston H.	3.47.17	3. Springburn H.	3.55.25
1955	1. Shettleston H.	3.46.13(rec)	2. Vic. Park AAC	3.47.58	3. Springburn H.	3.51.32
1956	1. Vic. Park AAC	3.47.40	2. Shettleston H.	3.50.10	3. Bellahouston H.	3.51.01
1957	1. Vic. Park AAC	3.44.12(rec)	2. Bellahouston H	3.48.23	3. Shettleston H.	3.48.46
1958	1. Bellahouston H.	3.49.29	2. Shettleston H.	3.50.43	3. Vic. Park AAC	3.51.54
1959	1. Shettleston H.	3.49.17	2. Bellahouston H.	3.49.35	3. Vic. Park AAC	3.50.49
1960	1. Shettleston H.	3.44.32	2. Bellahouston H.	3.49.23	3. Glasgow Univ.	3.50.24
1961	1. Shettleston H.	3.43.47(rec)	2. Edinburgh Sth. H.	3.45.50	3. Motherwell YMCA	3.46.15
1962	1. Motherwell YMCA	3.44.50	2. Edinburgh Sth. H.	3.46.15	3. Glasgow Univ.	3.48.35
1963	1. Motherwell YMCA	3.45.31	2. Edinburgh Sth. H.	3.47.16	3. Aberdeen AAC	3.48.01
1964	1. Motherwell YMCA	3.46.01	2. Edinburgh Univ.	3.48.30	3. Edinburgh Sth. H.	3.49.17
1965	1. Edinburgh Univ.	3.36.32(rec)	2. Motherwell YMCA	3.37.52	3. Vic. Park AAC	3.38.02
1966	1. Edinburgh Univ.	3.36.53	2. Vic. Park AAC	3.40.35	3. Motherwell YMCA	3.41.42
1967	1. Edinburgh Univ.	3.44.30	2. Equal Aberdeen AAC and Shettleston H. both 3.45.20			
1968	1. Shettleston H.	3.36.34	2. Aberdeen AAC	3.38.40	3. Edinburgh Sth. H.	3.40.54
1969	1. Edinburgh Sth. H.	3.44.57	2. Shettleston H.	3.48.06	3. Edinburgh Univ.	3.52.52
1970	1. Shettleston H.	3.53.39	2. Edinburgh Sth. H.	3.53.52	3. Vic. Park AAC	3.59.15
1971	1. Shettleston H.	3.39.08	2. Vic. Park AAC	3.40.07	3. Edinburgh Sth. H.	3.41.07
1972	1. Shettleston H.	3.39.14	2. Aberdeen AAC	3.41.44	3. Edinburgh Sth. H.	3.41.52
1973	1. Edinburgh Sth. H.	3.39.14	2. Edinburgh AC	3.41.23	3. Aberdeen AAC	3.41.33
1974	1. Edinburgh Sth. H.	3.47.34	2. Edinburgh AC	3.48.06	3. Clyde Valley AC	3.53.13
1975	1. Edinburgh Sth. H.	3.33.52(rec)	2. Edinburgh AC	3.36.36	3. Clyde Valley AC	3.39.46
1976	1. Shettleston H.	3.46.20	2. Edinburgh AC	3.47.34	3. Falkirk Vic. H.	3.49.35
1977	1. Edinburgh Sth. H.	3.40.24	2. Edinburgh AC	3.41.01	3. Shettleston H.	3.42.08
1978	1. Edinburgh Sth. H.	3.48.42	2. Vic. Park AAC	3.51.35	3. Shettleston H.	3.52.29
1979	1. Clyde Valley AC	3.52.53	2. Edinburgh AC	3.54.51	3. Edinburgh Sth. H.	3.55.33
1980	1. Clyde Valley AC	3.57. 19	2. Cambuslang H.	3.58.43	3. Vic. Park AAC	4.00.45
1981	1. Edinburgh Sth. H.	3.43.59	2. Clyde Valley AC	3.45.38	3. Aberdeen AAC	3.47.51
1982	1. Edinburgh Sth. H.	3.42.32	2. Edinburgh AC	3.43.37	3. Aberdeen AAC	3.44.45
1983	1. Aberdeen AAC	3.35.30	2. Bellahouston H	3.36.10	3. Clyde Valley AC	3.37.35
1984	1. Falkirk Vic. H.	3.40.16	2. Cambuslang H.	3.41.52	3. Spango Valley AC	3.41.59
1985	1.*Edinburgh Sth. H.	3.38.23	2. Falkirk Vic. H.	3.40.23	3. Cambuslang H.	3.40.48
1986	1. Aberdeen AAC	3.55.49	2. Cambuslang H.	3.56.55	3. Edinburgh Sth. H.	3.57.45
1987	1. Cambuslang H.	3.46.07	2. Edinburgh AC	3.47.35	3. Aberdeen AAC	3.49.32
1988	1. Aberdeen AAC	3.49.08	2. Edinburgh Sth. H.	3.49.29	3. Cambuslang H.	3.50.47
1989	1. Dundee Hawkhill H.	3.39.03	2. Cambuslang H.	3.40.33	3. Aberdeen AAC	3.41.43

* The Kangeroos from U.S.A., running as guests, finished in 3.37.40.

Edinburgh to Glasgow 8 Stage Relay —
Overall Medal Table 1930 to 1989

	GOLD	SILVER	BRONZE	TOTAL
Shettleston Harriers	11	10	4	25
Edinburgh Southern Harriers	9	5	7	21
Victoria Park AC	7	6	5	18
Bellahouston Harriers	3	5	5	13
Aberdeen AAC	3	3	6	12
Edinburgh AC	-	8	-	8
Maryhill Harriers	1	3	3	7
Motherwell YMCA Harriers	3	1	2	6
Clyde Valley AC	2	1	3	6
Cambuslang Harriers	1	4	2	7
Edinburgh University H & H	3	1	1	5
Plebian Harriers	3	-	2	5
Dundee Thistle Harriers	2	2	1	5
Falkirk Victoria Harriers	1	1	1	3
Springburn Harriers	-	-	3	3
Edinburgh Northern Harriers	1	1	-	2
Dundee Hawkhill Harriers	1	-	-	1
Garscube Harriers	-	1	1	2
Glasgow University H & H	-	-	2	2
Greenock Glenpark Harriers	-	-	1	1
Spango Valley AC	-	-	1	1
	51	52*	50*	153#

* In 1967 there was a dead heat for second place between Aberdeen AAC and Shettleston Harriers with both clubs being awarded silver medals and no bronze medals being awarded that year. Hence the extra silver medal in the table.

\# There was no race held in 1932 and, due to the Second World War, no races during the period 1940 to 1948 inclusive. However in 1949, on the restart of the event after the War, races were held in both April and November of that year. Thus 50 races were held in the 60 year history of the race from 1930 to 1989.

1. Only 21 clubs in the 51 race history of the event have ever won a medal.

2. Fifteen of these twenty one clubs have actually won the event.

3. Of the other six clubs in the medal table Edinburgh Athletic Club have finished runners up 8 times without ever winning since their formation in 1972.

4. Of the remaining clubs only Garscube Harriers have ever won a silver medal the others have all been bronze medallists.

5. Shettleston Harriers, as well as being the club with the greatest number of overall medals, have the greatest total of race victories.

**Edinburgh to Glasgow 8 Stage Relay —
Medal Table by Decade**

1930 - 39 (9 races)	**GOLD**	**SILVER**	**BRONZE**	**TOTAL**
Maryhill Harriers	1	3	3	7
Plebian Harriers	3	-	2	5
Dundee Thistle Harriers	2	2	1	5
Bellahouston Harriers	2	1	1	4
Edinburgh Northern Harriers	1	1	-	2
Garscube Harriers	-	1	1	2
Shettleston Harriers	-	1	1	2
	9	**9**	**9**	**27**

1949 - 59 (12 races)	**GOLD**	**SILVER**	**BRONZE**	**TOTAL**
Victoria Park AAC	7	3	2	12
Shettleston Harriers	4	7	1	12
Bellahouston Harriers	1	2	4	7
Springburn Harriers	-	-	3	3
Edinburgh Southern Harriers	-	-	1	1
Greenock Glenpark Harriers	-	-	-	1
	12	**12**	**12**	**36**

1960 - 69 (10 races)	**GOLD**	**SILVER**	**BRONZE**	**TOTAL**
Motherwell YMCA Harriers	3	1	2	6
Edinburgh Southern Harriers	1	3	2	6
Shettleston Harriers	3	2	-	5
Edinburgh University H & H	3	1	1	5
Aberdeen AAC	-	2	1	3
Victoria Park AAC	-	1	1	2
Glasgow University H & H	-	-	2	2
Bellahouston Harriers	-	1	-	1
	10	**11**	**9**	**30**

1970 - 79 (10 races)	**GOLD**	**SILVER**	**BRONZE**	**TOTAL**
Edinburgh Southern Harriers	5	1	3	9
Shettleston Harriers	4	-	2	6
Edinburgh AC	-	6	-	6
Clyde Valley AC	1	-	2	3
Victoria Park AAC	-	2	1	3
Aberdeen AAC	-	1	1	2
Falkirk Victoria Harriers	-	-	1	1
	10	**10**	**10**	**30**

1980 - 89 (10 races)

	GOLD	SILVER	BRONZE	TOTAL
Aberdeen AAC	3	-	4	7
Cambuslang Harriers	1	4	2	6
Edinburgh Southern Harriers	3	1	1	5
Clyde Valley AC	1	1	1	3
Falkirk Victoria Harriers	1	1	-	2
Edinburgh AC	-	2	-	2
Dundee Hawkhill Harriers	1	-	-	1
Bellahouston Harriers	-	1	-	1
Spango Valley	-	-	1	1
Victoria Park AAC	-	-	1	1
	10	**10**	**10**	**30**

CROSS COUNTRY IN THE NORTHERN DISTRICT

Cross country in the North of Scotland is of relatively recent origin when compared to the 100 years history of the Scottish Cross Country Union. There is little evidence of competitive cross country running in the North during the first fifty years of this century, despite the popularity - mainly through Highland Games - of amateur athletics. Indeed in the Thirties the North had a Scottish Sprint Champion, Ian Young of Inverness, who went on to represent Scotland and Great Britain in International athletics meetings. A North of Scotland Amateur Athletic Association was in being prior to the outbreak of the 1939 - 45 War but appears to have gone out of existence then, and it was not until 1949 that this Association was resurrected. The newly-formed Association was an autonomous body, controlling its own finances, and was affiliated to the Scottish Amateur Athletic Association and the Scottish Cross Country Union. It drew together, under one administrative body, the few athletic clubs in existence in the North at that time, together with one or two Services Organisations, the Schools Athletic Associations in Inverness-shire and Moray, as well as Gordonstoun and Fort Augustus Abbey Schools, both of which had athletics as an important feature of their curriculum.

In 1951 the North of Scotland A.A.A. introduced cross country running amongst clubs on a regular basis, and for the remainder of the 1950's there were occasional cross country runs between clubs and schools affiliated to the Association during the months of January, February and March, culminating at the end of March with the North of Scotland Cross Country Championships for Seniors and Youths which were inaugurated by the Association in 1953. In 1960 the Association also brought in Championships for Juniors and Senior Boys. Some time later the Junior Boys age group was added to the Championships.

Among the officials who were prominent in cross country in those early years were Donald Duncan, the Association's Secretary, who is now the Hon. President of the Scottish Cross Country Union, and Tom MacKenzie, his successor as Secretary of the Association who held that position for many years. Two of the leading North track and cross country athletes at that time were Forbes MacKenzie of Forres Harriers and Marshall Notman of Inverness Harriers, who had many interesting tussles over the country, with Notman often getting the better of the exchanges. In 1954 Forbes MacKenzie, running for Shettleston Harriers, succeeded in his first attempt at the National Cross Country Championship in gaining 5th place, and selection for Scotland in the International event at Birmingham that year, where he finished as third counter for the Scottish team. Unfortunately his promising career in cross country was brought to a sudden halt later that year when his legs were badly shattered in a motor cycle accident while returning from training with his club. Although he took up competitive running again some four years later and did, in fact, win the North of Scotland Cross Country Championship in 1962 and 1963, his injuries proved too great a handicap to enable him to reach International standard again. Another North athlete who gained prominence in the early 1960's was Calum Laing of Inverness Harriers. He was North of Scotland Champion in 1960 and again in 1961 ; and that year, while at Glasgow University, also won the Scottish

Universities Cross Country Championship. In 1962 he finished 3rd in the National Cross Country Championships at Hamilton Racecourse and was selected to represent Scotland in International events in 1962 and 1963.

The MacKenzie family in Forres played an important part in the local club's successes in cross country at that time, and Forbes MacKenzie was succeeded by his younger brother Iain, who took over from Forbes as North of Scotland Cross Country Champion. Between 1963 and 1978 Iain MacKenzie recorded eleven victories in North Junior and Senior Championships. He was well supported by Forres Harrier clubmates Duncan Davidson, Mike Scott, Hamish Cameron and Donnie McLean in keeping the club as a dominant force in North Cross Country events for many years. During the 1960's the Services stations at R.A.F. Kinloss and R.N.A.S. Lossiemouth also provided several good cross country runners, and won North team championships on several occasions. Gordonstoun School dominated the younger age group championships and much of their success can be attributed to the enthusiasm of George Welsh, the School's Sports Master at that time. A new athletic club was formed in Caithness and, coached by Sandy Gunn, became a force in cross country events in the 1960's and 1970's, dominating the younger age groups for a number of years. Regular inter-club meetings for cross country became more spasmodic during the latter part of the 1960's and, apart from the annual North of Scotland Championships, there was a decline for a period in cross country running in the North.

The revival of competitive cross country on a regular basis had its origins at the Knockfarrel Hill Race at Strathpeffer in 1971. Over a cup of tea at the conclusion of the race a few of the athletes got together with Walter Banks, President at that time of the North of Scotland A.A.A., who is now the Secretary of the Northern District of the Scottish Cross Country Union, and asked him to organise some regular competition between clubs in the North during the winter season, with the prospect of a League being formed if the venture proved successful. The first winter programme of cross country races at various venues was for Seniors only, and was so popular that, following meetings with interested clubs prior to the start of the cross country season in 1972, the North District Cross Country League was formed, with competitions for Seniors/Juniors and for Youths. In setting up the League Walter Banks did not have far to look for guidance as his father-in-law, the late George K Aithie, had been Secretary of the Eastern District Cross Country League for nearly 50 years! Six clubs (Forres Harriers, Lochaber A.C., Ross-shire A.C., Caithness A.A.C., R.A.F. Kinloss and Gordonstoun School) took part in the original League during the 1972/73 cross country season. Over the next few years the popularity of the League resulted in a steady increase in the number of clubs taking part, and the League was extended to cover the Senior Boys and Junior Boys age groups. As there was no cross country competition in the North of Scotland for females, the Girls and Women's age groups were also added. There are now six meetings in the League programme each year, all at different venues throughout the North, and each meeting has seven races with anything up to 250 athletes taking part.

The North of Scotland Cross Country Championships continued to be well supported but, above all, the 1973 Senior race will long be remembered for its premature end. The Championships that year were held in Inverness, and having battled through 5 miles of sleet, snow and hazards, and with the finishing line virtually in sight, the runners suddenly came across a final obstacle which was insurmountable. Before their eyes, on the run-in, the bridge over the Caledonian Canal was being opened to let a boat pass through. Officials at the finishing line some 200 yards away, having been assured that there would be no traffic for the duration of the race, could only watch in dismay - helpless to avert the crisis. One of the leading athletes, in sheer frustration, took the plunge into the chilly waters of the Canal but quickly turned back. The race was abandoned and re-run at Forres later in the season.

In 1975 the North of Scotland Amateur Athletic Association was disbanded, and the Northern District of both the Scottish Amateur Athletic Association and the Scottish Cross Country Union was formed. Since that time cross country running has gone from strength to strength, and is now a well established feature of athletics in the North, with 18 clubs in the District now affiliated to the Scottish Cross Country Union.

The greatest problem faced by the Northern District is the widely dispersed area it covers, with a population which is less than that of the City of Edinburgh. The area covered by the clubs under the District's jurisdiction stretches from Peterhead and Fraserburgh in the east (both of those clubs elected to be part of the Northern rather than the Eastern District), to Stornoway in the Outer Isles and from Orkney in the North to Lochaber in the South. The enthusiasm of the clubs and their athletes for competition has to be admired, for it can involve some clubs in a round trip of four or five hundred miles to take part in a League or Championship event. It is doubtful if clubs participating in the other two Scottish Districts require overnight accommodation for their athletes, as was the case for a few of the North clubs when the District Championships were held in Caithness recently! Consequently, travelling costs to cross country events, both within the Northern District and to venues in the South, plays a significant part in the finances of clubs in the District.

Adverse weather conditions in the North during the winter months can also, at times, play havoc with cross country events, and here again it is the distance clubs have to travel which can cause problems if the area has been affected by heavy falls of snow. It is not necessarily the underfoot conditions on a course which can result in events being cancelled, but rather ice-bound or snow-covered roads which can make travel to an event dangerous and an unnecessary risk. Between 1982 and 1986 the Northern District Cross Country Championships had to be cancelled on three occasions due to snow, and run later in the Season. Because of those cancellations the Northern District Committee decided to depart from the recognised January date for District Cross Country Championships to a date at the end of November, when the event was less likely to come under the threat of adverse weather conditions. In the first year of the change the course at Kinloss was covered in snow!

The North of Scotland frequently loses promising young athletes when they leave the area to study at University or College, and some of those athletes have gone on to gain top honours in cross country running. Calum Laing of Inverness Harriers and Glasgow University has already been mentioned. Elgin-born Alistair Wood won the National Senior Championship in 1959, and represented Scotland on six occasions from 1959 to 1964. A member of Aberdeen A.A.C., he still holds the record which he set in 1968 for the Alves to Forres Road Race, the first event each year in the North winter programme. Ross Arbuckle (Keith), when at

Start of the Alves to Forres road race in 1974, traditionally the opening event of the winter season in the North District. North of Scotland athletes in the line-up from the left, include: D. Shepherd, D. Davidson, I. Johnstone, F. Clyne, E. Campbell, D. McLean, R. Maughan, A. Pratt, W.E. Elliot, D. McLean, G. Laing, D. Bow, I. Johnston, A. Wood, D. Ritchie, R. Macdonald, M. Scott and G. Milne.

Aberdeen University in 1980, and Jamie Bell (Inverness Harriers) while also at Aberdeen University in 1986, both represented Scotland at Junior level in the World Cross Country Championships. The record would not be complete without a mention of one or two other prominent North club athletes such as Donald Ritchie (Forres Harriers), who has helped his club to many victories in cross country, but who is now better known for his outstanding feats in long distance road running. And cross country, road and hill running events in the North would not be the same if the ageless Eddie Campbell of Lochaber A.C. failed to appear. Eddie has been an inspiration to members of his club, and to other athletes in the North, from the time he first won the Ben Nevis Hill Race in 1952 and the North of Scotland Cross Country Championship in 1958.

The athletic clubs of longer standing in the District such as Forres Harriers, Inverness Harriers, Lochaber A.C., Caithness A.A.C. and Elgin A.C. are still well to the fore in the cross country scene, although all of them have had their lean periods as well as their triumphs in past years. The mid Seventies saw a remarkable revival in cross country of Inverness Harriers who had been in the doldrums for a few years. Under the guidance of Brian Turnbull, a former Teviotdale Harrier who had moved to Inverness, the Club emerged as a strong force in the Northern District, particularly in the younger age groups, and this development has broadened into the national scene during the Eighties. The Elgin club, with ex-Royal Navy man and former Scottish Wire Hammer Champion, Alex Valentine, at the helm, is presently undergoing a difficult period with a falling membership limiting its cross country interests. It is probably also feeling some effect from the recent emergence of a new athletic club in the area, Moray Road Runners, with cross country fast becoming a significant part of that club's activities. The Services stations at Kinloss and Lossiemouth no longer compete as clubs within the District. Many of the athletes at those stations now live within the local community and have allied themselves to local clubs. Ross-shire A.C. disbanded a few years ago but a new club, Black Isle A.A.C., led by Ray Cameron, has been set up at Muir of Ord, and is already producing several promising athletes. Peterhead A.A.C. and Fraserburgh Running Club are welcome recent additions to the Northern District, as is the East Sutherland Running Club, based at Dornoch, the first amateur athletic club to be based in the County of Sutherland. A special mention must be made of two of the Island-based clubs in the Northern District. Both Orkney Islands A.A.A. and the Nicolson Institute School, Stornoway, find that to compete at an event in the District, their athletes can be involved in staying for three nights on the mainland because of the timing of weekend ferry services. Competition for those clubs is difficult to come by and their efforts to encourage cross country running amongst their athletes is highly commendable.

The strength of cross country running in the North over the past twenty years or so has, in the main, been in the younger age groups. By and large, clubs have found difficulty in fielding strong teams of Juniors and Seniors, particularly when competing against clubs in the Central Belt. For this reason the Northern District has, for the past few years, been allowed by the General Committee of the Union to enter a composite team in the prestigious Edinburgh to Glasgow road relay race. Several good individual athletes have, however, emerged from the North in recent years such as Ross Arbuckle (Keith and District A.C.); Alan Reid (Coasters Running Club); Danny Bow (Nairn and District A.C.); Neil Martin and Bruce Chinnick (Forres Harriers); Chris Armstrong (Elgin A.A.C.); John Bowman (Inverness Harriers); Willie Miller (Caithness A.A.C.); and Graham Milne (Peterhead A.A.C.), now the North's leading veteran. All of them have made their mark in Northern District cross country events and have also fared well in competitions in the south. It should also be mentioned that North clubs occasionally benefit from having a prominent athlete come to reside in this area through his work. Over the past few years Paul Kenney, who competed for Scotland at International events in 1976 and 1977 while at Dundee University, and again in 1983 while with Inverness Harriers, and Simon Axon, also of Inverness Harriers, a Welsh international cross country runner, both won Northern District Championships during the time they were resident in the North.

The 1980's has seen tremendous improvements in road communication between the North and the Central Belt of Scotland and it has been easier in recent years for North clubs to take part in cross country events in the south. The rule, approved in 1976, which allowed athletes in the Northern District to compete as 'secondary first claim" members of clubs based outwith the District has also given North athletes the opportunity for better competition at top level. The benefits obtained from a better standard of competition at all levels have shown some good results, particularly in the Young Athletes age groups. Inverness Harriers won the Senior Boys team event in the National Cross Country Championships in 1982, took second place in the Youths team championships in 1984, and in 1987 and 1988 were 3rd in the Junior Boys team championships. At Hawick in 1989 the newest club in the Northern District - Fraserburgh Running Club - took 2nd place in the Junior Boys team championship on the first occasion in which the club had competed in a National Cross Country Championship.

In 1980 Inverness was the venue for the first-ever National Championships held in the Northern District when the National Relays were held there. Inverness hosted the National Centenary Relay Championships in 1989, firm indication that the Northern District has been accepted as a well-established part of the Scottish cross country scene. Hopefully, cross country running will continue to flourish, and the Northern District of the Union look forward with a realistic expectation that more clubs and individual athletes from this area will gain honours at National level in the final decade of this century.

NATIONAL CROSS COUNTRY SENIOR CHAMPIONSHIPS

Sub Committee of Management for National Championships

	INDIVIDUAL		TEAM
1886	A P Findlay	(Clydesdale H.)	Edinburgh H.
1887	J Campbell	(Clydesdale H.)	Edinburgh H.

Scottish Cross Country Association Championships

1888	A P Findlay	(Clydesdale H.)	Clydesdale H.
1889	C McCann	(Clydesdale H.)	Clydesdale H.
1890	A Hannah	(Clydesdale H.)	Clydesdale H.

Scottish Harriers Union Championships

1889	J W McWilliams	(Clydesdale H.)	Paisley
1890	C Pennycook	(Clydesdale H.)	Glasgow

Scottish Cross Country Union Championships

1891	A Hannah	(Clydesdale H.)	Edinburgh H.
1892	C Pennycook	(Clydesdale H.)	Clydesdale H.
1893	A Hannah	(Clydesdale H.)	Clydesdale H.
1894	A Hannah	(Clydesdale H.)	Clydesdale H.
1895	R A Hay	(Edinburgh H.)	Edinburgh H.
1896	A Hannah	(Clydesdale H.)	Clydesdale H.
1897	S Duffus	(Clydesdale H.)	Clydesdale H.
1898	J Paterson	(Watsonians CCC)	Clydesdale H.
1899	J Paterson	(Watsonians CCC)	Watsonians CCC.
1900	J Paterson	(Watsonians CCC)	Watsonians CCC.
1901	D W Mill	(Clydesdale H.)	Clydesdale H.
1902	D W Mill	(Clydesdale H.)	Clydesdale H.
1903	P J McCafferty	(West of Scotland H.)	Edinburgh H.

National Cross Country Union of Scotland Championships

1904	J Ranken	(Watsonians CCC)	Edinburgh H.
1905	J Ranken	(Watsonians CCC)	West of Scotland H.
1906	S Stevenson	(Clydesdale H.)	Clydesdale H.
1907	T Jack	(Edinburgh Southern H.)	Clydesdale H.
1908	T Jack	(Edinburgh Southern H.)	Motherwell YMCA H.
1909	A McPhee	(Clydesdale H.)	West of Scotland H.
1910	A McPhee	(Clydesdale H.)	West of Scotland H. & Clydesdale H. (tie)
1911	S S Watt	(Clydesdale H.)	Edinburgh H.
1912	T Jack	(Edinburgh Southern H.)	West of Scotland H.
1913	A Craig	(Bellahouston H.)	Bellahouston H.
1914	G C L Wallach	(Greenock Glenpark H.)	Bellahouston H.

No Championships were held in 1915, 1916, 1917, 1918, 1919 due to the First World War.

1920	J Wilson	(Greenock Glenpark H.)	Shettleston H.
1921	J H Motion	(Eglinton H.)	Shettleston H.
1922	G C L Wallach	(Greenock Glenpark H.)	Shettleston H.
1923	D McL.Wright	(Clydesdale H.)	Greenock Glenpark H.
1924	D McL.Wright	(Shettleston H.)	Shettleston H.
1925	D McL.Wright	(Shettleston H.)	Garscube H.
1926	J Mitchell	(Kilmarnock H.)	Garscube H.
1927	D McL.Wright	(Shettleston H.)	Maryhill H.
1928	J Suttie Smith	(Dundee Thistle H.)	Maryhill H.
1929	J Suttie Smith	(Dundee Thistle H.)	Maryhill H.
1930	J Suttie Smith	(Dundee Thistle H.)	Maryhill H.
1931	J Suttie Smith	(Dundee YMCA H.)	Maryhill H.
1932	J Suttie Smith	(Dundee YMCA H.)	Maryhill H.
1933	J C Flockhart	(Shettleston H.)	Shettleston H.
1934	J C Flockhart	(Shettleston H.)	Dundee Thistle H. and Plebian H. (tie)
1935	W C Wylie	(Darlington H.)	Edinburgh North H.
1936	J C Flockhart	(Shettleston H.)	Springburn H.
1937	J C Flockhart	(Shettleston H.)	Dundee Thistle H.
1938	J E Farrell	(Maryhill H.)	Maryhill H.
1939	R Reid	(Doon H.)	Bellahouston H.

No Championships were held in 1940, 1941, 1942, 1943, 1944, 1945, 1946 due to the Second World War.

1947	A Forbes	(Victoria Park AAC)	Bellahouston H.
1948	J E Farrell	(Maryhill H.)	Shettleston H.
1949	J Fleming	(Motherwell YMCA H.)	Shettleston H.
1950	R Reid	(Doon H./Birchfield H.)	Shettleston H.
1951	A Forbes	(Victoria Park AAC)	Victoria Park AAC.
1952	E Bannon	(Shettleston H.)	Victoria Park AAC
1953	E Bannon	(Shettleston H.)	Victoria Park AAC
1954	E Bannon	(Shettleston H.)	Shettleston H.
1955	D Henson	(Victoria Park AAC)	Shettleston H.
1956	E Bannon	(Shettleston H.)	Victoria Park AAC.
1957	H Fenion	(Bellahouston H.)	Victoria Park AAC.
1958	A H Brown	(Motherwell YMCA H.)	Victoria Park AAC.
1959	A J Wood	(Shettleston H.)	Shettleston H.
1960	G E Everett	(Shettleston H.)	Shettleston H.
1961	J Connolly	(Bellahouston H.)	Shettleston H.
1962	J N C Alder	(Morpeth H.)	Shettleston H.
1963	J Linaker	(Motherwell YMCA H.)	Motherwell YMCA H.
1964	A F Murray	(Edinburgh University H & H)	Edinburgh Southern H.

Scottish Cross Country Union

1965	A F Murray	(Edinburgh University H & H)	Edinburgh Southern H.
1966	A F Murray	(Edinburgh University H & H)	Edinburgh Univ H & H
1967	J L Stewart	(Vale of Leven AAC)	Edinburgh Univ H & H
1968	J L Stewart	(Vale of Leven AAC)	Edinburgh Univ H & H

1969	R T Wedlock	(Shettleston H.)	Edinburgh Southern H.
1970	J N C Alder	(Edinburgh AC)	Edinburgh Southern H.
1971	J N C Alder	(Edinburgh AC)	Shettleston H.
1972	I McCafferty	(Law & District AC)	Shettleston H.
1973	A McKean	(Edinburgh University H & H)	Edinburgh AC.
1974	J Brown	(Monkland H.)	Edinburgh AC.
1975	A McKean	(Edinburgh AC)	Edinburgh AC.
1976	A McKean	(Edinburgh AC)	Edinburgh AC.
1977	A McKean	(Edinburgh AC)	Shettleston AC.
1978	A Hutton	(Edinburgh Southern H.)	Edinburgh AC.
1979	N Muir	(Shettleston H.)	Edinburgh Southern H.
1980	N Muir	(Shettleston H.)	Edinburgh Southern H.
1981	N Muir	(Shettleston H.)	Edinburgh AC.
1982	A Hutton	(Edinburgh Southern H.)	Edinburgh Southern H.
1983	N Muir	(Shettleston H.)	Edinburgh Southern H.
1984	N Muir	(Shettleston H.)	Edinburgh Southern H.
1985	N Muir	(Shetleston H.)	Edinburgh Southern H.
1986	N Muir	(Shettleston H.)	Edinburgh Southern H.
1987	N Muir	(Shettleston H.)	Edinburgh Southern H.
1988	N Tennant	(Edinburgh Southern H.)	Cambuslang H.
1989	T Murray	(Greenock Glenpark H.)	Cambuslang H.
1990	P McColgan	(Dundee Hawkhill H.)	Cambuslang H

SCOTTISH NATIONAL TEAM CHAMPIONSHIP RESULTS 1886 - 1990

1886	1. Edinburgh H 35pt (only club to finish a team)		
1887	1. Edinburgh H 42 pt	2. Clydesdale H 49 pt	3. West of Scotland H 89 pt
1888	1. Clydesdale H 23 pt	2. Edinburgh H 62 pt	3. West of Scotland H 139 pt
1889(SHU)	1. Glasgow 40 pt	2. Ayrshire 55 pt	3. Lanarkshire 77 pt.
1889(SCCA)	1. Clydesdale H 31 pt	2. Edinburgh H 53 pt	3. West of Scotland H 113 pt
1890(SHU)	1. Glasgow	2. Renfrewshire	3. Dunbartonshire
1890(SCCA)	1. Clydesdale H 34 pt	2. Edinburgh H 44 pt	3. West of Scotland H 137 pt
1891	1. Edinburgh H 38 pt	2. Clydesdale H 44 pt	3. Motherwell YMCA H 148 pt
1892	1. Clydesdale H 37 pt	2. Edinburgh H 44 pt	3. West of Scotland H 113 pt
1893	1. Clydesdale H 48 pt	2. Edin.North H 60 pt	3. Edinburgh H 66 pt
1894	1. Clydesdale H 46 pt	2. Edin North H 56 pt	3. Edinburgh H 79 pt
1895	1. Edinburgh H 34 pt	2. Clydesdale H 44 pt (only 2 clubs finished teams)	
1896	1. Clydesdale H 24 pt	(Only club to finish a team)	
1897	1. Clydesdale H 36 pt	2. Edin North H 54 pt (only 2 clubs finished teams)	
1898	1. Clydesdale H 44pt	2. Watsonians CCC 71 pt	3. Motherwell YMCA H 102 pt
1899	1. Watsonians CCC 55 pt	2. Maryhill H 68 pt	3 Edinburgh H 92 pt
1900	1. Watsonians CCC 37 pt	2. Clydesdale H 65 pt(only clubs finished teams)	
1901	1. Clydesdale H 51pt	2. Edinburgh H 52 pt	3. Coatbridge H 75 pt
1902	1. Clydesdale H 38 pt	2. Edinburgh H 77 pt	3. Maryhill H 147 pt
1903	1. Edinburgh H 72 pt	2. Clydesdale H 103 pt	3. West of Scotland H 118 pt
1904	1. Edinburgh H 60 pt	2. Clydesdale H 103 pt	3. Garscube H 114 pt
1905	1. West of Scot H 79 pt	2. Edinburgh H 115 pt	3. Clydesdale H 127 pt
1906	1. Clydesdale H 53 pt	2. Edinburgh H 63 pt	3. West of Scotland H 97 pt
1907	1. Clydesdale H 84 pt	2. West of Scot H 93 pt	3. Motherwell YMCA H 102 pt
1908	1. Motherwell YMCAH 79pt	2. Clydesdale H 82 pt	3. West of Scotland H 97 pt

Year	1st	2nd	3rd
1909	1. West of Scot H 64 pt	2. Clydesdale H 65 pt	3. Edinburgh H 108 pt
1910	1 equal West of Scotland H & Clydesdale H 83 pt		3. Edinburgh H 106 pt
1911	1. Edinburgh H 54 pt	2. Clydesdale H 82 pt	3. West of Scotland H 91 pt
1912	1. West of Scot H 69 pt	2. Clydesdale H 81 pt	3. Edinburgh H 101 pt
1913	1. Bellahouston H 50 pt	2. West of Scot H 51 pt	3. Clydesdale H 89 pt
1914	1. Bellahouston H 29 Pt	2 West of Scot H 62pt	3. Edin. North H 128 pt

No Championship held in 1915 - 1919 due to First World War

Year	1st	2nd	3rd
1920	1. Shettleston H 76 pt	2. M/well YMCAH 125pt	3. Bellahouston H 126 pt
1921	1. Shettleston H 93 pt	2. Garscube H 112 pt	3. Green Glenpark H 179 pt
1922	1. Shettleston H 88 pt	2. Green Glenpark 98 pt	3. Garscube H 127 pt
1923	1. Green Glenpark H 95pt	2. Garscube H 100 pt	3. Shettleston H 174 pt
1924	1. Shettleston H 62pt	2. Garscube H 67 pt	3. Edin South H 135 pt
1925	1. Garscube H 65 pt	2. Shettleston H 130 pt	3. Maryhill H 192 pt
1926	1. Garscube H 78 pt	2. Maryhill H 112 pt	3. Shettleston H 193 pt
1927	1. Maryhill H 62 pt	2. Edin North H 124 pt	3. Monkland H 145 pt
1928	1. Maryhill H 55 pt	2. Plebian H 122 pt	3. Garscube H 171 pt
1929	1. Maryhill H 90 pt	2. Dundee This H 150pt	3. Plebian H 167 pt
1930	1. Maryhill H 86 pt	2. Dundee This H 94 pt	3. Plebian H 172 pt
1931	1. Maryhill H 55 pt	2. Garscube H 114 pt	3. Plebian H 192 pt
1932	1. Maryhill H 105 pt	2. Dundee This H 135pt	3. Plebian H 162 pt
1933	1. Shettleston H 154 pt	2. Springburn H 167 pt	3. Maryhill H 175 pt
1934	1 equal Dundee This H & Plebian H both 138 pt		3. Edin North H 142 pt
1935	1. Edin North H 125 pt	2. Dundee This H 138pt	3. Garscube H 186 pt
1936	1. Springburn H 106 pt	2. Maryhill H 142 pt	3. Bellahouston H 144 pt
1937	1. Dundee This H 78 pt	2. Maryhill H 125 pt	3. Plebian H 198 pt
1938	1. Maryhill H 99 pt	2. Shettleston H 125 pt	3. Bellahouston H 156 pt
1939	1. Bellahouston H 110 pt	2. Maryhill H 114 pt	3. Shettleston H 135 pt

No Championships held in 1940 - 46 due to Second World War

Year	1st	2nd	3rd
1947	1. Bellahouston H 59 pt	2. Vict Park AAC 90 pt	3. Maryhill H 120 pt
1948	1. Shettleston H 57 pt	2. Bellahouston H 90 pt	3. Garscube H 150 pt
1949	1. Shettleston H 69pt	2 equal Bellahouston H & Vict. Park AAC both 164 pt	
1950	1. Shettleston H 79 pt	2. Edin Univ H&H 140 pt	3. Vict. Park AAC 143 pt
1951	1. Vict Park AAC 50 pt	2. Springburn H 81 pt	3. Shettleston H 94 pt
1952	1. Vict Park AAC 36 pt	2. Springburn H 90 pt	3. Shettleston H 106 pt
1953	1. Vict Park AAC 60 pt	2. Shettleston H 91 pt	3. Springburn H 158 pt
1954	1. Shettleston H 90 pt	2. Vict Park AAC 113 pt	3. Edin South H 233 pt
1955	1. Shettleston H 106 pt	2. Vict Park AAC 122 pt	3. Clydesdale H 164 pt
1956	1. Vict Park AAC 80 pt	2. Green Wellpark H 155	3.Shettleston H 171 pt
1957	1. Vict Park AAC 93 pt	2. Bellahouston H 125pt	3. Edin South H 175 pt
1958	1. Vict. Park AAC 86 pt	2. Bellahouston H 94 pt	3. Shettleston H 147 pt
1959	1. Shettleston H 55 pt	2. Vict Park AAC 137 pt	3. Bellahouston H 159 pt
1960	1. Shettleston H 73 pt	2. Bellahouston H 118	3. Vict Park AAC 165 pt
1961	1. Shettleston H 114 pt	2. Edin South H 150 pt	3. Vict Park AAC 219 pt
1962	1. Shettleston H 115 pt	2. Aberdeen AAC 164 pt	3. Edin South H 192 pt
1963	1. Motherwell YMCAH 108pt	2. Edin South H 116 pt	3. Vict Park AAC 181 pt
1964	1. Edin South H 81 pt	2. Aberdeen AAC 148 pt	3. Motherwell YMCAH 221 pt
1965	1. Edin South H 147 pt	2. Aberdeen AAC 252 pt	3. Edin Univ H&H 252pt
1966	1. Edin Univ H&H 75 pt	2. Vict Park AAC 184	3. Edin South H 212 pt
1967	1. Edin Univ H&H 109 pt	2. Edin South H 253 pt	3. Vict Park AAC 260 pt
1968	1. Edin Univ H&H 93 pt	2. Aberdeen AAC 94 pt	3. Edin South H 167 pt
1969	1. Edin South H 80 pt	2. Shettleston H 102 pt	3. Edinburgh AC 131 pt
1970	1. Edin South H 122 pt	2. Edinburgh AC 152 pt	3. Shettleston H 193 pt

1971	1. Shettleston H 80 pt	2. Edin South H 105 pt	3. Edinburgh AC 267 pt
1972	1. Shettleston H 99pt	2. Edinburgh AC 190 pt	3. Aberdeen AAC 204 pt
1973	1. Edinburgh AC 124 pt	2. Shettleston H 168 pt	3. Edin South H 214 pt
1974	1. Edinburgh AC 75 pt	2. Edin South H 115 pt	3. Aberdeen AAC 209 pt
1975	1. Edinburgh AC 37 pt	2. Edin South H 101 pt	3. Shettleston H 199 pt
1976	1. Edinburgh AC 57 pt	2. Edin South H 99 pt	3. Shettleston H 162 pt
1977	1. Shettleston H 117 pt	2. Edin South H 125 pt	3. Edinburgh AC 126 pt
1978	1. Edinburgh AC 102 pt	2. Edin South H 110 pt	3. Shettleston H 204 pt
1979	1. Edin South H 112 pt	2. Edinburgh AC 172 pt	3. Vict Park AAC 215 pt
1980	1. Edin South H 103 pt	2 Clyde Valley AC 122	3. Cambuslang H 209 pt
1981	1. Edinburgh AC 121 pt	2. Edin South H 133 pt	3. Clyde Valley AC 195 pt
1982	1. Edin South H 89 pt	2. Clyde Valley AC 195	3. Aberdeen AAC 237 pt
1983	1. Edin South H 135 pt	2. Edinburgh AC 176 pt	3. Aberdeen AAC 188 pt
1984	1. Edin South H 111 pt	2. Cambuslang H 194 pt	3. Falkirk Vic H 224 pt
1985	1. Edin South H 81 pt	2. Falkirk Vic H 150 pt	3. Cambuslang H 180 pt
1986	1. Edin South H 78 pt	2. Cambuslang H 146 pt	3. Aberdeen AAC 294 pt
1987	1. Edin South H 133 pt	2. Bellahouston H 172	3. Cambuslang H 191 pt
1988	1. Cambuslang H 63 pt	2. Teviotdale H 162 pt	3. Aberdeen AAC 282 pt
1989	1. Cambuslang H 128 pt	2. Edin South H 162 pt	3. Shettleston H 353 pt
1990	1. Cambuslang H 126 pt	2. Edin South H 159 pt	3. Dundee Hawkhill 183 pt

NATIONAL JUNIOR CHAMPIONSHIP
INDIVIDUAL

			TEAM
1891	W J Lowson	(Dundee H.)	Edinburgh H.
1892	P T Lewis	(Clydesdale H.)	Edinburgh Northern H.
1893	S Duffus	(Abroath H.)	Edinburgh Northern H.
1894	W Robertson	(Clydesdale H.)	Clydesdale H.
1895	F W Bruce	(Edinburgh University H & H)	Watsonian CCC.
1896	C McCracken	(Carrick H.)	Clydesdale H.
1897	J Paterson	(Watsonians CCC)	Watsonian CCC.
1898	A Pitt	(Motherwell H.)	Motherwell H.
1899	W T Marshall	(West of Scotland H.)	Maryhill H.
1900	A Forrester	(Coatbridge H.)	Clydesdale H.
1901	J L McCafferty	(West of Scotland H.)	Coatbridge H.
1902	J Bathgate	(Edinburgh Northern H.)	Motherwell H.

First Junior to finish in the National Senior Championship.

1903	P J McCafferty	(West of Scotland H.)
1904	G McKenzie	(West of Scotland H.)
1905	P C Russell	(Bellahouston H.)
1906	D Cather	(Hamilton H.)
1907	T Jack	(Edinburgh Southern H.)
1908	A McPhee Jnr	(Clydesdale H.)
1909	J Duffy	(Edinburgh H.)
1910	R F Gilbert	(West of Scotland H.)
1911	J G Aitchison	(Gala H.)
1912	A Loch	(Clydesdale H.)
1913	A MacDonald	(Monkland H.)
1914	J Lindsay	(Bellahouston H.)

No Championships were held in 1915, 1916, 1917, 1918, 1919 due to the First World War.

1920 D McL.Wright   (Clydesdale H.)
1921 J H Motion   (Eglinton H.)
1922 J W Riach   (Maryhill H.)
1923 J G McIntyre   (Shettleston H.)
1924 R B McIntyre   (West of Scotland H.)
1925 J Mitchell   (Mauchline H.)
1926 F L Stevenson   (Monkland H.)
1927 C H Johnston   (Glasgow University H & H)
1928 R R Sutherland   (Garscube H.)
1929 D T Muir   (Maryhill H.)
1930 M Stobbs   (Catrine AC)
1931 J Addison   (Greenock Glenpark H.)
1932 P Peattie   (Monkland H.)
1933 J C Flockhart   (Shettleston H.)
1934 A Dow   (Kirkcaldy YMCA H.)
1935 J Freeland   (Hamilton H.)
1936 A MacPherson   (Airdrie H.)
1937 A Craig   (Shettleston H.)
1938 T W Lamb   (Bellahouston H.)
1939 R Reid   (Doon H.)

No Championships were held in 1940, 1941, 1942, 1943, 1944, 1945, 1946 due to the Second World War.

1947 A Forbes   (Victoria Park AAC)
1948 G B Craig   (Shettleston H.)
1949 J Fleming   (Motherwell YMCA H.)

National Junior (18 to 21 years of age) Championship

INDIVIDUAL			TEAM
1950	G Adamson	(West Kilbride ASC)	Edinburgh Univ H & H
1951	E Bannon	(Shettleston H.)	Edinburgh Univ H & H
1952	D Nelson	(Motherwell YMCA H.)	Victoria Park AAC.
1953	A D Breckenridge	(Victoria Park AAC)	Victoria Park AAC.
1954	J McLaren	(Shotts Miners Welfare)	Edinburgh Univ H & H
1955	J McLaren	(Shotts Miners Welfare)	Edinburgh Univ H & H
1956	P McParland	(Springburn H.)	Bellahouston H.
1957	J Wright	(Clydesdale H.)	Shettleston H.
1958	J Wright	(Clydesdale H.)	St Andrews University
1959	W Goodwin	(Bellahouston H.)	Edinburgh Univ H & H
1960	J H Linaker	(Pitreavie AAC)	St Andrews University
1961	J McLatchie	(Doon H.)	Teviotdale H.
1962	A Heron	(Edinburgh Southern H.)	Glasgow Univ H & H
1963	A F Murray	(Edinburgh University H & H)	Edinburgh Univ H & H
1964	M Edwards	(Aberdeen University)	Edinburgh Univ H & H
1965	I McCafferty	(Motherwell YMCA H.)	Edinburgh Univ H & H
1966	I McCafferty	(Motherwell YMCA H.)	Victoria Park AAC.
1967	E Knox	(Springburn H.)	Edinburgh Univ H & H
1968	J K Myatt	(Strathclyde University AC)	Shettleston H.

1969	N Morrison	(Shettleston H.)	Shettleston H.
1970	C Falconer	(Springburn H.)	Larkhall YMCA H.
1971	R MacDonald	(Monkland H.)	Shettleston H.«
1972	J Brown	(Monkland H.)	Monkland H.
1973	J Brown	(Monkland H.)	Monkland H.
1974	L Reilly	(Victoria Park AAC)	Springburn H.
1975	A Hutton	(Edinburgh Southern H.)	Shettleston H.
1976	N Muir	(Shettleston H.)	Aberdeen AC.
1977	N Muir	(Shettleston H.)	Shettleston H.
1978	N Muir	(Shettleston H.)	Edinburgh AC.
1979	B McSloy	(Strathclyde University	Strathclyde Univ AC
1980	G Williamson	(Springburn H.)	Edinburgh Southern H.
1981	A Douglas	(Victoria Park AAC)	Edinburgh Southern H.
1982	C Henderson	(Edinburgh Southern H.)	Victoria Park AC.
1983	J McNeill	(Law & District AC)	Cambuslang H.
1984	R Quinn	(Kilbarchan AC)	Cambuslang H.
1985	R Quinn	(Kilbarchan AC)	Cambuslang H.
1986	S Begen	(Springburn H.)	Kilbarchan AC.
1987	A Russell	(Law & District AC)	Cambuslang H.
1988	C Murphy	(Pitreavie AAC)	Motherwell YMCA H.
1989	C Murphy	(Pitreavie AAC)	J W Kilmarnock H.
1990	M Campbell	(Clydebank AC)	Clydebank AC

N.B. Between 1891 and 1902 a separate Junior Championship race over 9 miles was held with a team championship included.

Between 1903 and 1949 the first "Junior" to finish in the Senior 9 mile championship race was awarded the Junior title. A "Junior" during this period 1891 to 1949 was by qualification, not by age. An athlete of any age, who had not finished in the first three in a District Championship race or been a member of a winning team in a District Championship, was thus not in a "Senior" category and was eligible for "Junior" Competition.

From 1950 onwards to date the team championship was re-introduced and the Junior age category was under 21 (generally 18 - 21 years) up to 1966 after which it became 17 to 20 years. The distance in the Junior race from 1950 to 1962 was 6 miles and from 1963 to date it was 5 miles.

NATIONAL YOUTH CHAMPIONSHIP

INDIVIDUAL   TEAM

1933	J J McDonald	(St Peters AC)	Maryhill H.
1934	A Whitecross	(Dundee Thistle H.)	Springburn H
1935	G Craig	(Shettleston H.)	Springburn H.
1936	G Craig	(Shettleston H.)	Shettleston H.
1937	R Reid	(Doon H.)	Carntyne a.
1938	R Reid	(Doon H.)	Garscube H.
1939	A Haddow	(West of Scotland H.)	Teviotdale H.

No Championships were held in 1940, 1941, 1942, 1943, 1944, 1945, 1946 due to the Second World War.

1947	W Young	(Victoria Park AAC)	Victoria Park AAC.
1948	H Fenion	(Lochwinnoch AAC)	Kirkcaldy YMCA H.
1949	G Adamson	(West Kilbride ASC)	West Kilbride ASC.
1950	J Finlayson	(Hamilton H.)	Victoria Park AAC.
1951	J Finlayson	(Hamilton H.)	Hamilton H.
1952	J Lyle	(Cambuslang H.)	Cambuslang H.
1953	P McParland	(Springburn H)	Bellahouston H.
1954	I Cloudsley	(Shettleston)	Shettleston H.
1955	W Goodwin	(Bellahouston H.)	Shettleston H.
1956	W Goodwin	(Bellahouston H.)	Springburn H.
1957	J Messer	(Edinburgh Northern H.)	Shettleston H.
1958	N Biggs	(South Shields H.)	Shettleston H.
1959	A Fleming	(St Modans AC)	Bellahouston H.
1960	J Finn	(Monkland H.)	Shettleston H.
1961	J Finn	(Monkland H.)	Victoria Park AAC.
1962	A P Brown	(Motherwell YMCA H.)	Shettleston H.
1963	I McCafferty	(Motherwell YMCA H.)	Kirkcaldy YMCA H.
1964	E Knox	(Springburn H.)	Edinburgh AC.
1965	E Knox	(Springburn H.)	Edinburgh AC.
1966	M McMahon	(Shettleston H.)	Shettleston H.
1967	J Cook	(Garscube H.)	Springburn H.
1968	I Picken	(Springburn H.)	Shettleston H.
1969	J Lees	(Edinburgh AC)	Shettleston H.
1970	R MacDonald	(Monkland H.)	Monkland H.
1971	L Reilly	(Victoria Park AAC)	Victoria Park AAC.
1972	J Lawson	(Springburn H.)	Springburn H.
1973	M Watt	(Shettleston H.)	Law & District AC.
1974	J Graham	(Motherwell YMCA H.)	Springburn H.
1975	N Muir	(Shettleston H.)	Shettleston H.
1976	A Smith	(Shettleston H.)	Edinburgh AC.
1977	G Williamson	(Springburn H.)	Edinburgh AC.
1978	A Douglas	(Victoria Park AAC)	Clyde Valley AC.
1979	P Fox	(Clyde Valley AC)	Clyde Valley AC.
1980	R Copestake	(Dundee Hawkhill H.)	Springburn H.
1981	G McMillan	(Ayrshire AAC)	Kilbarchan AC.
1982	D McShane	(Cambuslang H.)	Cambuslang H.
1983	R Quinn	(Kilbarchan AC)	Cambuslang H.
1984	S Begen	(Springburn H.)	Cambuslang H.
1985	A Russell	(Law & District AC)	Cambuslang H.
1986	A Russell	(Law & District AC)	Law & District AC.
1987	T Reid	(Dundee Hawkhill H.)	Clydebank AC.
1988	M Campbell	(Clydebank AC)	Clydebank AC.
1989	M Campbell	(Clydebank AC)	Clydebank AC.
1990	M McBeth	(Cambuslang H)	Victoria Park AAC.

NATIONAL SENIOR BOYS CHAMPIONSHIP
INDIVIDUAL   TEAM
1958 J L Stewart   (Vale of Leven AAC)   George Heriots School
1959 G B Brownlee   (Edinburgh Southern H.)   George Heriots School
1960 H Barrow   (Victoria Park AC)   George Heriots School
1961 R Wedlock   (Shettleston H.)   Shettleston H.
1962 D Middleton   (Springburn H.)   St Modan's AAC.
1963 W Donaldson   (Edinburgh AC)   Edinburgh AC.
1964 W G Kerr   (Edinburgh AC)   Edinburgh AC.
1965 J M McLennan   (Edinburgh Southern H.)   Paisley H.
1966 G Jarvie   (Springburn H.)   Shettleston H.
1967 J Gallacher   (Bathgate AC)   Shettleston H.
1968 J E McGill   (Blackburn H.)   Monkland H.
1969 J Mulvey   (Shettleston H.)   Victoria Park AAC.
1970 J Mulvey   (Shettleston H.)   Springburn H.
1971 M Watt   (Shettleston H.)   Shettleston H.
1972 M Watt   (Shettleston H.)   Shettleston H.
1973 K McCartney   (Law & District AC)   Shettleston H
1974 I Murray   (Springburn H.)   Springburn H.
1975 T Young   (Central Region AC)   Central Region AC.
1976 G Adams   (Victoria Park AAC)   Victoria Park AAC.
1977 J Gladwin   (Edinburgh Southern H.)   Edinburgh Southern H.
1978 I Steel   (Edinburgh Southern H.)   Springburn H.
1979 R Hawkins   (Kilbarchan AC)   Cambuslang H.
1980 D McShane   (Cambuslang H.)   Springburn H.
1981 D Russell   (Law & District AC)   Springburn H.
1982 S Holden   (Falkirk Victoria H.)   Inverness H.
1983 T Hanlon   Edinburgh Southern H.)   Edinburgh Southern H.
1984 A Russell   (Law & District AC)   Bellahouston H.
1985 S Mathieson   (Law & District AC)   Clydebank AC.
1986 G Stewart   (Clydebank AC)   Clydebank AC.
1987 G Reid   (Kilmarnock H.)   Clydebank AC.
1988 N Freer   (Clydebank AC)   Victoria Park AAC.
1989 M McBeth   (Cambuslang H.)   Clydebank AC.
1990 G Gillies   (Moir Ayr Seaforth AC)   Moir Ayr Seaforth AC.

N.B. Up to 1967 there was only one "Boys" race for competitors under 15 years of age with the distance being 1½ miles. From 1968 the 'Boys" race was split between Senior Boys (13 to 15 years) at 3 miles and Junior Boys (11 to 13 years) at 2 miles.

NATIONAL JUNIOR BOYS CHAMPIONSHIPS
INDIVIDUAL   TEAM
1968 J Mulvey   (Shettleston H.)   Springburn H.
1969 J Thomson   (Law & District AC)   Law & District AC.
1970 M Watt   (Shettleston H.)   Shettleston H.
1971 S Elder   (Victoria Park AAC)   Monkland H.
1972 W McColl   (Bellahouston H.)   Bellahouston H.
1973 A Adams   (Clydesdale H.)   Edinburgh AC.

1974	J Egan	(Larkhall YMCA H.)	Springburn H.
1975	G Millar	(St Columba's H.S.)	St Columba's H.S.
1976	P Martin	(Clyde Valley AC)	Springburn H.
1977	S McPherson	(Springburn H.)	Falkirk Victoria H.
1978	D McShane	(Cambuslang H.)	Falkirk Victoria H.
1979	D McShane	(Cambuslang H.)	Edinburgh Southern H.
1980	S Holden	(Falkirk Victoria H.)	Shettleston H.
1981	D Boyd	(St Columba's H.S.)	St Columba's H.S.
1982	A Russell	(Law & District AC)	Clyde Valley AC.
1983	A Walsh	(Kilbarchan AC)	Clyde Valley AC.
1984	C Murphy	(Teviotdale H.)	Victoria Park AAC.
1985	T Graham	(Kilbarchan AC)	Kilbarchan AC.
1986	J Hemmings	(Pitreavie AAC)	Dumfries AAC.
1987	E McCafferty	(Cambuslang H.)	Clydebank AC.
1988	D Whiffen	(Dumfries AAC)	Clydebank AC.
1989	D Kerr	(IBM Spango Valley AC)	Law & District AC.
1990	K Daley	(Edinburgh S.P.C. AC)	Victoria Park AAC.

NATIONAL VETERANS CHAMPIONSHIP

INDIVIDUAL   TEAM

OVER 40 YEARS
1985	R Hodelet (Greenock Glenpark H)	Shettleston Harriers
1986	B Scobie (Maryhill H)	Pitreavie AAC
1987	B Scobie (Maryhill H)	Pitreavie AAC
1988	C Youngson (Aberdeen AAC)	Aberdeen AAC
1989	C Youngson (Aberdeen AAC)	Aberdeen AAC
1990	G Meredith (Victoria Park AAC)	Aberdeen AAC

OVER 45 YEARS   **OVER 60 YEARS**
1989	A Adams (Dumbarton AAC)		1989	W Marshall (Motherwell YMCA)
1990	A Adams (Dumbarton AAC)		1990	W Marshall (Motherwell YMCA)

OVER 50 YEARS   **OVER 65 YEARS**
1989	J Maitland (Lochaber AC)		1989	T Harrison (Maryhill H)
1990	J Linaker (Pitreavie AAC)		1990	No competitor

OVER 55 YEARS   **OVER 70 YEARS**
1989	H Gibson (Hamilton H)		1989	D Morrison (Shettleston H)
1990	H Rankin (J W Kilmarnock H)		1990	No competitor

INDIVIDUAL AND TEAM CHAMPIONSHIPS OF THE SCOTTISH VETERAN HARRIERS CLUB WERE HELD FROM 1972 AND WERE REGARDED AS "UNOFFICIAL" SCOTTISH CHAMPIONSHIPS.
FROM 1985 THE SCOTTISH CROSS COUNTRY UNION HELD AN OFFICIAL CHAMPIONSHIP FOR ALL ATHLETES OVER 40 YEARS OF AGE AND IN 1989 FURTHER AGE GROUP CATEGORIES IN FIVE YEAR BANDS FROM 40 YEARS OF AGE UPWARDS WERE ADDED TO THE CHAMPIONSHIP PROGRAMME.

SCOTTISH NATIONAL CHAMPIONSHIP DATES AND VENUES
1886 - 1990

1886	27th March, Lanark Racecourse	1937	6 March, Redford Barracks, Edinburgh
1887	19 March, Hampden Park, Glasgow	1938	5 March, Ayr Racecourse
1888	10 March, Hawkhill Stadium Edin.	1939	4 March, Lanark Racecourse
1889	23 February, SHU, Celtic Park,Glw	1940 - 1946 No Championships Held	
1889	22 March, SCCA, Hamilton Park Rccrse	1947	1 March, Lanark Racecourse
1890	22 February, SHU, Cathkin Park, Glw	1948	6 March, Ayr Racecourse
1890	8 March, SCCA, Tynecastle Park, Edin	1949	5 March, Ayr Reaccourse
1891	14 March, Cathkin Park, Glw	1950	4 March, Hamilton Park Racecourse
1892	12 March, Tynecastle Park, Edin	1951	3 March, Hamilton Park Racecourse
1893	8 March, Hampden Park, Glw	1952	1 March, Hamilton Park Racecourse
1894	10 March, Musselburgh Racecourse	1953	28 February, Hamilton Park Racecourse
1895	9 March, Queens Park, Glasgow	1954	6 March, Hamilton Park Racecourse
1896	14 March, Inverleith, Edinburgh	1955	28 February, Hamilton Park Racecourse
1897	6 March, Underwood Park, Paisley	1956	3 March, Hamilton Park Racecourse
1898	5 March, Musselburgh Racecourse	1957	26 February, Hamilton Park Racecourse
1899	5 March, Hampden Park, Glasgow	1958	5 March, Hamilton Park Racecourse
1900	4 March, Musselburgh Racecourse	1959	2 March, Hamilton Park Racecourse
1901	9 March, Maryhill, Glasgow	1960	5 March, Hamilton Park Racecourse
1902	8 March, Myreside, Edinburgh	1961	4 March, Hamilton Park Racecourse
1903	14 March, Scotstoun Showgrds, Glw	1962	3 March, Hamilton Park Racecourse
1904	5 March, Scotstoun Showgrds, Glw	1963	23 Feb, Hamilton Park Racecourse
1905	4 March, Scotstoun Showgrds, Glw	1964	29 Feb, Hamilton Park Racecourse
1906	3 March, Scotstoun Showgrds, Glw	1965	27 Feb, Hamilton Park Racecourse
1907	9 March, Portobello, Edinburgh	1966	26 Feb, Hamilton Park Racecourse
1908	8 March, Scotstoun Showgrds, Glw	1967	25 Feb, Hamilton Park Racecourse
1909	7 March, Scotstoun Showgrds, Glw	1968	24 Feb, Hamilton Park Racecourse
1910	5 March, Scotstoun Showgrds, Glw	1969	22 Feb, Duddingston Park, Edin
1911	4 March, Scotstoun Showgrds, Glw	1970	21 February, Ayr Racecourse
1912	3 March, Scotstoun Showgrds, Glw	1971	20 Feb, Bellahouston Park, Glw.
1913	1 March, Scotstoun Showgrds, Glw	1972	19 February, Currie, Midlothian
1914	7 March, Carntyne Racecourse, Glw	1973	17 Feb, Drumpellier Park, Coatbge
1915 - 1919 No Championships Held		1974	16 Feb, Drumpellier Park, Coatbge
1920	6 March, Rouken Glen Park, Glasgow	1975	14 February, Drumpellier Park, Coatbrge
1921	5 March Rouken Glen Park, Glasgow	1976	14 February, Drumpellier Park, Coatbrge
1922	4 March, Musselburgh Racecourse	1977	12 February, Glenrothes
1923	3 March, Bothwell Castle Policies	1978	4 March, Bellahouston Park, Glasgow
1924	1 March, Musselburgh Racecourse	1979	10 February, Livingston New Town
1925	7 March, Ayr Racecourse	1980	9 February, Beach Park, Irvine
1926	6 March, Hamilton Park Racecourse	1981	28 February, Callandar Park, Falkirk
1927	5 March, Redford Barracks, Edinburgh	1982	27 February, Beach Park, Irvine
1928	3 March, Hamilton Park Racecourse	1983	26 February, Jack Kane Centre, Edin.
1929	2 March, Hamilton Park Racecourse	1984	25 February, Beach Park, Irvine
1930	1 March, Hamilton Park Racecourse	1985	23 February, Jack Kane Centre, Edin.
1931	7 March, Hamilton Park Racecourse	1986	22 February, Beach Park, Irvine
1932	5 March, Hamilton Park Racecourse	1987	28 February, Callandar Park, Falkirk
1933	4 March, Hamilton Park Racecourse	1988	27 February, Beach Park, Irvine
1934	3 March, Hamilton Park Racecourse	1989	25 February, Wilton Lodge Park, Hawick
1935	2 March, Hamilton Park Racecourse	1990	24 February, Beach Park, Irvine
1936	5 March, Lanark Racecourse		

NATIONAL 4 × 2½ MILE CROSS COUNTRY RELAY CHAMPIONSHIP

1974	Clyde Valley AC	1982	Edinburgh Southern Harriers
1975	Edinburgh Southern Harriers	1983	Cambuslang Harriers
1976	Shettleston Harriers	1984	Edinburgh Southern Harriers
1977	Clyde Valley AC	1985	Spango Valley AC
1978	Edinburgh Southern Harriers	1986	Edinburgh Southern Harriers
1979	Clyde Valley AC	1987	Cambuslang Harriers
1980	Cambuslang Harriers	1988	Greenock Glenpark Harriers
1981	Edinburgh Southern Harriers	1989	Teviotdale Harriers

OPEN TO SENIORS AND JUNIORS THE CHAMPIONSHIP IS HELD OVER FOUR EQUAL LAPS TOTALLING 10 MILES.

NATIONAL 3 × 2 MILE YOUNG ATHLETES CROSS COUNTRY RELAY CHAMPIONSHIP

1977	Springburn Harriers	1984	Clydebank AC
1978	Clyde Valley AC	1985	Clydebank AC
1979	Falkirk Victoria Harriers	1986	Pitreavie AAC
1980	Livingston & District AC	1987	Clydebank AC
1981	Cambuslang Harriers	1988	Victoria Park AAC
1982	Edinburgh AC	1989	Victoria Park AAC
1983	Ayr Seaforth AC		

TEAMS OF THREE RUNNERS COMPETE IN THE RUNNING ORDER OF JUNIOR BOY, SENIOR BOY AND YOUTH WITH EACH COMPETITOR COVERING AN EQUAL LAP FOR A TOTAL OF 6 MILES.

NATIONAL SIX STAGE ROAD RELAY CHAMPIONSHIP

1979	Edinburgh Southern Harriers	1985	Bellahouston Harriers
1980	Edinburgh Southern Harriers	1986	Cambuslang Harriers
1981	Edinburgh Southern Harriers	1987	Edinburgh Southern Harriers
1982	Edinburgh Southern Harriers	1988	Springburn Harriers
1983	Edinburgh Southern Harriers	1989	Edinburgh Southern Harriers
1984	Edinburgh AC	1990	Dundee Hawkhill Harriers

OPEN TO SENIORS AND JUNIORS THE RACE CONSISTS OF SIX LAPS, THREE SHORT LAPS OF THREE MILES AND THREE LONG LAPS OF SIX MILES, TOTALLING 27 MILES AND NOT GREATER THAN 30 MILES IN TOTAL. THE FIRST RUNNER COVERS A SHORT LAP AND THE NEXT RUNNER A LONG LAP, CONTINUING WITH SIMILAR ALTERNATE LAPS UNTIL THE TOTAL DISTANCE IS COVERED.

NATIONAL NOVICE CHAMPIONSHIP

INDIVIDUAL

1919	W S Brown (Maryhall H)
1920	R S McMillan (Greenock Glenpark H)
1921	W S Moor (Edinburgh Univ. H & H)

TEAM

Maryhill Harriers
Shettleston Hariers
Shettleston Harriers

1922	W N Neilson (West of Scotland H)	Garscube Harriers
1923	J W Stanley (Shettleston H)	Shettleston Harriers
1924	T M Riddell (Shettleston H)	Garscube Harriers
1925	S K Tombe (Plebian H)	Garscube Harriers
1926	H Gilchrist (Paisley H)	Eglinton Harriers
1927	M Stobbs (Catrine AAC)	Doon Harriers
1928	J Hood (Shettleston H)	Shettleston Harriers
1929	J Miller (Beith H)	Shettleston Harriers
1930	R Simpson (Motherwell YMCA)	Garscube Harriers
1931	J K Hewitt (Edinburgh Univ. H & H)	Shettleston Harriers
1932	W Hinde (Edinburgh Northern H)	Springburn Harriers
1933	A. McGregor (Plebian H)	Maryhill Harriers
1934	C Smith (Dundee Hawkhill H)	Eglinton Harriers
1935	W G Black (Plebian H)	Plebian Harriers
1936	D Fyfe (Springburn H)	Shettleston Harriers
1937	R Reid (Doon H)	Springburn Harriers
1938	G Craig (Shettleston H)	South Glasgow AAC

No Championships held between 1939 and 45 due to World War 2

1946	J J Stuart (Shettleston H)	Vale of Leven AAC
1947	J J Duffy (Garscube H)	Victoria Park AAC
1948	T McNeish (Irvine YMCA)	Victoria Park AAC

Event discontinued in 1949.

EASTERN DISTRICT CHAMPIONSHIP

INDIVIDUAL — TEAM

1899	J Harcus (Kirkcaldy H)	Edinburgh Harriers
1900	J Ranken (Watsonian SCCC)	Stirlingshire Central Harriers
1901	A Suttie (Dundee Thistle H)	Waverley Harriers
1902	A Kinnaird (Edinburgh H)	Edinburgh Harriers
1903	G McMurtrie (Stirling Central H)	Stirlingshire Central Harriers
1904	J A Jamieson (Watsonians CCC)	Falkirk Victoria Harriers
1905	T Robertson (Edinburgh H)	Edinburgh Harriers
1906	P J Melville (Watsonians CCC)	Watsonians CCC
1907	A J Grieve (Teviotdale H)	Edinburgh Southern Harriers
1908	J S Matthew (Dundee Thistle H)	Edinburgh Northern Harriers
1909	J Torrie (Gala H)	Edinburgh Harriers
1910	W S Grant (Waverley H)	Edinburgh Northern Harriers
1911	J G Aitchison (Gala H)	Falkirk Victoria Harriers
1912	W Menzies (Edinburgh Northern H)	Edinburgh Harriers
1913	J Grierson (Teviotdale H)	Gala Harriers
1914	A Ledingham (Waverley H)	Edinburgh Northern Harriers

NO CHAMPIONSHIP RACES WERE HELD IN 1915, 1916, 1917, 1918, 1919 DUE TO THE FIRST WORLD WAR

1920	G Lumsden (Gala H)	Edinburgh Southern Harriers
1921	J Currie (Gala H)	Edinburgh Harriers
1922	F C Dobbie (Grange H)	Grange Harriers
1923	W G S Moor (Edin University H & H)	Falkirk Victoria Harriers

1924	A P Hamilton (Heriots CCC)	Edinburgh Northern Harriers
1925	T Whitton (Dundee Thistle H)	Gala Harriers and Kirkcaldy YMCA Harriers finished equal first.
1926	G A Farquharson (Dundee Thistle H)	Edinburgh Northern Harriers
1927	J Suttie Smith (Dundee Thistle H)	Edinburgh Southern Harriers
1928	J F Wood (Heriots CCC)	Edinburgh Harriers
1929	J M Petrie (Dundee Thistle H)	Dundee Thistle Harriers
1930	W A P Sanderson (Gala H)	Edinburgh Southern Harriers
1931	J Mercer (Penicuik H)	Edinburgh Northern Harriers
1932	J K Hewitt (Edin University H & H)	Dundee Thistle Harriers
1933	A Hay (Dundee Thistle H)	Dundee Hawkhill Harriers
1934	A Dow (Kirkcaldy YMCA H)	Dundee Thistle Harriers
1935	C Smith (Dundee Hawkhill H)	Dundee Thistle Harriers
1936	A W Carfrae (Edinburgh H)	Edinburgh Southern Harriers
1937	G A Smith (Edin University H & H)	Dundee Hawkhill Harriers
1938	A Archer (Edinburgh Southern H)	Edinburgh University H & H
1939	G M Carstairs (Edin University H & H)	Edinburgh University H & H

NO CHAMPIONSHIP RACES WERE HELD IN 1940, 1941, 1942, 1943, 1945, 1946 DUE TO THE SECOND WORLD WAR.

1947	C D Robertson (Dundee Thistle H)	Dundee Thistle Harriers
1948	T H Braid (Edin University H & H)	Edinburgh Southern Harriers
1949	J Sanderson (Gala H)	Edinburgh University H & H

BETWEEN 1899 AND 1949 THE DISTRICT CHAMPIONSHIP WAS CONTESTED ONLY BY "JUNIOR" ATHLETES. THESE WERE "JUNIORS", NOT BY AGE CLASSIFICATION, BUT BY CATEGORY OF NOT HAVING WON HONOURS IN THE "JUNIOR" DISTRICT INDIVIDUAL AND TEAM CHAMPIONSHIPS.

FROM 1950 ONWARDS THE DISTRICT CHAMPIONSHIP WAS OPEN TO ALL.

1950	C D Robertson (Dundee Thistle H)	Edinburgh University H & H
1951	W G Hunter (H.M.S. Condor)	Edinburgh University H & H
1952	G Reid (Edinburgh Southern H)	Edinburgh University H & H
1953	A Black (Dundee Hawkhill H)	Edinburgh Southern Harriers
1954	W A Robertson (Edinburgh Southern H)	Edinburgh University H & H
1955	J B Wilkinson (Edinburgh Northern H)	Edinburgh University H & H
1956	A C Horne (Edin University H & H)	Edinburgh University H & H
1957	A S Jackson (Edin University H & H)	Edinburgh Southern Harriers
1958	A S Jackson (Edin University H & H)	Edinburgh Southern Harriers
1959	A S Jackson (Edin University H & H)	Edinburgh Southern Harriers
1960	J Linaker (Pitreavie AAC)	Edinburgh Southern Harriers
1961	A S Jackson (Braidburn AC)	Edinburgh Southern Harriers
1962	A J Wood (Aberdeen AAC)	Teviotdale Harriers
1963	J C Douglas (Teviotdale H)	Edinburgh Southern Harriers
1964	A F Murray (Edin University H & H)	Edinburgh Southern Harriers
1965	A F Murray (Edin University H & H)	Edinburgh University H & H
1966	W Ewing (Aberdeen University H & H)	Edinburgh University H & H
1967	M Edwards (Aberdeen AAC)	Aberdeen AAC
1968	G Bryan-Jones (Edin University H & H)	Edinburgh University H & H

1969 A P Weatherhead (Heriot Watt Univ)   Edinburgh Southern Harriers
1970 A Blamire (Edin University H & H)   Edinburgh Southern Harriers
1971 A P Weatherhead (Octavians AC)   Edinburgh Southern Harriers
1972 S Downie (Falkirk Victoria H)   Edinburgh Southern Harriers
1973 A McKean (Edin University H & H)   Edinburgh Southern Harriers
1974 A McKean (Edinburgh AC)   Edinburgh Southern Harriers
1975 A Hutton (Edinburgh Southern H)   Edinburgh Southern Harriers
1976 A P Weatherhead (Edinburgh AC)   Edinburgh AC
1977 A McKean (Edinburgh AC)   Edinburgh AC
1978 A McKean (Edinburgh AC)   Edinburgh AC
1979 I Elliot (Edinburgh Southern H)   Edinburgh Southern Harriers
1980 J Robson (Edinburgh Southern H)   Edinburgh Southern Harriers
1981 F Clyne (Aberdeen AAC)   Edinburgh Southern Harriers
1982 G Laing (Aberdeen AAC)   Aberdeen AAC
1983 C Henderson (Tayside AC)   Aberdeen AAC
1984 T Mitchell (Fife AC)   Falkirk Victoria Harriers
1985 C Hume (Edinburgh Southern H)   Falkirk Victoria Harriers
1986 J Robson (Edinburgh Southern H)   Falkirk Victoria Harriers
1987 T Mitchell (Fife AC)   Teviotdale Harriers
1988 P McColgan (Dundee Hawkhill H)   Teviotdale Harriers
1989 S Hale (Perth Strathtay H)   Edinburgh AC
1990 S Hale (Perth Strathtay H)   Dundee Hawkhill Harriers

IN 1984 THE DISTANCE WAS INCREASED FROM 6 MILES TO 7½ MILES.

EASTERN DISTRICT JUNIOR CHAMPIONSHIP

FIRST JUNIOR, AGED 18 TO 21 YEARS, TO FINISH IN THE DISTRICT CHAMPIONSHIPS WAS AWARDED THE DISTRICT JUNIOR TITLE.

1959 J Linaker (Pitreavie AAC)
1960 G B Brownlee (Edinburgh Southern H)
1961 K Harley (Teviotdale H)
1962 J C Douglas (Teviotdale H)
1963 J C Douglas (Teviotdale H)
1964 M Edwards (Aberdeen AAC)
1965 J R Young (Edinburgh University H & H)
1966 J McKay (Edinburgh Southern H)
1967 D Logue (Edinburgh University H & H)
1968 G Richardson (Teviotdale H)
1970 J Dingwall (Edinburgh University H & H)
1971 S Downie (Falkirk Victoria H)
1972 D Lorimer (St. Andrews University CCC)
1973 D Lorimer (St. Andrews University CCC)
1974 A Hutton (Edinburgh Southern H)
1975 A Hutton (Edinburgh Southern H)
1976 P Kenney (Dundee University)
1977 I Brown (Falkirk Victoria H)
1978 I Brown (Falkirk Victoria H)

1979 N Jones (Edinburgh AC)
1980 C Donnelly (Aberdeen University H & H)
1981 J Gladwin (Edinburgh Southern H)
1982 C Henderson (Tayside AAC)
1983 A Currie (Edinburgh University H & H)

FROM 1959 TO 1966 JUNIOR AGE CATEGORY WAS 18 TO 21 YEARS, AND FROM 1967 TO 1983 THE AGE CATEGORY WAS CHANGED TO 17 TO 20 YEARS. THE JUNIOR CHAMPIONSHIP WAS RUN IN CONJUNCTION WITH THE SENIOR RACE, BUT IN 1984 A SEPARATE JUNIOR RACE WAS INTRODUCED OVER A DISTANCE OF 6 MILES WITH A SEPARATE TEAM CHAMPIONSHIP.

INDIVIDUAL   **TEAM**
1984 S Marshall (Dundee University)   Aberdeen AAC
1985 S Marshall (Dundee University)   Dundee University Harriers
1986 G Phillip (Edinburgh AC)   Edinburgh AC
1987 D Arnott (Pitreavie AAC)   Aberdeen AAC
1988 C Murphy (Pitreavie AAC)   Pitreavie AAC
1989 T Reid (Dundee Hawkhill H)   Pitreavie AAC
1990 I Falconer (Harmeny AC)   Edinburgh SPC AC

EASTERN DISTRICT YOUTH CHAMPIONSHIP

INDIVIDUAL   **TEAM**
1950 I Morrison (Edinburgh Rover Scouts)   Edinburgh Rover Scouts
1951 T Connolly (Gala H)   Gala Harriers
1952 D Dunn (Edinburgh Rover Scouts)   Edinburgh Rover Scouts
1953 I Drever (Braidburn AAC)   Braidburn AAC
1954 W H Watson (Edin University H & H)   Braidburn AAC
1955 G Wilson (Aberdeen AAC)   Braidburn AAC
1956 J Gray (Aberdeen AAC)   Falkirk Victoria Harriers
1957 J Messer (Edinburgh Northern H)   Falkirk Victoria Harriers
1958 J Linaker (Kirkcaldy YMCA H)   H.M.S. Caledonia
1959 K G Kinghorn (Edinburgh Southern H)   Aberdeen AAC
1960 G B Brownlee (Edinburgh Southern H)   Edinburgh Southern Harriers
1961 G B Brownlee (Edinburgh Southern H)   Edinburgh Southern Harriers
1962 R Carroll (Edinburgh AC)   Kirkcaldy YMCA Harriers
1963 R Carroll (Edinburgh AC)   Kirkcaldy YMCA Harriers
1964 J W Raeburn (Teviotdale H)   Teviotdale Harriers
1965 F Steel (Edinburgh AC)   Edinburgh AC
1966 R Heron (Dundee Hawkhill H)   Dundee Hawkhill Harriers
1967 J Grieve (Pitreavie AAC)   George Heriots School
1968 C Falconer (Forth Valley AC)   Edinburgh AC
1969 C Falconer (Forth Valley AC)   Kirkcaldy YMCA Harriers
1970 J McGill (Lewisvale Spartans AC)   Lewisvale Spartans AC
1971 A Hutton (Edinburgh Southern H)   Bathgate AAC
1972 A Hutton (Edinburgh Southern H)   Bathgate AAC
1973 J McGarva (Falkirk Victoria H)   Edinburgh AC
1974 C Haskett (Dundee Hawkhill H)   Edinburgh AC

1975	C Haskett (Dundee Hawkhill H)	Edinburgh AC
1976	D Ross (Edinburgh AC)	Central Region AC
1977	N Jones (Edinburgh AC)	Edinburgh AC
1978	C Hume (Edinburgh Southern H)	Edinburgh Southern Harriers
1979	C Henderson (Tayside AAC)	Edinburgh Southern Harriers
1980	R Copestake (Dundee Hawkhill H)	Central Region AC
1981	A O'Hara (Livingston & District AC)	Falkirk Victoria H
1982	I Matheson (Aberdeen AAC)	Edinburgh AC
1983	S Doig (Fife Southern H)	Fife Southern Harriers
1984	T Hanlon (Edinburgh Southern H)	Edinburgh Southern Harriers
1985	T Hanlon (Edinburgh Southern H)	Edinburgh Southern Harriers
1986	M Currie (Dollar Academy)	Aberdeen AAC
1987	T Reid (Dundee Hawkhill H)	Falkirk Victoria Harriers
1988	I White (Falkirk Victoria H)	Falkirk Victoria Harriers
1989	A Kinghorn (Edinburgh AC)	Aberdeen AAC
1990	S Cook (Queen Victoria School)	Queen Victoria School

EASTERN DISTRICT SENIOR BOYS CHAMPIONSHIP

	INDIVIDUAL	TEAM
1958	J A Robertson (Edinburgh Southern H)	George Heriots School
1959	G B Brownlee (Edinburgh Southern H)	George Heriots School
1960	R Masson (Edinburgh Southern H)	Edinburgh Southern Harriers
1961	R Carroll (Edinburgh Eastern H)	Kirkcaldy YMCA Harriers
1962	D Smith (Kirkcaldy YMCA H)	Dundee Hawkhill Harriers
1963	R Nicol (Teviotdale H)	Edinburgh Southern Harriers
1964	J Worrell (Edinburgh Southern H)	Edinburgh AC
1965	J M McLennan (Edinburgh Southern H)	Pitreavie AAC
1966	I Elliot (Teviotdale H)	Edinburgh AC
1967	J Lees (Edinburgh AC)	Edinburgh AC
1968	J A McGill (Blackburn AC)	Kirkcaldy YMCA Harriers
1969	R Wallace (Blackburn H)	Bathgate AC
1970	A McGill (Lewisvale Spartans AC)	Bathgate AC
1971	F Coyle (Edinburgh AC)	Edinburgh AC
1972	C Haskett (Dundee Hawkhill H)	Edinburgh Southern H
1973	C Haskett (Dundee Hawkhill H)	Edinburgh Southern H
1974	T Cole (Edinburgh AC)	Edinburgh AC
1975	N Jones (Edinburgh AC)	Edinburgh AC
1976	C Hume (Teviotdale H)	Teviotdale Harriers
1977	J Gladwin (Edinburgh Southern H)	Edinburgh Southern Harriers
1978	J Steel (Edinburgh Southern H)	Edinburgh AC
1979	D Slessor (Edinburgh Southern H)	Edinburgh Southern Harriers
1980	I Matheson (Aberdeen AAC)	Edinburgh AC
1981	F Boyne (Aberdeen AAC)	Edinburgh Southern Harriers
1982	S Holden (Falkirk Victoria H)	Livingston & District AC
1983	C Nichol (Teviotdale H)	Edinburgh Southern Harriers
1984	G McCusker (Teviotdale H)	Aberdeen AAC
1985	M Currie (Dollar Academy)	Edinburgh Southern Harriers

1986 S Rankin (Falkirk Victoria H)   Falkirk Victoria Harriers
1987 P Robertson (Dundee Hawkhill H)   Pitreavie AAC
1988 P McArthur (Central Region AC)   Edinburgh Southern Harriers
1989 M Kelso (Pitreavie AAC)   Falkirk Victoria Harriers
1990 M Kelso (Pitreavie AAC)   Pitreavie AAC

EASTERN DISTRICT JUNIOR BOYS CHAMPIONSHIP

INDIVIDUAL   **TEAM**
1966 J McGill (Lewisvale Spartans AC)   Edinburgh AC
1967 J A McGill (Blackburn H)   Teviotdale Harriers
1968 J A McGill (Blackburn H)   Bathgate AC
1969 J Campbell (Bathgate AC)   Bathgate AC
1970 P Forbes (Edinburgh AC)   Edinburgh AC
1971 D Walker (Edinburgh AC)   St. Mary's Academy
1972 T Cole (Edinburgh AC)   Edinburgh AC
1973 N Jones (Edinburgh AC)   Edinburgh AC
1974 C Hume (Teviotdale H)   Teviotdale Harriers
1975 J Pentecost (Falkirk Victoria H)   Falkirk Victoria Harriers
1976 J Steel (Edinburgh Southern H)   Falkirk Victoria Harriers
1977 M Walker (Central Region AC)   Falkirk Victoria Harriers
1978 K Maxwell (Falkirk Victoria H)   Falkirk Victoria Harriers
1979 C Little (Fife AC)   Edinburgh Southern Harriers
1980 S Holden (Falkirk Victoria H)   Edinburgh AC
1981 S Campbell (Livingston & District AC) Livingston & District AC
1982 V Hughes (Fauldhouse Miners H)   Pitreavie AAC
1983 G McCusker (Teviotdale H)   Teviotdale Harriers
1984 P Fettes (Lasswade AC)   Aberdeen AAC
1985 J Hemmings (Pitreavie AAC)   Falkirk Victoria Harriers
1986 B McMillan (Central Region AC)   Central Region AC
1987 M Kelso (Pitreavie AAC)   Edinburgh Southern Harriers
1988 A Tulloch (Falkirk Victoria H)   Pitreavie AAC
1989 R Wilson (Central Region AC)   Edinburgh AC
1990 K Daley (Edinburgh SPC AC)   Edinburgh SPC AC

EASTERN DISTRICT 4 × 2½ MILE RELAY CHAMPIONSHIP

AFTER THE FIRST WORLD WAR GEORGE MACKENZIE PRESENTED A TROPHY TO THE NATIONAL CROSS COUNTRY UNION OF SCOTLAND FOR TEAM COMPETITION BETWEEN EASTERN DISTRICT CLUBS. A RELAY RACE FOR THE MACKENZIE TROPHY WAS FIRST HELD IN 1919 AND CONTINUED FOR THE NEXT SEVEN YEARS AS AN OPEN RELAY RACE BETWEEN EASTERN DISTRICT CLUBS UNTIL THE FIRST OFFICIAL DISTRICT RELAY CHAMPIONSHIP WAS HELD IN 1926.

1926 Edinburgh Northern Harriers   1930 Edinburgh Northern Harriers
1927 Edinburgh Northern Harriers   1931 Edinburgh Northern Harriers
1928 Dundee Thistle Harriers   1932 Edinburgh Northern Harriers
1929 Dundee Thistle Harriers   1933 Edinburgh Northern Harriers

1934	Edinburgh Northern Harriers	1937	Edinburgh Northern Harriers
1935	Edinburgh Northern Harriers	1938	Edinburgh Northern Harriers
1936	Dundee Thistle Harriers		

NO CHAMPIONSHIP RACES WERE HELD IN 1939, 1940, 1941, 1942, 1943, 1944, 1945, 1946 DUE TO THE SECOND WORLD WAR.

1947	Dundee Hawkhill Harriers	1969	Edinburgh University H & H
1948	Edinburgh Southern Harriers	1970	Edinburgh Southern Harriers
1949	Edinburgh University H & H	1971	Edinburgh Southern Harriers
1950	Edinburgh Southern Harriers	1972	Edinburgh Southern Harriers
1951	Edinburgh Southern Harriers	1973	Edinburgh Southern Harriers
1952	Edinburgh University H & H	1974	Edinburgh Southern Harriers
1953	Dundee Hawkhill Harriers	1975	Edinburgh Southern Harriers
1954	Edinburgh Southern Harriers	1976	Edinburgh AC
1955	Edinburgh University H & H	1977	Edinburgh Southern Harriers
1956	Edinburgh University H & H	1978	Edinburgh Southern Harriers
1957	Edinburgh University H & H	1979	Aberdeen AAC
1958	Edinburgh Southern Harriers	1980	Edinburgh AC
1959	Edinburgh Southern Harriers	1981	Falkirk Victoria Harriers
1960	Aberdeen AAC	1982	Falkirk Victoria Harriers
1961	Edinburgh Southern Harriers	1983	Falkirk Victoria Harriers
1962	Teviotdale Harriers	1984	Falkirk Victoria Harriers
1963	Teviotdale Harriers	1985	Edinburgh Southern Harriers
1964	Teviotdale Harriers	1986	Edinburgh Southern Harriers
1965	Edinburgh Southern Harriers	1987	Edinburgh Southern Harriers
1966	Edinburgh University H & H	1988	Aberdeen AAC
1967	Edinburgh University H & H	1989	Dundee Hawkhill Harriers
1968	Edinburgh University H & H		

EASTERN DISTRICT YOUNG ATHLETES 3 × 2 MILE RELAY CHAMPIONSHIP

1975	Falkirk Victoria Harriers	1983	Teviotdale Harriers
1976	Edinburgh AC	1984	Edinburgh Southern Harriers
1977	Edinburgh Southern Harriers	1985	Falkirk Victoria Harriers
1978	Edinburgh Southern Harriers	1986	Pitreavie AAC
1979	Falkirk Victoria Harriers	1987	Pitreavie AAC
1980	Aberdeen AAC	1988	Pitreavie AAC
1981	Falkirk Victoria Harriers	1989	Pitreavie AAC
1982	Edinburgh Southern Harriers		

RUNNING ORDER IN RELAY CHAMPIONSHIPS IS JUNIOR BOY, SENIOR BOY AND YOUTH.

NORTHERN DISTRICT CHAMPIONSHIP

	INDIVIDUAL	TEAM
1976	I. Mackenzie (Forres H)	R.A.F. Kinloss
1977	B Finlayson (Lochaber AC)	Lochaber AC
1978	I Mackenzie (Forres H)	R.A.F. Moray
1979	A Lamb (R.A.F. Moray)	Lochaber AC
1980	D Smith (Forres H)	Lochaber AC
1981	D Lang (Elgin AAC)	Lochaber AC
1982	I Moncur (Forres H)	Forres Harriers
1983	P Kenny (Inverness H)	Forres Harriers
1984	W Miller (Caithness AAC)	Forres Harriers
1985	S Axon (Inverness H)	Inverness Harriers
1986	M Turner (Elgin AAC)	Forres Harriers
1986/87	B Chinnick (Forres H)	Elgin AAC
1987/88	R Arbuckle (Keith & Dist AC)	Caithness AAC
1988/89	R Arbuckle (Keith & Dist AC)	Forres Harriers
1989/90	A Reid (Coasters AC)	Forres Harriers

NORTHERN DISTRICT JUNIOR CHAMPIONSHIP

	INDIVIDUAL	TEAM
1976	S Cassells (Caithness AAC)	
1977	R Macdonald (Inverness H)	
1978	R Macdonald (Inverness H)	
1979	D McMillan (Inverness H)	
1980	A Stubbs (Lochaber AC)	
1981	A Stubbs (Lochaber AC)	
1982	J Watson (Lochaber AC)	
1983	N Martin (Forres H)	
1984	K Foulis (Orkney AAA)	Orkney Islands AAA
1985	J Bell (Inverness H)	None
1986	C Armstrong (Elgin AAC)	None
1986/87	D Rodgers (Lochaber AC)	None
1987/88	S Garland (Inverness H)	None
1988/89	No Contest	
1989/90	G McDowall (Inverness H)	Inverness Harriers

NORTHERN DISTRICT YOUTH CHAMPIONSHIP

	INDIVIDUAL	TEAM
1976	A Millar (Gordonstoun Sch)	Gordonstoun School
1977	D Taylor (Caithness AAC)	Caithness AAC
1978	C Voice (Caithness AAC)	Caithness AAC
1979	J McMaster (Lochaber AC)	Lochaber AC
1980	P Gunn (Lochaber AC)	Orkney Islands AAA
1981	N Martin (Forres H)	Inverness Royal Academy
1982	N Martin (Forres H)	Forres Harriers
1983	R Matheson (Caithness AAC)	Inverness Harriers
1984	J Bell (Inverness H)	Inverness Harriers
1985	G Worship (Inverness H)	Inverness Harriers

1986	I Dunn (Inverness H)	Inverness Harriers
1986/87	D Young (Forres H)	Inverness Harriers
1987/88	S Jarvie (Inverness H)	Inverness Harriers
1988/89	C Jack (Inverness H)	Inverness Harriers
1989/90	B Fraser (Min. Black Isle AAC)	Inverness Harriers

NORTHERN DISTRICT SENIOR BOYS CHAMPIONSHIP

	INDIVIDUAL	TEAM
1976	S Jarvie (Inverness H)	Inverness Harriers
1977	D Taylor (Caithness AAC)	Caithness AAC
1978	J McMaster (Lochaber AC)	Lochaber AC
1979	J Odie (Shetland AAA)	Caithness AAC
1980	N Martin (Forres H)	Inverness Royal Academy
1981	C Martin (Inverness H)	Inverness Royal Academy
1982	N McLennan (Inverness H)	Inverness Harriers
1983	C Donald (Elgin AAC)	Elgin AAC
1984	A Mackenzie (Forres H)	Orkney Islands AAA
1985	I Dunn (Fort Augustus Sch)	Inverness Harriers
1986	S Beaton (Peterhead AC)	Inverness Harriers
1986/87	S Jarvie (Inverness H)	Inverness Harriers
1987/88	B Fraser (Black Isle AAC)	Lochaber AC
1988/89	I Murray (Inverness H)	Inverness Harriers
1989/90	D Miller (Inverness H)	Inverness Harriers

NORTHERN DISTRICT JUNIOR BOYS CHAMPIONSHIP

	INDIVIDUAL	TEAM
1976	K Macleod (Millburn Acad)	Lochaber AC
1977	J Watson (Lochaber AC)	Lochaber AC
1978	N Martin (Forres H)	Dingwall Academy
1979	R Matheson (Caithness AAC)	Inverness Royal Academy
1980	C Martin (Inverness R A)	Inverness Royal Academy
1981	E Scott (Inverness H)	Orkney Islands AAA
1982	C Donald (Elgin AAC)	Elgin AAC
1983	I Mackenzie (Forres H)	Inverness Harriers
1984	S Jarvie (Caithness AAC)	Orkney Islands AAA
1985	S Jarvie (Caithness AAC)	Lochaber AC
1986	T Nixon (Lochaber AC)	Inverness Harriers
1986/87	D Sutherland (Inverness H)	Inverness Harriers
1987/88	A Macrae (Inverness H)	Inverness Harriers
1988/89	S Allan (Min. Black Isle AAC)	Fraserburgh RC
1989/90	M Johnstone (Min. Black Isle AAC)	Minolta Black Isle AAC

SENIOR 4 x 2½ MILES CROSS COUNTRY RELAY CHAMPIONSHIP

1976	Forres Harriers	1983	Inverness Harriers
1977	Forres Harriers	1984	Inverness Harriers
1978	Forres Harriers	1985	Elgin AAC
1979	Forres Harriers	1986	Elgin AAC
1980	Forres Harriers	1987	Lochaber AC
1981	Forres Harriers	1988	Forres Harriers
1982	Forres Harriers	1989	Inverness Harriers

YOUNG ATHLETES 3 x 2 MILE CROSS COUNTRY RELAY CHAMPIONSHIP

1976	Lochaber AC	1983	Elgin AAC
1977	Caithness AAC	1984	Orkney Islands AAA
1978	Caithness AAC	1985	Inverness Harriers
1979	Forres Harriers	1986	Inverness Harriers
1980	Inverness Harriers	1987	Inverness Harriers
1981	Elgin AAC	1988	Inverness Harriers
1982	Elgin AAC	1989	Min. Black Isle AAC

NEW WESTERN DISTRICT CHAMPIONSHIP

	INDIVIDUAL	TEAM
1976	L Reilly (Victoria Park AAC)	Shettleston Harriers
1977	J Brown (Clyde Valley AC)	Shettleston Harriers
1978	L Spence (Shettleston H)	Shettleston Harriers
1979	B McSloy (Clyde Valley AC)	Victoria Park AAC
1980	B McSloy (Clyde Valley AC)	Clydesdale Harriers
1981	J Brown (Clyde Valley AC)	Clydesdale Harriers
1982	L Spence (Shettleston H)	Bellahouston Harriers
1983	G Braidwood (Bellahouston H)	Cambuslang Harriers
1984	N Muir (Shettleston H)	Cambuslang Harriers
1985	L Spence (Spango Valley AC)	Cambuslang Harriers
1986	P Fox (Motherwell YMCA H)	Spango Valley AC
1987	C Robison (Spango Valley AC)	Spango Valley AC
1988	N Muir (Shettleston H)	Cambuslang Harriers
1989	T Murray (Greenock Glenpark H)	Cambuslang Harriers
1990	T Murray (Greenock Glenpark H)	Cambuslang Harriers

IN 1984 THE DISTANCE WAS INCREASED FROM 6 TO 7½ MILES.

NEW WESTERN DISTRICT JUNIOR CHAMPIONSHIP

1976	N Muir (Shettleston H)
1977	N Muir (Shettleston H)
1978	G Braidwood (Bellahouston H))
1979	B McSloy (Clyde Valley AC)
1980	A Douglas (Victoria Park AAC)
1981	A Callan (Springburn H)
1982	R Rioch (East Kilbride AC)
1983	J McNeill (Law & District AC)

FROM 1976 TO 1983 THE JUNIOR AGE CATEGORY WAS 17 TO 20 YEARS, WITH THE JUNIOR CHAMPIONSHIP BEING RUN IN CONJUNCTION WITH THE SENIOR RACE.

IN 1984 A SEPARATE JUNIOR RACE WAS INTRODUCED OVER A DISTANCE OF 6 MILES WITH A SEPARATE TEAM CHAMPIONSHIP.

INDIVIDUAL **TEAM**
1984 R Quinn (Kilbarchan AC) Cambuslang Harriers
1985 R Quinn (Kilbarchan AC) Cambuslang Harriers
1986 S Begen (Springburn H) Kilbarchan AC
1987 P Mayles (Kilbarchan AC) Motherwell YMCA Harriers
1988 A Russell (Law & District AC) Motherwell YMCA Harriers
1989 A Currie (Maryhill H) J W Kilmarnock H & AC
1990 M Campbell (Clydebank AC) Clydebank AC

NEW WESTERN DISTRICT YOUTHS CHAMPIONSHIP
INDIVIDUAL **TEAM**
1976 I Murray (Springburn H) Clyde Valley AC
1977 G Williamson (Springburn H) Victoria Park AAC
1978 G Millar (Clydesdale H) Clydesdale Harriers
1979 P Fox (Clyde Valley AC) Clyde Valley AC
1980 A Callan (Springburn H) Springburn Harriers
1981 R Hawkins (Kilbarchan AC) Kilbarchan AC
1982 D McShane (Cambuslang H) Dumbarton AAC
1983 S Marshall (Clyde Valley AC) Dumbarton AAC
1984 J Graham (Ayr Seaforth AC) Cambuslang Harriers
1985 A Russell (Law & District AC) Law & District AC
1986 A Russell (Law & District AC) Law & District AC
1987 D McGinley (Clydebank AC) Motherwell YMCA
1988 M Campbell (Clydebank AC) Victoria Park AAC
1989 M Campbell (Clydebank AC) Clydebank AC
1990 M McBeth (Cambuslang H) Victoria Park AAC

NEW WESTERN DISTRICT SENIOR BOYS CHAMPIONSHIP
INDIVIDUAL **TEAM**
1976 G Williamson (Springburn H) Victoria Park AAC
1977 I Doole (Clyde Valley AC) Clyde Valley AC
1978 A Anderson (Victoria Park AAC) Springburn Harriers
1979 A Anderson (Victoria Park AAC) Cambuslang Harriers
1980 D McShane (Cambuslang H) Cambuslang Harriers
1981 D Russell (Law & District AC) Shettleston Harriers
1982 R Skilling (Ayrshire AAC) Cambuslang Harriers
1983 A Russell (Law & District AC) Kilbarchan AC
1984 A Russell (Law & District AC) Law & District AC
1985 D McGinley (Clydebank AC) Clydebank AC
1986 G Stewart (Clydebank AC) Clydebank AC
1987 G Reid (Kilmarnock H) Victoria Park AAC
1988 N Freer (Clydebank AC) Clydebank AC
1989 M McBeth (Cambuslang H) Cambuslang Harriers
1990 I Richardson (Cambuslang H) Moir Ayr Seaforth AC

NEW WESTERN DISTRICT JUNIOR BOYS CHAMPIONSHIP

	INDIVIDUAL	**TEAM**
1976	R Barr (Springburn H)	Springburn Harriers
1977	S McPherson (Springburn H)	Springburn Harriers
1978	J Miller (Victoria Park AAC)	Cambuslang Harriers
1979	D McShane (Cambuslang H)	Springburn Harriers
1980	R Skilling (Ayrshire AAC)	Shettleston Harriers
1981	D Boyd (St. Columba's HS)	St. Columba's High School
1982	A Russell (Law & District AC)	Ayr Seaforth AC
1983	A Walsh (Kilbarchan AC)	Clyde Valley AC
1984	G Stewart (Dumbarton AAC)	Nith Valley AC
1985	W Adams (Kilbarchan AC)	Clydebank AC
1986	D McPherson (Cambuslang H)	Dumfries AAC
1987	E McCafferty (Cambuslang H)	Ayr Seaforth AC
1988	D Whiffen (Nith Valley AC)	Clydebank AC
1989	D Kerr (IBM Spango Valley AC)	Victoria Park AAC
1990	S Schendel (Cumnock & District AC)	Clydesdale Harriers

NEW WESTERN DISTRICT 4 × 2½ MILE RELAY CHAMPIONSHIP

1976	Shettleston Harriers	1983	Bellahouston Harriers
1977	Shettleston Harriers	1984	Shettleston Harriers
1978	Shettleston Harriers	1985	Spango Valley AC
1979	Spango Valley AC	1986	Spango Valley AC
1980	Law & District AC	1987	Cambuslang Harriers
1981	Cambuslang Harriers	1988	Greenock Glenpark Harriers
1982	Law & District AC	1989	Springburn Harriers

NEW WESTERN DISTRICT YOUNG ATHLETES 3 × 2 MILE RELAY CHAMPIONSHIP

1976	Springburn Harriers	1983	Cambuslang Harriers
1977	Springburn Harriers	1984	Victoria Park AAC
1978	Springburn Harriers	1985	Clydebank AC
1979	Springburn Harriers	1986	Clydebank AC
1980	Springburn Harriers	1987	Clydebank AC
1981	Clydesdale Harriers	1988	Cambuslang Harriers
1982	Cambuslang Harriers	1989	Victoria Park AAC

FORMER WESTERN DISTRICT CHAMPIONSHIP

	INDIVIDUAL	TEAM
1895	A McCallum (Partick H)	Wishaw Harriers
1896	W Rainey (Wishaw H)	Bellahouston Harriers
1897	W Love (Elderslie Wallace H)	Elderslie Wallace Harriers
1898	W T Marshall (Springburn H)	Springburn Harriers
1899	J J McCafferty (Celtic H)	Wishaw Harriers
1900	G Cunningham (Greenock Wellpark H)	Greenock Glenpark Harriers
1901	P J McCafferty (Celtic H)	Bellahouston Harriers
1902	H Gavin (Celtic H)	Greenock Glenpark Harriers
1903	J A Ure (Greenock Wellpark H)	Larkhall YMCA Harriers
1904	S Kennedy (Garscube H)	Garscube Harriers
1905	T W Young (Motherwell YMCA H)	Motherwell YMCA Harriers
1906	D McCafferty (St. Cuthbert H)	Hamilton Harriers
1907	A McPhee Jr. (Paisley H)	Motherwell YMCA Harriers
1908	G Culbert (Monkland H)	Motherwell YMCA Harriers
1909	W G Rodger (West of Scotland H)	Glasgow YMCA Harriers
1910	G Dallas (Maryhill H)	Maryhill Harriers
1911	D Peat (Motherwell YMCA H)	Paisley Junior Harriers
1912	A Loch (Clydesdale H)	Bellahouston Harriers
1913	R Bell (Monkland H)	Monkland Harriers
1914	J Lindsay (Bellahouston H)	Bellahouston Harriers

NO CHAMPIONSHIP RACES WERE HELD IN 1915, 1916, 1917, 1918, 1919 DUE TO THE FIRST WORLD WAR.

1920	S Small (Bellahouston H)	Shettleston Harriers
1921	D Cummings (Greenock Glenpark H)	Garscube Harriers
1922	A Young (Renfrew H)	Maryhill Harriers
1923	W N Neilson (West of Scotland H)	Garscube Harriers
1924	C H Freshwater (West of Scotland H)	Shettleston Harriers
1925	R Miller (Mauchline H)	Greenock Wellpark Harriers
1926	T M Riddell (Shettleston H)	Maryhill Harriers
1927	C H Johnston (Glasgow Univ H & H)	Motherwell YMCA Harriers/ Plebian Harriers (equal)
1928	R Henderson (Glasgow H)	Maryhill Harriers
1929	C P Wilson (Irvine YMCA H)	Shettleston Harriers

FROM 1895 TO 1929 THE DISTRICT CHAMPIONSHIP WAS CONTESTED ONLY BY "JUNIOR" ATHLETES. THESE WERE "JUNIORS", NOT BY AGE CLASSIFICATION, BUT BY CATEGORY OF NOT HAVING WON HONOURS IN THE "JUNIOR" DISTRICT INDIVIDUAL AND TEAM CHAMPIONSHIPS.

FORMER WESTERN DISTRICT 4 × 2½ MILE RELAY CHAMPIONSHIP

WILLIAM STRUTHERS PRESENTED A SHIELD FOR RELAY TEAM COMPETITION BETWEEN WESTERN DISTRICT CLUBS. A RELAY RACE WAS FIRST HELD IN 1925 IN OPEN COMPETITION BEFORE THE FIRST OFFICIAL DISTRICT CHAMPIONSHIP WAS HELD IN 1926

1926 Shettleston Harriers
1927 Shettleston Harriers
1928 Plebian Harriers

IN SEASON 1929/30, DUE TO THE LARGE NUMBER OF CLUBS IN MEMBERSHIP OF THE WESTERN DISTRICT, THERE WAS A DIVISION OF THE DISTRICT INTO TWO NEW DISTRICTS. THE MIDLAND DISTRICT COMPRISED THE CLUBS IN LANARKSHIRE, GLASGOW AND DUNBARTONSHIRE AND THE SOUTH WESTERN DISTRICT COMPRISED THE CLUBS IN RENFREWSHIRE, AYRSHIRE AND THE SOUTH WEST OF SCOTLAND.

MIDLAND DISTRICT CHAMPIONSHIP

	INDIVIDUAL	TEAM
1930	J Campbell (Bellahouston H)	Springburn Harriers
1931	D Urquhart (Garscube H)	Shettleston Harriers
1932	J C Ross (Shettleston H)	Plebian Harriers
1933	J C Flockhart (Shettleston H)	Springburn Harriers
1934	A McGregor (Plebian H)	Bellahouston Harriers
1935	J Gillies (Shawfield H)	Garscube Harriers
1936	J Kelly (Springburn H)	Shawfield Harriers
1937	W Donaldson (Shettleston H)	Shettleston Harriers
1938	T W Lamb (Bellahouston H)	Bellahouston Harriers
1939	J Morton (Springburn H)	Victoria Park AAC

NO CHAMPIONSHIP RACES WERE HELD IN 1940, 1941, 1942, 1943, 1944, 1945, 1946 DUE TO THE SECOND WORLD WAR.

1947	A Forbes (Victoria Park AAC)	Victoria Park AAC
1948	R Boyd (Clydesdale H)	Garscube Harriers
1949	J J Barry (St. Machan's AC)	Shettleston Harriers

BETWEEN 1930 AND 1949 THE DISTRICT CHAMPIONSHIP WAS CONTESTED ONLY BY "JUNIOR" ATHLETES. THESE WERE "JUNIORS", NOT BY AGE CLASSIFICATION, BUT BY CATEGORY OF NOT HAVING WON HONOURS IN THE "JUNIOR" DISTRICT INDIVIDUAL AND TEAM CHAMPIONSHIPS.

FROM 1950 ONWARDS THE DISTRICT CHAMPIONSHIP WAS OPEN TO ALL.

1950	W Lennie (Vale of Leven AAC)	Shettleston Harriers
1951	T Tracey (Springburn H)	Victoria Park AAC
1952	E Bannon (Shettleston H)	Shettleston Harriers
1953	E Bannon (Shettleston H)	Victoria Park AAC
1954	H Fenion (Bellahouston H)	Victoria Park AAC
1955	J McLaren (Shotts Miners Welfare)	Shettleston Harriers

1956 J McLaren (Victoria Park AAC)   Shettleston Harriers
1957 J McLaren (Victoria Park AAC)   Shettleston Harriers
1958 J McLaren (Victoria Park AAC)   Victoria Park AAC
1959 G E Everett (Shettleston H)   Shettleston Harriers
1960 G E Everett (Shettleston H)   Victoria Park AAC
1961 G E Everett (Shettleston H)   Shettleston Harriers
1962 A H Brown (Motherwell YMCA H)   Motherwell YMCA Harriers
1963 A H Brown (Motherwell YMCA H)   Motherwell YMCA Harriers
1964 I McCafferty (Motherwell YMCA H)   Motherwell YMCA Harriers
1965 I McCafferty (Motherwell YMCA H)   Motherwell YMCA Harriers
1966 J L Stewart (Vale of Leven AAC)   Victoria Park AAC
1967 I McCafferty (Motherwell YMCA H)   Motherwell YMCA Harriers
1968 P McLagan (Victoria Park AAC)   Shettleston Harriers
1969 J K Myatt (Strathclyde Univ AC)   Springburn Harriers
1970 I McCafferty (Law & District AC)   Strathclyde University AC
1971 J Brown (Monkland H)   Shettleston Harriers
1972 J Brown (Monkland H)   Shettleston Harriers
1973 J Brown (Monkland H)   Clydesdale Harriers
1974 D Logue (Glasgow Univ H & H)   Springburn Harriers
1975 S Easton (Shettleston H)   Victoria Park AAC

MIDLAND DISTRICT JUNIOR CHAMPIONSHIP

FIRST JUNIOR ATHLETE TO FINISH IN THE DISTRICT CHAMPIONSHIP WAS AWARDED THE DISTRICT JUNIOR TITLE.

1959 W Goodwin (Bellahouston H)
1960 F McPherson (Victoria Park AAC)
1961 M Ryan (St. Modans AC)
1962 M Ryan (St. Modans AC)
1963 J L Stewart (Vale of Leven AAC)
1964 I McCafferty (Motherwell YMCA H)
1965 I McCafferty (Motherwell YMCA H)
1966 E Knox (Springburn H)
1967 J Brennan (Maryhill H)
1968 J K Myatt (Strathclyde Univ AC)
1969 I Picken (Springburn H)
1970 C Falconer (Springburn H)
1971 J Brown (Monkland H)
1972 J Brown (Monkland H)
1973 J Brown (Monkland H)
1974 R L Spence (Strathclyde Univ AC)
1975 J Graham (Clyde Valley AC)

FROM 1959 TO 1966 JUNIOR AGE CATEGORY WAS 18 TO 21 YEARS, AND FROM 1967 TO 1975 THE AGE CATEGORY WAS CHANGED TO 17 TO 20 YEARS. THE JUNIOR CHAMPIONSHIP WAS RUN IN CONJUNCTION WITH THE SENIOR RACE.

MIDLAND DISTRICT YOUTH CHAMPIONSHIP

	INDIVIDUAL	TEAM
1947	W Young (Victoria Park AAC)	Victoria Park AAC
1948	C Hagan (St Modans AAC)	Shettleston Harriers
1949	D Nelson (Motherwell YMCA H)	Hamilton Harriers
1950	J Finlayson (Hamilton H)	Hamilton Harriers
1951	J Finlayson (Hamilton H)	Hamilton Harriers
1952	J Stevenson (Larkhall YMCA H)	Cambuslang Harriers
1953	P McParland (Springburn H)	Bellahouston Harriers
1954	G Kerr (Victoria Park AAC)	Shettleston Harriers
1955	W Goodwin (Bellahouston H)	Springburn Harriers
1956	W Goodwin (Bellahouston H)	Springburn Harriers
1957	E Smith (Victoria Park AAC)	Victoria Park AAC
1958	F McPherson (Victoria Park AAC)	Shettleston Harriers
1959	J Bogan (Glasgow Univ H & H)	Vale of Leven AAC
1960	W Fleming (St. Modans AC)	Monkland Harriers
1961	J Finn (Monkland H)	Victoria Park AAC
1962	A P Brown (Motherwell YMCA H)	Victoria Park AAC
1963	I McCafferty (Motherwell YMCA H)	Motherwell YMCA Harriers/ Springburn Harriers (equal)
1964	A D Middleton (Springburn H)	Springburn Harriers
1965	E Knox (Springburn H)	Springburn Harriers
1966	J Farrell (Springburn H)	Shettleston Harriers
1967	J Cook (Garscube H)	Springburn Harriers
1968	R McLean (Shettleston H)	Larkhall YMCA Harriers
1969	D McMeekin (Victoria Park AAC)	Larkhall YMCA Harriers
1970	R MacDonald (Monkland H)	Monkland Harriers
1971	L Reilly (Victoria Park AAC)	Victoria Park AAC
1972	J Thomson (Law & District AC)	Springburn Harriers
1973	J Graham (Motherwell YMCA H)	Law & District AC
1974	N Muir (Shettleston H)	Springburn Harriers
1975	N Muir (Shettleston H)	Shettleston Harriers

MIDLAND DISTRICT SENIOR BOYS CHAMPIONSHIP

	INDIVIDUAL	TEAM
1958	W McCulloch (Shotts Miners Welfare)	Shotts Miners Welfare Club
1959	J L Stewart (Vale of Leven AAC)	Bellahouston Harriers
1960	H Barrow (Victoria Park AAC)	Victoria Park AAC
1961	R Wedlock (Shettleston H)	Shettleston Harriers
1962	R Wedlock (Shettleston H)	Shettleston Harriers
1963	J Fleming (St. Modans AC)	St. Modans AC
1964	J Farrell (Springburn H)	Shettleston Harriers
1965	T Patterson (Shettleston H)	Shettleston Harriers
1966	G Jarvie (Springburn H)	Springburn Harriers
1967	A Gibson (Shettleston H)	Shettleston Harriers
1968	D McMeekin (Victoria Park AAC)	Monkland Harriers

1969	J Mulvey (Shettleston H)	Shettleston Harriers
1970	J Mulvey (Shettleston H)	Springburn Harriers
1971	J Thomson (Law & District AC)	Shettleston Harriers
1972	J Graham (Motherwell YMCA H)	Shettleston Harriers
1973	K McCartney (Law & District AC)	Shettleston Harriers
1974	T Young (Grangemouth Olympiades)	Springburn Harriers
1975	G Braidwood (Bellahouston H)	Springburn Harriers

MIDLANDS DISTRICT JUNIOR BOYS CHAMPIONSHIP

	INDIVIDUAL	TEAM
1966	A Trench (East Kilbride AC)	Springburn Harriers
1967	J Gallacher (Clydesdale H)	Clydesdale Harriers
1968	J Thomson (Law & District AC)	Springburn Harriers
1969	J Thomson (Law & District AC)	Law & District AC
1970	M Watt (Shettleston H)	Shettleston Harriers
1971	N Muir (Shettleston H)	Monkland Harriers
1972	A Renfrew (Springburn H)	Springburn Harriers
1973	A Adams (Clydesdale H)	Cambuslang Harriers
1974	G Williamson (Springburn H)	Springburn Harriers
1975	G Miller (St. Columba's HS)	St. Columba's High School

MIDLAND DISTRICT 4 × 2½ MILE RELAY CHAMPIONSHIP

1929	Plebian Harriers		1934	Shettleston Harriers
1930	Motherwell YMCA Harriers		1935	Plebian Harriers
1931	Plebian Harriers		1936	Shettleston Harriers
1932	Shettleston Harriers		1937	Shettleston Harriers
1933	Plebian Harriers		1938	Maryhill Harriers

NO CHAMPIONSHIP RACES WERE HELD IN 1939, 1940, 1941, 1942, 1943, 1944, 1945, 1946 DUE TO THE SECOND WORLD WAR.

1947	Bellahouston Harriers		1962	Motherwell YMCA Harriers
1948	Shettleston Harriers		1963	Motherwell YMCA Harriers
1949	Shettleston Harriers		1964	Motherwell YMCA Harriers
1950	Shettleston Harriers		1965	Motherwell YMCA Harriers
1951	Victoria Park AAC		1966	Motherwell YMCA Harriers
1952	Springburn Harriers		1967	Motherwell YMCA Harriers
1953	Shettleston Harriers		1968	Shettleston Harriers
1954	Shettleston Harriers		1969	Shettleston Harriers
1955	Shettleston Harriers		1970	Shettleston Harriers
1956	Shettleston Harriers		1971	Shettleston Harriers
1957	Shettleston Harriers		1972	Shettleston Harriers
1958	Victoria Park AAC		1973	Victoria Park AAC
1959	Bellahouston Harriers		1974	Strathclyde University AC
1960	Victoria Park AAC		1975	Clyde Valley AC
1961	Motherwell YMCA Harriers			

SOUTH WESTERN DISTRICT CHAMPIONSHIP

	INDIVIDUAL	TEAM
1930	M Stobbs (Catrine AAC)	Irvine YMCA Harriers
1931	K Davidson (Eglinton H)	Beith Harriers
1932	T Todd (Kilmarnock H)	Kilmarnock Harriers
1933	W O'Neill (Doon H)	Eglinton Harriers
1934	J Miller (Beith H)	Greenock Glenpark Harriers
1935	A K McDonald (Auchmountain H)	Auchmountain Harriers
1936	W Kennedy (Kilbarchan AC)	Beith Harriers
1937	W Fulton (Ardeer Recreation Club)	Irvine YMCA Harriers
1938	H Livingston (Kilmarnock H)	Greenock Glenpark Harriers
1939	R Reid (Doon H)	Greenock Wellpark Harriers

NO CHAMPIONSHIP RACES WERE HELD IN 1940,1941, 1942, 1943, 1944, 1945, 1946 DUE TO THE SECOND WORLD WAR.

1947	J Reid (West Kilbride AAC)	Auchmountain Harriers
1948	J B Fisher (Ayr AAC)	Greenock Glenpark Harriers
1949	T McNeish (Irvine YMCA H)	Irvine YMCA Harriers

BETWEEN 1930 AND 1949 THE DISTRICT CHAMPIONSHIP WAS CONTESTED ONLY BY "JUNIOR" ATHLETES. THESE WERE "JUNIORS", NOT BY AGE CLASSIFICATION, BUT BY CATEGORY OF NOT HAVING WON HONOURS IN THE "JUNIOR" DISTRICT INDIVIDUAL AND TEAM CHAMPIONSHIPS.

FROM 1950 ONWARDS THE DISTRICT CHAMPIONSHIP WAS OPEN TO ALL.

1950	J Reid (West Kilbride AAC)	Greenock Glenpark Harriers
1951	G Adamson (West Kilbride AAC)	Irvine YMCA Harriers
1952	T Stevenson (Greenock Wellpark H)	Greenock Glenpark Harriers
1953	T Stevenson (Greenock Wellpark H)	Irvine YMCA Harriers
1954	J Stevenson (Greenock Wellpark H)	Irvine YMCA Harriers
1955	J Stevenson (Greenock Wellpark H)	Greenock Wellpark Harriers
1956	T Stevenson (Greenock Wellpark H)	Paisley Harriers
1957	A Small (Plebian H)	Greenock Wellpark Harriers
1958	W J More (Kilmarnock H)	Greenock Wellpark Harriers
1959	T Stevenson (Greenock Wellpark H)	Greenock Wellpark Harriers
1960	T Cochrane (Beith H)	Beith Harriers
1961	I Harris (Beith H)	Greenock Wellpark Harriers
1962	J McLatchie (Ayr Seaforth AC)	Greenock Wellpark Harriers
1963	T Cochrane (Beith H)	Beith Harriers
1964	I Harris (Beith H)	Greenock Glenpark Harriers
1965	T Cochrane (Beith H)	Greenock Glenpark Harriers
1966	T Cochrane (Beith H)	Greenock Wellpark Harriers
1967	T Cochrane (Beith H)	Greenock Wellpark Harriers
1968	T Cochrane (Beith H)	Ayr Seaforth AC
1969	T Cochrane (Beith H)	Greenock Glenpark Harriers
1970	W J Stoddart (Greenock Wellpark H)	Greenock Wellpark Harriers
1971	W J Stoddart (Greenock Wellpark H)	Greenock Wellpark Harriers
1972	J Ferguson (Ayr Seaforth AC)	Greenock Glenpark Harriers
1973	R L Spence (Greenock Glenpark H)	Greenock Glenpark Harriers

1974   B Morrison (Irvine AC)   Paisley Harriers
1975   C Spence (Spango Valley AC)   Greenock Wellpark Harriers

SOUTH WESTERN DISTRICT JUNIOR CHAMPIONSHIP
INDIVIDUAL
FIRST JUNIOR ATHLETE TO FINISH IN DISTRICT CHAMPIONSHIP RACE
1959   W Thomas (Irvine YMCA H)
1960   P Bradley (Paisley H)
1961   P Bradley (Paisley H)
1962   J McLatchie (Ayr Seaforth AC)
1963   J Wilson (Ayr Seaforth AC)
1964   J Millar (Beith H)
1965   K Laurie (Ailsa AAC)
1966   M Pollard (Greenock Wellpark H)
1967   R Love (Greenock Glenpark H)
1968   J Ferguson (Ayr Seaforth AC)
1969   J Ferguson (Ayr Seaforth AC)
1970   J Ferguson (Ayr Seaforth AC)
1971   J Trainer (Babcock & Wilcox AC)
1972   R L Spence (Greenock Glenpark H)
1973   R L Spence (Greenock Glenpark H)
1974   J Smith (Kilmarnock H)
1975   A Gourlay (Beith H)

FROM 1959 TO 1966 JUNIOR AGE CATEGORY WAS 18 TO 21 YEARS AND FROM 1967 TO 1975 THE AGE CATEGORY WAS CHANGED TO 17 TO 20 YEARS. THE JUNIOR CHAMPIONSHIP WAS RUN IN CONJUNCTION WITH THE SENIOR RACE.

SOUTH WESTERN DISTRICT YOUTH CHAMPIONSHIP
INDIVIDUAL   TEAM
1951   D Lapsley (West Kilbride AAC)   West Kilbride AAC
1952   D Lapsley (West Kilbride AAC)   West Kilbride AAC
1953   I Harris (Beith H)   Greenock Wellpark Harriers
1954   J Simpson (Plebian H)   Irvine YMCA Harriers
1955   R Black (Kilbarchan AC)   Irvine YMCA Harriers
1956   W Thomas (Irvine YMCA H)   Greenock Wellpark Harriers
1957   W Thomas (Irvine YMCA H)   Irvine YMCA Harriers
1958   J Orr (Greenock Wellpark H)   Greenock Wellpark Harriers
1959   C Shepherd (Greenock Wellpark H)   Greenock Wellpark Harriers
1960   C Shepherd (Greenock Wellpark H)   Beith Harriers
1961   J Millar (Beith H)   Paisley Harriers
1962   K Shepherd (Greenock Wellpark H)   Ayr Seaforth AC
1963   J Simpson (Paisley H)   Greenock Wellpark Harriers
1964   T Dobbin (Greenock Glenpark H)   Greenock Glenpark Harriers
1965   T Dobbin (Greenock Glenpark H)   Paisley Harriers

1966	J Young (Paisley H)	Greenock Glenpark Harriers
1967	J Young (Paisley H)	Paisley Harriers
1968	R Hainey (Ailsa AAC)	Ailsa AAC
1969	T Wallnutt (St. Joseph's Academy)	St. Joseph's Academy
1970	R L Spence (Greenock Glenpark H)	Babcock & Wilcox AC
1971	R L Spence (Greenock Glenpark H)	Eastwood High School
1972	J Golder (Beith H)	Eastwood High School
1973	I Kerr (Kilmarnock H)	Greenock Glenpark Harriers
1974	A Gourlay (Beith H)	Eastwood High School
1975	H Cox (Greenock Glenpark H)	Ayrshire AAC

SOUTH WESTERN DISTRICT SENIOR BOYS CHAMPIONSHIP

INDIVIDUAL — TEAM

1958	A Dallas (Greenock Wellpark H)	No team race
1959	S Hyde (Doon H)	Doon Harriers
1960	S Hyde (Doon H)	Paisley Harriers
1961	K Shepherd (Greenock Wellpark H)	Greenock Wellpark Harriers
1962	R Arthur (Greenock Glenpark H)	Greenock Glenpark Harriers
1963	T Dobbin (Greenock Glenpark H)	Greenock Glenpark Harriers
1964	T Findlay (Beith H)	Kilbarchan AC
1965	J Burton (Greenock Glenpark H)	Paisley Harriers
1966	J Gebbie (Kilmarnock Academy)	Ayr Seaforth AC
1967	D Taylor (Ayr Seaforth AC)	Ailsa AAC
1968	R L Spence (Greenock Glenpark H)	Greenock Glenpark Harriers
1969	R L Spence (Greenock Glenpark H)	Paisley Harriers
1970	J Donnelly (Ayr Seaforth AC)	Eastwood High School
1971	R Foy (Johnston HS)	Kilmarnock Harriers
1972	M Higgins (Kilmarnock H)	Eastwood High School
1973	H Cox (Greenock Glenpark H)	Eastwood High School
1974	B Aird (Kilmarnock H)	Eastwood High School
1975	R Lynch (Ayrshire AAC)	Eastwood AAC

SOUTH WESTERN DISTRICT JUNIOR BOYS CHAMPIONSHIP

INDIVIDUAL — TEAM

1966	D Taylor (Ayr Seaforth AC)	Kilmarnock Academy
1967	T Ferguson (Paisley H)	Irvine YMCA Harriers
1968	G Collie (Paisley H)	Paisley Harriers
1969	R Foy (Johnston HS)	Johnston High School
1970	J Kerr (Kilmarnock H)	Paisley Harriers
1971	I Robb (Johnston HS)	Johnston High School
1972	P McCarney (Greenock Glenpark H)	Paisley Harriers
1973	E MacDonald (Greenock Glenpark H)	Greenock Glenpark Harriers
1974	D Smith (Paisley H)	Paisley Harriers
1975	W Smith (Paisley H)	Spango Valley AC

SOUTH WESTERN DISTRICT 4 × 2½ MILE RELAY CHAMPIONSHIP

1929	Irvine YMCA Harriers	1934	Beith Harriers
1930	Barleith Harriers	1935	Beith Harriers
1931	Beith Harriers	1936	Beith Harriers
1932	Eglinton Harriers	1937	Ardeer Recreation Club
1933	Greenock Glenpark Harriers	1938	Beith Harriers

NO CHAMPIONSHIP RACES WERE HELD IN 1939, 1940, 1941, 1942, 1943, 1944, 1945, 1946 DUE TO THE SECOND WORLD WAR.

1947	West Kilbride AAC	1962	Ayr Seaforth AC
1948	Greenock Glenpark Harriers	1963	Ayr Seaforth AC
1949	Greenock Wellpark Harriers	1964	Beith Harriers
1950	West Kilbride AAC	1965	Beith Harriers
1951	West Kilbride AAC	1966	Greenock Glenpark Harriers
1952	Irvine YMCA Harriers	1967	Greenock Wellpark Harriers
1953	Greenock Wellpark Harriers	1968	Beith Harriers
1954	Greenock Wellpark Harriers	1969	Beith Harriers
1955	Greenock Wellpark Harriers	1970	Greenock Wellpark Harriers
1956	Greenock Wellpark Harriers	1971	Greenock Wellpark Harriers
1957	Greenock Wellpark Harriers	1972	Ayr Seaforth AC
1958	Irvine YMCA Harriers	1973	Ayr Seaforth AC
1959	Beith Harriers	1974	Paisley Harriers
1960	Beith Harriers	1975	Ayrshire AAC
1961	Greenock Wellpark Harriers		

IN 1976, DUE TO THE SMALL NUMBER OF CLUBS IN THE SOUTH WESTERN DISTRICT, THERE WAS AN AMALGAMATION OF THE SOUTH WESTERN AND MIDLAND DISTRICTS TO FORM THE NEW WESTERN DISTRICT WHICH COMPRISED ALL THE CLUBS IN THE AREA OF WESTERN AND SOUTH WESTERN SCOTLAND

ATHLETES WHO HAVE REPRESENTED SCOTLAND IN THE ANNUAL ICCU CHAMPIONSHIP SINCE THE FIRST CHAMPIONSHIP RACE WAS HELD AT HAMILTON PARK RACECOURSE IN SCOTLAND ON 28th MARCH 1903:-

J ALDER	(Edinburgh AC)	(10)	1962 (36)* - 64 (30)* - <u>65 (15)</u>* - 66 (16)* - 67 (23)* - 68 (23)* - 69 (DNF) - 70 (31)* - 71 (38)* - 72 (20)*
R ALLISON	(Springburn H)	(1)	1929 (DNF)
P J ALLWELL	(Ardeer R.C.)	(2)	1938 (36)* - 39 (23)*.
G ANDERSON	(Bellahouston H)	(1)	1947 (38).
G ARNOTT	(Falkirk Vic. H)	(2)	1904 (31) Edinburgh H 1905 (36).
E BANNON	(Shettleston H)	(7)	1951 (49) - <u>52 (14)</u>* - <u>53 (4)</u>* - <u>54 (14)</u>* - <u>55 (35)</u>* - 56 (33)* - 57 (37)*.
A BARRIE	(Shettleston H)	(3)	1920 (26)* - 21 (12)* - 22 (27).
J BARRIE	(Motherwell. YMCA H)	(1)	1904 (13)*.
F G V BATHGATE	(Ballydrain H)	(1)	1948 (52).
B BICKERTON	(Shettleston H)	(1)	1950 (49)*.
I BINNIE	(Vic. Park AAC)	(2)	1952 (62) - 55 (DNF).
J A BLAMIRE	(Shettleston H)	(4)	1967 (63) - 68 (92) - 71 (58)* - 72 (DNF).
W BOWMAN	(West of Scot. H)	(4)	1907 (17)* - 08 (40) - <u>09 (11)</u>* - 10 (DNF).
A D BRECKENRIDGE	(Vic. Park AAC)	(1)	1953 (50)*.
J BRENNAN	(Maryhill H)	(1)	1967 (88).
A H BROWN	(Motherwell YMCA H/Law & District AC)	(12)	1955 (52)* - 56 (50) - 58 (54) - 60 (34)* - 61 (28)* - <u>62 (9)</u>* - <u>63 (11)</u>* - <u>64 (29)</u>* - 65 (43)* - 66 (48)* - 67 (47)* - 68 (19)*.
A P BROWN	(Moth YMCA H/Law & District AC)	(3)	1965 (78)* - 67 (60)* - 68 (67).
T M BUTTERS	(Maryhill H.)	(1)	1903 (40).
R C CALDERWOOD	(Vic. Park AAC)	(2)	1956 (41)* - 57 (77).
W H CALDERWOOD	(Maryhill H.)	(4)	1922 (18)* - 23 (DNF) - 26 (DNF) - 28 (37).
J CAMPBELL	(Bellahouston H)	(2)	1935 (42) - 36 (30)*.
S CARSON	(Garscube H.)	(1)	1907 (24).
D CATHER	(Hamilton H.)	(1)	1906 (13)*.
T COCHRANE	(Beith H.)	(2)	1963 (57)* - 64 (57).
J CONNOLLY	(Bellahouston H)	(5)	1957 (64) - 58 (34)* - 59 (57)* - 60 (44)* - 61 (21)*.
A CRAIG (Snr)	(Bellahouston H)	(7)	1913 (14)* - 14 (12)* - 20 (20)* - 21 (32)* - 22 (10)* - 23 (13)* - <u>24 (16)</u>*.

A CRAIG (Jnr)	(Shettleston H)	(2)	1938 (24)* - 39 (DNF).
G B CRAIG	(Shettleston H)	(3)	1948 (38)* - 49 (32)* - 50 (55).
M G CRAVEN	(Edinburgh Sth H)	(1)	1963 (70).
J CROSBIE	(Larkhall H.)	(1)	1903 (10)*.
D CUMMINGS	(Green Glenpark H)	(1)	1921 (30)*
G CUMMINGS	(Bellahouston H)	(1)	1914 (DNF).
J CUTHBERT	(Garscube H.)	(1)	1922 (21)*.
D DICKSON	(Bellahouston H)	(1)	1958 (56).
A M DONNETT	(Dundee Hawkhill H)	(1)	1938 (47).
A DOW	(Kirkcaldy YMCA H)	(5)	1934 (12)* - 35 (10)* - 36 (3)* - 37 (17)* - 38 (27)*.
J DUFFY	(Edinburgh H.)	(3)	1909 (17)* - 10 (15)* - 11 (35).
G A DUNN	(Garscube H.)	(1)	1956 (60).
G EADIE	(Cambuslang H.)	(1)	1961 (42)*.
M EDWARDS	(Aberdeen Univ)	(1)	1964 (50)*.
S ELLIOT	(Green Glenpark H)	(1)	1905 (23)*.
J ELLIS	(Vic. Park AAC)	(1)	1951 (46)*.
G E EVERETT	(Shettleston H)	(4)	1959 (31)* - 60 (22)* - 61 (18)* - 62 (71).
W E EWING	(Aberdeen Univ)	(1)	1965 (192).
J E FARRELL	(Maryhill H.)	(10)	1937 (23)* - 38 (8)* - 39 (7)* - 46 (25)* - 47 (19)* - 48 (29)* - 49 (56) - 50 (48)* 51 (44)* - 53 (59).
H FENION	(Bellahouston H)	(3)	1954 (24)* - 57 (51)* - 58 (42)*.
A FLEMING	(Cambuslang H)	(1)	1958 (50)*.
J A FLEMING	(Motherwell YMCA H)	(1)	1949 (37)*.
J C FLOCKHART	(Shettleston H)	(11)	1933 (12)* - 34 (6)* - 35 (13)* - 36 (20)* - 37 (1)* - 38 (37)* - 39 (12)* - 46 (15)* - 47 (7)* - 48 (37)* - 49 (40)*.
A FORBES	(Vic. Park AAC)	(6)	1947 (26)* - 49 (15)* - 50 (29)* - 51 (38)* - 52 (25)* - 53 (12)*.
J FREELAND	(Hamilton H.)	(2)	1935 (28)* - 38 (44).
C FRESHWATER	(West of Scot H)	(2)	1924 (DNF) - 26 (24)*.
D FRY	(Irvine YMCA H)	(1)	1931 (22)*.
J GARDINER	(Edinburgh H)	(1)	1921 (DNF).
J N H GARDINER	(Motherwell YMCA H)	(3)	1929 (78) - 30 (52) - 31 (48).
A C GIBSON	(Hamilton H.)	(4)	1951 (42)* - 52 (52) - 53 (30)* - 54 (37)*.
T GIBSON	(Bellahouston H)	(2)	1938 (45) - 46 (46).
R F GILBERT	(West of Scot H)	(1)	1910 (19)*.
J GILCHRIST	(West of Scot H)	(1)	1906 (28).
J GIRVAN	(Garscube H)	(2)	1927 (31)* - 33 (44).
T GLANCY	(Edinburgh North H)	(1)	1924 (47).

A J GREIVE	(Teviotdale H)	(1)	1907 (43).
W J GUNN	(Plebian H.)	(6)	1928 (29)* - 29 (77) - 30 (20)* - 31 (21)* - 32 (24)* - 36 (48).
I HARRIS	(Beith H.)	(1)	1961 (75).
R HENDERSON	(Glasgow H.)	(1)	1928 (31).
D HENSON	(Vic Park AAC)	(1)	1955 (42)*.
A I C HERON	(Edinburgh South H)	(1)	1964 (39)*.
W HINDE	(Edinburgh North H)	(4)	1933 (29) - 34 (26)* - 35 (30) - 37 (32).
H HOWARD	(Shettleston H)	(1)	1946 (36)*.
H HUGHES	(West of Scot H)	(2)	1912 (15)* - 13 (33).
J D HUGHES	(Edinburgh H)	(2)	1911 (33) - 12 (13)*.
R E HUGHES	(Edinburgh H)	(1)	1906 (16)*.
T C HUGHES	(Edinburgh H)	(1)	1903 (21)*.
R IRVING	(Bellahouston H)	(3)	1959 (60) - 60 (41)* - 62 (58)*.
T JACK	(Edinburgh South H)	(5)	1907 (5)* - 08 (33) - 09 (37) - 10 (26) - 12 (20)*.
A S JACKSON	(Edinburgh Univ)	(3)	1958 (46)* - 59 (30)* - 61 (51).
J R JOHNSTONE	(Monkland H)	(2)	1964 (48)* - 66 (78).
T JOHNSTONE	(Clydesdale H)	(6)	1903 (34) - 05 (11)* - 07 (16)* - 08 (12)* - 09 (18)* - 11 (24)*.
G BRYAN-JONES	(Edinburgh South H)	(3)	1968 (47)* - 69 (24)* - 70 (57).
R KANE	(Vic Park AAC)	(1)	1954 (40)*.
S KENNEDY	(Garscube H.)	(2)	1904 (28)* - 05 (27).
W KENNEDY	(Kilbarchan AAC)	(2)	1937 (DNF) - 39 (54).
A KERR	(Motherwell YMCA H)	(4)	1911 (22)* - 12 (28) - 20 (18)* Bellahouston H. - 13 (11)*.
A KIDD	(Garscube H.)	(1)	1951 (55).
A KINNAIRD	(Edinburgh H.)	(1)	1903 (41).
J P LAIDLAW	(Edinburgh North H)	(1)	1934 (27)*.
C LAING	(Glasgow Univ)	(2)	1962 (37)* - 63 (63)*.
T W LAMB	(Bellahouston H)	(1)	1938 (32)*.
A B LAWRIE	(Garscube H.)	(2)	1921 (DNF) - 23 (30).
J LINAKER	(Motherwell YMCA H)	(3)	1963 (36)* - 66 (34)* - 68 (57).
J LINDSAY	(Bellahouston H)	(1)	1914 (8)*.
W F LINDSAY	(Gala H.)	(1)	1955 (51)*.
A LOCH	(Clydesdale H.)	(1)	1912 (25).
A MANN	(Clydesdale H.)	(3)	1909 (15)* - 10 (24)* - 11 (27)*.
A M MATTHEWS	(Edinburgh Univ)	(1)	1906 (35).
J S MATTHEWS	(Dundee Thistle H)	(1)	1908 (29).
P J MELVILLE	(Watsonians CCC)	(2)	1907 (14)* - 08 (25)*.
D W MILL	(Green Glenpark H)	(1)	1904 (18)*.

R MILLER	(Mauchline H.)	(2)	1926 (22)* - 27 (13)*.
T MILLER	(Motherwell YMCA H)	(1)	1908 (28)*.
J MITCHELL	(Mauchline H.)	(2)	1925 (16)* - 26 (5)*
J H MOTION	(Eglinton H.)	(1)	1921 (31)*.
N MORRISON	(Shettleston H)	(2)	1970 (46)* - 71 (25)*.
P MOY	(Vale of Leven AC)	(3)	1956 (14)* - 57 (28)* - 58 (37)*.
W MUIRDEN	(Hamilton H.)	(1)	1906 (32).
W MULLETT	(Shettleston H)	(3)	1969 (54)* - 70 (25)* - 71 (114).
T MULRINE	(West of Scot H)	(2)	1903 (23)* - 05 (DNF).
J MYATT	(Law & District AC)	(1)	1972 (76)*.
A F MURRAY	(Dundee Hawkhill H)	(5)	1964 (40)* Edinburgh University H & H - 65 (39)* - 66 (90) Edinburgh Southern H. - 69 (23)* - 71 (115).
E McALLISTER	(Shettleston H)	(1)	1946 (54).
I McCAFFERTY	(Motherwell YMCA H Law & District AC)	(7)	1965 (71)* - 66 (14)* - 67 (DNF) - 68 (10)* - 69 (3)* - 70 (DNF) - 72 (81).
J McCORMACK	(Springburn H)	(2)	1956 (45) - 57 (58).
A McDONALD	(Monkland H)	(1)	1913 (28)*.
A McDOUGALL	(Vale of Leven AC)	(1)	1957 (53)*.
J McGHEE	(Shettleston H)	(3)	1954 (50) - 55 (54)* - 59 (47)*.
A McGREGOR	(Bellahouston H)	(1)	1947 (37)*.
D F MACGREGOR	(Edinburgh South H)	(2)	1965 (100) - 69 (74).
A J McGUFFIE	(West of Scot H)	(1)	1909 (35).
H McINTOSH	(Edinburgh North H)	(2)	1932 (16)* - 33 (11)*.
J McINTYRE	(Garscube H)	(3)	1923 (32) - 24 (DNF) - 25 (36).
J G McINTYRE	(Shettleston H)	(2)	1923 (2)* - 24 (17)*.
R B McINTYRE	(West of Scot H)	(1)	1924 (40)*.
R McKAY	(Motherwell YMCA H)	(1)	1963 (68)*.
A McKEAN	(Edinburgh AC)	(2)	1971 (69) - 72 (44)*.
F McKENZIE	(Shettleston H.)	(1)	1954 (27)*.
G McKENZIE	(West of Scot H)	(9)	1904 (29) - 05 (16)* - 07 (18)* - 08 (27)* - 09 (20)* - 10 (16)* - 12 (22)* - 13 (32) - 14 (13)*.
P McLAGAN	(Vic Park AAC)	(1)	1967 (51)*.
J McLAREN	(Vic Park AAC)	(6)	1955 (48)* - 56 (12)* - 57 (35)* - 58 (68) - 59 (58)* - 62 (80).
A McLEAN	(Bellahouston H)	(1)	1948 (25)*.
W McLEAN	(Green Glenpark H)	(1)	1948 (49).
C McLENNAN	(Shettleston H)	(1)	1946 (49).
A J T McMORRAN	(Garscube H.)	(2)	1925 (27)* - 27 (32)*.
T McNEISH	(Irvine YMCA H)	(1)	1949 (44)*.
A McPHEE	(Clydesdale H.)	(3)	1909 (34) - 10 (8)* - 11 (31)*.

R McPHERSON	(Airdrie H.)	(1)	1939 (22)*.
W N NEILSON	(West of Scot H)	(2)	1923 (29)* - 25 (26)*.
D NELSON	(Motherwell YMCA H)	(1)	1952 (29)*.
D PEAT	(West of Scot H)	(1)	1914 (19)*.
P PEATTIE	(Monkland H.)	(1)	1932 (47).
J M PETRIE	(Dundee Thistle H)	(3)	1930 (40) - 31 (31) - 32 (35)*.
A S PIRIE	(South London H)	(1)	1926 (30).
W C PLANT	(Monkland H.)	(1)	1927 (42).
G PORTEOUS	(Maryhill H.)	(1)	1946 (43)*.
D QUINN	(Garscube H.)	(1)	1926 (21)*.
J RANKEN	(Watsonians CCC)	(6)	1903 (14)* - 04 (11)* - 05 (12)* - 06 (25)* - 07 (23) - 08 (24)*.
M RAYNE	(Plebian H.)	(1)	1930 (33)*.
J REID	(West Kilbride AC)	(2)	1947 (43) - 49 (48).
R REID	(Doon H.)	(8)	1939 (31) - 46 (26)* - 47 (20)* - 48 (12)* - 49 (29)* - 50 (45)* - 51 (32)* - 52 (26)*.
J RESTON	(Clydesdale H.)	(2)	1903 (22)* - 04 (20)*.
J W RIACH	(Maryhill H.)	(1)	1922 (26)*.
C D ROBERTSON	(Dundee Thistle H)	(4)	1948 (20)* - 50 (44)* - 51 (51) - 52 (34)*.
T ROBERTSON	(Edinburgh H.)	(4)	1905 (35) - 06 (27)* - 07 (15)* - 08 (20)*.
W ROBERTSON	(Clydesdale H.)	(2)	1903 (DNF) - 04 (39).
W J RODGER	(West of Scot H)	(1)	1913 (34).
A ROSS	(Edinburgh Sth H)	(1)	1960 (56).
J C ROSS	(Shettleston H)	(1)	1939 (29)*.
R ROXBURGH	(Garscube H)	(1)	1927 (38).
J RUSSELL	(Vic Park AAC)	(2)	1957 (38)* - 58 (25)*.
P C RUSSELL	(Bellahouston H)	(2)	1905 (14)* - 06 (15)*.
J SANDERSON	(Gala H.)	(1)	1950 (85).
A SEMPLE	(Shettleston H)	(1)	1920 (DNF).
D SIMPSON	(Motherwell YMCA H)	(1)	1962 (66).
E SINCLAIR	(Springburn H)	(1)	1960 (55).
F SINCLAIR	(Green Wellpark H)	(4)	1947 (28)* - 48 (53) - 50 (46)* - 53 (52)*.
W D SLIDDERS	(Dundee Thistle H)	(1)	1933 (16)*.
A SMITH	(Clydesdale H)	(1)	1920 (DNF).
C SMITH	(Dundee Hawkhill H)	(3)	1935 (47) - 36 (38) - 37 (31)*.
J SUTTIE SMITH	(Dundee Thistle H)	(10)	1927 (18)* - 28 (2)* - 29 (16)* - 30 (13)* Dundee YMCA H. 1931 (10)* - 32 (7)* Canon ASC 1933 (3)* Edinburgh Northern H. 1934 (23)* - 35 (12)* Dundee Hawkhill H. 1936 (24)*.

J A SOMMERVILLE	(Motherwell YMCA H)	(1)	1905 (DNF).
W S SOMMERVILLE	(Motherwell YMCA H)	(2)	1946 (33)* - 47 (44).
G R STEPHENS	(Bellahouston H)	(2)	1912 (14)* - 14 (DNF).
F L STEVENSON	(Monkland H)	(5)	1926 (16)* - 27 (4)* - 28 (14)* - 29 (21)* - 30 (22)*.
J STEVENSON	(Green Wellpark H)	(4)	1953 (DNF) - 54 (28)* - 55 (60) - 56 (38)*.
S STEVENSON	(Clydesdale H)	(3)	1904 (36) - 05 (6)* - 06 (10)*.
T STEVENSON	(Green Wellpark H)	(6)	1949 (54) - 52 (45) - 53 (65) - 54 (54) - 55 (57) - 56 (39)*.
I STEWART	(Birchfield H)	(2)	1971 (9)* - 72 (3)*.
J L STEWART	(Vale of Leven AAC) (Shettleston H)	(10)	1964 (69) - 65 (58)* - 66 (12)* - 67 (4)* - 68 (18)* - 69 (20)* - 70 (12)* - 71 (60)* - 72 (27)*.
M STEWART	(Edinburgh North H)	(1)	1927 (41).
M STOBBS	(Catrine AC)	(3)	1930 (21)* - 31 (34) - 32 (DNF).
W STODDART	(Green Wellpark H)	(1)	1970 (85).
J STRAIN	(Shettleston H)	(2)	1920 (27)* - 22 (DNF).
R R SUTHERLAND	(Garscube H)	(7)	1928 (18)* - 30 (2)* - 31 (8)* - 33 (2)* - 34 (11)* - 36 (13)* - 37 (20)*.
W SUTHERLAND	(Shettleston H)	(4)	1932 (40) - 35 (19)* - 36 (52) - 39 (27)*.
S TAYLOR	(Aberdeen AAC)	(3)	1960 (45) - 61 (58) - 62 (35).
J W TEMPLEMAN	(Bellahouston H)	(4)	1910 (20)* - 11 (DNF) - 13 (18)* - 14 (38).
T TODD	(Kilmarnock H)	(1)	1934 (48).
S K TOMBE	(Plebian H)	(3)	1928 (39) - 33 (18)* - 34 (30).
T TRACEY	(Springburn H.)	(4)	1950 (75) - 51 (24)* - 52 (23)* - 54 (51).
R TREW	(Clydesdale H.)	(1)	1903 (DNF).
M B S TULLOH	(Portsmouth AC)	(2)	1960 (23)* - 61 (46)*.
J A URE	(Green Wellpark H)	(2)	1903 (17)* - 04 (24)*.
D URQUHART	(Garscube H)	(1)	1932 (20)*.
R C WALLACE	(Shettleston H)	(1)	1953 (33)*.
G C L WALLACH	(Green Glenpark H)	(9)	1910 (DNF) - 11 (3)* - 12 (4)* - 13 (8)* - 14 (2)* - 21 (8)* - 22 (4)* - 23 (22)* - 24 (23)*.
S S WATT	(Clydesdale H)	(5)	1909 (26)* - 11 (14)* - 12 (DNF) - 13 (17)* - 14 (20)*.
A WEATHERHEAD	(Octavians AC)	(1)	1970 (42)*.
R WEDLOCK	(Shettleston H)	(4)	1969 (36)* - 70 (45)* - 71 (24)* - 72 (73)*.
A T WHITECROSS	(Dundee Th H)	(4)	1937 (41).

A T WHITELAW	(Green Glenpark H)	(2)	1922 (29) - 23 (23)*.
T WHITTON	(Dundee H)	(3)	1925 (19)* - 26 (27) - 29 (50)*.
J WIGHT	(Edinburgh AC)	(1)	1972 (91).
C P WILSON	(Irvine YMCA H)	(2)	1929 (30)* - 31 (28)*.
F WILSON	(Larkhall H)	(1)	1903 (30).
J WILSON	(Green Glenpark H)	(4)	<u>1920 (1)*</u> - 21 (DNF) - 24 (19)* -25 (14)*.
J WILSON	(Birchfield H)	(2)	1933 (23) - 34 (45).
A J WOOD	(Shettleston H)	(6)	<u>1959 (20)*</u> - <u>60 (7)*</u> - 61 (33)* - 62 (25)* - 63 (31)* - 64 (53).
J F WOOD	(Heriots CCC)	(4)	1928 (21)* - 29 (26)* - 31 (13)* - 32 (8)*.
D McL.WRIGHT	(Clydesdale H)	(11)	1920 (22)* - 21 (9)* - 22 (11)* - 23 (24)* Shettleston H. 1924 (18)* - <u>25 (5)*</u> - 26 (13)* Caledonian H. 1927 (14)* Maryhill H. 1928 (20)* - 29 (46)* - 30 (39).
J WRIGHT	(Edinburgh AC)	(3)	1967 (42)* - 68 (20)* - 69 (98).
W C WYLIE	(Darlington H)	(3)	<u>1935 (2)*</u> - 36 (22)* - 37 (30)*.
T S YOUNG	(Motherwell H)	(1)	1905 (37).

The record number of appearances for Scotland in the International Cross Country Union Championships in the period 1903 to 1972 is held by Andrew Brown of Motherwell YMCA Harriers. He competed on 12 occasions (1955 - 56 - 58 - 60 - 61 - 62 - 63 - 64 -65 - 66 - 67 - 68) between 1955 and 1968, missing only 1957 and 1959. He was a counter in Scotland's team on 10 of the 12 occasions and was the leading Scot to finish on 3 occasions in 1962, 63 and 64.

SCOTTISH MEDAL WINNERS IN I.C.C.U. CHAMPIONSHIP 1903 - 1972

SCOTTISH GOLD MEDALLISTS (3)

Arthur J Robertson * (Birchfield H)   At Colombes Stadium near Paris on 26th March 1908.

James Wilson (Greenock Glenpark H.)   At Belvoir Park, Belfast on 3rd April 1920.

James C Flockhart (Shettleston H.)   At Hippodrome de Stockel, Brussels on 20th March 1937.

Representing England though of Scottish qualification.

SCOTTISH SILVER MEDALLISTS (6)

George C L Wallach (Greenock Glenpark H.)   At Chesham Park, England on 28th March 1914.

James G McIntyre (Shettleston H.)   At Maison Lafite, Paris on 23rd March 1923.

John Suttie Smith (Dundee Thistle H.)   At Ayr Racecourse, Scotland on 24th March 1928.

Robert R Sutherland (Garscube H.)   At Royal Leamington Spa, England on 22nd March 1930.

Robert R Sutherland (Garscube H.)   At Caerleon Racecourse, Newport, Wales on 25th March 1933.

W C Wylie (Darlington H.)   At Hippodrome d'Auteuil, Paris on 23rd March 1935.

SCOTTISH BRONZE MEDALLISTS (5)

George C L Wallach (Greenock Glenpark H.)   At Caerleon Raceourse, Newport, Wales on 25th March 1911.

John Suttie Smith (Canon A.S.C.)   At Caerleon Racecourse, Newport, Wales on 25th March 1933.

Alexander Dow (Kirkcaldy YMCA H.)   At Squire Gate Stadium, Blackpool, England on 28th March 1936.

Ian McCafferty (Motherwell YMCA H.)   At Dalmuir Public Park, Clydebank, Scotland on 22nd March 1969.

Ian Stewart (Birchfield H.)   At Coldhams Park, Cambridge, England on 18th March 1972.

ATHLETES WHO HAVE REPRESENTED SCOTLAND IN THE ANNUAL IAAF WORLD CROSS COUNTRY CHAMPIONSHIP SINCE THE FIRST CHAMPIONSHIP RACE WAS HELD AT THE HIPPODROME DE WAREGEM, BELGIUM ON 17th MARCH 1973.

J ALDER	(Edinburgh AC)	(4)	1973 (57)* - 74 (88) - 75 (101) - 76 (96)*.
S BEGEN	(Springburn H)	(1)	1986 (235).
A BLAMIRE	(Shettleston H)	(1)	1974 (66)*.
G BRAIDWOOD	(Bellahouston H)	(3)	1983 (201) - 84 (DNF) - 85 (162)*.
J BROWN	(Monkland H)	(7)	1974 (4)* - 75 (75)* - 76 (24)* - 77 (36)* - 78 (114) - 80 (31)*. - 81 (DNF)
A CALLAN	(Springburn H)	(1)	1986 (193)*.
E CAMERON	(Edinburgh Sth H)	(1)	1983 (198).
G CLARK	(Spango Valley AC)	(2)	1980 (128)* -82 (145).
F CLEMENT	Bellahouston H)	(2)	1975 (111) - 78 (67)*.
F CLYNE	(Aberdeen AAC)	(5)	1981 (DNF) - 82 (127)* - 83 (97)* - 84 (149)* - 86 (173)*.
R COPESTAKE	(Dundee Hawkhill H)	(3)	1984 (131)* - 85 (DNF) - 87 (192).
G CRAWFORD	(Springburn H)	(1)	1983 (182)*.
J DINGWALL	(Edinburgh AC)	(3)	1979 (164) - 83 (180)* - 85 (213).
S DOIG	(Fife South H)	(1)	1986 (217).
P DOLAN	(Clydesdale H)	(2)	1976 (126) - 78 (DNF).
A DOUGLAS	(Vic Park AAC)	(2)	1981 (192)* - 82 (135)*.
J EGAN	(Larkhall YMCA H)	(1)	1984 (170).
C FALCONER	(Springburn H)	(2)	1973 (115) - 74 (47)*.
D FRAME	(Law & District AC)	(1)	1983 (122)*.
A GILMOUR	(Cambuslang H)	(1)	1984 (168)*.
I GILMOUR	(Clyde Valley AC)	(4)	1973 (74)* - 75 (110) - 78 (84)* - 81 (122)*.
J GRAHAM	(Clyde Valley AC)	(3)	1977 (89) - 78 (90)* - 80 (73)*.
D GUNSTONE	(Edinburgh AC)	(1)	1974 (79)*.
C HASKETT	(Dundee Hawkhill H)	(4)	1984 (175) - 85 (164)* - 86 (147)* -87 (181)
C HUME	(Edinburgh South H)	(2)	1985 (147)*
A HUTTON	(Edinburgh South H)	(10)	1974 (109) - 75 (38)* - 76 (34)* - 77 (14)* - 78 (24)* - 79 (105)* - 80 (29)* - 81 (48)* - 82 (30)* - 87 (196).
P KENNEY	(Dundee Univ AC)	(2)	1976 (98) - 77 (68)*.
R MacDONALD	(Clyde Valley AC)	(2)	1974 (31)* - 82 (95)*.
A McKEAN	(Edinburgh AC)	(6)	1973 (30)* - 74 (46)* - 75 (53)* - 76 (41)* - 77 (49)* - 78 (19)*.
B McSLOY	(Clyde Valley AC)	(2)	1979 (164) - 80 (167).
T MITCHELL	(Fife AC)	(4)	1983 (159)* - 84 (146)* - 85 (DNF) - 86 (134)* - 87 (137)*.

N MORRISON	(Shettleston H)	(1)	1973 (13)*.
N MUIR	(Shettleston H)	(8)	1978 (7)* - 79 (10)* - 80 (DNF)* - 81 (26)* - 82 (26)* - 83 (11)* - 85 (49)* - 87 (40)*.
T MURRAY	(Green Glenpark H)	(1)	1987 (152)*.
J K MYATT	(Law & District AC)	(1)	1973 (83).
J PATTON	(Edinburgh AC)	(2)	1976 (72)* - 79 (99)*.
R QUINN	(Kilbarchan AAC)	(2)	1985 (197)
L REILLY	(Vic Park AAC)	(6)	1974 (97) - 75 (43)* - 76 (81)* - 77 (41)* - 78 (97) - 79 (146)*.
G RIMMER	(Cambuslang H)	(2)	1979 (158) - 80 (131).
C ROBISON	(Spango Valley AC)	(2)	1986 (170)* - 87 (149)*.
J ROBSON	(Edinburgh Sth H)	(8)	1977 (94)* - 70 (52)* - 80 (5)* - 81 (54)* - 82 (85)* - 85 (42)* - 86 (122)* - 87 (146)*.
L SPENCE	(Shettleston H)	(8)	1976 (134) - 77 (141) - 79 (74)* - 80 (46)* - 81 (134)* - 82 (138)* - 83 (193) - 84 (112)*.
E STEWART	(Cambuslang H)	(3)	1982 (148) - 84 (143)*
I STEWART	(Birchfield H)	(1)	1975 (1)*.
J L STEWART	(Shettleston H)	(1)	1973 (45)*.
N TENNANT	(Edinburgh Sth H)	(3)	1985 (144)* - 86 (DNF) - 87 (180)*.
R WARD	(Shettleston H)	(2)	1975 (82)* - 77 (62)*.
A WEATHERHEAD	(Edinburgh AC)	(1)	1973 (72)*.
R WEDLOCK	Shettleston H)	(1)	1973 (120).
G WILLIAMSON	(Springburn H.)	(1)	1981 (DNF).

*   Signifies a counting member of the Scottish team of 6 runners in the race.
(3)   After name and club signifies number of international appearances.
(DNF)   The athlete did not finish the race.
(93)   Position of athlete in race.
(15)*   First Scots runner to finish in the race.

The International Amateur Athletic Federation took over the organisation and control of the Championship and the race became a World Championship, with the first Championship race being held at the Hippodrome de Waregem, Belgium on 17th March 1973.

SCOTTISH MEDAL WINNERS IN I.A.A.F. CHAMPIONSHIP 1973 - 1987

SCOTTISH GOLD MEDALLIST (1)

Ian Stewart (Birchfield H.)   At Souissi Racecourse, Rabat, Morocco on 16th March 1975.

The record number of appearances for Scotland in the I.A.A.F. Championships in the period 1973 to 1987.

The record number of appearances for Scotland in the International Amateur Athletic Federation Championships in the period 1973 to 1987 is held by

Allister Hutton of Edinburgh Southern Harriers. He competed on 10 occasions (1974-1987), missing only the 4 years betwen 1983 and 1986. He was a counter in Scotland's team on 8 of the 10 occasions and was the leading Scot to finish in 1977.

Allister Hutton (Edinburgh Southern Harriers) 1974 - 75 - 76 - 77 - 78 - 79 - 80 - 81 - 82 - 87 (10 appearances).

It should be noted that the record number of appearances for Scotland in the International Championships of the ICCU and the IAAF combined is James Alder of Edinburgh AC who competed on 14 occasions between 1962 and 1976 as follows :

ICCU 1962 - 64 - 65 - 66 - 67 - 68 - 69 - 70 - 71 - 72 (10 appearances)
IAAF 1973 - 74 - 75 - 76 (4 appearances)

He was a scoring counter in Scotland's team on 9 of the 10 occasions in the I.C.C.U. Championships between 1962 and 1972 and was the leading Scot to finish in 1965. He was a scoring counter in Scotland's team on 2 of the 4 occasions in the I.A.A.F. Championships between 1973 and 1976.

ATHLETES WHO HAVE REPRESENTED SCOTLAND IN THE I.C.C.U. JUNIOR CROSS COUNTRY INTERNATIONAL BETWEEN 1962 AND 1972

P BANNON	(Shettleston H.)	(1) 1972 (13)*
A BLANEY	(Springburn H.)	(2) 1968 (31)* 69 (38)*
A BLAMIRE	(Edinburgh Univ.)	(1) 1966 (15)*
J BRENNAN	(Maryhill H.)	(1) 1966 (10)*
A BROWN	(Motherwell YMCA H.)	(2) 1963 (11)* 64 (7)*
J BROWN	(Monkland H.)	(2) 1971 (3)* 72 (2)*
W BURNS	(Larkhall YMCA H.)	(2) 1970 (19)* 71 (20)*
F CLEMENT	(Bellahouston H.)	(1) 1971 (34)
J COOK	(Garscube H.)	(2) 1967 (27) 68 (18)*
W DAY	(Falkirk Victoria H.)	(1) 1967 (20)*
C DOUGLAS	(Teviotdale H.)	(2) 1962 (21) 63 (10)*
W EADIE	(Strathclyde Univ.)	(1) 1965 (22)*
C FALCONER	(Springburn H.)	(1) 1970 (5)*
J FINN	(Monklands H.)	(1) 1962 (16)*
D GILLANDERS	(Shettleston H.)	(1) 1969 (9)*
I GILMOUR	(Birmingham Univ.)	(1) 1971 (13)*
D GUNSTONE	(Dundee Hawkhill H.)	(1) 1970 (25)*
A HERON	(Edinburgh South H.)	(1) 1962 (11)*
G JARVIE	(Springburn H.)	(1) 1969 (32)*
J JOHNSTON	(Monkland H.)	(1) 1963 (22)*
E KNOX	(Springburn H.)	(3) 1965 (5)* 66 (3)* 67 (1)*
A MOODY	(Teviotdale H.)	(1) 1962 (18)*
B MORRISON	(Irvine YMCA H.)	(1) 1969 (19)*
N MORRISON	(Shettleston H.)	(2) 1967 (13)* 68 (13)*
J MYATT	(Strathclyde Univ.)	(1) 1967 (19)*
I McCAFFERTY	(Motherwell YMCA H.)	(1) 1964 (1)*
R MacDONALD	(Monkland H.)	(3) 1970 (13)* 71 (14)* 72 (23)*
M McMAHON	(Shettleston H.)	(1) 1968 (17)*
T PATTERSON	(Shettleston H.)	(1) 1968 (35)
I PICKEN	(Strathclyde Univ.)	(1) 1969 (40)
J REILLY	(Victoria Park AAC)	(1) 1964 (9)*

L REILLY	(Victoria Park AAC)	(1) 1972 (20)*
R L SPENCE	(Strathclyde Univ.)	(1) 1972 (50)
F STEEL	(Edinburgh AC)	(1) 1966 (28)*
J L STEWART	(Vale of Leven AC)	(2) 1962 (10)* 63 (3)*
I YOUNG	(Springburn H.)	(2) 1964 (22)* 65 (17)*
R WEDLOCK	(Shettleston H.)	(1) 1965 (25)*

SCOTTISH MEDAL WINNERS IN I.C.C.U. CHAMPIONSHIP 1962-72

SCOTTISH GOLD MEDALLISTS (2)

Ian McCafferty (Motherwell YMCA H.) at Leopardstown Racecourse, Dublin, Ireland — 1964
Edward Knox (Springburn H.) at Barry, Wales — 1967

SCOTTISH SILVER MEDALLIST (1)

James Brown (Monkland H.) at Coldhams Common, Cambridge, England — 1972

SCOTTISH BRONZE MEDALLISTS (3)

James Laughlin Stewart (Vale of Leven AC) at Hippodrome de Lasarte, San Sebastian, Spain — 1963
Edward Knox (Springburn H.) at Souissi Racecourse, Rabat, Morrocco — 1966
James Brown (Monkland H.) at Hippodrome de Lasarte, San Sebastian, Spain — 1971

N.B. 1963 Championships declared null and void as a number of athletes were over age, but L Stewart was the only one of the three medallists to be the correct age.

ATHLETES WHO HAVE REPRESENTED SCOTLAND IN THE I.A.A.F. WORLD JUNIOR CROSS COUNTRY CHAMPIONSHIP BETWEEN 1973 AND 1987

R ARBUCKLE	(Aberdeen Univ.)	(1) 1980 (74)*
D ARNOTT	(Pitreavie A.A.C.)	(1) 1987 (40)
S BEGEN	(Springburn H.)	(2) 1984 (66)* 85 (107)
J BELL	(Inverness H.)	(1) 1986 (135)
I BROWN	(Falkirk Victoria H.)	(2) 1977 (68) 78 (17)*
J BROWN	(Monkland H.)	(1) 1973 (1)*
J BURNS	(Shettleston H.)	(1) 1975 (11)*
A CALLAN	(Springburn H.)	(1) 1980 (47)*
R CAMERON	(Central Region AC)	(2) 1982 (29)* 83 (48)*
I CAMPBELL	(East Kilbride AC)	(2) 1978 (27)* 79 (10)*
R CAREY	(Annan & District AC)	(1) 1986 (61)*
P CONGHAN	(Spango Valley AC)	(1) 1983 (64)*
R COPESTAKE	(Dundee Hawkhill H.)	(1) 1980 (65)*
A CURRIE	(Dumbarton A.A.C.)	(1) 1984 (90)
D DONNETT	(Springburn H.)	(1) 1987 (138)*
A DOUGLAS	(Victoria Park A.A.C.)	(3) 1977 (59) 78 (36)* 79 (11)*

P FORBES	(Edinburgh AC)	(1) 1975 (56)
P FOX	(Clyde Valley AC)	(2) 1979 (57)* 80 (85)
J GLADWIN	(Edinburgh South H.)	(2) 1980 (69)* 81 (31)*
J GRAHAM	(Clyde Valley AC)	(1) 1975 (51)*
J GRAY	(Edinburgh AC)	(1) 1978 (64)
T HANLON	(Edinburgh South H.)	(2) 1985 (47) * 86 (134)*
C HASKETT	(Dundee Hawkhill H.)	(2) 1975 (53) 76 (69)
T HEARLE	(Kilbarchan AC)	(1) 1986 (102)*
C HENDERSON	(Tayside A.A.C.)	(1) 1981 (74)*
N JONES	(Edinburgh AC)	(1) 1978 (60)*
P KENNEY	(Dundee Univ.)	(1) 1974 (13)*
D KIRK	(Dumbarton A.A.C.)	(1) 1979 (68)
C MARR	(Sheffield Univ.)	(1) 1977 (46)
S MARSHALL	(Motherwell YMCA H.)	(1) 1984 (55)*
P MAYLES	(Kilbarchan AC)	(1) 1986 (DNF)
G MILLER	(Clydesdale H.)	(1) 1980 (78)
G MITCHELL	(Falkirk Victoria H.)	(1) 1982 (44)*
P MORRIS	(Cambuslang H.)	(1) 1985 (87)*
N MUIR	(Shettleston H.)	(4) 1974 (19)* 75 (12)* 76 (3)* 77 (8)*
K McCARTNEY	(Law & District AC)	(2) 1975 (21)* 76 (42)*
R MacDONALD	(Monkland H.)	(1) 1973 (14)*
C McFADYEAN	(Nith Valley AC)	(1) 1987 (103)*
C McINTYRE	(Edinburgh Univ.)	(1) 1981 (84)*
R McKAY	(Shettleston H.)	(1) 1982 (76)
D McMEEKIN	(Victoria Park A.A.C.)	(1) 1973 (17)*
G McMILLAN	(Ayrshire A.A.C.)	(1) 1981 (96)
J McNEIL	(Law & District AC)	(1) 1983 (77)*
D McSHANE	(Cambuslang H.)	(2) 1982 (81) 84 (76)
B McSLOY	(Clyde Valley AC)	(2) 1976 (63)* 77(39)*
D McTAVISH	(Bellahouston H.)	(1) 1979 (86)
R McWATT	(Clydesdale H.)	(1) 1978 (81)
J ORR	(Cambuslang H.)	(1) 1984 (64)*
S PATON	(Belgrave H.)	(1) 1982 (50)*
A PUCKRIN	(Kilbarchan A.C.)	(1) 1983 (78)*
A RUSSELL	(Law & District AC)	(3) 1985 (60)* 86 (59)* 87 (84)*
J QUINN	(Motherwell YMCA H.)	(1) 1987 (145)
R QUINN	(Kilbarchan A.C.)	(1) 1984 (20)*
B SCALLY	(Shettleston H.)	(1) 1985 (116)
W SHERIDAN	(Glasgow Univ.)	(1) 1974 (12)*
R L SPENCE	(Strathclyde Univ.)	(1) 1973 (27)*
J STEEL	(Edinburgh South H.)	(2) 1981 (78)* 82 (61)*
M TAGGART	(Shettleston H.)	(1) 1983 (89)
M WALLACE	(Victoria Park A.A.C.)	(1) 1987 (124)*
G WILLIAMSON	(Springburn H.)	(2) 1977 (43)* 79 (23)*
A WILSON	(Victoria Park A.A.C.)	(1) 1983 (96)

N.B. Clark Murphy of Pitreavie A.A.C. represented the combined United Kingdom Team in the 1988 I.A.A.F. World Cross Country Championships in New Zealand.

SCOTTISH MEDAL WINNERS IN I.A.A.F. CHAMPIONSHIP 1973-87

SCOTTISH GOLD MEDALLIST (1)

James Brown (Monkland H.) at Hippodrome de Waregem, Belgium 1973

SCOTTISH BRONZE MEDALLIST (1)

Nathanial Muir (Shettleston H.) at Chepstow Racecourse, Wales 1976

Nathanial Muir of Shettleston Harriers has the greatest number of Scottish International appearances, having competed on 4 occasions between 1974 and 1977, and been a counting member of the Scottish team on all 4 occasions. He was the leading Scot to finish the race on 2 occasions in 1976 and 1977, gaining a bronze medal in 1976.

Ronald MacDonald of Monkland Harriers also represented Scotland on 4 occasions between 1970 and 1973, and was a counting member of the Scottish team on all 4 occasions. His first 3 appearances, from 1970 to 1972, were in the I.C.C.U. Championships, with the final appearance in 1973 being in the inaugural I.A.A.F Championships.

INTERNATIONAL CHAMPIONSHIPS HELD IN SCOTLAND 1903 - 1978

1903	28 March (ICCU)	Hamilton Park Racecourse (Inaugural race)
1907	23 March (ICCU)	Scotstoun Showgrounds, Glasgow
1912	30 March (ICCU)	Saughton Park, Edinburgh
1922	1 April (ICCU)	Hampden Park, Glasgow
1928	24 March (ICCU)	Ayr Racecourse
1934	24 March (ICCU)	Ayr Racecourse
1946	30 March (ICCU)	Ayr Racecourse
1952	22 March (ICCU)	Hamilton Park Racecourse
1960	20 March (ICCU)	Hamilton Park Racecourse
1969	22 March (ICCU)	Dalmuir Public Park, Clydebank
1978	25 March (IAAF)	Bellahouston Park, Glasgow.

PRINCIPAL OFFICERS OF THE UNION 1885 - 1990

PAST PRESIDENTS 1887 - 1955

SUB COMMITTEE OF MANAGEMENT
1885-86   None appointed
1886-87   None appointed

SCOTTISH CROSS COUNTRY ASSOCIATION
1887-88   J M Bow, Edin H.
1888-89   S. Lawrie, West of Scot H
1889-90   J. M. Bow, Edin H.

SCOTTISH CROSS COUNTRY UNION
1890-91   T. Fraser, Edin H.
1891-92   D.C. Brown, West of Scot H.
1892-93   D.S. Duncan, Ed. Univ H&H
1893-94   A. McNab, Clydesdale H.
1894-95   A. Forrest, Dalkeith H.
1895-96   L Hamilton, West of Scot H.
1896-97   R.K. Kinnimont, Watsonians CCC
1897-98   A. Hannah, Clydesdale H.
1898-99   G. Hume, Berwick & Dist. H.
1899-01   A.M. Bryson, West of Scot H.
1901-03   J. Bartlement, Edin. H.

NATIONAL CROSS COUNTRY UNION OF SCOTLAND
1903-05   W.A. McCaa, Garscube H.
1905-07   G. Hume, Berwick & Dist. H.
1907-09   J. McCulloch, Maryhill H.
1909-10   W. A. Batchin, Waverley H.
1910-11   W. Bain, West of Scot H.
1911-12   W. Laing, Edinburgh H.
1912-14   W. Struthers, Green Glenpark H
1914-20   M Dewar, Edin. Southern H.
1920-21   J.D. McKinlay, Maryhill H
1921-22   A.F. Dickson, Heriots CCC
1922-24   J. Howieson, Shettleston H
1924-25   R. Porteous, Grange H.
1925-26   R.F. Murray, Motherwell YMCA H
1926-27   J.W. Dickson, Heriots CCC
1927-28   J.C.A. Bodie, West of Scot H.
1928-29   G.M. Grant, Edin Northern H.
1929-30   T. Fraser, Olympic H.
1930-31   T. Jack, Edin. Rover Scouts
1931-32   T. McAllister, Glasgow H.
1932-33   W. Murdoch, Auchmountain H
1933-34   C. Chalmers, Garscube H.
1934-35   H.J. Scott, Edinburgh H.
1935-36   D. McSwein, Green Wellpark H
1936-37   W.S. McCarthy, Springburn H.
1937-38   W. Carmichael, Edin.Eastern H
1938-46   J. Follon, Kilbarchan AAC
1946-47   J.O.Hepburn, Bellahouston H.
1947-48   A.M. Donnett, Dundee Thistle H
1948-49   A.F. Neilson, Bellahouston H.
1949-50   J.C. Scott, Hamilton H.
1950-51   A.N. Crosbie, Edin. Southern H
1951-52   P.E.M. Leggat, Ayr AAC
1952-53   D. Scott, Monkland H.
1953-54   J.T. Mitchell, Braidburn AC
1954-55   G. Pickering, Renfrew YMCA
1955-56   J W C Armour, Victoria Park AAC
1956-57   G. K. Horsburgh, Edin Northern H
1957-58   E Thursby, Ayr AAC
1958-59   T. D. McKie, Glasgow Police
1959-60   I Ross, Edin Southern H.
1960-61   A. K. MacDonald, Auchmountain H.
1961-62   G. Dallas, Maryhill H.
1962-63   A. Falconer, Edinburgh A.C.
1963-64   J.C.R. Morton, Springburn H.
1964-65   W. S. Lawn, Bellahouston H.
1965-66   A.S. Stevenson, Shettleston H.
1966-67   L G. Kapelle, Edin Southern H.
1967-68   J.H. Gardiner, Nat. Coun. YMCAs
1968-69   W. Diverty, Glas. Univ. H&H
1969-70   J.M. Hamilton, Teviotdale H
1970-71   A Johnston, Strathclyde Univ AC
1971-72   R.L. McSwein, Paisley H.
1972-73   E.S. Murray, Garscube H.
1973-74   C.M. Meldrum, Stirling AAC
1974-75   J. R. Scott, Tayside AC
1975-76   D.M. Duncan, Inverness H.
1976-77   B.A. Goodwin, Bellahouston H.
1977-78   J.E. Clifton, Edin. Southern H.
1978-79   D. McSwein Jnr, Green Wellpark H.
1979-80   R. Devon, Scottish Veteran H.
1980-81   D.F. Macgregor, Fife AC
1981-82   W. Banks, Inverness H.
1982-83   J.M. Young, Ayrshire AAC
1983-84   C.R. Jones, Edinburgh AC
1984-85   J. G. Cherry, Shettleston H
1985-86   R. Morrison, St Andrews Univ.
1986-87   W.C. Robertson, Bellahouston H.
1987-88   F. McCluskie, Livingston & Dist AC
1988-89   H. Quinn, East Kilbride AC
1989-90   R. M. Dalgleish, Annan & Dist AC

HONORARY SECRETARY/TREASURERS
1885-87   D.S. Duncan, Edinburgh Univ. H&H
1892-97   W. M. Carment, Edinburgh H.
1897-98   D. McNaughton, Motherwell YMCAH
1898-11   A. Ross Scott, Clydesdale H.
1911-21   W. Roxburgh, Hamilton H.
1921-46   G. Dallas, Maryhill H.

HONORARY TREASURERS
1946-72   D. McSwein, Green Wellpark H.
1972-   R.L. McSwein, Paisley H.

HONORARY SECRETARIES
1946-60   G. Dallas, Maryhill H.
1960-64   A.S. Stevenson, Shettleston H
1964-72   E.S. Murray, Garscube H.
1972-82   R.M. Dalgleish, Springburn H.
1982-   J.E. Clifton, Edin. Southern H

HONORARY ASSISTANT SECRETARIES
1972-79   J. M Hamilton (Teviotdale H)
1979-82   J.E. Clifton (Edin. Southern H.)
1982-85   C.A. Shields (Green Glenpark H)
1985-   D.V. McLaren (Penicuik H)

HONORARY PRESIDENTS
1921-28   W. Struthers
1928-70   Sir T.C.R. Moore Bart, CBE, OBE, M.P.
1970-71   Dr. C.A. Hepburn
1971-83   G. McKenzie
1984-   D.M. Duncan

CLUBS AFFILIATED TO THE SCOTTISH CROSS COUNTRY UNION
as at 1st January 1990

EASTERN DISTRICT
Aberdeen AAC (White vest with two red hoops)
Aberdeen University H & H (Yellow vest)
Arbroath & District AC (Black vest with left hand vertical yellow stripe)
Banchory AC (Royal blue vest with one white horizontal hoop "Banchory")
Bathgate AAC (Red vest with grey and white horizontal hoops on front)
Blackburn AAC (Blue vest with red band)
Blackhill Harriers (White vest with royal blue diagonal)
Blairgowrie Roadrunners (Yellow vest with black lettering)
Bo'ness Harriers (Light blue vest, white and amber bands)
Carnethy Hill Running Club (Yellow vest)
Central Region AC (Yellow vest with blue trim)
Corstorphine AAC (White vest with black facings and 2" black vertical stripe at sides)
Dunbar Running Club (Green vest with white trims and screened castle and DUNBAR)
Dundee Hawkhill Harriers (Vest with blue and white quarters)
Dundee Roadrunners AC (Blue top, white lower half diagonally separated vest)
Dundee YMCA Roadrunners Club (Gold vest with bottle green broad hoop, DUNDEE)
Edinburgh Southern Harriers (White vest with two blue hoops)
Edinburgh Spartans (Red and white vertical striped vest)
Edinburgh University H & H (Green vest with white side panels)
Ellon and District AAC (White vest with ELLON in black)
Espc AC (White vest with two black diagonal bands)
Falkirk Victoria Harriers (Black vest with gold band)
Fauldhouse Miners Harriers (Black vest)
Ferranti AAC (Yellow vest with black letters)
Fife AC (White vest with red band)
Gala Harriers (White vest with green hoop)
Haddington East Lothian Pacemakers (Red and white half horizontal vest)
Harmeny AC (Red vest with green diagonal)
Herriot Watt University CCC (Royal blue vest with yellow trim)
Hunters Bog Trotters (Brown vest)
Ladywood Runners (Green and gold vest)
Lasswade AC (White vest with two blue bands linked by single red band)
Linlithgow AC (White vest with royal blue, gold and blue hoops)
Livingston & District AC (Yellow vest with green vertical stripe)
Lochgelly AAC (Dark blue vest with sky blue and white bands)
Lothian AC (Light blue vest with dark blue trim)
Lothian & Borders Police AC (Blue vest with Lothian and Borders police badge)
Montrose AC (White vest with upper red and lower black hoops)
Peebleshire AAC (Red vest)
Penicuik Harriers (White vest with purple panel)
Perth Roadrunners (Green, white and black vest)
Perth Strathtay Harriers (Orange vest with blue trim)
Pitreavie AAC (White vest with badge and gold trim)
St. Andrews University CCC (White vest with two blue bands and blue cross)
Tayside AAC (Blue vest with black T on front)
Teviotdale Harriers (White vest with maroon band)
Whitburn AAC (Claret vest with amber hoops).

NORTHERN DISTRICT

Caithness AAC (White vest with diagonal blue stripe)
Coasters Running Club (White vest with 4" blue band and trimming)
East Sutherland Running Club (Red vest with yellow band and trimming)
Elgin AAC (Black vest with white trim)
Forres Harriers (Red vest)
Fraserburgh Running Club (Black vest with white side panels and trimming)
Inverness Harriers (Gold vest with maroon diagonal band)
Lochaber AC (White vest with two blue hoops)
Minolta Black Isle AAC (Black vest with red diagonal)
Moray Roadrunners (Grey and blue vest)
Nairn & District AAC (Orange vest with black badge NDAAC in black letters)
Northern Constabulary (Navy vest with white horizontal band and Force Crest)
Orkney Isles AAA (Red vest with narrow black band on white hoop)
Peterhead AAC (Sky blue best)
Skye & Lochalsh Harriers (Silver grey vest with maroon/red stripe)
Stornoway Running Club (Red vest with gold band)

WESTERN DISTRICT

A.C Moir Ayr Seaforth AC (White vest with red diagonal cross)
Afton Water AAC (Red vest with white diagonal)
Airdrie Harriers (Grey and Sky blue vest with 3" black diagonal)
Annan & District AC (Yellow vest with ADAC in black)
Ardrossan AC (White vest with red horizontal band and club name)
Avonside Track Club (Black vest with dark blue diagonal)
Barr & Stroud Harriers (Royal blue vest with two white hoops)
Bellahouston Harriers (Dark Blue vest with light blue cross)
Bellshill YMCA Harriers (Red vest with white facings)
Calderglen Harriers (Vest with vertical amber and black stripes)
Cambuslang Harriers (Red vest with white band)
Clydebank AC (Vest with yellow top and white bottom halfs)
Clydesdale Harriers (White vest with black C and black trim)
Cowal AC (Dark blue vest and light blue facings)
Cumbernauld AAC (Sky blue vest with maroon hoop)
Cumnock AAC (Black vest with red diagonal)
Dalry Thistle Boys Club (Royal blue vest with badge, white trim)
Dumbarton AAC (Black vest with red band)
Dumfries AAC (Sky blue vest with 4" navy band)
Dumfries Running Club (White vest with sky blue and burgundy hoops)
East Kilbride AAC (Gold vest with two black bands)
Forth Road Runners (White vest with two red and one black band on front)
Galloway Harriers (Black vest with two white bands)
Garscube Harriers (White vest with blue band)
Giffnock North AAC (Amber vest with royal blue hoops)
Girvan AAC (White vest with blue and green horizontal stripes)
Glasgow University H & H (Black vest with yellow 'G' on back)
Greenock Glenpark Harriers (Sky blue vest with royal blue and gold hoops)
Greenock Wellpark Harriers (White vest with black band and badge)
Hamilton Harriers (White vest with red facings)
Helensburgh AAC (Gold vest with red horizontal band "HELENSBURGH")
I.B.M. Spango Valley AC (Vest with royal blue and yellow vertical stripes)

Irvine Cable AC (Red vest with navy blue trim)
J.W. Kilmarnock H & AC (Royal blue vest with two diagonal white stripes)
Kilbarchan AAC (Gold vest with bold black band)
Kirkintilloch Olympians AC (Sky blue vest with black and white hoops)
Larkhall YMCA Harriers (Red vest with two white bands)
Law & District AAC (Amber vest with red and white bands)
Linwood Pentastar AC (Blue vest with white band)
Loudoun Runners (Blue vest with one broad and two narrow amber hoops)
L & L Track Club (Lemon vest with scarlet trim)
Maryhill Harriers (Royal blue vest and badge)
Mid Argyll AC (Yellow vest with 1" black vertical strip on left)
Milburn Harriers (Light blue vest with dark blue diagonal)
Motherwell YMCA Harriers (Yellow vest with two vertical red stripes)
Nith Valley AC (Blue vest with yellow diagonal)
Oban Area AAC (White vest with diagonal navy and red stripe)
Paisley Harriers (Red vest with blue band)
Renfrew AC (Amber vest with red and blue hoops)
Scottish Veteran Harriers (Amber vest)
Shettleston Harriers (Blue vest with gold band)
Springburn Harriers (Navy blue vest with white diamond badge)
Sri Chinmoy AC (Scotland) (Purple vest)
Stewartry AC (Sky blue vest with black diagonal)
Stirling University CCC (Yellow vest with STIRLING UNIVERSITY in green)
Stonehouse AAC (Maroon vest with sky blue and dark blue hoops)
Strathclyde Fire Brigade AC (Blue vest with white trim)
Strathclyde Police AA (Royal blue vest with black and white diagonals)
Strathclyde University AC (Maroon vest with gold and blue bands)
Troon Tortoises AC (Yellow vest with black trim)
Vale of Leven AAC (Vest of red and white bands)
Victoria Park AAC (Vest of blue and white bands)
Westerlands CCC (Gold vest with black W on back)

AFFILIATED SCHOOLS

Berwickshire HS (Red vest)
Dollar Academy (Navy vest with large letter 'D')
Eastwood HS (Scarlet vest with green cross)
Fettes College CCC (White vest with chocolate and magenta hoops)
Forfar Academy (Maroon and blue vest)
George Heriots School (White vest with blue bands)
Hutcheson GS (Royal blue vest with white trim)
Larbert HS (Navy blue vest with white trim)
Larkhall Academy (Gold vest with two navy blue horizontal bands)
Merchiston Castle School (Dark blue vest with white laurel)
Nicolson Institute (Royal blue vest with horizontal gold band)
Park Mains HS (Royal blue vest)
Queen Victoria School (White vest with red, amber and green bands)
St. Aloysius College (Green vest with yellow eagle and yellow piping)
St. Brides HS (Yellow vest with purple and white horizontal bands)
St. Pius SS (White vest with brown and gold bands)
St. Columba's HS (Green and amber vest)
St. Luke's HS (White vest)
St Ninian's HS (Burgundy vest with pale blue, white and burgundy bands)

AFFILIATED ASSOCIATIONS

Ayrshire Harrier Clubs Association
Boys Brigade
Scottish National Council of YMCA's.